THE RECEPTION
OF VATICAN II

THE RECEPTION OF VATICAN II

Edited by Giuseppe Alberigo,
Jean-Pierre Jossua, and
Joseph A. Komonchak

Translated by
Matthew J. O'Connell

The Catholic University of America Press
Washington, D.C.

Originally published by L'Editions du Cerf
under the title *La Réception de Vatican II*
Edited by G. Alberigo and J.-P. Jossua
Coll. Théologie et Science Religieuse/Cogitatio Fidei 734
Paris, 1985

LIBRARY OF CONGRESS
CATALOGING-IN-PUBLICATION DATA
Reception de Vatican II. English.
  The reception of Vatican II.
  Translation of: La réception de Vatican II.
  1. Vatican Council (2nd : 1962–1965) 2. Catholic
Church—Doctrines—History—20th century. 3. Catholic
Church—History—1965-   . I. Alberigo, Giuseppe.
II. Jossua, Jean Pierre. III. Komonchak, Joseph A.
IV. O'Connell, Matthew J. v. Title.
BX8301962.R3813   1987   262'.52   87-15175
ISBN 0-8132-0647-2
ISBN 0-8132-0654-5 (pbk.)

Contents

Foreword   vii

Abbreviations   ix

1. *Giuseppe Alberigo*
   The Christian Situation after Vatican II   1

I. THE CONTEXTS OF THE RECEPTION

2. *Hermann J. Pottmeyer*
   A New Phase in the Reception of Vatican II: Twenty
   Years of Interpretation of the Council   27

3. *Louis de Vaucelles*
   The Changing Social Contexts of Postconciliar
   Catholicism   44

4. *Segundo Galilea*
   Latin America in the Medellín and Puebla
   Conferences: An Example of Selective and
   Creative Reception of Vatican II   59

II. CENTRAL THEMES IN THE RECEPTION

5. *Joseph A. Komonchak*
   The Local Realization of the Church   77

6. *Giuseppe Ruggieri*
   Faith and History   91

7. *Enzo Bianchi*
   The Centrality of the Word of God   115

8. *René Girault*
   The Reception of Ecumenism   137

III. THEMES TAKEN FURTHER IN THE RECEPTION

9. *Gustavo Gutiérrez*
   The Church and the Poor: A Latin American
      Perspective   171

10. *Pierre Toulat*
    Peace: Between the Good News and the Lesser Evil   194

11. *Adrien Nocent*
    The Local Church as Realization of the Church of
       Christ and Subject of the Eucharist   215

IV. THEMES INSUFFICIENTLY RECEIVED

12. *Lukas Vischer*
    The Reception of the Debate on Collegiality   233

13. *Eugenio Corecco*
    Aspects of the Reception of Vatican II in the Code
       of Canon Law   249

14. *Christian Duquoc*
    Clerical Reform   297

15. *Luis Maldonado*
    Liturgy as Communal Enterprise   309

V. REJECTIONS OF THE COUNCIL

16. *Daniele Menozzi*
    Opposition to the Council (1966–84)   325

Appendix

Avery Dulles, S.J.
The Reception of Vatican II at the Extraordinary
   Synod of 1985   349

Foreword

Vatican II has rightly been described as the most important event in the history of the Roman Catholic Church since the Protestant Reformation. This is a judgement shared by those enthusiastic about the Council's effects, by those with very pessimistic assessments of that impact, and by those whose evaluation falls somewhere between those two extremes. Many different assumptions—ecclesiological, cultural, historical—lie behind these different evaluations, of course. Among them are different judgements about the Council itself, indeed even about what is meant by the term "Vatican II." Is the Council simply the sixteen documents it issued? the event of the conciliar meeting itself? the official implementation of its reforms? the various ways in which the documents and the reforms were received? all of these together?

Twenty years of history have passed since the Council ended its work. In one sense, that is a long period of time, time enough, as Emile Poulat has put it, for the Church to have changed more than it had in the previous hundred years. In another sense, however, twenty years is not a long enough period of time for one to be able to speak confidently of what the Council was as a historic event. To anyone who knows the history of the Church, this should not be surprising. Within twenty years of their close, the spiritual power of the Councils of Chalecedon and of Trent had not yet been fully revealed. Those Councils today have the significance they enjoy among Catholics precisely because of effects which only became clear hundreds of years afterwards. When today we think of those two Councils, we think also of their "reception," that is, of what the Church made of them, of what in their work the Church tested and found good and retained or wanting and discarded. In a defensible meaning of the word, the history of those Councils is also the history of their effects in the Church.

It is as a contribution to a similar evaluation of the Second Vatican Council that this volume of studies is offered. It is a first assessment of the initial impact of the Council, of the early stages of its reception by the whole Church. It makes no claims to being definitive, and it is offered only as a critical analysis of a process of reception which has by no means come to an end. The editors and authors, to the contrary, agree that the Council's spiritual force has by no means been exhausted in the succeeding twenty years; and they make this claim against both those who believe the Council may now be put behind us while we prepare for a possible "Vatican III" and those who are so critical of the post-conciliar developments that they reduce the Council itself to a nearly incidental moment in the history of the Church. Vatican II is and will be what the Church makes of it. The reception of the Council is only just beginning; and, if this volume is offered as a first assessment of its reception, it offers that assessment also as a critical contribution to a dynamic process for which, in the end, the whole Church will be responsible.

The studies published in this volume were commissioned before Pope John Paul II convoked the second extraordinary session of the Synod of Bishops to celebrate the twentieth anniversary of the close of the Second Vatican Council. But the publication of the original Italian and French editions of this work on the very eve of the Synod of 1985 was a good symbol of the coincidence of the volume's themes and the topics which were to concern the members of the Synod. Because the work of the 1985 Synod of Bishops is so relevant to our theme, we are pleased to be able to publish as an appendix to the English edition an analysis of the Synod by Fr. Avery Dulles, S.J.

Besides the original editions in French and Italian, this volume has also been published in German. As editor of the English edition, I wish to acknowledge with gratitude the assistance received for the translation from Mrs. J. de Menil of Process, Inc. and from the First Catholic Slovak Ladies Association and the Pennsylvania Slovak Catholic Union.

JOSEPH A. KOMONCHAK

Abbreviations

AA	*Apostolicam actuositatem*
AAS	*Acta Apostolicae Sedis*
AfkKR	*Archiv für katholisches Kirchenrecht*
AG	*Ad gentes*
Cath	*Catholica*
CD	*Christus Dominus*
CollTheol	*Collectanea Theologica*
DC	*Documentation catholique*
DMC	*Discorsi, messaggi, colloqui del santo padre Giovanni XXIII*
DOL	International Commission on English in the Liturgy, *Documents on the Liturgy 1963–1979. Conciliar, Papal, and Curial Texts* (Collegeville, Minn., 1982)
DS	*Enchiridion symbolorum*, H. Denzinger, ed.; 32d ed., A. Schönmetzer, ed. (Freiburg, 1963)
DTC	*Dictionnaire de théologie catholique*
DV	*Dei Verbum*
EcumRev	*Ecumenical Review*
ES	*Ecclesiae sanctae*
ETL	*Ephemerides Theologicae Lovanienses*
FZPT	*Freiburger Zeitschrift für Philosophie und Theologie*
GS	*Gaudium et spes*
ICI	*Information catholique internationale*
Inf. Serv.	*Information Service*
Irén	*Irénikon*
JES	*Journal of Ecumenical Studies*
Jur	*Jurist*
LEF	*Lex ecclesiae fundamentalis*
LG	*Lumen gentium*
LTK	*Lexikon für Theologie und Kirche* (2d ed.)
NRT	*Nouvelle revue théologique*
OAKR	*Österreichisches Archiv für Kirchenrecht*
OE	*Orientalium ecclesiarum*
OT	*Optatam Totius*
PC	*Perfectae caritatis*
Per	*Periodica de re morali canonica liturgica*
PO	*Presbyterorum ordinis*

QL	*Questions Liturgiques*
RB	*Revue biblique*
RDC	*Revue de droit canonique*
RHE	*Revue d'histoire ecclésiastique*
RSPT	*Revue des sciences philosophiques et théologiques*
SacMundi	*Sacramentum Mundi*
SC	*Sacrosanctum Concilium*
SCatt	*Scuola cattolica*
TGl	*Theologie und Glaube*
TLZ	*Theologische Literaturzeitung*
TPS	*The Pope Speaks*
TQ	*Theologische Quartalschrift*
TS	*Theological Studies*
TTZ	*Trierer theologische Zeitschrift*
UR	*Unitatis redintegratio*
ZEE	*Zeitschrift für evangelische Ethik*
ZRGG	*Zeitschrift für Religion und Geistesgeschichte*

Giuseppe Alberigo

1. The Christian Situation after Vatican II

Phenomenology and History of the Postconciliar Period

A synthetic view of the interrelationships between Vatican II and Christianity is possible, in my opinion, only if we considerably expand our
temporal horizons. That is, it would be inadequate and even misleading
to assess these relationships in terms that are too narrow and in a temporal framework that includes only the twenty years since the solemn
closing of the Council[1] or even only the period since John XXIII first
announced a council on January 25, 1959, at St. Paul's outside the Walls,
in Rome.

Closer examination shows that the period of Christian history involved in the phenomenon of Vatican II is much more extensive. It includes not only Vatican I (1869–70), the immediate predecessor of Vatican II, but to some extent even the Council of Trent (1544–63) insofar as
it was a strictly monoconfessional and monocultural council.[2] For Vatican II was, in contrast, "open" to the other Christian confessions and to
a variety of cultural influences; it also aimed at restoring both a real sub-
ordination of ecumenical councils to the word of God and a real involvement in human history, to the point even of recognizing in this history

---

1. Volumes have begun to appear with appraisals of various types: M. Simone, ed., *Il
Concilio venti anni dopo*. Vol. 1, *Le nuove categorie dell'autocomprensione della chiesa* (Rome,
1984); P. Giglioni, ed., *Concilio e riforma liturgica* (Milan, 1984); G. Jarczyk, *La liberté religieuse
20 ans après le concile* (Paris, 1984); *La riforma liturgica in Italia. Realtà e speranze* (Padua, 1984);
J. Thomas, "Les fruits de Vatican II, vingt ans après *Lumen gentium*," *Etudes*, 361 (1984)
253–63; G. Fagin, ed., *Vatican II. Open Questions and New Horizons* (Wilmington, 1984); G.
Ruggieri, ed., *A venti anni dal concilio. Prospettive teologiche e giuridiche* (Palermo, 1984). Also
of interest: Y. Congar, *Le concile de Vatican II* (Paris, 1984).

2. See H. Jedin, "Das Konzil von Trient in der Schau des 20. Jahrhunderts," *Jahres- und
Tagungsbericht der Görres-Gesellschaft 1963* (Cologne, 1964), pp. 11–24; my own "Prospettive
nuove sul Concilio di Trento," *Critica storica*, 5 (1966) 267–82; and G. B. Winkler, "Vorrefor-
matorische und 'Gegenreformatorische' Kategorien im II. Vatikanischen Konzil," in
E. Klinger and K. Wittstadt, eds., *Glaube im Prozess. Christsein nach dem II. Vatikanum. Für
Karl Rahner* (Freiburg, 1984), pp. 137–42.

"signs" pregnant with the gospel. To that extent, Vatican II represents a recovery of directions—neglected but not abandoned—that are profoundly imbedded in Christian tradition as understood in its fullest Catholic sense.[3]

In proposing to assess Vatican II against this background, it is not my intention to exalt it or give it the stamp of unconditional approval. On the contrary, when the Council is seen in this perspective, historical judgment necessarily becomes much more critical, and the demands to which Vatican II should have responded are seen to grow at an ever-increasing rate.

Instead of this exacting approach, we find today a widespread lack of interest in the Council and even, at times, a hostility toward it. Not only those who have reached maturity since the 1970s but those as well who experienced the Council when they were young have other concerns.[4] They seem to have little interest in understanding whether and to what extent the Council has influenced the life of the churches; they even resist acknowledging that their own Christian experience is indebted to the Council. There seems at first sight to be, on the one hand, a "silent majority" of Christians for whom Vatican II is a past event that has no real, vital impact on the present,[5] and, on the other, an aggressive minority whose aim is to play down the importance of the Council and to point out its lamentable effects.[6] Vatican II seems, paradoxically, to have called forth a militant opposition but no convinced supporters.

If I am to avoid Manichaean simplifications and analyze adequately the place of Vatican II in the history of modern and contemporary Christianity, I must first recall certain facts regarding the relationship between the Church and its councils in the past and then formulate some methodological criteria that will help ensure a correct approach to this same relationship in the case of Vatican II.

Implementation, Reception, Consent

Christianity and the institutions it has produced have endured for a long time, and their duration has been marked by a ceaseless dialectic of the old and the new. Within this dialectic, in turn, the set of rela-

3. See A. Dulles, "Das II. Vatikanum und die Wiedergewinnung der Tradition," in Klinger and Wittstadt, *Glaube im Prozess*, pp. 546–62.

4. Of special interest in this context are the observations made by J.-P. Jossua at a symposium in Bologna on occasion of the tenth anniversary of the close of the Council; see his "Il metodo teologico conciliare e la teologia oggi," *Il Regno–Documenti*, 21 (1976) 132–33. In my opinion, the periodical *Concilium* has increasingly moved away from its original conciliar inspiration; see my note, "History and Theology: An Open Challenge," *Concilium*, 170 (1983) 66–72.

5. See A. Filippi, "Concilio vent'anni luce," *Il Regno–Attualità*, 27 (1982) 413–16.

6. See, for example, the harsh attacks of A. Lorenzer, *Das Konzil der Buchhalter. Die Zer-*

tionships that goes by the name of reception or consent has always played a major role. These relationships have been very important especially on occasion of the great conciliar assemblies held down through the centuries. Each council has been followed by a more or less lengthy, more or less intense and important period in which the conciliar decisions have been assimilated by the Church (I understand "Church" here both as community of believers and as set of organizational structures). There have thus been stages of application and implementation of conciliar decrees, that is, processes of reception or rejection by way of consent or dissent.

These processes have been called into play on numerous and varied occasions, so much so indeed that the Church can plausibly be described as the communion of those who "receive" the gospel.[7] In the case of the major (ecumenical or general) councils, however, the process of implementation and reception has acquired distinctive traits of its own.[8] From a formal viewpoint, the conciliar decisions of antiquity had the force of juridical norms that were binding in virtue of imperial approval, whereas in the Middle Ages papal approval was combined with a forwarding of decrees to the universities, so that approval from above was combined with reception at the university level.[9] An exception to this practice was the Council of Constance, the decisions of which progressively won the consent of a Christendom to which they had restored a single legitimate pope.[10] The Council of Florence evidently had an opposite effect: its decree of union between East and West did not win the consent of the Church and remained a dead letter.

At the end of the Council of Trent Pius IV took upon himself the re-

störung der Sinnlichkeit. Eine Religionskritik (Frankfurt, 1981), as well as the vast literature cited by D. Menozzi in his contribution to the present volume.

7. See the very penetrating comments of J. Zizioulas, "The Theological Problem of 'Reception,' " Centro Pro Unione Bulletin, 26 (1984) 3–6.

8. See A. Grillmeier, "Konzil und Rezeption," Théologie und Philosophie, 45 (1970) 321–52; Y. Congar, "La 'réception' comme réalité ecclésiologique," RSPT, 56 (1972) 369–403, with abbreviated version in Concilium, 77 (1972); W. Hryniewicz, "Die ekklesiale Rezeption in der Sicht der orthodoxen Theologie," TGl, 65 (1975) 242–66; idem, "The Process of Reception of Truth in the Church: Hermeneutic and Ecumenical Significance," CollTheol, 45/2 (1975) 19–34; H. Müller, "Rezeption und Konsensus in der Kirche: Eine Anfrage an die Kanonistik," OAKR, 27 (1976) 3–21; G. King, "The Acceptance of Law by the Community: A Study in the Writings of Canonists and Theologians 1500–1750," Jur, 37 (1977) 233–65; F. Wolfinger, "Die Rezeption theologischer Einsichten und ihre theologische und ökumenische Bedeutung," Cath, 31 (1977) 202–33; A. Houtepen, "Reception-Tradition-Communion," in M. Thurian, ed., Ecumenical Perspectives on Baptism, Eucharist and Ministry (Geneva, 1982), pp. 140–60; E. J. Kilmartin, "Reception in History: An Ecclesiological Phenomenon and Its Significance," JES, 21 (1984) 34–54.

9. See G. Alberigo, "Una cum patribus. La formula conclusiva delle decisioni del Vaticano II," in Ecclesia a Spiritu Sancto edocta, Lumen gentium 53. Mélanges théologiques (Hommage à Mgr. G. Philips) (Gembloux, 1970, pp. 291–319.

10. I refer the reader to my Chiesa conciliare. Identità e significato del conciliarismo (Brescia, 1981), pp. 241–56.

sponsibility of full and complete approval of the conciliar decisions. However, their effective juridical force, which was still limited to the Roman Catholic world, depended, especially in the case of disciplinary decrees, on the approval of the various political authorities, which by this time were jealously asserting their respective territorial sovereignties.[11]

These various modalities of reception were operative, however, only at the juridical and formal level. The real and effective power of conciliar decisions has always depended on the intrinsic validity of the deliberations themselves, a validity verified concretely through a comparison with the needs of the ecclesial community and the consciousness of faith.

Beginning with the very first general council, Nicaea, decisions have been distinguished as doctrinal or disciplinary, depending on whether they have to do with the formulation of the faith or with the establishment of behavioral and organizational criteria.[12] The processes by which these two types of decision have been assimilated have often varied, in a number of ways. Doctrinal decisions have had an immediate impact on the main body of the faithful and have usually been received by way of a consent that was at least implicit.

Dissent from doctrinal decisions, as in the case of the Arians, Monophysites, or Old Catholics, has been a radical dissent that finds expression in opposing views and ends in heterodox positions. In these cases dissent has been centered in a confessing community supported by theologians who have had the burden of formulating the refusal of a believing people. It can therefore be said that the assimilation of doctrinal conciliar decisions has come about through reception of these decisions, in their original formulation, by the people of God giving consent to a "fixed" object, namely, a conciliar decision or, at times, conciliar definition. An especially relevant instance is the reception of the Nicene-Constantinopolitan creed by all Christian traditions.[13]

In the case of disciplinary decisions, scholars often speak of their implementation, application, or introduction, to the extent that such decisions, whether sanctioning preconciliar practices or, more often, prescribing changes or reforms in the existing situation, have had as their immediate recipients the authorities in charge of the life of the Church.

11. See L. Willaert, *Après le concile de Trente. La restauration catholique* (Paris, 1960), pp. 65–75, and the classic study by V. Martin, *Le gallicanisme et la réforme catholique en France. Essai historique sur l'introduction en France des décrets du Concile de Trente (1563–1615)* (Paris, 1919).

12. The formal qualification to be assigned to conciliar decrees, so as clearly to determine the greater or lesser degree of obligation attaching to them, is another and distinct problem. As is well known, Vatican II decided that it would not publish any dogmatic definitions.

13. See G. L. Dossetti, *Il simbolo di Nicea e di Costantinopoli* (Rome, 1967); A. M. Ritter, *Das Konzil von Konstantinopel und sein Symbol. Studien zur Geschichte und Theologie des II. Ökumenischen Konzils* (Göttingen, 1965); idem, "Il secondo concilio ecumenico e la sua ricezione: Stato della ricerca," *Cristianesimo nella storia* 2 (1981) 341–65.

These authorities were obliged to comply with the new discipline settled on by the Council and to see to it that others also complied with it. They were the subjects called upon to implement the decisions by applying them to the daily life of the churches and thereby making them part of the living fabric of these churches. It must be said, however, that in the final analysis even disciplinary decisions were the object of a process of reception by the people of God, for unless they were received by the people they were destined to remain lifeless dictates and achieve nothing. This was all the more true because, unlike doctrinal decisions, disciplinary decisions could be the object of a selectivity that gave consent to some and refused it to others.

In attending to these distinctions we must not lose sight of the sameness of the process by which the decisions of each council have been received: each has been followed by a complex and somewhat lengthy period of tensions caused by readjustments in the life of the Church. The only councils not followed by such periods are those which for various reasons have not had a profound impact on the life of the Church, namely, Florence, Lateran V, and even Vatican I. On the other hand, the conciliar assemblies that have produced decisions of importance for the Church have had a postconciliar stage that was both demanding and fruitful.

For examples I need only cite two councils that have had an exceptional influence on the development of Christianity through the centuries: Chalcedon[14] and Trent.[15] Both were followed by a very difficult and painful process of reception, although we today profit chiefly by the positive ways in which they shaped the life of the Church. Their decisions have become the "flesh and blood" of the Church to such an extent that a church in which these two councils had not occurred would be unrecognizable to us. I state the obvious, therefore, when I say that for Christian consciousness Chalcedon and Trent are today more than past events; they are two crucial moments in the development of Christianity and have profoundly shaped our very way of understanding the gospel message.

It is important to realize that these results came by way of a long-term historical process that was neither linear nor uniform. In the course of this process the conciliar event itself and the body of decisions that it produced were, as it were, purified and reduced to essentials. Contingent or secondary elements fell away and what was left was unforesee-

---

14. See A. Grillmeier, "The Reception of Chalcedon in the Roman Catholic Church," *EcumRev*, 22 (1970) 383–411; J. Coman, "The Doctrinal Definition in the Council of Chalcedon and Its Reception in the Orthodox Church in the East," ibid., 363–82; and M. Ashjian, "The Acceptance of the Ecumenical Councils by the Armenian Church, with Special Reference to the Council of Chalcedon," ibid., 348–62. Of interest with regard to reception in the Palestinian area is L. Perrone, *La Chiesa di Palestina e le controversie cristologiche. Dal concilio di Efeso (431) al secondo concilio di Costantinopoli 553* (Bologna, 1980).

15. See my article, "Du concile de Trente au tridentisme," *Irén*, 54 (1981) 192–210.

ably and unexpectedly fruitful. As a result of the dynamics operative in the postconciliar period, the energies mobilized or elicited by the Council itself altered the previous framework.[16] The context inside and outside the Church gradually changed as the conciliar event receded into the past; people in the postconciliar period often had the impression that the Council had revealed more problems than it had resolved. The assimilation of the conciliar spirit as something transcending the letter and particular contents of the deliberations was usually a slow and irregular process and followed, as it were, a broken line that sometimes gave the impression of failure rather than success.[17]

These postconciliar stages that the Church has had to endure, and which have been so fruitful, represent a privileged phase in the life of the Church. Their function has been to authenticate the harmony between conciliar decisions and ecclesial consciousness by setting in motion latent forces and sleeping energies present in the people of God and bringing into play a dynamic rarely found in political societies. It is because of this evocative power of the great councils that the *sensus fidei* has come to have such profound confidence in the lifegiving effectiveness of conciliar assemblies. There is question here not of a fetishism regarding such assemblies but of a trust that has been repeatedly justified, and this explains why every convocation of a council raises expectations and feeds hopes.[18] Every postconciliar period has been an occasion for extending the conciliar experience to the Church as a whole. As at the Council itself, this sharing comes in a process that is not one-directional but circular and intertwined, and in which every believer and every community is simultaneously subject and object.[19]

16. A typical and especially significant example is Charles Borromeo, whose work as archbishop of Milan (1564–84) enormously influenced the implementation of the Council of Trent.

17. Of great interest is the inquiry that Emperor Leo I conducted among the Eastern bishops in 457 with regard to the reception of the decisions of Chalcedon; see Th. Schnitzler, *Im Kampfe um Chalkedon. Geschichte und Inhalt des Codex Encyclicus von 458* (Rome, 1938), and, more recently, H. Sieben, *Die Konzilsidee der alten Kirche* (Paderborn, 1979), pp. 258–63.

18. In his *History of the Council of Trent*, vol. 1 (New York, 1957), Jedin has written with exceptional clarity on the ecclesial esteem for the idea of a council. See also my *Chiesa conciliare* (n. 10, above).

19. It is worth noting that the proceedings of Vatican II had important repercussions in the Protestant world, where it stirred great interest in the idea of "conciliarity" as a permanent dimension of the life of the Church. The conference of the World Council of Churches at Uppsala (1968) formally adopted this perspective and launched the idea of "conciliarity." The theme was given a fuller treatment at the Faith and Order Conference in Louvain, where the fourth commission adopted the resolution that "conciliarity represents the future of the ecumenical movement"; see "Conciliarity and the Future of the Ecumenical Movement," *EcumRev*, 24 (1972) 88–90. See also the comments made on this resolution in K. Raiser, "Konziliarität. Die Disziplin der Gemeinschaft," *ZEE*, 16 (1972) 371–76, as well as the essays of L. Vischer, "Die Kirche als konziliare Bewegung," in R. Nelson and W. Pannenberg, eds., *Um Einheit und Heil der Menschheit* (Frankfurt, 1973), pp. 235–48, and "Drawn and Held Together by the Reconciling Power of Christ," *EcumRev*, 26 (1974) 166–

There have been occasions when some one agency has aspired to be sole director of this complex development by regulating its spontaneity and freedom. In the long run, such undertakings have shown themselves to be promethean; the irrepressible power of the Spirit that aids the Council does not abandon the Church in the postconciliar period, nor does it submit to "regulation" by anyone.[20]

From Pre–Vatican II to Post–Vatican II

Keeping in mind the information presented above, we will be helped in analyzing the twenty years since Vatican II. But first a caution: twenty years is too short a period for satisfactorily assessing the results of a great conciliar event. Twenty years are hardly enough even for beginning to perceive the process of historical purification that is going on thanks to Vatican II. It is interesting to see how the events of these two decades have been influenced by the workings of the Council[21] (often to a greater extent than by its decisions) and how at the same time the very

---

90. The theme was taken up again in the Salamanca Colloquium of 1973 (see *What Kind of Unity?* [Geneva, 1974]), and the Nairobi Assembly of 1975 received an important report from J. Deschner on "Visible Unity as Conciliar Fellowship" (published in *EcumRev*, 28 [1976] 22–27), the substance of which was incorporated in the conclusions of the second section, "What Unity Requires" (in D. M. Paton, ed., *Breaking Barriers: Nairobi 1975, The Official Report of the Fifth Assembly of the World Council of Churches* [Grand Rapids, 1976], pp. 59–69.) See also G. Larentzakis, "Die dogmatische Begründung der Synodalität," in *Konziliarität und Kollegialität* (Innsbruck, 1975), pp. 64–69; *Ecumenismo in Italia. Conciliarità* (Camaldoli, 1978); G. Conte and P. Ricca, *Il futuro dell'ecumenismo: un concilio di tutte le chiese?* (Turin, 1978); G. Nagy, ed., *Die konziliare Gemeinschaft* (Frankfurt, 1978); R. Mehl, "L'unité conciliaire de l'Eglise," in L. Hein, ed., *Die Einheit der Kirche, Dimension ihrer Heiligkeit, Katholizität und Apostolizität. Festgabe P. Meinhold* (Wiesbaden, 1977), pp. 69–79; H. M. Biedermann, "Die Synodalität, Prinzip der Verfassung und Leitung der Orthodoxen Kirchen und Kirche," ibid., pp. 296–314; and W. Beinert, "Konziliarität der Kirche. Ein Beitrag zur ökumenischen Epistemologie," *Cath*, 33 (1979) 81–108.

20. The most interesting case is perhaps the post-tridentine situation in which the Roman papacy undertook with great determination to implement the decrees of the Council (see P. Prodi, "Note sulla genesi del diritto nella chiesa post-tridentina," in *Legge e vangelo. Discussione su una legge fondamentale per la chiesa* [Brescia, 1972], pp. 191–223), but its leadership proved to be conditioned by other agencies, from Charles Borromeo and Francis de Sales to the political authorities of the great modern states.

21. We still do not have studies of participation in Vatican II and on the development of a common consciousness in the assembly, whether occasioned by the labors of the Council proper (in general meetings and commissions) or resulting from the vast network of contacts and exchanges made possible by the bishops being together in Rome for three months each year. Some aspects of the subject have been brought out in connection with one of the participants, G. Lercaro; see "L'esperienza di un vescovo," in *Per la forza dello Spirito. Discorsi conciliari* (Bologna, 1984), pp. 7–62. See especially the report that Cardinal Lercaro presented to Paul VI, in the name of the moderators, on Nov. 15, 1963, concerning the progress of the Council's labors (ibid., pp. 265–74, esp. pp. 271–73).

image of Vatican II is changing as we are better able to put it in historical perspective.[22]

It can be said that, strictly speaking, we are coming to the end of only a first phase in post–Vatican II history. In fact, not a few of those who were protagonists at the Council or who took part in it in any way (like John Paul II) are still alive and active. This first phase will be completed only when that generation has departed from the scene and both the remembrance and the effectiveness of the Council are determined solely by its own intrinsic power. At present, the postconciliar period is marked largely by a continuation of the tensions experienced at the Council itself; nor is it an accident that almost all the leading figures on all sides today attended the Council.[23] This same phenomenon can be observed after other councils, for example, Chalcedon and Trent; it is facilitated today by the increase in the average length of life.

Also influential today is a special circumstance peculiar to Vatican II. The centralization of disciplinary decisions and doctrinal directives stimulated by Vatican I and intensified by the experience of the anti-Modernist decade, led to the exercise of a de facto monopoly by the Curia and Roman theologians in the pontificate of Pius XII. The result was that almost all other bishops and theologians were shunted into a marginal position in which they became irrelevant, if not suspect. Movements, sensitivities, suggestions for new directions—whether pastoral, doctrinal, or organizational—could survive only if their representatives would settle for a marginal existence that was both humiliating and repressive, or if they could manage to win a benevolent hearing in narrow but "authoritative" Roman circles.[24] In these circumstances the announcement and celebration of Vatican II had to end either in the further ratification and definitive sacralization of the Roman monopoly or in the dismantling of that anomalous situation and the reestablishment ("restoration"?) of a normal and healthy dynamic of ideas and tendencies. We know now, of course, that the Council chose the second alternative and that the decisive moment came with its rejection of the preparatory

22. The publication of the three series of *Acta Synodalia*, devoted respectively to the ante-preparatory proceedings, the proceedings of the preparatory phase, and the proceedings of the general meetings (nothing has been published concerning the all-important work of the commissions), has not as yet influenced historical studies of Vatican II. I can only express my hope that it will do so.

23. The leaders of the traditionalist wing came chiefly from the ranks of the minority bishops at the Council. Moderate critics of the Council, on the other hand, came chiefly from among the theologians who attended the Council as "experts" (*periti*). It would be of interest to know what percentage of the bishops who played a part in the Council are still active twenty years later.

24. An adequate historical knowledge of preconciliar movements will be an indispensable point of reference for understanding the course of the Council, especially if it proves possible to show the extent to which each movement influenced the development of the key points relating to it. Some light on this subject can be gotten from M.-D. Chenu's *Le Saulchoir. Una scuola di teologia* (Casale Monferrato, 1982). See G. Alberigo, "Cristianesimo come storia e teologia confessante," ibid., pp. vii–xxx.

schemata submitted to it.[25] Had the conciliar fathers done nothing else, that action alone would have been credited to Vatican II—and John XXIII—as a meritorious deed of the first importance: a refusal to succumb to an oligarchy, and the restoration of full freedom in the Church.

But this happy outcome, which was responsible for the climate of joyful hope created by Vatican II, also had its negative side. On the one hand, resentment built up among those who for decades had enjoyed unlimited authority and had become convinced that they had a right to it.[26] On the other hand, all those who had been outsiders in preconciliar days rushed to join what soon came to be known as the "majority" at the Council.[27] It will be worth our while to dwell on this last point for a moment, because clarification of it may help in understanding certain aspects of the postconciliar situation. It is in fact becoming increasingly clear that the phrase "majority of council fathers" was an ambiguous one. The group to which it refers was at once too small and too large.

The group was never large enough completely to overcome the resistance of the preconciliar oligarchy, especially when the latter managed to take advantage of Paul VI's anxieties.[28] As a result, the rest of the conciliar fathers had to join ranks in a solidarity that was indispensable for ensuring the right of all to speak freely, but at the same time was

25. This event has thus been the object primarily of sweeping judgments that make it either the decisive point of reference for understanding the development of the Council or, on the contrary, the original sin of the Council and the explanation of its limitations. Only a careful historical study of the event and a detailed analysis of its significance, schema by schema, will make possible a more balanced assessment of it. In fact, the history of the councils shows no other instance in which such extensive and detailed preparation had results so affecting the successive activities of the council. As for the actual relationship between preparatory redactions and conciliar redactions, a detailed comparison in the case of the "Constitution on the Church" has brought to light broad areas of agreement between the two; see G. Alberigo and F. Magistretti, eds., *Synopsis historica constitutionis dogmaticae Lumen gentium* (Bologna, 1975).

26. An analysis of the participation in Vatican II of Cardinal Ottaviani, the principal spokesman for these circles, would be quite valuable (see the biographical sketch of Ottaviani by A. Riccardi in *Dizionario storico del movimento cattolico in Italia* II [Casale Monferrato, 1982], pp. 435–39). The reader must remember, however, that above and beyond the positions taken by individuals, a mute institutional resistance built up in wide circles of the Curia during the years of the Council. This resistance found expression not only in acts of hostility to John XXIII but subsequently also in opposition to the Secretariat for Christian Unity and the commission for liturgical reform as being creations of the Council and means whereby it was influencing the life of the Church. Paul VI's plan to change this situation by internationalizing the Curia was based on an insufficient analysis of the Curia's institutional structure, and its inadequacy soon became clear.

27. As everyone knows, at one moment of major tension—i.e., in the voting of Oct. 30, 1963 on directions to be taken—the least number of votes achieved by the majority was 1,588 as opposed to 525 by the minority on the question of establishing a permanent diaconate; see *Acta Synodalia*, 2/3, p. 575. P. Levillain's book, *La mécanique politique de Vatican II* (Paris, 1975), is of only limited usefulness. It would be helpful to have detailed analyses of the extent to which the majority presented a consistent front in various situations and especially in the commissions and subcommissions, where confrontations with the minority were more concrete and direct.

28. Ten years ago B. Ulianich offered a first analysis of the attitude of Paul VI during the

burdensome and led to equivocations to the extent that it obliged all to accept a common denominator.[29]

As the Council proceeded apace in its labors, there was not enough time for mature reflection;[30] as a result, the forced acceptance of a common denominator led to decreasing vigor in conciliar decisions and thus prepared the way for the "changes of field" that, from de Lubac to Ratzinger, were to mark the 1970s. It would be a mistake to interpret these phenomena as pathological; they were in fact only an interesting proof of the liberating role that the Council played.[31]

---

postconciliar years (*Il Regno–documenti*, 21 [1976] 136–40), but there is still no study of relationships between Paul VI and Vatican II. There is some evidence, however, to justify hypothesizing a connection between the demands of the conciliar minority and some especially sensitive interventions of Paul VI in the work of the Council. I am thinking of the amendments to *Lumen gentium* and the decree on ecumenism, of his attitude in the disagreements regarding the declaration on religious freedom, and, above all, to the request for an interpretive note on episcopal collegiality (the *Nota explicativa praevia* or "Prefatory Note of Explanation" by the doctrinal commission), which was made up essentially of extracts from speeches given by the minority bishops at the Council.

29. Almost without its being realized, there developed during the Council an either-or atmosphere that was summed up in the title of a famous article by Mgr. G. Philips, "Deux tendances dans la théologie contemporaine. En marge du IIe concile du Vatican," *NRT*, 85 (1963) 225–38. This cliché about two theologies and two ecclesiologies exerted no little pressure on the work of the Council and especially on the theologians, who sometimes had the impression that a rigid schematization was being adopted that left many nuances unheeded. Account should also be taken of the fact that the fruitful climate established at the beginning of the Council's labors nourished doctrinal tendencies that were destined to emerge into the open only after the close of the Council and the dissipation of the esprit du corps that had grown up especially among the European theologians.

30. Not to be forgotten is the effort of some circles at the Council to show the opportuneness of a pause for riper reflection between the third (1964) and fourth (1965) sessions. According to this point of view, the pace of the Council's labors had been extremely rapid, and the new trends and directions proposed to the bishops had come in an even hastier sequence; on both counts it seemed advisable to let a substantial interval pass before continuing the Council and bringing it to a close. The delay, it was said, would make it possible to take advantage of the positive effects of liturgical reform; it would also enable the bishops to check the state of their churches in the new climate that had been created; it might also lead to a weeding out of the many schemata for possible declarations that still burdened the assembly's agenda. It would also be possible to give a more mature form to the important schema XIII on the Church in the world, which was in danger of being drawn up without mature deliberation. But the proposal to postpone the continuation of the Council ran into two obstacles: the anxiety of the bishops to return to full-time residence in their dioceses, and the concern that the proposal might conceal a desire to make the Council a quasi-permanent part of the Church's life by prolonging it indefinitely. As early as the end of October, 1964, Paul VI decided to have the fourth and final session of the Council the following year; apparently he did so without consulting the presidents (see G. Lercaro's letter of Oct. 25, 1964, in G. Lercaro, *Lettere dal Concilio 1962–1965*, G. Battelli, ed., [Bologna, 1980], p. 306). In other words, the pope seems to have held tenaciously to the program set down in a letter of Oct. 18, 1962 (published in *Notiziario dell'Istituto Paolo VI*, 7 [1983] 11–14), and did not allow the experience of the work of the first two sessions to exercise any influence on the future program for the Council.

31. I hardly need remind the reader that the pontificate of John XXIII and the celebration of Vatican II put an end to the marginal status of theologians who had been directly or

I said that the "majority" was in fact never large enough. But it was also too large and therefore too heterogeneous a group to have a vision of its own. Its productivity therefore remained high as long as it was dealing with aspects and perspectives that had been thematized, developed, and even given experimental form in preconciliar movements (liturgical, biblical, ecumenical), or with demands developed in opposition to the emphasis on papal prerogatives that had resulted from Vatican I (for example, the upgrading of the position of the bishops). When, on the other hand, there was question of moving beyond the limits of preconciliar developments and passing from the recognition of collegiality to an ecclesiology of communion, from the authorization of ecumenism to a surmounting of Eastern uniatism, or from the immobilism of a "perfect society" to a frank acceptance of human history, this same majority ran into difficulties.[32] There had not been enough prior study of these subjects. Even more important, however, were the cultural limitations of the conciliar fathers who were the mainstay of the majority: they were all Central Europeans and a good many of them had been educated and trained before the Second World War.[33]

From this point of view Vatican II labored under an unresolved tension between, on the one hand, themes and tendencies that had been elaborated in silence and amid suspicion between 1930 and 1960, and, on the other, the much more profound and complex demands produced by the very holding of the Council.[34] Clear evidence of this tension is the discrepancy between the viewpoints expressed by hundreds of bishops

---

indirectly affected by *Humani generis*. It now became possible to appreciate the harm—to say nothing of the injustice—that methods of suspicion and repression had done to the Church as a whole. The shift from condemnation to generosity that John XXIII proposed as he opened the Council was applied first and foremost to the internal life of the Church; it liberated energies that had previously been sacrificed, and restored a healthy atmosphere of responsible confrontation and thus of pluralism as well. See my essay, "Dal bastone alla misericordia. Il magistero nel cattolicesimo contemporaneo (1830–1980)," *Cristianesimo nella storia*, 2 (1981) 487–521.

32. In this context it is worth recalling a generally known fact: that the eschatological dimension was introduced into chap. 8 of *Lumen gentium* at the express request of John XXIII, but it had no widespread influence on the theology of the Council. References to evangelical poverty remained peripheral and embryonic, despite the presence of a sizable pressure group that existed alongside the Council throughout its duration. The idea that faith exists in history was likewise expressed more as a theme worth attention than as a position that had already been given theological development, and this despite Pope John's inclination to a theology of the signs of the times.

33. One of the tensions at Vatican II was due precisely to the presence in large numbers of the third world episcopates, which, however, had quite limited influence on the work and decisions of the Council. The African, Latin American, and Asian bishops acted rather as supporters of the Central European leadership and were unable effectively to influence it, much less go beyond it. This does not mean that they participated passively; on the contrary, the experience of these bishops at the Council was the basis for the role that they and their churches are now playing in the final decades of the twentieth century.

34. The best way to shed light on this aspect of the conciliar experience would be to analyze the various groups making up the assembly. A comparison of the pastoral activity

in preparatory consultations and the attitude of these same bishops during the labors of the Council itself. It seems that the only possible way out of that impasse would have been to follow the courageous course outlined in the address *Gaudet mater ecclesia* with which John XXIII opened the Council on October 11, 1962.[35] But perhaps the very atmosphere of freedom the pope fostered, together with the feeling of satiety left by the heavy-handedness of Pius XII in the exercise of his teaching office, prevented the bishops from adequately appreciating the vistas opened to them by John. In any case the vision presented in the opening address was so rooted in tradition and at the same time so focused on eschatological fulfillment that it was alien to almost all the council fathers.[36]

The Substantive Focal Points of the Postconciliar Period

We meet here one of the most important problems to be faced in reflection on the postconciliar period. I am convinced that the decisive factor in this period is not the confusions[37] that were inevitable in a Christian world that had for centuries been accustomed to a pervasive immobilism and had been led to regard this condition as synonymous with fidelity and as a guarantee of divine grace. I would say the same about the facile optimism that infected the late 1960s and about the radical and continuous changes that occurred in the political, economic, and cultural spheres in the 1970s.[38] Similar confusion, optimism, and changes have followed every council, and we are naive if we are surprised by them or regard them as very important: in fact they are only variable constants.[39]

of the same bishops before and after the Council would be an especially fruitful way of checking the real results of their participation in Vatican II.

35. See G. Alberigo and A. Melloni, "L'allocuzione *Gaudet mater ecclesia* di Giovanni XXIII (11 ottobre 1962)," in *Fede Tradizione Profezia. Studi su Giovanni XXIII e sul Vaticano II* (Brescia, 1984), pp. 185–283.

36. It can be said that the views that the pope set forth were controlled by the idea of the ending of one era and the beginning of another, whereas the bishops were concerned primarily to overcome the lag created in recent decades and, as a result, were less keenly aware of long-term changes.

37. The sense of alarm that dominated the apostolic exhortation of Paul VI on the fifth anniversary of the close of the Council (Dec. 8, 1970) seems to me a typical expression of a concentration on postconciliar confusions; see *Insegnamenti di Paolo VI*, 8 (Vatican City, 1970), 1408–18. It is significant in this context that a scheme for a *Lex ecclesiae fundamentalis* had been published the preceding summer.

38. These aspects have been stressed by J. Kerkhofs, "Principali mutamenti nell'area euro-atlantica dopo il Vaticano II," *Cristianesimo nella storia*, 2 (1981) 5–22, and A. Acerbi, "Receiving Vatican II in a Changed Historical Context," *Concilium*, 146 (1981) 77–84.

39. It seems to me, that is, that every postconciliar period brings changes that must be

I maintain, on the other hand, that the postconciliar period has essentially had two focal points, which are so closely connected as to give the impression of being two aspects of the same problem. On the one hand, there is the underlying energy or *dynamis* at the heart of Vatican II, beyond, and perhaps despite, the limitations of the Council, beyond, too, the contradictions and errors into which it fell. On the other hand, there is the ability of postconciliar Christianity to recognize this power or energy, and to distinguish the living substance from the accidentals that are lifeless or at least lacking in vitality and that therefore become encumbrances and distractions.[40] The twenty years since 1965 have shown that this recognition does not come easily or quickly and, above all, that it requires openness and a commitment to conversion and reform.

How are we, twenty years later, to identify the substantive, dynamic heart of Vatican II: that which turns the Council into a powerful, driving force for Christian development or, in other words, serves as a criterion for judging the link between the directives of the Council and the foundational gospel message?[41]

The perspective provided by the twenty years that have passed since the closing of the Council enables us to see with growing clarity how the very decision of John XXIII to convoke it had immense historical importance precisely within the Roman Catholic tradition. After the medieval Western councils, the Council of Trent suffered, and approved, a drastic narrowing, both qualitative and quantitative, of the Catholic horizon. Rarely had a major council been attended by so small a number of bishops, and by bishops who came almost exclusively from the Latin and Mediterranean world.[42] Despite this limited representation, the council happily succeeded in damming the flood waters that were threatening to destroy Catholicism and in starting a revival. But the price paid for this successful orientation cannot be overlooked; it can be summed up as a drastic isolation of Roman Christianity, now cut off and insulated from any interaction with the other Christian traditions of East

---

measured and evaluated in each case, but without succumbing to the confusion of regarding these changes as determinative of the process of reception.

40. John XXIII, who was especially fond of the classic distinction between substance and accidents, revived it and applied it to the purposes of the Council. Vatican II itself and the postconciliar period found it quite difficult, however, to make practical application of the distinction and tried to eliminate it, at least in practice. As seen from this vantage point, the prolixity of the conciliar documents seems to be the expression of a phenomenological mentality inclined to reduce the distinction. The official postconciliar line seems still to be imprisoned within the same limitations; the documents embodying it fill six volumes in the edition published by the Centro Dehoniano of Bologna!

41. The Councils of Nicaea and Constantinople I entered Christian life by way of symbols (creeds); Chalcedon became identified with christology; Constance (and Florence) with church unity; Trent was the basis for the reorganization of Roman Catholicism.

42. As is well known, no Protestants attended; unfortunately, even the Catholics of non-Mediterranean Europe and of Latin America were missing at Trent, where for practical purposes only the Iberian, French, and Italian bishops played an active part.

and West, condemned to an attitude of defensiveness toward the modern world, and, finally, surrounded by a *cordon sanitaire* to prevent contamination from alien cultures. Never in the history of Christianity had the *massa damnata* been made to include so much and so many; never had Christianity so extended and exacerbated its own estrangement from the fortunes of the human race.[43]

Catholicism was thus launched in a direction that was new by comparison with previous tradition. From the sixteenth to the nineteenth centuries the new trend became increasingly radical, especially because the struggle with the Protestant Reformation on the one side and with modern culture on the other was transformed from a war on an ever-shifting field into one of resistance and defense of a fixed position. Repeated attempts to break out of this fortress mentality by opening up lines of communication with various cultures (in the Far East and in Latin America) were systematically blocked. The same fate lay in wait for the "sorties" attempted by saintly pioneers (from St. Philip Neri to Charles de Foucauld) whose talent was that of building bridges between the Christian condition and the common human condition.

The new order adopted by modern Catholicism entered a critical period when the French Revolution swept away the still existent shadowy remnants of "Christian society" and started the so-called "dechristianization" of modern culture.[44] Over a century later, the October Revolution was seen as the historical personification of evil itself and as a kind of confirmation that the right choice had been made centuries before when the Church moved toward a "closed" concept of itself and a corresponding organizational structure.[45] In keeping with this thinking, Pius IX entrusted a "final"[46] council—Vatican I (1869–70)—with the task of ratifying this conception of the Church as a society in which authority "descends" from the top, and communion among the members is mediated through the dependence of all on the authority of the pope alone. The result was an ecclesiology not unknown before, but never sanctioned either in its structure or in the central place given to it in the

43. See K. Rahner, "Istanze teologiche disattese del Vaticano II," *Rassegna di teologia*, 25 (1984) 1–17.

44. See G. Micoli, "Chiesa e società in Italia tra Ottocento e Novecento: il mito della 'Cristianità,' " in *Chiese nelle Società* (Turin, 1980) 151–245, and, more generally, D. Menozzi, "La chiesa e la storia. Una dimensione della cristianità da Leone XIII al Vaticano II," *Cristianesimo nella storia*, 5 (1984) 69–106.

45. See O. F. Piazza, "Dalla 'Societas perfecta' alla 'Chiesa-Mistero.' Il dibattito conciliare su *Lumen gentium* 8," in Simone, *Il Concilio* (n. 1, above), pp. 49–69; G. Mucci, "La dimensione giuridica della Chiesa nella manualistica preconciliare," ibid., pp. 13–40; and Congar's book cited in n. 1, above.

46. The conviction that no more general councils would be needed was developed after the definition of papal primacy and especially of papal infallibility. And in fact the pope's ability, attributed to him by theologians and canonists alike, to pronounce definitive and irreformable definitions did seem to render superfluous the convocation of councils, the latter being looked upon as bodies whose role was to approve universally binding and definitive decisions.

Christian economy. Ecclesiocentrism thus reached levels that were new in relation to the entire Christian tradition.[47]

Such was the background for John XXIII's decision to convoke a new council. His intention was to call into council not only Catholicism but the whole of Christianity, within the limits possible in a situation so compromised and intractable. His purpose was that, by dint of joint commitment and effort, the Church should emerge from a lengthy historical stage that now seemed finished and without any possible future.[48] The crises that would become public knowledge by the end of the 1960s and that some would try to blame on Vatican II, were already incubating when John summoned the Council: problems ranging from the identity of the priest as a sacral figure to the identification of the sacrament of penance with auricular confession. These were only the perceptible symptoms of a deeper and wider malaise that even Pius XII had sensed, although he diagnosed it as a disease to be suppressed and eliminated rather than as an uneasiness caused by an increasingly intolerable historical lag.[49] For John XXIII there was no longer any question of correcting deviations and manifestations of impatience; the need now was to come to grips with the fact that the lengthy post-tridentine stage of history was being challenged and that fidelity to the central Christian tradition was possible only by an effort to rethink the "today" of faith, in the light of the eternal gospel and tradition itself.[50]

From a distance of twenty years it is increasingly clear that this epochal shift was both the cause and the purpose of Vatican II. Those who interpreted John XXIII's decision as a desire to complete Vatican I or as an ecclesial response to the Kennedy-Khrushchev détente or as a desire to adapt the Church to neocapitalist society can be seen now to have adopted a false perspective. It is true that Vatican II was not convoked to reject a heresy or to settle a dogmatic dispute, as some earlier

47. See R. Aubert, "La geografia ecclesiologica del XIX secolo," in *Sentire Ecclesiam*, 2 (Rome, 1964) 49–120, and Y. Congar, "Cristologia e pneumatologia nella ecclesiologia del Vaticano II," *Cristianesimo nella storia*, 2 (1981) 97–110.

48. Here as elsewhere a great deal of interest attaches to the original Italian redaction of the pope's opening address at Vatican II (see the edition cited above in n. 35).

49. The critical reconstruction of the pontificate of Pius XII is still in an embryonic stage, but it can fairly be said that he had a vivid and even tragic sense of a profound crisis in contemporary society, which he saw as ruled by conflicting ideological systems and in which the Church's role was to be a bulwark of civilization. The pessimism that dominated the pope's vision led him to prefer an attitude of great caution toward movements of renewal and even to opt for immobilism. It is easier to understand the historical limitations of this pontificate when we compare the pope's outlook with the theological optimism of a churchman like E. Suhard, the Archbishop of Paris, whose pastoral letter on the youthfulness of the Church inspired a great surge of hope; see J. Vinatier, *Le cardinal Suhard. L'évêque du renouveau missionaire 1874–1949* (Paris, 1983).

50. It is well known how the Modernist crisis at the beginning of the century poisoned the wells and made valid reflection on this problem extremely difficult, and how the harsh repressiveness of that time strangled all Catholic initiatives in this direction. Only in the next generation would it be possible to tackle the problem in a new spirit and with more adequate critical tools.

councils were, but this should not make us overlook the historical need that Roncalli saw. It was not by chance that the announcement of the Council led to talk of the end of the Constantinian era and of moving beyond Trent.[51] Anyone who wants to discuss the historical opportuneness of Pope John's decision must do so at that level rather than dwell on the inadequacy of the approach taken in *Gaudium et spes* to the crisis of sociological Christianity as this has shown itself in recent decades.

The council fathers soon came to feel this need of getting out of the post-tridentine shoals, out of numbness and passivity. At the same time, however, only a few in the assembly grasped the full dimensions of John's vision. The age-old predominance of the post-tridentine pastoral and theological mentality continued in fact to set limits to the labors of the council and, in particular, to its constructions, especially whenever there was question of moving beyond positions developed in the immediately preceding decades. It proved more difficult to recover a profound contact with pre-tridentine traditions and with the vital impulses coming to light on the periphery of or outside the citadel of Roman Catholicism. I hardly need add that the retreat of the conciliar (and post-conciliar) minority into the fortress of a late tridentine traditionalism[52] is not only not a historically feasible alternative, but in addition contributes nothing to the Council's response to the epochal challenge voiced by John XXIII.

The "Call" of Vatican II

We can begin to see clearly today that Vatican II had sufficient acumen to grasp the historical need of a "forward leap" by the Church in fidelity to the gospel, and that it managed to glimpse some important directions in which to move, although on other points it remained deaf and could produce no more than stammering utterances that, at a distance of twenty years, prove useless and embarrassing. When we look back from this vantage point, it is not difficult to see that the Council did not impose on the Church a program of readjustment containing clear and distinct norms to be followed.[53] (I observe in passing that this accounts for

51. See M. D. Chenu, "La fin de l'ère constantinienne," an essay of 1961 that was reprinted in his *La Parole de Dieu*. Vol. 2, *L'évangile dans le temps* (Paris, 1964), pp. 17–36.
52. Roman Catholicism had gradually withdrawn into an ever narrower attitude of self-sufficiency and deceived itself that it could overcome the limitations imposed by an almost exhausted cultural dynamism and by institutional procedures that were to an irritating degree centered upon and, as it were, personified in the person of the pope. This attitude had produced an objective arrogance that sought to give the appearance of strength to what was in fact an increasingly serious weakness and isolation. The paradoxical result was not only a hostility to what the Syllabus kept calling "modern civilization," but also a growing deafness to the most ancient and venerable Christian traditions.
53. The "pastoral" character that John XXIII assigned to the Council has often been

the subsequent desperate attempt to translate the decisions of the Council into a new Code of Canon Law, something that by definition is destined to be a hopelessly inadequate repository of those decisions.)[54]

What the Council brought home to the Church was the need of realizing without delay that Christianity had finished its tridentine age and must henceforth break new ground and take new forms. Vatican II saw that if a creative response was to be possible, that is, a response arising out of renewed fidelity to the gospel, the Church must shake off its inertia[55] and realize that the walls surrounding the Christian citadel had fallen and that further resistance would be oppression rather than self-defense.[56] The Church must set out anew and seek in freedom the Lord who always goes on before his disciples. Nothing could be more diametrically opposed to this new quest than the itch for novelty, a mundane optimism, or indifference to tradition.[57] The task indeed demands much of Christians and the churches, though not more than was demanded at the time when the barbarian peoples were brought in or again when the Gregorian reform was going on, or when the decrees of Trent were being implemented.[58] It is a very demanding task and not without its

---

underestimated, as though it were a peculiar idea of the pope or a device to exclude any dogmatic element. In fact, in Roncalli's vocabulary "pastoral" was an exceptionally rich term and undoubtedly referred to the highest level of the Church's life. By using this adjective, then, he was giving Vatican II an ecclesial scope that was not solely dogmatic or solely disciplinary but all-embracing. An adequate understanding of this kind of council is essential if we are to take a correct view of the postconciliar period. When a council is a pastoral council, postconciliar activity cannot be restricted to "implementation" or even principally to "reception" but must necessarily find expression in an active and creative "consensus." According to E. Klinger, "Der Glaube des Konzils. Ein dogmatischer Fortschritt," in Klinger and Wittstadt, *Glaube im Prozess* (n. 2, above) 615–26 the pastoral outlook that John XXIII assigned to Vatican II was itself a genuine dogmatic advance.

54. See E. Corecco's essay in this volume (chap. 13, below).

55. As is well known, the popes of the first half of our century devoted special attention to Catholic Action and made it the only escape valve for ecclesial energies, so much so that it was in danger of exhausting itself in soulless activism. It could easily be foreseen that the renewed understanding and relevance of the people of God as the community of the faithful would undermine the very foundation of Catholic Action, because it was a surrogate for the healthy activity that had been denied to the Church. See my article, "Il popolo di Dio nell'esperienza di fede," *Concilium*, 20 (1984) 940–58.

56. This is true, for example, of "Christian culture," something that had a long and fruitful history but that in the modern cultural context can no longer have any real meaning, because Christians are drawing upon many cultures and there is an increasing awareness that no culture (or society) is more homogeneous with or closer to the gospel than others: the seeds of the gospel can germinate anywhere.

57. This does not mean, of course, that incompatible attitudes and errors of this kind do not exist. They were perhaps inevitable; it is nonetheless proper to criticize them. Frequently, however, the way in which critics speak gives the impression that they see a cause-and-effect connection between the Council and this kind of defect, thus making it permissible and even obligatory to attribute to the Council phenomena diametrically opposed to it.

58. Tensions and difficulties are inevitable when these and other epochal changes occur; the search for a new balance gives rise to fears and to a nostalgia that greatly ex-

dangers, but it is not unparalleled. In this case again the churches are being asked to look both backward and forward: back to tradition in all its rich variety, and forward to the signs of the gospel that are hidden in history but are decipherable if we commit ourselves to share in reading them under the sovereign guidance of God's word and in a fraternal communion of all Christians.

For the last two decades Christianity, and Catholicism in particular, has been faced with this call to commitment. The call is an invitation, inasmuch as Vatican II made nothing obligatory, but it also has a binding force, inasmuch as the historical situation imposes obligations of its own.[59] The response to the call has taken forms that have varied in intensity and have been given at different levels.

There was an initial response at the institutional level in the publishing and implementing of the Council's decisions. The creation of a special agency for liturgical reform, the reform of the Roman Curia, the assignment of ecumenical initiatives to the Secretariat for Unity, the introduction of a Synod of Bishops, and many comparable steps were the expression of a commitment (which, however, gradually lessened) by the central Catholic authorities to implement a certain number of conciliar directives. In areas more distant from the center, the response in this first phase took the form of establishing presbyteral and pastoral councils, strengthening the episcopal conferences, and preparing for synods in some places (Holland, Latin America).[60] When some voices were heard calling for more vigorous interventions in the organization of the local churches so as to ensure a renewal that would not be simply a decorous "conservative restoration," the authorities did intervene in drastic ways.[61] Paradoxically, this phase climaxed in the decision of Paul VI in

---

aggerates the security provided by familiar situations and the dangers the future will bring.

59. From this point of view the Council's refusal to issue new definitions has often been misunderstood to mean that Vatican II had no "strong" message to offer to Christians and churches. But the priority of the "pastoral" criterion over the "dogmatic" and the "disciplinary" seems rather to suggest a more thoughtful and carefully articulated classification of directives for Church authorities.

60. It is noteworthy that the importance assigned to episcopal conferences has elicited doctrinal opposition from those who maintain that the conferences detract from the responsibility of the individual bishops. In fact, however, the conferences have proved to be one of the few really effective agencies in eliminating or at least offsetting Roman centralization and restoring territorial awareness to local churches. The conferences provide bishops with an opportunity for otherwise unavailable experiences of collegiality; in them the bishops are developing new episcopal sensitivities and styles.

61. The best known case is the Church of Holland, whose episcopate was restructured in such a way as to destroy solidarity and perhaps even communion among the bishops. Less widely known are the penalties inflicted on Cardinal Giacomo Lercaro, Archbishop of Bologna, who was removed at the beginning of 1968, on Archbishop Baldassari of Ravenna, likewise dismissed, and on other bishops whose pastoral approach was considered to depart too much from the Roman model.

July, 1976, to suspend Archbishop Lefebvre from his sacred functions for his refusal to accept Vatican II.[62]

It is becoming increasingly clear that this first phase was one of instrumentalities, that is, one in which the intention was to set up institutional agencies that would implement some of the needs that had come to be recognized in the Council. But the wave of protests that occurred in 1968 and the parallel unrest within the Church caused these changes to be undertaken with timidity, if not with real fear.[63] What seems now especially worthy of note, however, is the distorted perspective that led not a few people to see in the protests of 1968 (and then in succeeding major crises: the energy crisis, the decline of ideologies, the destabilization caused by terrorism, the revival of consumerism, and so on) a proof of the failure of Vatican II, which had not foreseen any of these things, or at least the end of the conciliar springtime and the abrupt entrance into a new and quite different phase. This point of view was and still is a major obstacle to reception of the Council, especially because it indicates a radical misunderstanding of the historical meaning of the Council itself. There was no realization that the deep and turbulent malaise of 1968 was an especially noisy symptom of widespread cultural change. Men and women were protesting both against social immobilism, which made them impatient, and against possible changes, which made them fearful and insecure. But the very contradictory character of these feelings bore witness to an obscure and confused perception that a new historical phase was at hand, to be desired or feared precisely because it was impending.

It is surprising that credit should have been given to such a misunderstanding, namely, that Vatican II was contradicted by the appearance of the very needs and demands that played a normative role in its most enlightened decisions! The misunderstanding should, I think, be emphasized because it bears eloquent witness to the confusion that marked the beginning of the postconciliar phase, dominated, on the one hand, by an implementation focused on a return to normality, and, on the other, by expectations—soon dispelled by brutal contact with reality—of an easy renewal. Both positions were inspired by a myopic and reductive vision of the Council; they fastened on the letter alone and were unable to penetrate to the deeper motivation and universal, historical significance of the Council.[64] I may add that a similar lack of historical perspective was to be seen after the councils of Chalcedon and Trent.

62. The penalty imposed on this traditionalist bishop, like that imposed on the abbot of St. Paul's outside the Walls, seems excessive and had the effect of making the group seem more important than it was. The decision in the autumn of 1984 to permit celebration of the Tridentine Mass may help offset the severity of those punishments, provided it signifies the acceptance of a real liturgical pluralism.

63. The course of liturgical reform is a very clear illustration of this first postconciliar phase.

64. It is dismaying that since John XXIII the Bishops of Rome, despite the responsibility

The postconciliar period began at a different level and against a different cultural background in areas whose bishops were active at Vatican II but had played a marginal part. The decisive event here was the Latin American synod held at Medellín, Colombia, in 1968. As is well known, on that occasion, and precisely because of its historical situation of marginality and suffering, the Latin American Church was able to discern one of the characteristic aspects of the Council and to take responsibility for renewing its own presence in that part of the world. The attitude manifested there was a very fruitful one and turned the churches of Latin America into leading exponents of a renewed Christian life in these final years of the twentieth century. Similar developments are taking place, in varying degrees, in the other continents that throughout the modern period had been colonies and the objects of missionary dedication. There can be no denying that Vatican II has been given a much more open and convinced reception in these parts of the world than in lands whose Christianity had had a long history but whose churches, after being the leaders at the Council, seem to have lost their understanding of it.[65]

The places where postconciliar Christianity shows that it has been able to recognize the deeper dynamism at work in the conciliar event and to distinguish between its transient and its substantive aspects are also the places where an active and therefore creative reception has taken shape and is enduring. The Council is not looked upon there as a fixed historical datum and a set of norms that are to be taken over passively in the various parts of the Church. On the contrary, these local churches perceive the liberating power of the Council; they accept the stimulus to search out things "new and old"; seeds that had remained hidden are allowed to bear fruit.

This is true, for example, of poverty and peace as subjects for commitment and themes for Christian reflection.[66] Vatican II was reserved and,

laid on them by their primacy, have been unable to focus the Church's attention on the central core of the conciliar teaching.

65. It is possible that Vatican II will increasingly come to be seen as the historical occasion on which the European churches gave expression to their finest energies at the end of the twentieth century and thereby provided greater room for the current Christian experience of the peoples in other continents and especially in the Third World. When viewed from this standpoint, the conclave that elected a Polish pope in 1978 showed that it grasped the direction of historical evolution, though its interpretation of it was especially cautious and not free of all ambiguity. The election of a Polish prelate as bishop of Rome showed that the electors perceived the need of new blood, but at the same time they limited the thrust of this conviction by choosing a descendant of the Slavic tradition of Christianity—a tradition that is independent vis-à-vis European Catholicism but is at the same time profoundly conditioned by it. Whatever the ultimate significance of the present pontificate, it is already possible to stress its importance as a break with the unbroken Italian tradition of the post-tridentine papacy; this was one valuable product of the climate created by Vatican II.

66. It has become increasingly clear during these years that poverty and peace are two

in the final analysis, silent on these two key problems of contemporary life and Christian experience. Nonetheless it was this very fact that gave rise to a fevered inquiry that is beginning to bear fruit. In many cases, the fruits are undeniably still bitter and unsatisfactory, but they already light up the future and nourish hope to the extent that they are pledges of renewed fruitfulness in the womb of a church that for centuries had produced nothing but stereotyped repetition.[67] It would be surprising and even incredible to find mature fruits after so short a time and despite the tenacious resistance of the spiritual and intellectual habits characteristic of the very recent past. Those who think they must severely criticize the immaturity of today should remember that the deeper responsibility for it belongs to preconciliar lag and inertia, not to the feverishness of the postconciliar quest. It is not possible to exercise spiritual discernment except on a sufficiently broad basis of historical discernment.

One might be tempted to conclude that these twenty years have been dominated more by the long shadows of the preconciliar period than by energies released at the Council itself. And yet the Church has in fact changed, and to such an extent that it may be said to be unrecognizable when compared with the Church of the 1950s. On the other hand, the journey has hardly begun; we hear loud calls to return to the house we have abandoned; a deceitful nostalgia makes its way abroad; the task of advancing into the unknown and accepting the challenge of the gospel seems an unbearable one. According to Cardinal Ratzinger, it is possible for a council to be a failure; but the non-reception of an indispensable and lifegiving council is also a failure to be avoided.

The Struggle for Identity

Recent years have seen a surprising revival of positions that were characteristic of more conservative circles of the Roman Curia and the episcopate in the 1960s. There has been, in other words, a clear return to attitudes that Vatican II unequivocally disavowed and overcame, atti-

---

crucial elements in the contemporary human condition. Poverty and peace are economic and political problems, but they are more than that: they are also two dimensions that are keys to the very future of the human race. For this reason they are surely pregnant signs of the gospel as a message of divine love for human beings. John XXIII had directed attention to this point; Vatican II could not summon up the energy needed to deal with these matters but it did stimulate the churches to be sensitive to them.

67. It is not possible to deal here with the problems raised by the theology of liberation and with the criticisms directed at it by the Congregation for the Doctrine of the Faith; the same applies to the efforts that many episcopates have made in the twenty years since 1965 to rethink their catechetical texts. Both the theology of liberation and these new catechetical undertakings, though very different in character, have been inspired by the need of

tudes that had found refuge in tiny groups of nostalgic individuals. A pessimistic vision of history, poisoned by Manichaeism, seems to be spreading abroad. There is a rejection of the Council's call to the churches to become once again pilgrims and missionaries, as though it implied an abandonment of tradition, and, finally, a revival of the "closed" ecclesiology of the post-tridentine period in which the Church is a fortified castle, jealous of its own purity and bristling with condemnations.

Understandably, many ask how this revival could have taken place despite the vast evangelical ferment that has been at work everywhere in the life of the people and producing an unparalleled stage of Christianity, a stage that is planetary in extent and bears witness to an astonishing and perduring activity of the Spirit. They ask, again, how such attitudes can be reconciled with the spirit of the Council. Is this not an attempt to "bury the Council," as traditionalists of the Lefebvre stamp explicitly wanted to do?

Many who share these attitudes are in positions of authority in the Church. This fact necessitates a serious analysis of these attitudes. For we are clearly in the presence of a movement that, although calling for fidelity to Vatican II, in fact ends up striking at the central and distinctive substance of the Council. It would reorder the theological and spiritual plan of the Council, to the point even of completely subverting it.

A persistently negative judgment on the contemporary world emphasizes a multiplicity of incidents, circumstances, and tendencies that are undoubtedly present in modern societies and that often stifle, impede, and oppose Christian life and the proclamation of the gospel. It has become customary to insist that the naive optimism about development that is a constitutive element in the conciliar constitution *Gaudium et spes* is inadequate for dealing with such problems. Those who argue in this way think it legitimate simply to set Vatican II aside as being tainted by facile optimism. But they avoid coming to grips with the more radical position of the Council, which was stated by John XXIII in his opening address and shared by the vast majority of the conciliar fathers, namely, that the time had come for reviving an eschatological reading of history, and surmounting the myopic vision of the "prophets of doom." If the Church is to be capable of a "new Pentecost," it must shake off many age-old incrustations that seem to be adornments but are in fact simply dusty residues of a past that can never return. Only an internalized renewal focusing on the substance of the faith can enable the Church to live in history with an unadorned authenticity, protected only by the

giving revised form to the living heritage of Christian tradition. The Roman congregation just mentioned has judged it necessary to express serious reservations regarding both efforts, thereby casting dark clouds of suspicion over entire episcopates. It is impossible not to see its interventions as alien to Vatican II and inspired by forms of security-mindedness—or even of repressiveness—that were characteristic of the Church prior to its "choice of mercy."

poverty of the gospel. Visions of time and history as demonic in the Christian tradition have always been the product of fear and not of reverence for God, of an effort to achieve security by burying one's talents and not of the courage that accepts the human condition but calls for its transfiguration.

Pessimism at higher levels of the Church has rarely led to great ages of faith. More often it has been symptomatic of narrowed horizons and a criterion of judgment that replaces the *krisis* of the gospel with a wholly human and rational balance sheet, which has a descriptive reliability but is prisoner of concerns lacking in spiritual depth and Pauline discernment.

When this point of view is adopted, it is possible to draw up endless lists of drawbacks and deviations, while failing to see that a synthetic judgment on the historical moment cannot reflect simply the arithmetical sum of these lists. It is possible, therefore, and obligatory, to draw up other lists of positive factors and of instances of healthy, living growth, even though they are so inextricably combined with drawbacks and deviations that no effort of Manichaean rationalism can separate them. Above all, however, the pessimism of the "prophets of doom" is opposed to the most authentic Christian tradition and to Vatican II because it tries to ignore (or simply cannot see) the concentration of graces that the Spirit has poured out upon our age, of which the Council was one sign. The intense communion of faith that inspired the council fathers and, around them, the Catholic Church and the other Christian churches was an event that present generations are called upon to preserve and develop, not to repress and spoil. Ever since the experience of the first community in Jerusalem, "councils" have been privileged moments at which the Spirit has permeated the Church and taken possession of it in an exceptionally intense way. The ecumenical councils in particular have been experiences of joint quest and following of the Lord, experiences that are not the privilege of a minority but involve the ecclesial community as such. That is why the early Church venerated the first four councils as it did the four gospels; that is why the great councils have become the patrimony of all Christians, and why each Christian has the right and duty of defending the councils against any reductionist attack on their full meaning and message.

Reductionism is precisely the risk run by any assertion that the history of the Church has no before and after. A picture of church history as an even, unbroken line can indeed bring out the aspect of continuity, but it is also a picture of death, not of life, of inertia, not of a journey toward the heavenly homeland. Vatican II showed a deep and intense, concrete awareness that many preconciliar tendencies were not suitable expressions of the *sensus fidei*. On certain key points—such as the concept of revelation, the mystery of the Church, the relationship between the people of God and the ecclesiastical hierarchy, the acceptance of a Catholic ecumenism, and the vision of the Church as living *in* history—this awareness led the Council to move beyond the emergency formulations and controversialist approaches of the last few centuries and go back to the earliest and most authentic tradition.

But the most important novelty of Vatican II is not to be found in these various positions but rather in the very fact that it was convoked and held. From this point of view the Council represents a point of no return or, better, in the words of John XXIII, "a leap forward toward an understanding of doctrine and a formation of consciences, both of which are completely faithful to . . . authentic doctrine." An inability on the part of the Church to recognize this key moment in its own life would be a symptom of tragic sterility and blindness. No more insidious and effective "normalization" of the Council can be imagined than to deny its epochal importance. Such an emptying of its meaning would avoid the brutal rejection of the traditionalists but would nonetheless bury Vatican II in a post-tridentine "normality."

Those who want precisely this result fall back on an ingenious contrast between the "spirit of the council" and the "true council." The contrast is alien to any sound hermeneutic and seems meant to justify an authoritarian and univocal interpretation of Vatican II. But an approach of this kind contradicts the very nature of a council that was meant to be and is recognized as having been "pastoral," one that expressly shunned definitions and chose discourse as the literary genre for conveying its decisions. Rigid and univocal interpretations are alien to the whole conciliar tradition and have in fact been adopted only after polemical councils such as Trent, though with results that were far from satisfactory. In the case of Vatican II, that kind of interpretation would be an intolerable act of violence and would end in the most radical denial of the conciliar event. Only the *sensus fidei* of the Church as a whole can be the adequate interpreter of a major council. Such a *sensus fidei* can reach maturity only slowly, with the concurrence of the entire people of God; it cannot be replaced by an action of the hierarchy alone.

I. THE CONTEXTS OF THE RECEPTION

Hermann J. Pottmeyer

2. A New Phase in the Reception of Vatican II: Twenty Years of Interpretation of the Council

Vatican II, A Transitional Council

"There has seldom been a Council without great confusion after it": so wrote Newman in 1870 after Vatican I.[1] And Vatican II, in fact, was destined to provide confirmation of this experience. True enough, its agenda included no condemnations of errors in faith. But whereas the two preceding councils, Trent and Vatican I, had aimed at restoring internal stability and establishing a dogmatic front, Vatican II sought to relax rigid fronts and achieve an opening. As experience has shown, however, such an attempt leads to instability. For this reason, Vatican II has a place apart among the councils. Given this situation, the Catholic Church in the post–Vatican II period has proved surprisingly stable.

Vatican II can best be described as a *transitional council*. This is what the pope who convoked it and the majority of the council fathers intended it to be; this was the intention that determined the choice of subjects and the language. For this reason, Vatican II is a challenge to its interpreters. The rules customarily applied in interpreting dogmatic texts, especially those of the modern period, do not work here. The texts, even those that are doctrinal in character, lack the conceptual precision, the unambiguous definition of positions, the technical form, and the unity of literary genre to which Trent and Vatican I had accustomed us. Passages using the language of the Bible as no previous council had used it alternate with historical expositions, analyses of the contemporary situation, and, not least, citations of previous councils (half of them from Trent and Vatican I) and references to papal teaching (half of them to Pius XII). No wonder, then, that the interpretations given during the first twenty years after the council present a bewildering picture and display a great deal of insecurity.

1. C. S. Dessain and T. Gornall, eds., *The Letters and Diaries of John Henry Newman* (Oxford, 1979), 25:175.

From a statistical standpoint Vatican II again occupies a place apart among the councils. Of the 37,727 lines of text supplied by all the councils together, Vatican II alone provides 12,179, whereas Trent, the next closest in length, has 5,637. In Vatican II, 5,646 lines deal with pastoral and social problems, whereas in Trent only 431 lines are devoted to these concerns.[2] From this point of view the description of Vatican II as a "pastoral" council is justified. It must be noted, however, that its strictly dogmatic texts occupy 3,148 lines (out of a total of 8,521 for all the councils). It is wrong, therefore, even from a purely statistical standpoint, to say that Vatican II was *only* "pastoral."

In any case, the communication, reception, and interpretation of such a mass of texts present special problems. The "prolixity" and "verbosity" for which the Council has been criticized—and legitimately so in some of its texts—is again a consequence of its character as a transitional council that uses persuasive language to get the Church moving but at the same time wants to maintain continuity. Canonists in particular have complained about the lack of precision and the "ambiguity" of the conciliar texts.[3] And in fact the postconciliar codification of church law makes clear the special problems that the texts pose for canonical interpretation. But would it not have been inherently contradictory to give a fixed legal formulation to what was in fact the expression of a desire for transition and mobility?

Dogmatic theologians, on the other hand, find it easier to live with the Council. The reason is that they all, whether "conservative" or "progressive," feel able to base their own positions on the conciliar texts. But this kind of treatment of the Council, one not based on any common interpretive approach, will help little to agreement among theologians or in the Church at large. Many conflicts of the postconciliar period have their basis in the difficult and uncertain interpretation of Vatican II.

It is clear that the transitional character of Vatican II has also played a part in its reception. The condemnation of an error is immediately operative. And yet when earlier councils condemned errors it often took decades before orthodoxy prevailed. When the issue was church reform, centuries were sometimes required. This most recent council dealt precisely with church reform, with a movement toward a renewed church. True enough, Vatican II was blessed in that, thanks to the modern media, the entire world was able to attend its proceedings and be informed of its results—although admittedly in the fragmentary fashion proper to the media. Nonetheless its reception, its assimilation, by so

2. See J. van Laarhoven, "The Ecumenical Councils in the Balance: A Quantitative Review," *Concilium*, 167 (1983) 50–60.

3. See, e.g., K. Walf, "Lakunen und Zweideutigkeiten in der Ekklesiologie des II. Vatikanums," in G. Alberigo, Y. Congar, and H. J. Pottmeyer, eds., *Kirche im Wandel. Eine kritische Zwischenbilanz nach dem Zweiten Vatikanum* (Düsseldorf, 1982), pp. 195–207; in Italian: "Lacune e ambiguità nell'ecclesiologia del Vaticano II," *Cristianesimo nella storia*, 2 (1981) 187–201.

vast an ecclesial community, requires time: time for rethinking, time for conversion, time for developing a new self-understanding.

Those who invoke the transitional character of Vatican II and claim that we are already in a new situation about which the Council now has little more to say, fail to understand what it means to call the Council transitional and what the Council itself had in mind. For the younger generation the Council is indeed already history, and the situation that the Council had in mind has changed. But no one can deny that the beginnings of the new ecclesial self-understanding that the Council was attempting have not yet borne their fruit, and that the Council's invitation to make the Church a *communio* and a sign of salvation for the world is still very much the answer to the challenges of the present situation.

And what role did the Council assign to the transition it was making? It meant it not as a single once-and-for-all step but as an example of a passage to be made over and over again, in every moment, the signs of which must be read in the light of the gospel. The active reception of the Council's first steps toward a new ecclesial self-understanding is therefore a task that will take decades; *Ecclesia semper reformanda*, the reformation of the Church, is a perduring task. Thus far we have not even been able to agree on a proper hermeneutic for the Council.

Reception as Interpretation of Texts and as Movement

The process of the reception of Vatican II has thus far, like every reception, been a process of interpretation as well. This refers first of all to the reception and interpretation of the *documents* that the Council issued, that is, four constitutions, nine decrees, and three declarations. Interpretation of these documents has taken an unofficial as well as an official form. The official interpretation is found in postconciliar legislation for the universal Church and for the regional and local churches. It is in this way that postconciliar institutions and the new Code of Canon Law have come into being. But the Council has also received an official interpretive translation in pronouncements of a doctrinal or pastoral kind: papal encyclicals and addresses, decisions and declarations of curial agencies, and numerous episcopal synods and pastoral letters. Special mention must be made of the reception of the Council that has taken place through the introduction of new liturgical texts and forms. The Council has also been given a no less influential, even if not officially binding interpretation, by theologians, by religious literature, and by its reception in the practice of communities and the faithful. In fact, it is not least in this practical reception that the Council has demonstrated its fruitfulness.

The distinction between official and unofficial interpretation applies, therefore, only to the public recognition of them as binding in differing degrees. From the standpoint of an ecclesiology of communion, the entire people of God is the subject that receives. If reception is not a merely passive process, then the entire people of God, though in varying ways, plays an active role in interpreting a council. This is especially true of a council that does not condemn errors but aims at the active self-renewal of the entire Church in the Holy Spirit and at the fruitfulness of its members through faith, hope, and love.

The postconciliar process of reception and interpretation thus includes more than the reception and interpretation of conciliar texts. Vatican II was not only a body that turned out decisions; it was an event, an opening, a *movement* in the course of which the Church elaborated a new interpretation of itself. The Council was therefore first experienced, then understood and received. It launched a conciliar movement that manifested itself in a new kind of synod, in the establishment of permanent synodal structures, and in the rise of base communities, but also in the acceptance of dialogue with separated Christians and with non-Christians and, not least, in new liturgical forms that more adequately reflect the nature of God's people as a community. The movement derived its material stimulus both during and after the Council from the movements of renewal—liturgical, ecumenical, and biblical—that had already been under way before the Council. A particularly intense emotional stimulus was the preconciliar logjam of problems that made itself felt as an increasing lack of contemporaneity between Church and world and to which John XXIII replied with his programatic term "aggiornamento."

As an act of *setting out*, which found expression in the image of the Church as people of God, the Council had two aspects. On the one hand, it was a *religious and spiritual event*: John XXIII had announced it in advance as a "new Pentecost," and that is what the majority of the council fathers felt it to be. And it launched a corresponding movement that generated in many Catholics a readiness for a change of ideas, for renewal, for involvement in the Church, and an openness to the outside. On the other hand, the Council was an *act of comprehensive criticism*: John XXIII had announced it as a council that was to renew the Church and restate its tradition; the critical impulse was therefore already at work in the program for the Council. It led to the "rebellion" of the council fathers against the prepared drafts of its documents and, after the Council, to a movement of intra-ecclesial criticism that was both liberating and disintegrative.

The two aspects and movements are inseparable, yet it is not easy to determine their interaction and mutual relationships, especially because they are still in full swing. By the nature of the case, and under the added pressure of the New Enlightenment and the movement of emancipation in the 1960s and 1970s, the critical impulse initially made itself felt more strongly than did the religio-spiritual. This fact was of considerable importance for the reception of the Council. The heavy emphasis on criticism of tradition and authority that marked postconciliar discussion and focused on changing internal structures of the Church led to a reaction at the same level. An example of where the emphasis has been put in the reception of the Council is the little attention paid to the teaching of *Lumen gentium*, chapter 1, on the Church as a mystery, in comparison with the other parts of the same constitution.

The Dialectic of Reception and Interpretation

The movement thus discernible in the conciliar event itself and in postconciliar developments points to a dialectic that it will be helpful to take into consideration as we try to understand the phases and difficulties in the reception and interpretation of the Council. The critical impulse that can be seen at work during and after the Council was aroused because the official self-understanding of the Church, which right up to the Council had been formed by a counter-reformational and neo-scholastic theology, had become questionable. It had become increasingly alien to the real life of human beings and no longer met the needs of an effective pastoral practice. The way had been paved for the movement of critical rejection by the already mentioned preconciliar renewal movements and by the progress of theology, which, in its discovery of the historical dimension of faith and the Church and in the impulses to new systems that it learned from transcendental, existential, and personalist thinking, was making its own the typically modern "anthropological turn."

Pius XII had indeed ventured upon a cautious opening: to a new self-understanding of the Church in the encyclical *Mystici Corporis*; to biblical scholarship in *Divino afflante Spiritu*; and to liturgical reform in *Mediator Dei* and the restoration of the *Triduum sacrum*. On the other hand, in *Humani generis* he had come down strongly on the side of the ahistorical, juridico-intellectual approach that had been dominant since the Modernist controversy and that forbade any attempt to relativize, as simply a historical peculiarity, the theological self-understanding of the Church that had been shaped by the Counter-Reformation and neo-scholasticism.

When John XXIII in his address at the opening of the Council proclaimed history to be the "teacher of life" and recognized the historicity of expressions of faith and of theology, he took a decisive step. The council fathers then repeated it when they rejected the prepared drafts of documents that sought to give permanent validity to the neo-scholastic understanding of the Church. The length of the leap taken by the Council can be gauged by the fact that theologians who only a few years earlier were still subject to special ecclesiastical censorship now became the advisers who set the tone of the proceedings.

The historical relativization of the neo-scholastic understanding of the Church and the critical attitude adopted toward it were theologically possible only because the Council found a basis for its leap in an earlier phase of the Church's self-understanding, namely, in the period of the origins and early life of the Church as attested in sacred scripture and the Fathers of the Church. This basis had the further advantage that it enjoyed a normative status superior to that which modern ecclesiology could claim in and of itself. At this point the intrinsic connection between the "Constitution on Revelation" and the "Constitution on the Church" becomes visible: the advance in ecclesiology is supported by the way in which the "Constitution on Revelation" relates sacred scripture and tradition to each other.

The foundation in the Bible and the early Church was, however, only one point of reference for the new departure. Along with attention to "the treasure of truth that the Church has inherited from the fathers," John XXIII in his opening address assigned the Council the task of "taking the present into account as well." The "world of today" was the other reference point of the Council, and the determination of the Church's place in the modern world became the theme of the pastoral constitution *Gaudium et spes*. The two points of reference exercise a mutual control: the return to sacred scripture and the early Church cannot be made in a biblicist or classicist spirit; the need is rather for us to listen to the gospel as living human beings and relate it to the present age with an eye on the "signs of the times." On the other hand, the reference to sacred scripture and tradition will prevent aggiornamento from becoming simply conformity to the modern world. John XXIII stated still a third point of reference: "The unity of Christians and the human race."

It is characteristic of any movement of critical distancing to emphasize differences between itself and the immediately preceding historical phase, in order in this way to find its own distinct identity. In a phase of critical distancing, distinguishing elements predominate and develop a dynamism of their own, leading possibly to a complete rejection of the elements that played a determining role in the preceding phase. But when the new form develops into the contrary of the form that marked the preceding phase, it is still determined by the phase it seeks to reject, inasmuch as it is its contradictory. A classic example of such a process is the movement of the Reformation churches and the Counter-Reformation Catholic Church in opposite directions; the Council of Trent came too late to draw them together.

In the case of Vatican II the characteristic traits and perils of a movement of critical distancing emerged less at the Council itself (the participants were still too much shaped by the Pian era for this to happen) than in the postconciliar development. With its *communio* ecclesiology the Council laid the foundation for a new ecclesial self-understanding that takes seriously the dignity shared by all members, and with the aggiornamento that it promoted it opened the Church to the modern world. In the ensuing period the elements of the Council were emphasized that distinguished its teaching from Counter-Reformational and neo-scholastic ecclesiology. In the process some interpreters understood the Council to be calling for the leveling down of ecclesial office and its special responsibility, the complete autonomy of local churches, the adoption of forms in keeping with the age, such as democracy, the entrance of the Church into social conflicts, and service to the world instead of worship and prayer.

In general, such demands made their presence felt only as tendencies, and many did not even realize that in going along with these tendencies they were in danger of departing from the normative self-understanding of the Church and not merely from the neo-scholastic view of the Church. Nonetheless, some did expressly call for these changes, and it was these extreme positions that once again elicited reactions in the contrary direction. It was pointed out that Vatican II made no dogmatic claims but was purely pastoral in character; therefore in the area of dogma Trent and Vatican I were still in effect; Vatican II had taken them over unchanged and had reasserted their authority. In addition, many who reacted along these lines were certain that Vatican I also covered with the mantle of its authority the neo-scholastic understanding of the Church that had shaped it. As a result, the movement by which the reception of Vatican II is to be achieved cannot evade the task of clarifying the relationship of this council to the immediately preceding phase of ecclesial self-understanding; it cannot continue to be exclusively a movement of critical distancing.

This call for a new stage in the dialectical movement that characterizes the history of a reception springs from the central hermeneutical problem in the reception of Vatican II: Is Vatican II to be read in the light of Vatican I, or is the direct opposite the case, or will the as yet unachieved reconciliation of the two councils show the necessity of a further stage in the development of ecclesial self-understanding?

Two Phases in the Process of Reception and Interpretation

In speaking of the postconciliar movement and its dialectical structure I have described the two phases that we are in a position today to see as marking the history of the Council's reception up to now. The first phase can be described as a phase of excitement. It was completely under the immediate influence of the Council as a liberating event, and many believed that they were already living fully, and without challenge, in a new situation. They saw Vatican II as an utterly new beginning; they lost sight of the fact that the Council was, and intended to be, part of a continuum.

This phase was succeeded by a phase of *disillusionment* or, as others put it, a phase of *truth* and *realism*. All that was novel in Vatican II had developed its own dynamism, often without possessing the necessary religious and spiritual energies, and as a movement solely of critical distancing from what had gone before, but also, it must be said, in undertakings pregnant with the future and full of hope. The enthusiasts now discovered to their disillusionment the inertia characteristic of so great an institution and its historical forms. They came to realize the weight of tradition, even of immediately preconciliar tradition, present in the conciliar texts and their footnotes and often latent in an unmediated tension with the new beginnings. In this sense, too, Vatican II was a transitional council. At this point, what has been called the internal incoherence or two-sided character of the conciliar texts became the focus of attention. For it is the two faces of the Council itself, and not simply the continuing influence of a preconciliar mentality, that seem to be the essential cause of continuing postconciliar conflicts.

The task that must be faced at the end of the second phase of the postconciliar history of reception is to incorporate what is still binding in preconciliar theology into the newly acquired foundation, that is, into a *communio* ecclesiology and a Christian anthropology that calls for commitment to human dignity. The task is not one to be taken up simply for tactical reasons, that is, to restore consensus in the Church. It is also imposed by the self-understanding of the Catholic Church and by its understanding of its tradition. Unlike the Reformation with its more actualistic understanding of the Church and tradition, the Catholic Church cannot simply write off a phase of its development. It believes rather that in every phase of its development it is effectively led by the Spirit of God, even if in different degrees and even if it must make critical distinctions between what is binding, what is conditioned by the age, and what is perhaps even sinful.

The decisive question, therefore, is whether we are giving the new ecclesial self-understanding enough time and room to develop its own dynamism and shape, and thus to gain the strength it needs for creatively appropriating tradition and incorporating it into a continuity at a new level. Or, to put it differently, the decisive question is whether we are giving the Spirit of God enough freedom to lead the church along new paths. With this goes the freedom to make mistakes (though without adulterating the gospel) and learn from them.

Danger of Interrupting the Process of Reception

For some time now the call for stabilization has been heard in the Church. The normal life of the Church (it is said) must not be turned into a continual conciliar movement; rather a distinction must be made between the new conciliar departure, recorded in the conciliar texts, and postconciliar reception.

Paul VI had already called attention to this distinction at the general meeting of the Council on November 18, 1965: "From now on aggiornamento will mean for us an enlightened insight into the Council's spirit and a faithful application of the norms it has set forth in such a felicitous and holy manner." As a matter of fact, we would fail to understand the special position of a conciliar gathering if we were not to heed the line of demarcation that the end of a council represents. But, it is asked, is aggiornamento not an ongoing task of the Church, and does not the understanding of the Church as *communio* mean that the Church is essentially conciliar in nature? Do we not risk paralyzing the Church if we look on the Council and its decisions as a kind of parking lot? Furthermore, which of the divergent tendencies to be found in the conciliar statements is to be taken as the basis for stabilization?

These questions indicate the problem latent in the contemporary call for a stabilization faithful to the Council. The problem emerges clearly in connection with postconciliar legislation. The two faces or sides of the conciliar texts also leave their mark on postconciliar institutions and the new Code of Canon Law.[4] In fact, many regulations give the impression that the concerns of the conciliar minority, which made their way into the texts of the Council because the majority was willing to compromise, have been given greater weight than the new beginnings supported by the will of the majority. Is this "fidelity," which can indeed appeal to much of the letter of the Council, really a fidelity that regards itself as bound by the spirit of the Council? In short: Does the transitional nature of Vatican II permit any stabilization of a status quo? The twofold call of Paul VI reflects the full tension present in the task of the postconciliar period: faithful application of the norms of the Council and, at the same time, enlightened insight into the spirit of the Council. Unless both are respected, there will be an interruption of the process of reception.

A notable variant of the problem set by legislation for the universal Church is the way in which such legislation takes account of the special postconciliar developments in the particular churches. Completely in line with its ecclesiology of the local church, the Council (in LG 13) sees

4. See A. Acerbi, "Die ekklesiologische Grundlage der nachkonziliaren Institutionen," in Alberigo et al., *Kirche im Wandel*, pp. 208–40; in Italian: "L'ecclesiologia sottesa alle istituzioni ecclesiali post-conciliari," *Cristanesimo nella storia*, 2 (1981) 203–34.

catholicity as unity amid the multiplicity of particular churches and says that one task of the primatial office is to preserve legitimate differences and see to it that they contribute to unity. The vital movement issuing from Vatican II has led to independent developments in the particular churches, in keeping with the pastoral situation in each. If these developments are to continue, the particular churches need an indispensable measure of freedom, and the episcopal conferences must have a corresponding power to make regulations. The local churches must be able to conduct experiments and evaluate them. Was it not the case that the council could achieve its breakthrough to an ecclesiology of *communio* only because it first experienced itself as a *communio*? The same holds for the particular or local churches:

There must be the practice and experience of *communio* so that a corresponding ecclesiology may be able to develop and be accepted in the Church and so that the institutional conclusions of such an ecclesiology may be drawn and acquire the force of custom, in order finally to be turned into law (by the competent authority).[5]

There is, of course, a legitimate concern that if left to follow their own developmental dynamism, the particular churches may drift apart in a way that renders communication impossible at the level of the universal Church. Yet more to be feared today is that developments in the local churches may be too quickly subordinated to regulations issued for the universal Church, and that the reception of Vatican II may be halted because its interpretation has been monopolized by the lawgiver.

These misgivings would be groundless if it were true that the reception of Vatican II is now essentially completed. That it is not so will be argued below. Viewed both as interpretation of the conciliar texts and as movement of renewal, the reception of Vatican II is still incomplete. Everything possible must be done to allow the Church to enter a new phase in the process of reception.

The Dialectic of the Conciliar Texts: A Challenge to Interpretation and Reception

If we look back over the twenty years that have passed since the conclusion of the Council, we will see that for practical purposes no hermeneutic of Vatican II has been developed and therefore an adequate interpretation and reception of the conciliar decisions is still in its initial stages. Two interpretive approaches are in conflict, especially in the second phase of reception: one looks exclusively to the new beginnings produced by the conciliar majority, the other looks exclusively to state-

5. W. Böckenförde, "Der neue Codex Juris Canonici," *NJW*, 36 (1983) 254.

ments that were taken over from the preparatory draft schemata at the instigation of the minority and reflect preconciliar theology. The two approaches share the same method of selective interpretation. The opposition between them has its basis in what has been called the internal incoherence of the conciliar texts themselves. But this rather negative description of the texts will hardly promote the more objective reading of them that is required for the third phase of reception for which we are striving. Perhaps we grasp the objective situation better if we take the transitional character of Vatican II as our starting point and see the two sides of the conciliar texts less as a failure of the Council than as an indication of its limits.

It is customary in dogmatic hermeneutics to interpret the statements of a council as corresponding exactly to the errors the council intended to condemn. This principle cannot be applied to Vatican II, because this council did not intend to condemn any errors. As a reform council with a pastoral goal it aimed rather at a renewal of the Church by concentrating on the heart of the Christian message and in this way serving the Church in its mission, which is to be a sign of salvation in the modern world. Connected with this was the intention of correcting those developments in the life and structure of the Church that had proved themselves one-sided when judged by sacred scripture and the overall tradition of the Church or by the development of ecumenism.

Special attention must be paid here to the method the Council used in linking two concerns: renewal of the Church and preservation of continuity. The method is essentially that of juxtaposition: alongside a doctrine or thesis couched in preconciliar language is set a doctrine or thesis that formulates some complementary aspect. Here are three examples. In the "Constitution on Revelation" the theses on the unity of revelation and on the magisterium's mission of serving the word of God are set alongside the Tridentine thesis on scripture and tradition. In the "Constitution on the Church" the thesis of Vatican I on the primacy of the pope is followed by the thesis on the equally supreme authority of the episcopal college. In the "Decree on Ecumenism" the thesis on the truth of the Catholic Church stands side by side with the thesis on the elements of truth in the other churches.

We must not fail to see, however, that this juxtaposition was rendered possible by deeper insight into the teaching at issue in each instance: in the "Constitution on Revelation" by moving beyond an understanding of revelation based on an instructional model; in the "Constitution on the Church" by giving sacramental structures priority over jurisdictional structures; in the "Decree on Ecumenism" by distinguishing between the *una sancta catholica ecclesia* and the Roman Catholic Church. In addition to this deeper penetration there is a no less important new assessment of relative values. In the "Constitution on the Church," for example, the chapter on the Church as People of God is placed before the chapter on the hierarchy; elsewhere in the same document the teaching on the infallibility of the whole Church in its faith is placed before the teaching on the infallibility of the magisterium. More than that: in contrast to the preconciliar view that all dogmas are equally important, the Council speaks explicitly of a "hierarchy of truths," thus showing that this nuanced assessment of relative importance is expressly intended, and legitimating it as a hermeneutical principle.

The widespread view that sees in the juxtaposition of two theses nothing but a compromise (in the pejorative sense) at the level of formulas is therefore too superficial. The juxtaposition of two theses is doubtless the result of a struggle between majority and minority and of a compromise. But disagreement over how the truths of faith are to be formulated and how a renewal of the Church is to be undertaken is thoroughly legitimate. No less legitimate is compromise in such matters, because the will to compromise is simply the will to remain united as long as the truth of the faith itself is not at issue, and to preserve *communio* with one another and continuity in doctrine. On this point all the council fathers were in agreement; nothing was more distant from the mind of the majority than to do away with the dogmas of Trent and Vatican I.

The limitation of the Council was that it did not succeed, and probably could not have succeeded, in going beyond juxtaposition to a new synthesis. But in this respect there is hardly any difference between Vatican II and other councils. Despite all the theological expertise that is gathered at a council and accompanies its work, a conciliar text is not controlled by a unified systematic intention. Vatican II does indeed achieve the already mentioned insight and new assessment of relative values in not a few doctrinal areas; these, however, are only beginnings. But even juxtaposition is progress, because by being complemented the older thesis is relativized as one-sided and bearings are given for further development in understanding of the faith. The needed synthesis is a task the Council sets for the Church and for theologians; it is a task of reception, which is far from being a merely passive process.

By the very method it adopts the Council thus shows itself to be a transitional council. This approach caught the attention especially of Protestant commentators who speak of a dialectic of conciliar decisions[6] and judge it in a wholly positive way.[7] The dialectic at work in its decisions is at once the Council's strength and its limitation, though the latter is only to be noted objectively and not turned into a reproach. The reproach of internal contradiction can therefore be leveled not so much

6. See R. Weibel, "Konfessionelle Perspektiven in der Darstellung und Würdigung des 2. Vatikanischen Konzils," *Theologische Berichte*, 11 (Zürich/Einsiedeln/Cologne, 1982) 102f.

7. See, e.g., O. Cullmann, "Die Reformbestrebungen des 2. Vatikanischen Konzils im Lichte der Geschichte der katholischen Kirche," *TLZ*, 92 (1967) 1–22; in English: "The Reform of Vatican Council II in the Light of the History of the Catholic Church," in idem, *Vatican Council II: The New Direction* (New York, 1968), pp. 64–101.

at the Council itself as at the use that has subsequently been made of its documents and that has helped form the contemporary picture of a Church in conflict.[8] I am referring to the selective interpretation—"conservative" or "progressive," depending on the viewpoint of the interpreter—that seizes upon one thesis in a pair without attending to the other and incorporates it into a given line of argument. As a result, the conciliar battles between majority and minority, which the Council brought to an end by its method of juxtaposition, are still being fought. Fidelity to the Council requires that both juxtaposed theses be taken seriously and that an attempt be made through more penetrating theological reflection and a renewed ecclesial praxis to reconcile them in a synthesis that will allow further advances. Fidelity to the Council also requires that we pay heed to the stress that the Council itself laid on the one or the other thesis, according as a thesis was supported by the majority or the minority. The fact remains, however, that majority and minority alike agreed to both theses and in particular to their juxtaposition.

Toward a Proper Interpretation of the Conciliar Texts

The abandonment of selective interpretation and the resultant beginning of a third phase of reception require a hermeneutic that reflects fidelity to the Council, its intention, its procedure, and its transitional character. This hermeneutic will concern itself, first of all, with the interpretation of the conciliar texts.

Each of these texts has a preconciliar history, a history within the Council, and, since that time, a postconciliar history or history of influence exercised. The preconciliar history includes the texts drafted by the preparatory commissions; these reflect in varying degrees posttridentine, neo-scholastic, and post–Vatican I theology, but also preconciliar movements of renewal, such as the liturgical and biblical movements. The history of the texts within the Council includes the alternative drafts and suggestions for wording that were offered by the council fathers, the conciliar debates and votes, the addresses and wishes of John XXIII and Paul VI, the work of the commissions, and the successive redactions of the texts.

A development is discernible both in the overall history of the Council's work and in the history of the individual texts: a development, over the course of four years, in the council fathers' level of theological in-

---

8. I am here modifying the thesis I expounded in my article "Die zwiespältige Ekklesiologie des Zweiten Vatikanums—Ursache nachkonziliarer Konflikte," *TTZ*, 92 (1983) 272–83; see H. J. Pottmeyer, "Il concilio vent'anni dopo: retrospettive e prospettive," in *A venti anni dal Concilio. Prospettive teologiche e giuridiche* (Palermo, 1984), pp. 15–32.

formation, in their understanding of one another's positions, and in their awareness of the problems. Among the 2,200 Fathers who were in attendance on the average, this development brought with it the formation of an increasingly clear majority who found themselves united by a desire for renewal. This majority was opposed by a minority of about 220 Fathers, some of whom, especially those who were members of the Curia, exerted no little influence. The minority group was concerned primarily with the preservation of continuity and the abiding validity of Trent and Vatican I.

The wishes expressed regarding formulations and alterations, the interventions in which council fathers justified these wishes during the debates, and the votes taken all manifest a clear tendency that expresses the will of the Council no less than do the new approaches introduced into the text as a result of the tendency. An appropriate hermeneutic requires, therefore, that the texts be interpreted in light of the evolution both of the Council and its texts, and of the tendency manifested therein. When dealing with the juxtaposition of two theses, we must take into account the Council's will to continuity as well as its will to move in a new direction.

"Progressive" interpretations have occasionally forgotten that the Council retracted nothing in the dogmas of Trent and Vatican I. It did indeed relativize these dogmas in the sense that it no longer regarded their formulations as the absolutely final stage of development in the understanding of the faith, but instead located them within the whole tradition of faith. "Conservative" interpretations have occasionally forgotten that despite their will to continuity the council fathers attached differing values to the theses in question. The theses defended by the minority do not represent the will of the Council in the same degree as the theses that passed by an overwhelming majority.

In his excellent contribution to a hermeneutic of Vatican II, G. Thils has proposed two criteria for an objectively valid interpretation:

In principle, fidelity to Vatican II would require that we (a) bring to bear on a question under discussion all the doctrines accepted and promulgated, each in its proper relation to the whole; and (b) point out the trajectory these doctrines traveled in the course of the debates, so that we may see which acquired increasing importance and which consistently lost in importance.[9]

It follows from this that:

To use above all, and set an excessive value on, the doctrines favored by the "minority" or by what has survived from the preparatory schemata, and to neglect or minimize the significance of the changes and additions won by the "majority" at the end of the conciliar discussions would be a form of manipula-

9. G. Thils, ". . . en pleine fidélité au Concile du Vatican II," *La foi et le temps*, 10 (1980) 278; see idem, "Trois traits charactéristiques de l'Eglise postconciliaire," *Bulletin de théologie africaine*, 3 (1981) 233–45.

tion, in the pejorative sense of the term, the degree of which would have to be determined in each case.[10]

An interpretation of the kind that Thils calls for requires an intensive study of the conciliar acts and debates. To this end not only must the acts of the council be available, but suitable tools must also be forged. At present such a tool exists, in the form of a *Synopsis historica*,[11] only for *Lumen gentium*. Attention must also be paid to the personal accounts of the council fathers and theologians, which are already available in the form of diaries, exchanges of letters, and reports, or which, it is to be hoped, may yet be published.[12] After the important early commentaries on the Council, mostly by theologians who took part in it, it would be helpful to have a second generation of commentaries with a critical approach based not only on a detailed knowledge of the acts but also on the history of the Council's influence down to the present time. They would provide the basis for a new phase in the reception of Vatican II.

Beyond the Council out of Fidelity to the Council?

The reception of the Council as a movement is an equally unfinished business. This aspect of the Council is sometimes referred to as its "spirit"; what is meant is the intellectual and spiritual impulse toward renewal that animated the work of the Council itself and that emanates from it. "Spirit" is also a theologically appropriate description. For, just as the Council understood itself to be a Pentecostal event, so its authentic reception can only be a renewal of the Church in the Holy Spirit. Here the task confronting a hermeneutic of the Council goes far beyond an objective interpretation of the texts. Something more is needed: a *discretio spirituum*, a recognition and distinction or discernment of spirits.

I must call attention here to a danger connected with the reception of the Council as a movement, and a danger that "progressive" interpretations of the Council have not always avoided. I am referring to the hermeneutical misunderstanding summed up in the slogan: Beyond the Council out of fidelity to the Council! The slogan can indeed have an acceptable meaning if it refers to the new synthesis to which theologians and the Church are challenged by the unreconciled juxtapositions found in the conciliar statements. The slogan is erroneous, however, if it is meant as a call to leave the Council behind us. As I said earlier, no one can seriously claim that the transition the Council represents and at which it aimed is already behind us. Such a claim cannot be maintained

10. Thils, ". . . en pleine fidélité," p. 279.
11. G. Alberigo and F. Magistretti, eds., *Constitutionis Dogmaticae Lumen gentium Synopsis Historica* (Bologna, 1975).
12. See Weibel, "Konfessionelle Perspektiven," pp. 93–123.

with regard either to the religious and spiritual dimension of the Council or to its critical and ecclesial dimension. I have already called attention to the uneven development in reception of these two dimensions of the Council as a movement. As a result, the religious and spiritual depth of many conciliar texts has thus far really not been adequately appreciated and received. Yet, as Paul VI said, only an entrance into the "spirit" of the Council will make it possible to form the Church into a fruitful *communio* in the Spirit; but even the realization of this in structures and consciousnesses can hardly be said to be finished business.

The hermeneutical misunderstanding of which I am speaking finds expression in the attempt to separate the "spirit" of the Council from its letter and then leave the letter behind. The attempt does not represent fidelity to the Council. Despite the limitation, already described, of the conciliar texts, the "spirit" of the Council is tied to them, because without them it would lack any sense of direction. The "spirit" of the Council makes itself known from the direction given in the texts. Conversely, of course, it is only in this "spirit" that the texts are properly understood.

"Spirit" is to be understood here pneumatologically. The focus on the word of God in sacred scripture; the development of the Church as a *communio* and a sacrament of salvation for the whole world; solidarity with the poor; an opening to separated Christians and to non-Christians—all these elements that make up the Council as a movement and embody the "spirit" of the Council are nothing else than the gifts of the Holy Spirit. Above and beyond its technical meaning, therefore, "reception" means the reception, the acceptance, of the gifts of God that alone make his reign a reality. Rightly, then, does the Council urge pastors to discover and heed the charisms that the Spirit of God bestows on his church. New forms of charismatic experience, of community structures, of lay participation, and of commitment to the poor and social justice, as well as developments in the separated churches, can be gifts of the Holy Spirit, and reception of them can be part of the reception of the Council.

Critical attention must be given, finally, to the concept of aggiornamento, which became a programatic slogan for the Council as a movement and for its reception. It is remarkable to see the unanimity with which both "progressives" and "conservatives" criticize it today. With naive optimism the Council itself and the postconciliar period uncritically took over the bourgeois liberal ideals of the West as represented by the Kennedy era and the New Enlightenment; they even saw in them an expression of the gospel and the working of the Spirit of God. They paid too little attention to the fact that in vast areas of the world injustice and oppression—or, in theological terms, the powers of evil—reigned. The disillusionment that has settled in since then shows what a limited vision lay behind the optimism.

This criticism, which has been directed especially against the pastoral constitution *Gaudium et spes* and its influence, is not entirely unjustified.

In its legitimate effort to enter into dialogue with the modern world, the pastoral constitution occasionally overlooked the fact that such concepts as justice, progress, and human dignity do not necessarily have the same meaning in the Christian and the modern understanding of them. As a result, in the ensuing period not a few people imagined that fidelity to the Council required an unconditional solidarity with all forces that marched behind banners championing the attainment of a world more worthy of human beings. The danger in this outlook was that of interpreting the content of the gospel in terms of the common goal supposedly shared with others—for example, liberals or Marxists—and of reducing it to a common denominator.

Even at the Council, no less than later on, there were voices—including Protestant—that warned:

We as Christians may not be satisfied with simply saying the same thing that the world says—even if we say it with special urgency. We must say it differently and say different things whenever possible, even things that the world does not like to hear or has trouble understanding. . . . There should have been a stronger and more conscious reaction against the danger of eliminating the scandal that is part of the gospel.[13]

As a matter of fact, Vatican II, like any other council, was not only a Pentecostal event but also an event of its own time. It is reasonable to think, then, that not only the Holy Spirit but the spirit of the age speak in it—an assertion that is not derogatory but a statement of fact. In any case, critical attention to elements reflective of the age is part of the hermeneutic of a council. Many statements of Vatican II became possible only after historians had brought to light the ways in which Trent and Vatican I reflected their times. The passage of time and the change of historical situation allow us today to see how Vatican II was also tied to its temporal setting, and to take this into account in an interpretation of it that is objectively valid and true to its spirit. Not the least result of this realization will be an insight into the necessity and possibility of a new phase in the reception of Vatican II and of a corresponding hermeneutic. The *discretio spirituum* or ability to distinguish between the Holy Spirit and the spirit of the times and judge accordingly is part of this hermeneutic.

In fact, the reception of Vatican II is not yet complete. All attempts to break off the process of reception—whether through overly restrictive legislation or through a "progressive" interpretation—are incompatible with a professed fidelity to the Council. A new phase in the process of reception is certainly due, one that will end the conflict of selective interpretations and explain the letter of the conciliar texts in accordance with the "spirit" of the Council, aided by a hermeneutic that does justice to the character of Vatican II as a transitional council.

13. Cullmann, "Reform" (n. 7, above), p. 94 (translation somewhat modified).

Louis de Vaucelles

3. The Changing Social Contexts of Postconciliar Catholicism

Introduction

Every council has been profoundly marked by its environment and by the kinds of questions raised at the time. Furthermore, the basic principle by which it is possible to reconstruct the historical context of the discussion and to analyze the conditions in which a council was received is itself dependent on the way in which a particular civilization conceives of its relationship to religion.

In the era when Christendom was a reality, conciliar assemblies dealt with problems of faith, morality, and canonical discipline in a context in which Christian beliefs affected the entire life and culture of Western peoples. This was true at the level of how the world was experienced and the level of a rational approach that consisted essentially in theological reflection. Doctrinal conflicts, schisms, and heresies had to do less with the horizon of accepted truths than with their interpretation. Thus the great sixteenth-century break between Protestantism and Catholicism appears to us now to have been essentially a dispute over the proper way of understanding how the identity of the faith was to be maintained amid the socio-cultural upheavals of the Renaissance and over the conclusions to be drawn for ecclesiastical reform. Even though the crisis would eventually influence the entire religious evolution of the West, it had hardly any immediate effect on the social recognition and relevance of confessional Christianity.

Reception, for its part, was for both clergy and faithful essentially a matter of obedience; political considerations entered in only in regard to the acceptance by rulers of the canonical and disciplinary decrees of councils.

The situation changed radically as Western civilization gradually asserted its independence of Christian authorities in the areas of science and culture, ethics and social organization. The process began in the critical approach of the Enlightenment to religious tradition and moved into the socio-political order in the American and French revolutions. It continued throughout the nineteenth century, when it caused the Church to adopt an intransigent attitude to a society that was rejecting its former state of tutelage.

This attitude can be seen at work in Vatican I, at which the majority of the conciliar fathers, greatly disturbed by the growth of a liberal ideology and by secularizing interferences of the states in the life of the churches, adopted a strategy of withdrawal, condemnation, and defense against an ever more threatening environment. A fundamental concern of the episcopate of that day was to establish at the heart of the Church a power strong enough to resist the encroachments of political authorities; the bishops hoped to accomplish this by the proclamation of papal infallibility and primacy of jurisdiction. To the same end, the hierarchy emphasized the nature of the Church as a *societas perfecta* whose specific character should, they thought, be all the more respected by the various governments because, in the final analysis, it gave legitimacy to their own temporal authority.

Finally, the Council crowned its work by showing in the constitution *Dei Filius* how revelation presupposed and completed reason; the intention here was to answer the accusations of obscurantism directed against the Christian faith and to protect the faithful against the danger of contamination from the rationalism around them. In regard to the reception of Vatican I it must be said that the acceptance of conciliar decisions no longer concerned the civil authorities but had become an internal affair of Catholicism. Members of the Church were urged to submit to the doctrinal and practical directives of the supreme pontiff and the bishops.

At Vatican II the Church introduced a new type of relationship to its environment. Ratifying the changed attitude to modernity that various groups in the Church had already adopted, and drawing conclusions from the de facto reconciliation that had already taken place between the Church and Western democracies, the Council was to make openness to the world and attention to the realities of contemporary societies one of the cardinal points of its teaching. In this spirit it acknowledges, along with religious freedom, the values specific to other Christian confessions, other religions, and historical movements embodying an ideal of human liberation. It develops a basic anthropology that tries to take into account the new conditions affecting a human race that now shares one and the same scientific and technological civilization. In so doing, the bishops effect a historic shift of focus from an intransigent Catholicism to the positive aspects of the human adventure in our time. Instead of condemning the civilization that issued from the Enlightenment, the hierarchy tries to uncover and foster its valid elements in economic, social, and cultural life. It urges believers to play a part in the building of a world in which the prospects opened up by unprecedented progress and growth go hand in hand with a concern for greater justice in relationships between different social strata and among nations. In short, the Church as an institutional body involves itself in its environment by trying to know it, understand it, and serve it in accordance with the specifically spiritual character of the Church.

This new perspective and new scale of values have inevitably affected the reception of the Council, for reception is not a matter simply of obedience and discipline; other factors play a part. To begin with, there is the degree of attention and sensitivity that believers show to the social environment of Christianity. For the integralist Catholics whose spokesman Archbishop Lefebvre was to become some years after the Council, statements of faith are by their nature strictly independent of a historical context that is contingent and, in addition, has an ineradicable defect: the denial of the authority of God and his ministers, despite the fact that this is the only source of stability in human societies and of legitimacy for political power. Other believers will be led to adopt varying attitudes according to their situations and their involvements in society. The same phenomenon of diversified response is repeated on a larger scale in the local churches as they face the problems of the regions and continents within which they develop. As a result, the reception of Vatican II, which I shall now study in the light of the development of contemporary societies, suddenly becomes the source of an internal pluralism at the theological and pastoral levels.

Developments in the Several Third Worlds

One of the salient facts of contemporary history since the Bandung Conference (1955) has undoubtedly been the appearance of the Third World peoples on the world scene and their efforts to assert their place in the international community. At the moment when Vatican II was finishing its work, decolonization was almost complete. Other urgent needs were now determining the goals of the newly independent states: the building of national unity, the modernization of socio-economic structures, the effort to change relationships between North and South, and to unite the poor countries in a solidarity based on common interests. Though undertaken in very diverse contexts and by different methods, these endeavors had one and the same purpose: to meet the vast expectations of peoples who want more than anything else to escape from the scourge of destitution and ignorance and enjoy the benefits of progress.

Third World churches saw the critical importance of the efforts being made to improve the living conditions of these disinherited peoples and quickly realized that they too must take part in the process with the means at their disposal and in accordance with their position in society. As a result, these churches began to reread the conciliar documents and bring them to bear on their own environment. Vatican II had spoken of the Third World in very Western terms; the council fathers had conceived the general situation there as one of backwardness and had thought that improvement must come from an effort on the part of the rich nations to practice justice and solidarity with the poorer countries; this, after all, was in the real interests of the rich countries. On the initiative of the episcopates of Latin America, Africa, and Asia, three intercontinental meetings were held, at Medellín (1968), Kampala (1969), and Manila (1970), respectively, for the purpose of determining how the churches in these varying political and cultural zones should make "the struggle for justice and the transformation of the world . . . a constitutive dimension of the preaching of the gospel," as the Roman Synod of Bishops put it in 1971. The result of these various new readings of the conciliar documents and of Paul VI's encyclical *Populorum progressio* (1967) was a very rapid and wide-ranging mobilization of the vital forces of Catholicism and an involvement that varied in kind from region to region.

Social and Political Tensions in Latin America

The Church in Latin America and the Caribbean has been faced with a difficult situation by reason of its audience and its social responsibilities. Despite relatively satisfying results in the postwar period, growth slowed after 1980 and has been offset by the increase in population. Industrialization and economic expansion, though quite impressive in some countries, have not succeeded in reducing pockets of destitution in both rural and urban areas. Inequality, underemployment, and social tensions have increased; this was a point clearly emphasized at the Medellín meeting (1968), which also singled out the dependence of Latin America on the decision-making centers of the international economic system as one reason for the failure of the modernization being undertaken. This unsatisfying balance sheet highlights the failure not only of a policy of development but also of the reforms undertaken by populist governments and Christian Democratic political parties. At different dates the figures of Vargas, Perón, and Frei symbolize the collapse in Brazil, Argentina, and Chile of the popular hopes they had aroused.

The end of the 1960s saw a sudden heightening of discontent in many Latin American countries. Leftist forces, popular movements, and revolutionary groups, all more or less influenced by the Cuban experience, denounced the prevailing state of affairs and tried to create the conditions for a socialist alternative; they were strengthened by Allende's accession to power in 1970. Faced with mounting frustration and disorder, a large segment of the middle and upper classes considered it necessary to seek the help of the army. The result was the appearance of military regimes that appeal to the ideology of national security as justification for suppressing all opposition.

The majority of the hierarchy saw the seriousness of the situation and called for profound social changes as a cure for the institutionalized violence that was threatening the peace of Latin America. This explains the positions taken at Medellín. These were well received by the active elements of the Latin American churches and contributed greatly to the development of two often associated phenomena: the basic ecclesial communities and the theologies of liberation.

The success of the former in a number of countries and regions (there are said, for example, to be over 60,000 in Brazil alone) is due to the fact that these communities have managed to combine the basic religious experience of their members with an effort at emancipation and improvement of living conditions in which the people on the spot are the primary agents and benefactors. This type of association that integrates all aspects of life enables peoples traditionally submissive and even resigned to their lot to acquire confidence in their own ability to organize against the most widespread forms of institutionalized violence and to undertake modest but meaningful forms of development. In some areas, the attempts thus made were hampered by brutal and sometimes bloody interventions by the forces of repression and could not have succeeded and lasted without the rise at the local level of natural leaders and the aid of priests who were concerned to help establish Christian communities capable of taking independent control of their own religious and human development.

It was from this experience that the liberation theologians drew much of their inspiration, for it derives basically from the will to listen to the voice of the poor and to be at the service of an evangelization that cannot be carried out unless the social environment and real situation of those to whom it is addressed are taken into account. This explains the interest of these theologians in popular longings for justice and in the historical movement to which these longings give rise.

The rapid development of the basic communities and the theologies of liberation, though encouraged by a number of bishops, has aroused not only opposition from outside the Church but profound misgivings in other bishops and Christians. These circles, and the Vatican, criticize a development that, as they see it, is driving the Church along the road of secularization and political radicalism, and is thus deeply dividing it at the very time when its unity is more than ever necessary in the face of very authoritarian regimes. Several attempts to gain control of the situation have already been made: a change of direction at the head of CELAM (1972); efforts to modify the positions of Medellín during the preparation for the Puebla meeting (1979). Other attempts are being made at the present time: pressures on bishops regarded as too favorable to the movement, and appointment of bishops who are opposed to it. Proceedings have recently been started against some liberation theologians on the grounds that their reliance on Marxism has led them into a theological reductionism that is dangerous to the faith. More perhaps than elsewhere, political divisions have made their way into the churches of Latin America that are faced with formidable emergencies and especially tense situations, as in El Salvador and Nicaragua.

Whatever the future may bring, the postconciliar evolution of the Church in Latin America will have strongly emphasized the impossibility of separating faith from social responsibility, and will have raised a basic question that echoes throughout the other Third Worlds: What is to be done to prevent the exclusion of the disinherited and the poor from a development and modernization, the necessity of which no one questions?

The Special Challenges of Subsaharan Africa

After being subjected for several centuries to the slave trade and then to foreign occupation, the black continent achieved political independence in and around the 1960s. Exceptions were the Portuguese territories and Rhodesia, which became independent later on. At present, only Namibia, which is controlled by South Africa where apartheid still reigns, has not yet become a sovereign state. Working within the framework of boundaries inherited from the colonial period, the new states are concerned first and foremost to develop a national consciousness (a process slowed by the continuance of ethnic antagonisms) and to provide the conditions for a much more rapid development than in the period when the European powers exercised authority. The process, in which a variety of models and methods have been followed, is leading in our day to results that vary but for the most part are remote from the hopes that inspired them. Two major obstacles, one cultural, the other political, have impeded real progress.

The choices aimed at fostering development and a gradual integration into the dominant civilization have encountered the obvious difficulties of a lack of trained personnel, and insufficient capital for improving infrastructures and the means of production. They have also run up against the lack of education and instruction in populations in which the influence of traditional mentalities is a strong brake on the spread of various forms of learning and on the use of the practical experience developed in the modern age. The problem is extremely complex. It is not automatically solved by a deliberate and violent overthrow of ancient socio-cultural structures, as is evident when we look at the shattering and destruction of age-old modes of life and thought that inevitably occur with the introduction of progress, wages, monetary exchanges, and schooling. In other words, modernization irreversibly jeopardizes the cultural patrimony of ancient civilizations. It is being discovered that authentic development, if it is to be effective, requires a reliance on the

values and wisdom inherited from the past. The challenge is a formidable one and is especially pronounced in Africa; it explains the efforts
being made to foster a development from within.

In the field of religion the African churches are facing questions that
cut close to the bone: How are we to be Christians without renouncing
our own roots? The answer seems linked to a recovery of the essential
data of Judeo-Christian revelation as related to the special traditions and
values of African societies. The call for this kind of vision had already
been issued in the well-known book, *Des prêtres noirs s'interrogent* (Paris:
Cerf, 1956) and has been repeated ever since the Council, to the point of
profoundly influencing its reception.

Evangelization must have its starting point "within Africa, and no
longer outside it," writes Cameroon theologian Jean-Marc Ela, who goes
on to say: "We can no longer avoid the encounter between faith and our
radical contingency wherein God addresses Africans in the words of
their own land and tradition." These views have been repeated by African episcopates and echoed by Paul VI and John Paul II during their
travels in Uganda, Zaire, and Kenya.

There is often a long delay between the expression of desires or intentions and their fulfillment. The process of implementation challenges a
too immediately universalist conception of Christianity, upsetting many
who are attached to traditional canonical rules and to a very centralized,
Western functioning of the Church in the areas of liturgy, celebration of
the sacraments, and theological discourse. Undertakings in new directions are still limited; this includes marriage, an area of serious problems, as is well known. However, some reforms, connected in many
instances with the lack of priests, have made it possible to draw upon
traditional solidarities and, especially in recently created dioceses, to establish neighborhood and village communities in which the faith is lived
in a manner reflective of local contexts. Without being the only ones to
do so, these communities can turn outward to other inhabitants, who
belong to Islam or the traditional religions, and lay the foundations for a
mobilization of all in the service of an endogenous development. The
way in which the churches of Africa are trying to achieve a better inculturation of Christianity in the realities of their continent cannot fail to
have results for the kind of modernization that requires a raising of consciousness, a formation, and commitments adapted to the concrete situation of the people.

A further obstacle to development in Africa is, on the one hand, dependencies produced by the mechanisms of the world market and, on
the other, the malfunctioning of political authorities who, in many countries and regardless of their ideological persuasions, tend to run the state
for the profit of dominant minorities. This leads to many injustices
whose principal victims are the rural and urban poor, the unemployed,
and the unrooted young. In addition, there are the disastrous consequences of governmental instability and authoritarianism, of the con-

tempt shown by some leaders for human rights, and of civil wars and other conflicts with their retinue of victims and refugees. Some episcopates—in Zaire, Madagascar, and elsewhere—have courageously resisted these abuses by criticizing civil authorities, calling for reforms, and urging believers not to be resigned but to work to rectify the situation. They bear witness to the real conditions of the life of the people, and their words, passed on by pastors and theologians, are helping in no small degree to change the abusive ways of those in power.

Other Significant Cases

Under this heading I group various parts of Asia which have one thing in common: for demographic and cultural reasons, Christianity plays a minor role. This is the case in India and the Far East, except for the Philippines where the problems and the positions taken by Catholics tend to resemble those of Latin Americans. In this part of the world, the efforts of Vatican II toward openness to non-Christian religions and toward an attitude of positive tolerance have been taken up by the Manila Conference and the Federation of Asian Bishops' Conferences.

Theologians have begun to work on the problem of inculturating Christianity in the great Asiatic civilizations. Intercultural and interreligious dialogue has gotten off the ground and has been expanded. Its purpose is not simply to compare spiritual experiences and doctrines. In a number of cases, especially in India, it includes reflection on the responsibility of Hinduism, Buddhism, and the Christian churches for the improvement of the lot of those people for whom an intense religious spirit and a desire to escape insecure living conditions are not inherently incompatible. This suggests the importance of "practical ecumenism," that is, an orthopraxis that tries to meet developmental needs that vary from country to country.

The situation that the introduction of competitive, export-oriented industry has created in Taiwan, South Korea, Hong Kong, and Singapore entails special problems of social justice that are different from those of India with its dual economy, or the Philippines, which still suffers from serious internal tensions. It is to be noted, moreover, that in the latter two countries some Christian circles are providing a growing audience for theologies of liberation.

Not to be overlooked, finally, is the fact that the challenge that China represents for the universal Church is awakening distinctive echoes in the Christian churches of Southeast Asia as a result of their geographical nearness to China and the presence of a sizable population of Chinese origin.

At the end of this survey (in which I shall say nothing of the very special situation of minority Christian communities in the Arab-Muslim world) one fact is undeniable: in their practices and in their theologies, which display the creative character of the Christian tradition as they face the demands of their environment, the young churches have continued, on the one hand, the innovative intentions of Vatican II regarding openness to non-Western religions and cultures and, on the other, the Council's reflections on North-South relationships and the problems of the Third World. In their efforts at inculturation these churches are trying to be no longer mere assimilated appendages of a foreign religion, that of the West. They are likewise participating, and not without making original contributions, in the tasks of development and the struggles to overcome injustice, oppression, violence, and destitution. So serious an involvement is proving to be a source of profound conflicts within the ecclesial body, because in the last analysis it raises radical questions about the real loyalties of groups of believers and about the way they are to be accepted.

The progress the young churches have made in achieving integration into their respective societies has had repercussions in their internal life. Pastoral care is heavily influenced by a concern to form Christian communities that can help the baptized live and understand their faith in relation to the problems of their environs. This accounts for a number of practices not anticipated by Vatican II, especially in the area of ministerial responsibilities. Similarly, inasmuch as cultures differ no less than do socio-economic and political contexts, these churches have produced varied theological approaches to the same Christian mystery.

An important consequence of these manifestations has been that concern for union with the universal Church has taken a different form. The unity of Catholicism is no longer confused with uniformity or regarded as something ready-made. It is seen rather as a task that has several dimensions—institutional, theological, and pastoral. This is an extremely important issue, for it demands—as the Council clearly saw—a reform of ecclesial structures and of the spirit that guides their functioning. It is a fact, of course, that there has been no really serious effort at such a reform, as is clear from, for example, the recent appearance of a new Code of Canon Law. Despite the difficulties and reverses they meet within the Church, the Christian communities of the Third World seem nonetheless moved by a dynamism that forces the older Christian churches to examine their own vitality and their attitude toward the peoples of the South.

The Uncertainties of Western Modernity

Major Changes

As we all know, Vatican II was held at a time of material prosperity unmatched in the history of the West. This exceptional situation was due to the effectiveness of a particular socio-economic model—namely, neocapitalism—and to a set of advantageous conditions that worked in combination with it. It began on the morrow of the Second World War, when the urgent need for rebuilding and for renewing international exchanges (stimulated by the Marshall Plan) fitted in neatly with the necessary modernization of the various spheres of activity and a heavy demand for consumer goods on the part of peoples who had been sorely tested by the effects of depression and of the war that had ravaged Europe.

The response to this set of challenges—to which was added the need of reconversion and development in the United States—was made possible by the revolution in technology and tools, the spread of mechanization, the concentration of businesses, and transformations in the character of work, which was increasingly following the assembly-line model. These new conditions quickly resulted in a large-scale production of inexpensive goods, the sale of which was ensured by an increasingly solvent market. The reciprocal influence of supply and a demand stimulated by the increased buying power of wages led to ever greater profits and therefore to investments made more promising by the assimilation of technological advances and the creation of new products. Accumulation of capital, advances in productivity, and mass consumption went hand in hand.

The originality of the new system was not due solely to the factors mentioned; it was due also to the introduction, under the aegis of public authorities, of regulatory mechanisms that would prevent the whole from slipping out of control and would ensure a socially more balanced distribution of profits. An effort was made to harmonize technological progress and modernization, on the one side, with social justice and a higher living standard, on the other. On the European scene this explains, for example, the creation of social security systems, the establishment of a minimum wage, the extension of collective agreements, and the development of institutionalized relationships between employers, unions, and a state whose role was continually expanding because of its increasingly important interventions, regulations, and activity as financier. To these structural changes were added the liberalization of trade, increased exchanges, and the new ways in which these were organized under the direction of such institutions as the General Agreement on Tariffs and Trade (GATT), the International Monetary Fund (IMF), and the United Nations' Economic Commission for Europe (ECE).

An assessment of these changes reveals negative aspects, to which I shall return, but it also shows undeniable successes that were greatly aided by the inexpensiveness of raw materials and oil. Until the beginning of the 1970s the Western countries experienced a growth in gross national product and an unprecedented rise in the living standard. Given the tangible fruits of prosperity and the beginning of East-West détente, many Westerners were understandably optimistic about the accomplishments of technico-scientific civilization. At this same period the majority of the council fathers felt the same way, as can be seen from the pastoral constitution *Gaudium et spes.*

But the period immediately after the end of Vatican II saw the appearance of tensions and contradictions. It was increasingly difficult for the brilliant results being obtained to hide the social cost of the changes that had come about. In France, the exodus from the countryside and the call for foreign workers, both of them dictated by the need for unskilled labor, meant an extremely rapid urbanization in conditions that were poor and even less than poor. Changes in the modes of production led everywhere to a disqualification of the laboring class and the formation of a work force that was employed in repetitive piecework of a very simple kind. At the cultural level there was at the same time an increasingly vocal criticism of modern industrial societies whose specifically economic logic had invaded the entire socio-political sphere, thus causing the proper finalities of the latter to become blurred. The problem of restoring a public space and public debate in democracies began to be seen, although only confusedly. In large measure, the student rebellions in and around 1968 were a translation of this latent malaise as perceived chiefly in the institutional constraints of a system that was organized in subservience to the demands of production and consumption. This accounts for the surfacing of forms of rejection that were varied and ambiguous, but related to basic questions still not answered today.

In any case, we can see in all this the preliminary signs of wear and tear in the prevailing model whose malfunctionings, already perceptible as early as 1965 when the profits on capital began to decline, were to become evident in the monetary and economic crises of the following decade. The force of these blows was intensified by successive rises in the price of oil, the resurgence of East-West tensions, and the deterioration of the situation in the countries of the South, which found their difficulties aggravated by the crisis. The threats to their growth and the problems caused by their indebtedness had repercussions in the North Atlantic world. In short, the general climate of Western civilization had altered in about twenty years. The hopes aroused by progress and the possibilities it opened up for the rational organization and responsible development of our societies were succeeded by a sense of uncertainty and of relative powerlessness due to the difficulties of achieving a genuine political mastery of economic realities and a regulation of international relationships.

The difficult period through which modernity has been passing is felt all the more keenly because the great Western traditions are proving quite ineffective in the search for ways and means to cope with the problems of the present time. As the 1968 generation intuitively realized, the crisis is global: its economic and political forms point to an erosion in the visions of the world that were the bedrock of our societies. We have seen not only the limitations of a technico-scientific culture based on an instrumental mastery of nature but also the loss of credibility by Marxist-Leninist regimes in view of their record in Eastern Europe. The liberal democracies and their institutions are suffering the effects of a poorly controlled economic development and have lost both their authority and their capacity for social integration.

Because our contemporaries have no really dynamizing motives for collective life, many of them have retreated into private life, the desire for personal fulfillment, and the success of their children; at the same time they distance themselves from the great structures for the training and supervision of society, which are accepted as unavoidable necessities but not perceived as sources of inspiration and motivation. This development, which is very characteristic of the recent evolution of modernity, has gone hand in hand with the rise of an individualism intensified by the availability of education, the spread of culture, and advances in living standards that guarantee material security and the satisfaction of essential needs.

The Churches and Secularization

The churches seem to be no better equipped than other Western institutions to respond to the questions and changes of our age. To begin with, they experience the same difficulty in maintaining their internal cohesion and socio-religious ascendancy. In Catholicism, for example, the classic means of training and supervising the faithful are proving much less effective: urbanization and social mobility have profoundly altered the traditional parish unit, and the accentuation of cultural differences within communities has not been without influence on the vision that the baptized have of Christianity. Not only are a large number indifferent toward the official pronouncements of the Church, but even staunch believers themselves are picking and choosing among the norms set down by the ecclesial institution, especially in regard to the obligations of religious practice, traditional observances, and ethical precepts governing private life. The reactions to the encyclical *Humanae vitae* made clear the reservations of Catholic opinion about papal teaching on sexual morality. The attitude is not new, but it does have a new face: it is accompanied by criticism and at times even rejection of ecclesiastical teachings, especially when they are cast in an outdated language and rest on arguments from authority.

The increasing autonomy claimed by Catholic consciences is to be seen not only in contestation but in the area of divergent public expression; the synods of a number of European churches have provided the most striking example of this phenomenon. The national status of these agencies and the fact that the laity is associated with them made possible an effort at communication and dialogue that contrasted with the usual past practice in which teachings and directives used to make their way from the center to the periphery, from the top (the hierarchy) to the bottom (the faithful). The incidents to which I am referring have made clear the existence of tensions and differences of approach between the official positions taken by the institution and those of various groups of believers on points of morality, sacramental and liturgical pastoral practice, the organization of ministries, the status of women within the Church, and ecumenical relationships. From the Dutch Pastoral Council to the National Pastoral Congress at Liverpool, by way of the synods of West Germany, Switzerland, and Denmark, the same reformist aspirations have emerged. Although they have not been accepted by the Holy See, the fact is that in them a Catholic opinion has found open and responsible expression. The integration, now a reality, of Catholics into the life of the Western democracies has not been without its influence on an evolution that is likewise being fostered within the Church by the development of theological pluralism.

The consequences of secularization, defined here by the fact that the religious sphere is no longer either all-inclusive or a womb within which the universe develops, have a counterpart (I am still speaking of the postconciliar period) in the fact that Christianity in the West has suffered a palpable loss of relevance and social effectiveness. Thus, beginning in the 1960s, the model on which Catholic magisterial teaching on relationships between Church and society and between faith and politics is based has crumbled. The fundamental presupposition of this model—the quest for a specifically Christian model of society, one considered not to be subject to the errors and inadequacies of liberalism and Marxism—has not stood up against the changes brought about by contemporary modernity. This is clear in France, where the crisis affecting specialized Catholic Action youth movements (*Jeunesse Étudiante Chrétienne* and the *Mouvement Rural de la Jeunesse Chrétienne*) has shown the idealist character of a teaching whose abstract principles prove unable to cope with the working of modern societies.

In broader terms, Catholicism in the North Atlantic world finds itself facing a twofold danger: either adaptation pure and simple to its environment, or retreat into a religious life that is alien to the interests, issues, and risks of contemporary history. Adaptation of this kind calls into question the very originality of the Christian tradition, whereas withdrawal will end in cutting the Church off from society even more completely and in stripping its message of significance. Between recovery through adaptation and a withdrawal of a sectarian kind there is but a narrow passage. The official positions of the Holy See and part of the episcopate tend toward inevitable compromises with modernity (defense of human rights, assertion of the need of a revision of North-South relationships, concern to work for the establishment of peace between blocs and nations), even while maintaining a sacral vision of the world. This approach has not succeeded in surmounting the contradictions pointed out above.

As a result, we have seen other approaches developing alongside the unchanging theses of an intransigent Catholicism. The most fully developed come from theologies that recognize the inability of the *sacred* to infiltrate the contemporary world and *consecrate* it. They therefore tend, first of all, to reinterpret the history of Christianity by taking seriously the external constraints that have weighed upon the life of Christian communities, and the ways in which these communities have given concrete expression to the originality of the faith in the varying contexts that were theirs. This kind of hermeneutic of Christianity is leading scholars nowadays to study the influence exercised by the Church's social environment and to ascertain the conditions in which it is possible for the specific character of the gospel message to come to light. Those taking this approach are still very much in the minority, but its application, initiated here and there, is an effort to give the Church an existence at the heart of the complexities and questions of our civilization.

Problems of Conciliar Aggiornamento in Eastern Europe

The picture I have been sketching would not be complete if I did not touch on the role of Vatican II in the Catholic churches that are living under communist regimes. A basic characteristic of these regimes is that they will not countenance the coexistence of another vision of the world, be it religious or nonreligious, alongside their own. As a general rule, the situation of these Christian communities is extremely precarious, even if in a number of cases (Poland, East Germany, Hungary) the importance of Christianity in the national tradition has led the authorities to express its hostility in less direct and less visible ways.

The aggiornamento that Vatican II wanted has thus found itself confronted in these cases with a political and ideological environment deeply hostile to any reform and renewal of Catholic communities. Recognizing the permanence of religion and the failure of attempts to hasten its decline, the ruling oligarchy is concerned above all to exercise a close control over the Church, to limit its activities in a strict way, and to reduce it as far as possible to a marginal existence. It therefore opposes anything likely to cause believers to emerge from the ghetto in which the communist party has enclosed them and to become agents of social change. Consequently, as is clear from the interdiocesan synods of East Germany and Cracow, in the socialist world the postconciliar movement has been concerned largely with the preservation and strengthening of the faith itself by means of the liturgy, with a pastoral practice based on popular devotion, and with a Christian initiation supported by family life.

Fear that civil authorities will exploit any division within the Church has checked intraecclesial debates and favored the continuation of traditional clericalism. In addition, the local hierarchies invoke the character of the socio-political context as justification for their opposition to the spread and adaptation of theologies and correlative practices originating in the West. This they do at the risk of underestimating the effects of secularization, which is at work in the socialist world no less than elsewhere. This attitude is found even in Poland where Catholicism enjoys a privileged social position by reason of its links with the people and the national culture.

Conclusion

At the end of our journey one point is clear: the reception of Vatican II has been heavily influenced by the situation in human societies, their developments and setbacks, the questions they raise. In face of this fact Catholic circles have reacted in two opposed ways.

In the view of some, this real influence of the environment should not be exaggerated: the transformations history brings and their repercussions on the ecclesial body are in the final analysis only happenstances of minor importance that lead the Church from time to time to adapt itself in limited ways. The recent conciliar aggiornamento had for its purpose to meet only this need. We must limit ourselves strictly to this minimal updating and not let ourselves be contaminated by the secularistic extremes of modernity or commit ourselves imprudently to reforms that were not intended by the Council or that now show themselves quite inopportune. In a period of breakups and uncertainties the first priority is to safeguard the deposit of revelation and maintain the inner cohesion of the institution.

Others, however, think that Vatican II, though traditional in many ways, has laid the foundation for a renewed understanding by the Church of itself and its situation in the midst of human societies. In their view, the council was "the beginning of a beginning" (Karl Rahner). It began a period in which the Church explicitly recognizes that it is really and deeply affected by developments in its environment and that in its doctrines and practices it can no longer lead an abstract existence above and beyond history. The Council's innovative insights are a solid point of departure for living and thinking the faith even amid the changes with which the human race is continually faced. These insights make available to Christian communities, which willy-nilly are increasingly involved in the developments of modernity, room for innovation that will allow them to handle problems that the recent council did not resolve or perceive.

These two outlooks, which are the root of present divisions within Catholicism, make clear how crucial an issue is the part that the various social environments play in the reception of Vatican II.

Segundo Galilea

4. Latin America in the Medellín and Puebla Conferences: An Example of Selective and Creative Reception of Vatican II

ℐ

Situation of the Churches in Latin America during the Council

The Latin American Church differs in important ways from country to country and within each country as well. For this reason every statement about it needs to be qualified. Any generalization is only an approximation, though legitimate in my opinion, and this fact must be kept in mind during the following reflections.

It can be said that Latin America by and large was not prepared for the Second Vatican Council, that is, for the vast problems tackled there and for the pastoral and doctrinal reforms undertaken. The majority of the Latin American laity and clergy had not paid sufficient attention to the development of Christian thought during the previous few decades. The outcome of the Council was therefore a surprise, even if a pleasing and welcome one, for these churches as a whole.

It is also true, however, that many Catholic groups and elites had wanted changes in the Church (especially in its liturgical and pastoral practice) and were working for them. This dissatisfaction with the growing distance between "traditional" pastoral practice and the needs of the people was intensified by the social and cultural changes upon which Latin America had more or less recently embarked. "Social change" was the watchword of the 1950s, as the passage from a rural society to an increasingly urban society and a deepening critical awareness in the social and political spheres were creating a new situation for the traditional faith of the peoples. This desire for renewal in pastoral practice and ecclesial institutions was already intense among the elites of the 1950s, especially in the southern part and more particularly in Chile and Brazil. In these areas, specialized Catholic Action and the social encyclicals had strongly influenced important sectors of the laity, clergy, and episcopate. There was an emphasis on more intensive pastoral action, even among minorities; on the transformation of environments; on social and political involvement; on a church that acts as a leaven and a servant of the world and is more independent of political authorities. This was the prevailing mentality among those Latin American bishops who would later be prominent at the Council.

In addition, but still within a predominantly "conservative" ecclesial outlook, there were other factors that would contribute to the good reception subsequently given to the Council. Among these was the establishment in 1955 of CELAM (*Consejo Episcopal Latinoamericano*, Latin American Episcopal Council), which gradually created a common ecclesial consciousness, a sense of Latin American oneness even before it was cultivated by politicians and statesmen, and a practice of joining together to study and find solutions for the problems and challenges of the Christian faith. The Council would set its seal of approval on this joint search.

During the years of the Council the typical and original conditions (perhaps unmatched anywhere else in the universal Church) were being created in which Latin America received the stimulus of the Council. The foremost of these conditions was an intensification of the social change already mentioned, which had now taken on traits that were socially and culturally disintegrative for the peoples of Latin America: a sudden and chaotic urbanization unaccompanied by adequate industrialization, creating a subculture of rootlessness and urban destitution; widespread access to the communications media, which were alien to popular tradition and threatened unanimity among Catholics; accelerated economic development (begun in the 1940s), which increased the gulf between rich and poor, and created vast marginalized minorities.

A second condition was a consequence of the first: during the years of the Council Latin Americans, believers and unbelievers alike, became increasingly aware of the injustice about them and of the need of urgent and radical changes in society and the economy. It is this phenomenon that has come to be called a deepening "revolutionary consciousness" ("revolutionary" here has a very broad meaning that applies to all the influential ideologies of the period).

This was the human framework, the Christian consciousness, in which Latin America received a Council that was attentive to the world's needs and bent on the renewal of the Church. This background explains the success of the Council—at least at the level of reception—among the more active Christian circles of the continent. It also explains the widespread, even if always atypical, sense of urgency in regard to applying the Council in the Latin American context. In a part of the world where the vast majority were Catholics (at least culturally and sociologically), the felt need for ecclesial change went hand in hand with, and was stimulated by, the felt need for social change. In my opinion this convergence did not exist in other parts of the world. In North America and

Europe, basic social changes had already taken place; in Asia and Africa, which were likewise being battered by social and political transformations, Christian influence was still too weak for the Council to have played a decisive role in these changes. In Latin America, however, social change and "conciliar" Christianity formed a closely knit pair.

The Council had not yet ended when CELAM, which exercised a strong continental leadership at this period, organized meetings for the purpose of implementing conciliar reforms in liturgy, catechetics, and religious life (among other areas). Before the close of the Council, institutes for pastoral, liturgical, and catechetical training had arisen at the regional and continental levels under the direction of CELAM, and courses in renewal were multiplying. All this, however, would not be exempt from conflicts and excesses, inasmuch as the majority of priests and religious had not thought through the conciliar changes and new directions, for which they were therefore unprepared.

The Medellín Conference

During the final session of the Council the idea arose within CELAM of convoking a Latin American "synod" for the purpose of applying the conciliar decrees to the reality of Latin America. Such an undertaking would be completely feasible and productive, given the (relative) sameness of human and Christian problems throughout the region, and the consciousness of an ecclesial coordination that had been created in the 1950s and was being consolidated by numerous small-scale meetings during the years of the Council.

Pope Paul VI therefore convoked the Medellín Conference for 1968 and entrusted its organization to CELAM. The most representative and dynamic episcopal delegations of the continent took part in the conference, as did many experts (in this respect Medellín profited by the valuable experience of the Council). The express theme of Medellín was the reception of the Council by Latin America; the official formulation of the theme was: "The Church in the Transformation of Latin America in the Light of the Council."[1]

This official formulation of the theme for the Medellín Conference confirms what I said above: Medellín was a meeting point for the social transformation of Latin America and the ecclesial transformation wrought by the Council. It also enables us to understand the creative role played by the conference (Medellín aimed at translating the Council

1. Latin American Episcopal Council, *The Church in the Present-Day Transformation of Latin America in the Light of the Council*, L. M. Colonnese, ed., with official translation by the Latin American Bureau of the United States Catholic Conference and CELAM (Bogotá: General Secretariat of CELAM, 1970), vol. 1: Position Papers; vol. 2: Conclusions. All references are to vol. 2; for quotations the page number in vol. 2 is added.

into terms applicable to a socio-cultural area within Catholicism) as well as its selection of subjects: the bishops at Medellín were concerned primarily with those elements of the Council that would better enable the Church to keep pace with and apply the gospel to the social transformation of the continent. The theme explains the success and impact of Medellín, but also its limitations from the standpoint of a more integral reception of the Council. Thus we do not find Medellín showing any creativity in the theological, ecclesiological, and christological application of the Council. The same can be said of evangelization and culture, of missiology, and of other subjects to which other churches showed greater receptivity. The Medellín approach was eminently pastoral (in this it showed itself a child of the Council) and concentrated heavily on the reality of Latin America (here it was simultaneously creative and selective).

The impact and immediate influence of Medellín on more educated Latin American Catholic circles was enormous, but unequal. In some regions and churches, Medellín was more consciously accepted and assimilated only some years later as a result of the Puebla Conference, which in many respects was a continuation of Medellín.

Their judgment may not be accurate, but many think that the impact of Medellín was greater than that of the Council and that the Council entered Latin America via Medellín with its creativity and power to mobilize energies but also with its selectivity. Be that as it may, the closeness of the two events in time (little more than two years separated them) meant that to some extent the reception of the Council and the reception of Medellín were one and the same thing in the Latin American experience.

I must mention two other factors that contributed greatly to the success of Medellín as a localized reception of the Council. The first was the appearance of the encyclical *Populorum progressio* of Paul VI. As is well known, in this document the pope provides a most lucid set of Christian directives regarding the problems of justice and human development in the so-called Third World. It was not accidental that *Populorum progessio* was published immediately after the Council, for it served to complement and make up for a deficiency of Vatican II, which was still very European and weak in regard to Third World concerns. For the churches of Latin America the encyclical was to be an important aid in applying the Council to the realities in which their peoples were involved.

The second factor that helps explain Medellín was historical. As far as we know, Medellín was the third continent-wide "synod," if we exclude two or three analogous events in the colonial period, which in fact were heavily focused on two main regions (Peru and New Spain [Mexico]). The first of the three synods had taken place in 1889 at Rome (First Plenary Council of Latin America), and the second in 1955 on the occasion of the establishment of CELAM. These two synods, however, had no pastoral impact, nor did they provide a Christian reading of the Latin

American cultural and social world (I state this as a fact, not as a criticism: the necessary conditions for this impact and analysis did not exist as yet and would be created only later on by the Council). Medellín, on the contrary, would look at the signs of the times in Latin America in light of the Council and would thereby play a prophetic and foundational role in regard to the historical and missionary vocation of these churches.

Creativity and Selectivity at Medellín

A first general characteristic of the Medellín Conference was that it formulated the specific mission of the Latin American Church at this critical moment, on the basis not only of the Christian faith but also of the historical situations in which Latin Americans live. This explains its emphasis on anthropology and its inductive approach to theological and pastoral reflection.

Evident here is the influence of at least some of the conciliar decrees and constitutions, especially *Gaudium et spes* (which exerted an undeniable influence on the style of Medellín), and of the encyclical *Populorum progressio*. Medellín takes for granted the reality of Latin America and its historical processes and discerns the values, ambiguities, and sinfulness found therein, seeing them as playing a part in the history of salvation and as pointing the way for Christian experience and mission. This represents the most serious effort ever made in the history of the Latin American Church to incarnate evangelization in history. Medellín then requires that this attention to the real Latin American human being be carried into preaching, catechesis, liturgy, religious life, and ministries—areas in which the theme of inculturation was already very much present. The influence of the decree *Ad gentes* is evident here, especially when Medellín takes up (not always with the needed depth) the subject of the ethnic minorities, and especially the native peoples, of Latin America.

The closer relationship that the Council had established between the natural and the supernatural allowed Medellín to pursue the same line and construct a synthesis between history and salvation, human tasks and Christian tasks. I believe that in the post-Medellín period this synthesis—formulated in terms of the relationship between faith and justice, between human liberations and the eschatological liberation accomplished by Jesus Christ—will be one of the creative and universally valid themes of pastoral life and of the emerging "Latin American theology." Thus we read in the "Message to the Peoples of Latin America": "As Christians we believe that this historical stage of Latin America is intimately linked to the history of salvation" (p. 38).

A second general characteristic of the Medellín Conference is its reliance on the "signs of the times." Here it once again draws its inspiration from *Gaudium et spes*, but it also creatively translates this universally applicable conciliar theme. At the same time, Medellín finds itself obliged to select what it sees as signs of the times for Latin America. The bishops at Medellín make a frank and realistic analysis of Latin American social realities, but in their selection of signs they give a privileged place to those found in social injustices and forms of dehumanization. In this regard the Conference is both creative and legitimately selective. A Latin America that is already evangelized and has a basically Catholic culture but in which injustice is also institutionalized: this is the sign that most attracts the attention of the bishops at Medellín. This explains their call to the Church to take up once again its main historical function and to be more clearly critical of what the Conference calls "social sin" and help deliver human beings from it. This translates into an option for the evangelization and integral liberation of the poor and oppressed of Latin America.

Listen once again to the "Message to the Peoples of Latin America":

As Latin American men we share the history of our people. . . . In the light of the faith that we profess as believers, we have undertaken to discover a plan of God in the "signs of the times." We interpret the aspirations and clamors of Latin America as signs that reveal the direction of the divine plan operating in the redeeming love of Christ [pp. 37, 38].

We may sum up this typical and comprehensive option of Medellín as a decision by the Church to make its own, in the perspective of evangelization, and play a part in the efforts to liberate and humanize the peoples of Latin America. This synthesis of history and grace was to take shape increasingly in the ensuing years as "liberating evangelization."

The theme of Christian liberation of the poor and oppressed is thus a third general characteristic of Medellín. After the Conference it would be one of the most important ecclesial signs of the times. It would be the **response of faith (inspired by** *Gaudium et spes* **and** *Populorum progressio*) **to the negative picture revealed by an analysis of the signs of the times in Latin America society** ("sinful situation": Doc. II, § 1, p. 71; "institutionalized violence": Doc. II, § 16, p. 78).

At Medellín the word (and theme) "liberation" appears for the first time in an official document of the Church. I said earlier that "liberation" is a creative and "Latin American" application of the insight found in *Gaudium et spes* and *Ad gentes* (to speak only of these two documents), namely, that the task of evangelization is to bring deliverance to the human condition, to cultures, to social and familial relationships, and so on. Medellín's characteristic way (both creative and selective) of conceiving liberation is due both to its analysis of specific signs of the times and to *Populorum progressio*, in which the Church renews its commitment to the integral promotion of the poorest peoples (a point that was inadequately made at the Council).

The first documents drawn up at the Conference adhere closely to the terminology of *Populorum progressio* and speak of the "integral development" of the Latin American peoples (for example, Introduction to the Final Documents, §§ 4–6; Doc. I, §§ 11, 15; Doc. II, §§ 1, 14). But the "integral development" of *Populorum progressio* comes to be a synonym of liberation in the Christian sense of this word. As a result, Medellín increasingly shifts to the word "liberation," which in the final analysis is a richer term, more in harmony with the New Testament message, more humanistic, and therefore less freighted with socio-economic overtones. In the last documents of Medellín (last in order of composition) "liberation" appears four times. Thenceforth it would be naturalized in the pastoral practice and the theology of the the Latin American churches, and would exercise no little influence outside Latin America. The theology of liberation provides the theological development of the theme; the Medellín Conference may be regarded as the point of departure for this theology.

I have dwelt to some extent on the theme of liberation as it arose at Medellín because I think it is a typical example of how the Latin American churches made an important aspect of the Council their own in a creative and selective way. As I understand it, one of the dynamic dimensions or lines of thought of the Council is the idea of the Church as servant of the world. The Church renders this service in both the temporal and the "spiritual" orders, and always in ways coherent with evangelization. This conciliar synthesis of integral evangelization as service to the world is creatively translated at Medellín as "integral liberation." The translation reflects a selective choice that is legitimate, for the bishops realized that the Church's service to the world in Latin America must be characterized by service leading to the Christian liberation of the poor. In Latin America the "world" of *Gaudium et spes* is to be seen, first and foremost, as the "world" of the poor and marginalized.

This legitimate choice, like every choice, runs the risk of being separated from its wider context in Medellín and the Council, or of being taken as the whole rather than as a choice that puts a special emphasis within the whole. This explains some excesses and confusions, both theoretical and practical, that arose in later talk about liberation; it also explains the integral way in which Puebla tackled the subject.

A fourth general characteristic of Medellín as a translation of the Council is its emphasis on the local church or churches of Latin America, and on the personality and riches proper to them within the Catholic communion. The theme is an eminently conciliar one, and indeed one of the most creative developed by the Council. The ecclesiology of the Council here emphasizes a very important element of catholicism that had sometimes been lost from sight in recent centuries: that each local church is the universal Church in concentrated form, and that the variety of local churches yields a pluralism of cultures, spiritualities, expressions, and celebrations of the faith, and of theologies. Each local church enriches the universal Church and is in turn enriched by it and by the other churches.

Medellín represents for the Latin American Church a climactic moment in growth of awareness of its originality and vocation, a growth that has come not simply from development in ecclesiology but also and even more on the basis of the signs of Latin American Catholic reality and of the specific nature of the Church's mission. (Here again Medellín is both creative and selective: creative in making Latin Americans conscious of this conciliar theme, but selective in favoring the historico-cultural approach. To put the point in pastoral terms: Medellín tells us that cultural and historical roots explain the "localness" and diversity of the churches and that in becoming more aware of its localness and originality, thanks to the ecclesiology of the Council, Christian Latin America has reached an important new stage in its maturation.)

In my opinion the Medellín Conference will go down in history not only for having given broad and official recognition to the "local" characteristics of the Latin American Church, but also for having drawn the conclusions for pastoral practice and Christian life that this recognition implies. All this is especially important for churches that, despite already having more than four centuries of history behind them, have not only not produced anything specifically their own in the service of Catholicism (though this assertion requires a good deal of nuancing) but have also been characterized by an excessive dependence on European Catholicism in the areas of theology, pastoral practice, and mysticism.

Paul VI himself, in one of his Colombian addresses on the Conference, made this same point:

In this transformation, behind which lies the desire of integrating the entire scale of temporal values into the global vision yielded by the Christian faith, we become aware of the unique vocation of Latin America: its vocation of combining in a new and original synthesis the ancient and the modern, the spiritual and the temporal, what others give us and what is natively our own.

On the basis of this originality of the local church in Latin America, Medellín is once again both creative and selective in its reception of Vatican II as it develops three pastoral questions that, except for the first, were raised only in a very implicit manner at the Council: the question of ecclesial pluralism, the question of the base-level ecclesial communities, and the question of popular religion.

The second and third questions are typically Latin American, even if they have universal relevance. The most typical historico-cultural expression of Latin American Catholicism as a set of local churches is the popular character of its religion (its Catholicism); in fact, this will even provide an original way of evangelizing Latin America. The same can be said of the base-level ecclesial communities: they are at the same time a typical expression of the Catholic Church as localized in America and a pastoral form for its life.

The theme of ecclesial pluralism will perhaps be of greater interest to us in the present context because it is explicitly conciliar and is more relevant to postconciliar Catholicism worldwide. Medellín makes its own the conciliar teaching on Catholic pluralism (I need mention only *Lumen gentium*, *Ad gentes*, and the decrees on ecumenism and the Eastern churches, without forgetting the "Constitution on the Liturgy"). It does so, once more, not for ecclesiological reasons but to meet pastoral needs (thus showing once again its selectivity and the inevitable inadequacies this entails).

For Medellín the "localness" of the Latin American Church makes it simultaneously one and many, to the extent that it embraces many cultures, subcultures, and situations. (We touch here on the familiar theme of the cultural unity—in history, language, religion, ethos, etc.—and simultaneous cultural diversity of the Latin American continent.) Evangelizing activity must therefore likewise be diversified and adapted to the men and women of Latin America according to their circumstances. We find this pastoral pluralism at work at Medellín in regard to pastoral care of the young (Doc. V, § 14), the masses (or popular religion) (Doc. VI, § 11), the elites (Doc. VII, §§ 5–8, 17–21), and catechesis (Doc. VIII, §§ 5, 6, 8). This last document states:

It is also necessary to consider the demands of a pluralistic society in formulating a Latin American pastoral plan. . . . Catechetical teaching must be adapted to a diversity of languages and mentalities and to a variety of human conditions and cultures. It is impossible, in view of all this, to impose fixed and universal patterns [§ 8; p. 141].

Liturgical reform in the Latin American context makes the same demands: the liturgy "must be adapted and integrated into the spirit of different cultures. Therfore it should positively welcome plurality in unity, avoiding the establishment of uniformity as an 'a priori' principle" (Doc. IX, §§ 7–8; p. 152). The need of diversifying the priestly ministry reflects the same principle at work (Doc. XI, § 22, citing the Council). Medellín asks that, in view of the original and varied character of Latin America and its peoples, the orders and congregations of religious men and women be decentralized at every level so that the general norms of these groups may be applied in an adaptive way (Doc. XII, § 25). The training of permanent deacons (Doc. XIII, § 3) must likewise be pluralistic, as must the forms taken by the base-level ecclesial communities (Doc. XV, § 10).

In the pastoral practice of the post-Medellín period it has not always been an easy or peaceful task to implement this ecclesial and pastoral pluralism. On the one hand, it requires that all pass through a slow apprenticeship in collaboration with the universal Church. This apprenticeship in turn requires that the reflexes and attitudes of the Church in the post-tridentine period be slowly overcome. On the other hand, the Medellín call for pluralism, which resulted from its consciousness of being a local and unique Church, was perhaps excessively pragmatic and not based on an equally creative extension of the conciliar ecclesiology. This shortcoming of Medellín may serve as an occasion for recalling, after fifteen years of implementation, some other inadequacies in the area of our concern here, namely, the Latin American reception of the Council as it took shape at the Medellín Conference.

Shortcomings of Medellín

The extraordinary ecclesial importance of Medellín is generally acknowledged, as are also its shortcomings, which have become clearer with the passage of time and with further experience. Some brief mention of these is in place here: they have inevitably affected the manner in which the Council has been received in Latin America and the setting of emphases in this reception.

Medellín itself and, even more, the immediate post-Medellín period, show an excessive optimism vis-à-vis the various forms of social liberation in Latin America and vis-à-vis the leading role of the Church in the process. I am aware that my statement can be challenged, but certainly the discussion of liberation at Medellín seems to be too much limited to Latin America, and seems to pay too little heed to the world context. Excessive confidence in political changes as means of Christian liberation (a confidence somewhat muted at Medellín but more pronounced in Christian elites of the post-Medellín period) may be connected with a certain socio-political euphoria in vogue at the end of the 1960s and discernible to some degree at Medellín. The authority which Marxism acquired at one point as a force for liberation may be connected with the above.

Next, Medellín does not deal adequately with the theme of Latin American cultures as related to evangelization and to continental identity. The bishops did not see the value of making this conciliar theme their own in a creative way, as they were to do later on at Puebla, even if still in an inadequate way. Their attitude may have been due to the greater esteem that the social, economic, and political sciences enjoyed at that time as compared with the cultural, historical, and religious sciences, an esteem fostered by the urgent need of social change.

Medellín does not appear to have eased the priestly and vocational crisis (widespread throughout the Western Church) that arose in connection with the Council and reached serious proportions in Latin America. Perhaps Medellín came too early for a creative redefinition of priestly identity, or perhaps the Council itself fell short in this respect. In any case, this crisis marks one of the areas of weakness in a healthy and balanced reception of the Council by Latin America.

Connected with the vocational crisis is the crisis of spirituality in the postconciliar period; Medellín did not adequately face up to this (and Puebla showed itself equally weak). In the reception of the Council and of Medellín in the Latin American churches there was an evident imbalance between reforms in institutions, pastoral practice, and theological thought, on the one hand, and reform in mysticism and the quality of Christian life, on the other. This remains true, even though in the case of the priestly crisis we are clearly turning the corner today and trying to achieve a more creative synthesis, without the arbitrary selectivity that characterized us in the period immediately after the Council and Medellín.

At another level, the renewed and creative Church of Medellín seems to us still very much focused on itself. Its consciousness of being a unique local church is not sufficiently combined with a consciousness of its universal mission and its need of transcending its own borders.

Finally, Medellín's most noticeable shortcoming was that, although it had an excellent "Latin American pastoral plan," it was backed by an insufficiently renewed theology. This claim can perhaps be debated, but certainly there was at Medellín no creative reception of the (explicit or implicit) christology and ecclesiology of Vatican II. Key pastoral themes such as the base-level ecclesial communities or popular Catholicism did not receive sufficient theological support. Puebla would devote more attention to filling these lacunae. This would be much more feasible then than at Medellín because of the abundant theological production of the post-Medellín period. (More abundant indeed than theological writings that referred more directly to the Council. Or, more exactly: in Latin American theology of the postconciliar and post-Medellín period, references to the two events tended to be combined. This fact, which has no parallel in other churches, is perhaps a decisive characteristic of the reception of the Council in Latin America.)

The Puebla Conference

The conference held at Puebla in 1979 is relevant to these reflections on the reception of Vatican II in Latin America because Puebla was in fact a continuation of Medellín: it endeavored to complement Medellín or it responded to questions that had arisen since Medellín or that Medellín had neglected. As a result, Puebla became a vehicle for reception of the Council, especially in certain areas or countries where neither Vatican II nor Medellín had sufficiently penetrated. In other areas and countries where there had been a fuller assimilation of those two events,

Puebla would introduce—again in a creative and selective way—certain conciliar themes to which Latin America had hitherto not been responsive (e.g., culture and evangelization; mission "to the nations").

The central theme of Medellín had been the reception of Vatican II in a Latin America in process of transformation. The central theme of Puebla was to be "Evangelization in Latin America's Present and Future," a theme sufficiently broad to cover in practice the same human and ecclesial areas that Medellín had covered.[2]

The final document issued by Puebla has four major points of reference. The first is the Medellín Conference (see the opening address of John Paul II) and the Second Vatican Council. The teaching of the Council is not present only in the form of the continuity of Puebla with Medellín; as I have said, Puebla also takes up various themes that are new in relation to Medellín. The ecclesiological material in Puebla is extensively inspired by *Lumen gentium*, as are its anthropology, its conception of culture, its missiology, its teaching on the laity and the hierarchic ministries, and so on.

The second major point of reference for Puebla is the apostolic exhortation *Evangelii nuntiandi* of Paul VI. (Puebla's own theme made this reference inevitable.) *Evangelii nuntiandi* is to Puebla what *Populorum progressio* had been to Medellín. The two conferences strove for a "Latin American" reading and application of the two documents.

Puebla's third reference is to the human reality that is the life of God's people in Latin America, with the continuities and changes that mark it ten years after Medellín and within the historical framework of Latin America since the time of its first evangelization. The analysis of the reality of life in Latin America is made from a pastoral point of view, that is, the reality is analyzed for its impact on faith, Christian life, and the humanization (liberation) and cultural values of its peoples.

The fourth point of reference is the pastoral experience of the Latin American churches, especially since Medellín, and the theological thought that sprang from this experience. Latin America has had, though not everywhere equally or without blemishes, a rich and creative pastoral experience: solidarity with the poor, support of human rights, a proliferation of communities and lay ministries, the experience of persecution, the evangelization of native cultures, and so on.

On this broad basis Puebla attempts an evaluation of the way traveled by the post-Medellín Church; this amounts, in fact, to an evaluation (the first on a continental scale) of the reception and implementation of the Council in Latin America. The main choices made by Medellín, choices that are conciliar in origin, are left intact: the Church's prophetic vision of Latin American reality; its liberating response to the cry of the poor

---

2. The Final Document of Puebla, as well as the major addresses of John Paul II in Mexico, are in *Puebla and Beyond: Documentation and Commentary*, J. Eagleson and P. Scharper, eds. (Maryknoll, N.Y.: Orbis Books, 1979).

and abandoned; the unique identity and mission of the churches and of
Latin American Catholicism; a deeper understanding of this mission as
the very reason for the Church's existence as servant of Latin American
societies and cultures; and so on.

Let me dwell for a moment on the more significant elements in the
message of Puebla, and especially on those that are of greater importance as being an explicit or implicit reception of the teaching of Vatican II.

1. There is the primacy of evangelization in the life of the Church.
This represents a renewal of the Council's eminently pastoral outlook
and of its concern that evangelization should be a humanizing and redemptive service given to human beings and the human condition.

2. What Puebla says about authentic human dignity and the defense
of all human rights (a problem made more difficult by the increase in
regimes based on power) is very much related to the Council and especially to *Gaudium et spes*. In handling this theme Puebla, to a greater extent than Medellín, takes into account the international context and the
situation of Latin America within the universal Church and the modern
world.

3. Puebla takes over and repeats, in even more pointed and urgent
terms, the commitment of the Church to the poorest of its children and
to their integral and liberative evangelization. "Preferential option for
the poor" is the phrase Puebla uses in repeating this commitment. A
decade after Medellín, Puebla develops this theme more fully and enriches it by drawing on the theological work done in Latin America, especially on liberation and the service of the poor.

4. Puebla provides a more serious treatment than Medellín of the
Church and culture and, following *Evangelii nuntiandi*, of the evangelization of the Latin American cultures. It deals with the theme of indigenous and minority cultures (Amerindians, Afro-Americans, and others),
although still inadequately. The subject of popular religion, the discernment needed in regard to it, and the purification it requires appear once
again, though now in a more fully developed historical and cultural
framework. Reception of the questions raised at the Council regarding
mission and culture is evident here in the explicit references to *Ad gentes*
and *Gaudium et spes*. At the same time, this is a creative reception of the
conciliar teaching; on the subject of secularization, for example, Puebla
departs from interpretations reflective of the First World. It takes a more
critical and relational view of secularization, seeing it as opposed to the
identity of the Latin American peoples and to popular culture and religion.

5. For the first time since the Council, the Latin American hierarchy at
Puebla acknowledges in a creative way the theme of the universal mission of the local churches (*Ad gentes*). In the Puebla view, Latin America
must cross its own frontiers and go out to the still unevangelized peoples of Asia and Africa. The creative side of this decision is to be seen, in

my opinion, in the fact that this mission *ad gentes* must be undertaken despite, and even on the basis of, a lack of means and the relative scarcity of clergy in the Latin American churches. This introduces a new factor into the conciliar thinking on the universal mission of the Church, namely, the relationship between poverty and the proclamation of the gospel, and the missionary style proper to "poor" churches.

6. Puebla makes its own the conciliar ecclesiological thinking on the Church as sacrament of salvation and on the people of God as a community with a mission; it stresses "communion" as a way of life in the Church and as a manifestation of Christian mysticism. Communion is a unifying theme in the Puebla document and one of the axes of its ecclesiology. This is another simultaneously creative and selective aspect of the Latin American understanding of the renewed and fruitful idea that the Council offers of the church.

Unanswered Questions

The reception of Vatican II via the Medellín Conference and the supplementary work of Puebla has still left some matters unsettled as far as the assimilation and implementation of the Council in Latin America is concerned. I shall end my reflections with a short discussion of these points.

The churches of Latin America are still quite uninterested in important missionary questions; I am referring not only to the mission *ad gentes* (an especially serious matter in a continent possessed of so much Catholic vitality and such numbers) but also to dialogue with the great non-Christian religions and cultures. These areas, so fruitful and full of promise in relation to the mission of the Church that they were extensively developed in various conciliar documents, hardly enter the ecclesial consciousness of Latin America. This can be explained by the fact that Latin America has traditionally been a rather self-centered "Christendom" used to receiving and not repaying. The future of the faith in the world now demands, however, that these churches make their contribution and give their answer to these great questions raised by the Council and becoming more and more important with the passage of time.

Except in one area, ecumenism has likewise not followed a creative and productive path in Latin America. There has indeed been, here as in the rest of the Church, a good ecumenical relationship with the churches and confessions that issued from the Reformation. Serious difficulties remain, however, in regard to the "free churches" and the "sects" of Protestant origin. The question is very complex and affects ecumenism not only in Latin America but in all other parts of the world. Moreover, the responsibility for the situation lies, in my opinion, not with the

Catholic Church but with the proselytizing activity and aggressivity of these groups that have sprung from Protestantism. Be that as it may, their existence is a challenge that has not yet been met and is intensified today by the more or less veiled political plans of the sects entering Latin America.

Also unsettled as yet is the matter of the adaptation and inculturation of the liturgy (as called for by the Council), particularly in the minority ethnic groups of Latin America and in indigenous groups, especailly the blacks who practice a syncretistic Catholicism. The question of a reconciliation and synthesis between the official liturgy and popular Catholicism is a variant of the same issue. In these respects, the problem of liturgical reform in undoubtedly universal once again (at least in non-Western cultures), but in any case the relative pluralism approved at Medellín in continuity with the Council has not yet been adequately received in practice.

There are other areas of conciliar concern in which reception has been conscious and prompt (and was emphasized at Medellín) but has at the same time been very inconsistent, somethimes confused, and not always well conceived. I am thinking, for example, of renewal in religious life, despite the good work and contributions of the Latin American Conference of Religious (CLAR). Or of the renewal of priestly ministry and priestly training, although the initial crisis has been surmounted and the Latin American churches are today experiencing an unusual increase in vocations. Or of the identity and pastoral functions of permanent deacons. Or, finally, of collegiality and participation at all levels in the progress of the Church, and of dialogue in all its forms.

In these and other areas, the Christian communities of Latin America have come a long way since the Council, but much remains to be done and brought to maturity.

II. CENTRAL THEMES IN THE RECEPTION

Joseph A. Komonchak

5. The Local Realization of the Church

Those familiar with the considerable literature on the local Church that has appeared in the last twenty years may be surprised, on turning to the texts of Vatican II, to find there neither a systematic exposition of the theme nor even a consistent vocabulary in which to discuss it.[1] For reasons partially explained below, theologians devoted little attention to the local Church before the Council began. At the Council itself, both the agenda (even that of the reform-minded majority) and the drama of the Council's internal history were dominated by West European concerns. It would be only after the Council that other local churches would begin to make their presence felt in international church assemblies.[2]

Nevertheless, the Council did make a number of statements about the local Church that were to prove remarkably fruitful when the various churches throughout the world undertook the task of receiving and appropriating the Council within their various cultural contexts.[3] It asserted, first of all, that the one and universal Church is realized in and through the variety of local churches. Insofar as they come to be through the call of God, the word of Christ, the grace of the Spirit, and the exercise of the apostolic ministry, especially through the Eucharist, local churches are genuine churches, "formed after the image of the universal Church"; but rather than "parts" of some preexisting "whole," they are

---

1. For a discussion of the terminological issue, see H. Legrand, "La réalisation de l'Eglise en un lieu," in *Initiation à la pratique de la théologie*, B. Lauret and F. Refoulé, eds., Tome III, *Dogmatique 2* (Paris: Cerf, 1983), pp. 145–46, 157–59. In this essay, I simply use "local church" to refer to realizations of the Church in particular cultural spheres.

2. This is one of the main arguments of Jan Grootaers's book, *De Vatican II à Jean-Paul II: Le grand tournant de l'Eglise catholique* (Paris: Centurion, 1981).

3. For discussions of the Council's teaching on the local Church, see Legrand, "Réalisation," esp. pp. 146–55; J. A. Komonchak, "Ministry and the Local Church," in *Proceedings of the Catholic Theological Society of America*, 36 (1981) 56–82; S. J. Kilian, "The Meaning and Nature of the Local Church," ibid., 35 (1980) 244–55; P. Granfield, "The Local Church as a Center of Communication and Control," ibid., 35 (1980) 256–63; H. de Lubac, *Les églises particulières dans l'Eglise universelle* (Paris: Aubier, 1971), pp. 29–56; E. Lanne, "The Local Church: Its Catholicity and Apostolicity," *One in Christ*, 6 (1970) 288–313.

local realizations of all that the one Church is, and it is "in them and out of them that the one and holy catholic Church comes to exist."[4]

Because the universal Church exists only as the communion of local churches, the diversity of culture and circumstance enters into the very definition of the local Church. In numerous texts, the Council showed a great sense of respect for particularity and diversity.[5] Like Christ himself, the Church cannot be a stranger to anyone or to any place (AG 8); it must learn "to speak, understand, and lovingly embrace all languages and so overcome the dispersion of Babel" (AG 4). Avoiding both syncretism and ethnocentrism, "the Christian life will be adapted to the genius and character of every culture, and particular traditions, along with the distinctive gifts of every family of nations, will be illumined by the Gospel and taken up into the catholic unity. Thus, new particular Churches, with their own traditions, will take their place in the communion of the Church" (AG 22). The catholicity of the Church thus does not refer merely to the universal geographical spread of a single, uniform church:

The character of universality which adorns the People of God is the gift of the Lord himself, by which the catholic Church effectively and constantly seeks to recapitulate the whole of humanity with all its goods under the Headship of Christ, in the unity of his Spirit. In virtue of this catholicity, the several parts bring their own gifts to one another and to the whole Church, so that the whole and its several parts grow by the mutual sharing of all and by a common effort towards the fullness of unity [LG 13].

In other words, the Church is not an abstract but a *concrete* universal, one not in spite of but precisely in and because of the variety of the local churches. And this unity in concrete catholicity is something to be achieved every day, through an interchange in which all the churches are active and responsible subjects and recipients.

This view of the Church represents, as a number of commentators have pointed out, something like a Copernican revolution in ecclesiology.[6] Historically, it represents at least a counterweight to, if not a reversal of, a centuries-long process of institutional and administrative centralization and uniformity in almost all areas of church life. Despite the West European dominance of the Council's activities and themes,

4. LG 23; see also LG 26; SC 42; CD 11, which gives the following definition: "A diocese is a portion of the People of God which has been entrusted to the pastoral care of a bishop with the cooperation of the presbyterate, so that, adhering to their pastor and gathered by him in the Holy Spirit through the Gospel and the Eucharist, they might constitute a particular Church in which is truly present and active the one, holy, catholic and apostolic Church of Christ."

5. See SC 37–40, 123; OE 2, 5; UR 14, 16–18; LG 13, 23; AG 8–11, 16, 22–23, 26; GS 53–55, 58, 61, 91.

6. See E. Lanne, "L'Eglise locale et l'Eglise universelle: Actualité et portée du thème," *Irén*, 43 (1970) 481–511; L. Bouyer, *L'Eglise de Dieu: Corps du Christ et Temple de l'Esprit* (Paris: Cerf, 1970), pp. 333–43.

the conciliar statements on the local Church were to produce in a re-markably short time a refocusing of the tasks of the self-realization of the Church away from those that had dominated the recent history of a Eurocentric church to those that concern the existence of the Church in the many and varied circumstances—economic, social, political, and cultural—where it concretely exists and carries out its mission. That this shift has not occurred without difficulties and tensions is only what might have been expected, given the ideal of uniformity that had pre-vailed before the Council and the inevitable problems of communication and understanding that must attend serious efforts to inculturate the Gospel.

Vatican II and the Culture of Roman Catholicism[7]

The Council's call for cultural realizations of the Church forms part of a general cultural accommodation that represents the chief historical significance of Vatican II and deserves analysis before turning to more particular illustrations of the inculturation of the Church.

Under the comparatively innocuous banner of aggiornamento, Vati-can II represented a long-overdue effort by the Catholic Church to deal seriously and discriminatingly with the culture created in the West by the Enlightenment, the economic and political revolutions of the last two centuries, the development of the natural and human sciences, and the secularization and pluralization of society. The Church undertook this effort at what now appears to have been the term of one stage of that cultural transformation, when it had reached a moment of supreme self-confidence.

The Catholic Church, whose bishops met in council from 1962 to 1965, was a church that for the previous century and a half had been marked by an increased emphasis upon uniformity and by the centralization of all authority in Rome. It had practically defined itself by its suspicion of modernity, in response to which it created a world of its own, distinct in worldview and ethos, expressed in its own language and symbols, and defended and legitimated by a distinct mode of philosophy and theolo-gy. It retained, almost as a normative memory, a more than nostalgic affection for an idealized medieval Christendom, prior to the separa-

7. By "Roman Catholicism" in what follows I mean the sociological and cultural form that the Catholic Church assumed in the Counter-Reformation and especially since the French Revolution and in response to the challenges of modernity. This form is not iden-tical with the Church; it differs in important respects from earlier forms; and of it, one may say, with Louis Bouyer, "Il peut bien mourir" (La décomposition du Catholicisme [Paris: Aubier-Montaigne, 1968], p. 152), without thereby desiring or anticipating the death of the Church. The following footnotes will indicate some of the sources from which I have drawn my description.

tions that Protestantism, philosophism, liberalism, and secularization had introduced, when the Church possessed a monopoly of cultural definition, when social institutions embodied and confirmed its world-view and ethos, and political authorities sanctioned them with their power.[8]

In this way Roman Catholicism constituted a culture, or, where it had competitors, a subculture, of its own. In its official legitimations, in its pastoral practice, and in its theology, it embodied what Bernard Lonergan has called a "classicist" notion of culture.[9] It took the ideal of individual and civic culture created and transmitted in the West as a standard against which all other cultures were to be measured. It claimed to be universal, unchanging, necessary. It looked with suspicion on the differentiations introduced into thought by the Enlightenment and modern science, and on the variety and relativity uncovered by modern history and social science. It prided itself on the perennial character of its philosophy and theology. It regarded the culture that Christendom had created as an unsurpassable ideal, which only needed minor adaptations to be relevant to new historical eras or to newly discovered societies.

These classicist cultural assumptions were called into question by Vatican II. The Council was called for the sake of reform and aggiornamento, both slogans implying at least a qualified criticism of recent habits of church life and thought. It acknowledged, moreover, that "the human race is involved in a new age of its history" (GS 4), an age in which it "is passing from a more static notion of the order of things to a more dynamic and evolutionary notion" (GS 5), an age marked by the achievements of the modern sciences—natural, human, and historical—by the spread of technology and means of communication, by industrialization and urbanization, by a new respect for the variety and diversity of cultures. Hence it was calling for "a more universal form of human culture, which promotes and expresses the unity of the human race to the degree that it respects the particularities of different cultures" (GS 54), an age that requires a "new humanism, in which man is espe-

---

8. Among the most interesting efforts to describe this Roman Catholicism are the following: F. X. Kaufmann, *Kirche Begreifen: Analysen und Thesen zur gesellschaftlichen Verfassung des Christentums* (Freiburg: Herder, 1979); *Zur Soziologie des Katholizismus,* K. Gabriel and F. X. Kaufmann, eds. (Mainz: Grünewald, 1980); E. Poulat, "Le catholicisme comme culture" and "Catholicisme et modernité," in *Modernistica: Horizons, physionomies, debats* (Paris: Nouvelles Ed. Latines, 1982), pp. 58–101; G. Miccoli, "Chiesa e società in Italia tra Ottocento e Novecento: Il mito della 'cristianità,'" in *Chiese nelle Società: Verso un superamento della Cristianità* (Turin: Marietti, 1980), pp. 151–245; and D. Menozzi, "La chiesa e la storia: Una dimensione della cristianità da Leone XIII al Vaticano II," *Cristianesimo nella storia,* 5 (1984) 69–106.

9. B. Lonergan, *Method in Theology* (New York: Herder and Herder, 1972), pp. 300–302. For the description that follows, see also E. Poulat, "Le catholicisme comme culture," cited in the previous note.

cially defined by his responsibility for his brothers and for history" (GS 55). In almost all these respects, the Council was undermining the cultural presuppositions on which modern Roman Catholicism had been founded.

Even apart from its documents and the specific reforms to which it gave rise, then, Vatican II must be seen as a historic cultural turning point for Roman Catholicism. It sanctioned with the highest authority movements for institutional, liturgical, and theological reform that had been resisted if not repudiated for two centuries. It substantively altered the way in which the Church responded to the modern world and the fashion in which it was to deal with political problems and powers. It relativized the normative character of the language and habits of thought with which the Church had legitimated its teachings and activities. It called Catholics out of their cultural alienation to assume new and more positive relationships with Protestants, members of other religions, and the bearers of modern social, political, and cultural movements. It abandoned the idea of a single normative culture, identified with Western "Christian civilization,"[10] and called for an incarnation of Catholic Christianity in the variety of the world's cultures.

In the years after the Council, it soon became apparent that neither "aggiornamento" nor "adaptation" were adequate descriptions of what the Council had accomplished, especially as local churches took up the responsibility for the realization of the Church in their areas, which the Council had enjoined on them. Their efforts, by definition, could not but differ considerably. Here it will be possible only to outline some of the main lines of development, first among "the young churches" and then in the more established churches of Europe and North America. I will then conclude with some general observations.

The "Young Churches" and Inculturation

The years since the Council have seen a shift from the perspective in which the churches of the southern hemisphere were seen as missionary territories and dependencies of the European and North American churches. They are now regarded as equal members of the Church universal, with their own contribution to make to a church that, precisely because it is catholic, cannot be centered upon Europe. Karl Rahner was so struck by this development that he even spoke of the beginning of a "third age" of the Church, a transition no less significant than that in

10. For the origins and uses of the notion of "Christian civilization," see *Civilisation chrétienne: Approche historique d'une idéologie, XVIIIe-XXe siècle* (Paris: Beauchesne, 1975) and G. Miccoli, "Chiesa e società."

which the Church moved out from Judaism into the Hellenistic world of the Roman Empire.[11]

Although the Council had used the metaphor of a *plantatio Ecclesiae* to describe the first stage of missionary activity and had spoken of an "adaptation" of the Christian life to various cultures,[12] both terms were soon discarded after the Council because they suggested that local realizations of the Church in a new cultural area were simply a matter of adjustments to a pregiven model. After experiments with such terms as "contextualization," "accommodation," and "indigenization," the word "inculturation" has been commonly adopted both by members of such churches and by Roman authority.[13] The process includes an initial moment in which the Gospel is translated from the language of the received tradition into the language of the new culture, a second moment in which what Pope John Paul II calls "a dialogue of cultures" takes place,[14] and a third moment in which the Gospel has so entered into the local culture that it can help form and direct it. Many of the young churches are still engaged in the first or second of these stages, both of them requiring a more elastic notion of culture and of evangelization than was common when a Eurocentric model of the Church was considered an obligatory ideal.

It is not possible here to describe in detail the vast movement for inculturated realizations of the Church that are going on among the young churches. The most that can be offered is some notice of important moments in this effort since the Council and a summary of some of the major lines of force.

For the assumption of local self-responsibility for the Church, the Medellín Conference of CELAM (1968) had a paradigmatic character. At Medellín, the Latin American Church reflected on itself both "in the light of the Council" and in the context of "the present-day transformation of Latin America." Both foci of this hermeneutical endeavor need to be kept in mind. Medellín was a rereading and a reception of Vatican II, but it was not carried on in a private, introverted ecclesiastical sphere, but as at the same time a reading and interpretation of the economic, social, political, and cultural developments that were transforming the continent. It was not some mythical "church in general" that the

11. Karl Rahner, "Basic Theological Interpretation of the Second Vatican Council," in *Concern for the Church: Theological Investigations XX* (New York: Crossroad, 1981), pp. 77–89.

12. See AG 6, 15–16, 18–19, 22.

13. For example, Pope John Paul II, *Catechesi tradendae*, 53; *Familiaris Consortio*, 8. Ary A. Roest-Crollius offers the following definition: "The inculturation of the Church is the integration of the Christian experience of a local Church into the culture of its people, in such a way that this experience not only expresses itself in elements of this culture, but becomes a force that animates, orients and innovates this culture so as to create a new unity and communion, not only within the culture in question but also as an enrichment of the Church universal" ("What is so new about Inculturation? A Concept and its Implications," *Gregorianum*, 59 [1978] 735).

14. *Catechesi tradendae*, 53.

bishops considered, but a church in and for Latin America in the late twentieth century. Medellín revealed the degree to which the self-realization of local churches is always a hermeneutical achievement, in which text and context, word and situation, are brought together in an interpretative unity in which each both illumines and is illumined. The reception of Vatican II thus becomes for each local church the same act of self-examination and self-purification that the Council represented for the universal Church.[15]

Medellín and later Puebla became models for other churches to imitate or at least to envy. (One still hears people in the United States say: "What we need is a North American Medellín or Puebla!") Episcopal conferences in other areas of the Third World were not long in attempting their own readings of the Council in the light of their own situations. The first Pan-African Symposium of Bishops was held at Kampala in 1969 and has been followed by other important meetings of bishops, regional and continental. The Asian bishops first gathered at Manila in 1970 and then organized a Federation of Asian Bishops' Conferences, which has held several plenary assemblies since then.[16]

But the bishops of these local churches also brought the contributions and the problems of their peoples to the universal Church, especially through their participation in and effect upon successive meetings of the Synod of Bishops. Their presence was already felt in the 1969 and 1971 synods, but with the 1976 synod, devoted to evangelization, they became a force impossible to ignore, claiming an equal right to frame the questions to be considered and to contribute to their clarification and resolution. Neither that meeting nor those that followed in 1977, on catechesis, and in 1980, on the family, succeeded to everyone's satisfaction; but they have been significant expressions of the new self-confidence of the "young churches" and they portend even more dramatic developments.[17]

At the 1976 synod, Cardinal Malula expressed in terms of his own context what might be regarded as the banner for all the young churches' efforts: "Yesterday foreign missionaries christianized Africa. Today the Christians of Africa are called to africanize Christianity."[18] The

---

15. "The great turning point that Vatican II represented for Europe, Medellín represented for Latin America" (Grootaers, De Vatican II, p. 56).

16. For these "postconciliar rereadings of Vatican II," see Grootaers, ibid., pp. 52–67. For an illuminating summary of the Asian meetings, see C. G. Arévalo, "Further Reflections on Mission Today in the Asian Context," in Toward a New Age in Mission: The Good News of God's Kingdom to the Peoples of Asia (Manila: IMC/TCO, 1981), book 2, pp. 129–53.

17. See René Laurentin, L'évangélisation après le IVᵉ Synode (Paris: Seuil, 1975, whose bilan of the 1974 Synod (pp. 90–128) could be repeated in large part for the two following meetings. See also Grootaers, De Vatican II, pp. 72–87, with the remark of Bishop Sangu in 1975: "The last synod clearly showed that the former missionary countries have become particular churches with a right to their own existence. . . . We are partners and not just churches that receive" (p. 84).

18. Quoted in Laurentin, L'évangélisation, p. 52.

many efforts to inculturate Christianity follow certain general lines of force. The churches are attempting to produce liturgies that reflect their own local cultures not only in language, but also by introducing relevant symbols and rites. Questions are being asked about what is meant by the "substance" of the sacraments (e.g., the Eucharist and marriage). They are seeking to appropriate the religious elements of their own peoples, through both a finer appreciation of non-Christian religions and a greater respect for popular religion. They show a new respect and concern for elements of popular cultures that have not experienced the differentiations and rationalizations typical of Western culture. They are asking questions about the universal applicability of certain cultural and moral norms characteristic of the West. Almost all of them have committed themselves to constructing the Church from below, through vital grassroots communities. They have recognized the importance of developing an indigenous clergy and are experimenting with new articulations of ecclesial ministry. They have insisted that the inculturation of the Church cannot avoid sharing in the political and economic struggles of their peoples. And this has required them to face the problems created by the rapid modernization of their societies and their assumption into global economic and political systems, and to try to overcome the alienation caused by the Church's past associations with colonial powers and with local structures of domination.

The churches of these areas have also not been slow in attempting to produce new theologies to justify and to promote their efforts at self-realization. To the pluralism produced in the Church at large by the collapse of neo-scholasticism has been added the further pluralization that follows when theology is conceived as reflection on the role of a religion within a culture.[19] The Council itself called for such theologies when it proposed a new theological reflection to assist a new *fides quaerens intellectum*, making use of "the philosophy and wisdom of the peoples" (AG 22). Many theologians have taken up the challenge eagerly, even aggressively, effecting a sort of "decolonialization" of theology.[20] Many Latin American, Asian, and African theologians are challenging traditional notions of where theology is to be done, by whom, with what methods, in what terms, and for what purposes. They are not afraid to characterize their theology as "regional," that is, as African or Asian or Latin American, regretting only that so many other theologians neglect the re-

19. "A theology mediates between a cultural matrix and the significance and role of a religion in that matrix" (Lonergan, *Method*, p. xi).

20. See, for example, the "Final Communiqué" of the Pan-African Conference of Third World Theologians" held in Accra in 1977, in *African Theology en Route*, K. Appiah-Kubi and S. Torres, eds. (Maryknoll, N.Y.: Orbis, 1979), pp. 189–95. The literature on these efforts is by now enormous. For an introduction, see *Mission Trends No. 3: Third World Theologies*, G. H. Anderson and T. F. Stransky, eds. (New York: Paulist Press, 1976); *Doing Theology in New Places* (*Concilium*, 115), J.–P. Jossua and J. B. Metz, eds. (New York: Seabury, 1978); and J. S. Ukpong, "The Emergence of African Theologies," *Theological Studies*, 45 (1984) 501–36.

gional character of their own work, as when they apply such qualifications only to work undertaken outside Europe or North America or in terms unfamiliar to themselves.

These new theologies are not only marked by the attempt to make use of the cultural resources of their people, they are also undertaken as reflections on the commitments of their churches to the service of the poor and to the construction of a more decent human future. The best known of these efforts, of course, is the theology of liberation, which originated in Latin America but has found echoes in Asia and Africa as well. A socio-critical dimension is constitutive of such theologies, and not merely an edifying addendum to or a practical application of an already basically complete theological synthesis.

The Collapse of Roman Catholicism

The cultural crisis and challenge brought on by the Council had a different character in the older established churches and in the face of the secularizing and rationalizing forces of modern society. These were the social and cultural areas in and for which the distinctive culture of Roman Catholicism was created and these were the churches in which it was embodied. Some people expected that, inasmuch as the conciliar reforms were conceived primarily in view of these regions, Vatican II could provide a blueprint that would excuse these churches from tasks that young churches, more marginal at the Council, could not avoid. This did not prove to be the case, however, and in North America and in Europe also the Council provoked something like a cultural revolution within the Church.

The reforms in internal church life that the Council proposed might perhaps have been assimilable without great disturbance had the Council not also seriously qualified the Church's attitude toward the modern world. But when the basic motive for much of the logic, structure, and practice of Roman Catholicism was itself questioned, the subculture it had produced collapsed as if from its own weight.[21] In those regions of the West where modernity had made most progress, the Church underwent a major cultural crisis, as its members sought to achieve a more positive and a more accommodating presence in the modern world. All areas of Church life, it seemed, were affected: forms of worship, patterns of association, modes of thought and language, habits of devotion, everyday behavior, political relationships, the methods and locations of

21. There are many chronicles of this collapse or decomposition and just as many diagnoses. Phrases such as "the end of the Constantinian era" or "the end of Christendom" refer to the culturally decisive issue of the Church's relationship to the world. See the 1984 issue of *Christianesimo nella storia*, esp. the articles by G. Alberigo, D. Menozzi, and J.-P. Jossua.

theology, the relationships between local churches, individually and as national or regional bodies, and Rome.

Immediately after the Council, the reforms were begun in a spirit of cultural optimism and primarily as internal reforms to make the Church more effective in the context of a secular and pluralistic world. Although even these reforms put a certain strain on the Catholic sense of identity, the impact of the Council on the western churches was also greatly affected by the severe criticisms that had begun to be addressed to western culture in the late 1960s. The primary movements and legitimations of Western modernity came under attack: rationalization, bureaucracy, technology, capitalism, liberalism, the cult of progress, and so forth. The cultural, political, and economic hegemony of the West was called into question, and its sense of historical destiny was challenged. Social and cultural change seemed to accelerate, with profound effects upon Catholics, who were no longer immunized from the world and who had seen their own church embark upon significant self-criticism and change. The changes in the Church became almost inextricably intertwined with changes in society and culture, much to the chagrin of many Catholics who thought they had exchanged a rock for a raft![22]

The changes that the Council's new openness to the world at least permitted are too many to analyze in detail. But some major developments must be mentioned: liturgical reform and local adaptation; the criticism and decline of many traditional forms of personal piety; the replacement of Catholic Action by a new sense of lay ministry and responsibility; the collapse of many Catholic associations and movements; a redefinition, theoretical and practical, of the principle of authority; the growth of attitudes and habits of "confrontation"; calls for the sharing of responsibility in and for the Church at almost all levels; a greater sense of the distinct missions of local churches; redefinitions of the nature and roles of the ordained ministry and of the religious orders; a charismatic movement; a new respect for personal religious experience; urgent calls to give women equal rights (and even rites!) in the Church; movements in the direction of more communitarian notions and realizations of the Church, often accompanied, paradoxically enough, by a considerable increase in ecclesiastical bureaucracy; a rethinking of the political responsibilities of the Church in societies whose economic and political liberalism could no longer be accepted without question. This is obviously a very mixed bag of developments and it ignores the not inconsiderable differences between the experiences of the various churches of western Europe and North America; but most of them can be found in almost all the churches, and together they constitute the end of a uniform Roman

22. The simultaneity of the critiques of Western society and of the Church in the decade following the Council makes it very difficult, as some interpreters do, to "blame" the Council for certain perhaps unfortunate developments in the Church. The decade between 1965 and 1975 was not an ordinary decade in the history of western societies!

Catholicism and the emergence of quite new forms of the one Church, marked by the peculiarities of area and circumstance.

Theology in these areas both reflected and contributed to these developments. The Council can be read as an acceptance by the Church of the challenges of historical consciousness: acceptance of the need and role of critical history; a new awareness of and appreciation for cultural and historical diversity; a greater sense of individual and collective responsibility for the future of humanity. Catholic theology could not but be affected to its roots. The reign of neo-scholasticism ended with astonishing speed. History, social science, and hermeneutics became integral dimensions of the theological enterprise. The role of authority was reconceived in all areas of its application: the Bible, tradition, dogma, magisterium. Theology ceased to be a clerical monopoly to be carried out chiefly in seminaries. Theologians left their dogmatic corners and engaged the world, seeing their work as a moment in the interaction of faith and culture, and not simply a legitimizing function within a self-sufficient church. With this shift, their work became a political or public task, attempting to make the Gospel a critical challenge to society and culture.[23]

All this has given a direction and character to the attempts to localize the Church in western societies, a direction and character they might not have had in times of greater social and cultural stability. The tensions between the proponents and opponents of the Church's cultural accommodation to the modern world were complicated by certain similarities between the new cultural critiques and the old condemnations of Roman Catholicism. As a result, two great and perhaps only apparently dissimilar temptations have recently been experienced, both of them containing at least implicit criticisms of the Council. The first is a desire to retreat back into the former attitude toward modern culture, an attempt to re-create the distinct sociological form that was Roman Catholicism, with greater or lesser regret that the Church ever attempted any accommodation to modernity. If that temptation afflicts many conservatives and especially Catholic traditionalists, those who have taken the reforming plunge face the temptation so to accommodate themselves to the rapidly changing movements of society and culture that the Council again comes under criticism for a too eager détente with a now suspect economic and political order. In both cases, there lurks the danger of a return to the undifferentiated intransigence that used to characterize Roman Catholicism's attitude toward the modern world.[24]

23. By far the most important North American analysis of and contribution to this reconception of the role of theology is to be found in the two volumes of David Tracy, *Blessed Rage for Order: The New Pluralism in Theology* (New York: Seabury Press, 1975) and *The Analogical Imagination: Christian Theology and the Culture of Pluralism* (New York: Crossroad, 1981).

24. This totalizing Catholicism can tempt those on the political left as much as those on the right, both having in common an aversion to the differentiations that in part define

Difficulties and Challenges

Although I have described separately the developments of the local churches in the Third World and in the North Atlantic world, they did not, of course, take place without effects upon one another. The churches have given to and learned from one another. There have been many points of contact, official and unofficial. The dramatic political commitments of many Latin American churches have had considerable effect upon the North American and West European churches. The theology of liberation has challenged the Christians of Europe and North America to rethink their roles in those very countries from which many Third World nations wish to free themselves. The women's movements in the United States and Europe have forced questions upon the Christians of the Third World. The United States bishops' pastoral letter on nuclear weapons proved a stimulus for other hierarchies to address the issue. Pastoral practices found helpful in some areas are often quickly tried out in others.

In all these ways, something of what the Council defined as the concrete catholicity of the Church is being achieved: that mutual sharing by which the fullness of unity is realized (LG 13). The very effort to realize a genuinely local church becomes a model for other churches to emulate; one local church's self-realization, especially when it has a socially or culturally critical dimension, requires other churches to reconsider their role in their societies and cultures; the difficulties and the achievements of one church concern and challenge all the others. A different notion of the unity of the Church universal is thus being realized. It is no longer a unity based simply either upon a one-way dependency of other churches on those of the North Atlantic or upon the direction of Roman authority. The unity is to be achieved through an active common sharing, presided over by the bishop of the church at Rome, of all that the one Gospel of Jesus Christ brings to be in the various churches of the world.

This is an important point, for the difficulties in the task of local realizations of the Church, especially after generations of uniformity, should not be ignored. Each local church runs the danger of becoming closed in on itself, of such cultural assimilation that it loses its sense of belonging to the larger Catholic fullness. No local church—in Europe, North America, or the Third World—is exempt from the temptation to ethnic, racial, political, or nationalistic exclusivism. The Council's com-

modern political liberalism and pluralism. The later Lamennais and Louis Veuillot were at opposite ends of the political spectrum, but they shared a desire to see Christendom restored. See J.-M. Mayeur, "Catholicisme intransigéant, catholicisme social, démocratie chrétienne," *Annales*, 27 (1972) 483–99, and his *Des partis catholiques à la Démocratie chrétienne, XIXᵉ-XXᵉ siècles* (Paris: Armand Colin, 1981), pp. 233–39.

ment that "the things that unite the faithful are stronger than the things that divide them" (GS 92) should be applicable to the churches too. But the difficulties of applying the old adage, *in necessariis unitas, in dubiis libertas, in omnibus caritas* can be overcome only when "charity in all things" presides over a common effort to determine what the necessary things are and where differences may be allowed.

It is easy enough to say, as did Pope Paul VI, that there are "many secondary elements" in the Church's message, which may change, and an "essential content, a living substance, which cannot be modified or ignored."[25] But the real problem is in knowing how to separate that substance from culturally conditioned elements. Traditional Catholicism bears the marks of the long history through which it has transformed Western culture and been itself transformed in the process. There is not now, nor has there ever been, a Catholicism that represents some pure, transcultural quintessence of Christianity. Catholicism is what Catholicism has become through its history; and the power which it possesses is not felt only in its institutions but in the hold over minds and hearts that familiarity and habit produce.

Pope John Paul II described the dimensions of the issue:

On the one hand, the Gospel message cannot be purely and simply isolated from the culture in which it was first inserted (the biblical world or, more concretely, the cultural milieu in which Jesus of Nazareth lived), nor, without serious loss, from the cultures in which it has already been expressed down the centuries; it does not spring spontaneously from any cultural soil; it has always been transmitted by means of an apostolic dialogue which inevitably becomes part of a certain dialogue of cultures.

On the other hand, the power of the Gospel everywhere transforms and regenerates. When that power enters into a culture, it is no surprise that it rectifies many of its elements. There would be no catechesis if it were the Gospel that had to change when it came into contact with the cultures.[26]

In other words, we do not find, even in the scriptures and in the normative tradition, a noncultural expression of the Gospel; and we would have nothing left if we stripped away all cultural determinations of our message. Furthermore, faith comes from hearing the message of Jesus Christ; it may, indeed must, encounter *semina Verbi* in new cultures, but these are not the Gospel itself, which always must both purify and enrich. In the final analysis, evangelization and catechesis, the local realization of the Church, are an apostolic dialogue carried out as a "dialogue of cultures."

That phrase "dialogue of cultures" is not a bad description as well of an essential feature of a church that is both one and concretely universal. Concrete Catholicity needs a dialogue of churches, each of which has

25. *Evangelii Nuntiandi*, 25.
26. *Catechesi Tradendae*, 53.

had to undertake, willy-nilly, in quite different circumstances and often in quite different forms, the same challenge of a local dialogue of cultures. The willingness of local churches to engage in both dialogues is the best illustration of what the Council said in a slightly different context: "This variety of local Churches, seeking together to be one, shows all the more resplendently the catholicity of an undivided Church" (LG 23).

Giuseppe Ruggieri

6. Faith and History*

The idea that faith is anchored in history is not a novelty, as is clear when we recall that from the beginning Christian biblical faith has been the recognition of God's action in the history of a people (Israel) and the life of an individual (Jesus Christ). In addition, apart from this central aspect of the matter, there have always been individuals in the Christian biblical tradition who have been able to find God's will manifested in concrete events, whether extraordinary or everyday. If, then, we wish to understand what is specific to the Vatican II message regarding history, we must move beyond general formulations and determine exactly the problem that the Council faced and the problem that is making itself felt today.

Even at this point, before entering into the argument, we can say that the problem is not in the first place the problem of prophecy or the problem of lived experience; it is a problem of *recognition*. In fact, prophecy and lived experience by definition draw their sustenance from history. In the Hebrew and Christian tradition the prophets were and continue to be those who break through the crust formed by the commonplace attitudes that shelter the routine institutions and prevailing mentalities of any human group. Prophets do so because they have the ability to pronounce judgments that are at once awesome and ordinary: awesome, because they carry the authority of a will that is mightier than that of this world's rulers and is bent on tearing down and building, destroying and raising up (see Jer. 1:10); ordinary, because, unlike commonplace attitudes, this judgment brings to light the dimension of existence that is the most obvious and yet tends to be found reprehensi-

---

*In this essay "faith" means concrete, lived Christian faith with its ecclesial connotations. The relationship between faith and history will therefore be studied not from the viewpoint of the relationship between revelation and history, which has been the sole concern of theological discussion in recent centuries, but from the more limited and specific viewpoint of the relationship between, on the one hand, the experience of believers with its ecclesial determinants (to the extent that Christian faith gives rise to and at the same time arises out of an organized set of objective relationships and mediations) and, on the other, common human experience.

ble. Before the eyes of all, the prophet sets the suffering of the oppressed, the numbers who have died of hunger in a society that is regarded as opulent, and so on. Like prophecy, the lived experience of
Christians consists in the ability to examine *every* event of their own
lives, without sacrificing anything to universal definitions or to comfort-
able statements about "what has to be," but with the love of God who
makes the rain fall on just and unjust alike.

Here precisely is the problem: the recognition of prophecy and common experience. It is a profoundly ecclesial problem. In other words: we
need to know whether the Church is a human group whose relationship
to history is the same as that of any other group that, in order to give
permanence to certain aspects of its own experience and identity, establishes institutions for perpetuating and protecting these aspects, and in
which therefore the institutional element is primarily a defense against
anything unexpected that history may bring. Or is it rather that, although the Church does not ignore the need of safeguarding and continuing its own tradition but on the contrary revitalizes it in a fruitful
way, the eyes of its members are nonetheless focused primarily on
"whatever happens," on the common human condition, without fear or
censure. *Recognition* makes prophecy and lived experience the central
elements in the life of a group and does not restrict them to manifestations of a subculture or to secret messages marginal in relation to what
directs and conditions the life of the group as such.

My argument is therefore a challenge: Is it possible for prophets and
common men and women not to be reduced to wearisome incidentals or
to the vexing, even if continuous, buzz of insects that are to be extermi-
nated with a squirt of lethal poison in the form of meaningless assur-
ances, neglect, or repetition? Is history, that is, the real lives of human
beings (not theories about history or hermeneutics of history or theologies of history), the place where faith in the God of the living sinks its
roots, in imitation of him who emptied himself and became like human
beings in all things save sin? Or are we, like the king of Judah, going to
question the imprisoned prophet, but then be filled with fear at his plain
words and decide to take shelter in the rules of the institution and ignore
his message (see Jer. 38:14–28)?

History as Proof of What is Already Known

Melchior Cano (1509–60) had already included history among the *loci*
("places" or sources) of theology. If, however, we are to understand his
position, which can be regarded as representative of the prevailing outlook among Catholics until a few decades ago, we must keep in mind
two basic points in his theory. The first has to do with the very idea of a
theological *locus*. According to Cano, who bases his views on the *De in-*

ventione dialectica of Rudolf Agricola, the theological *loci* can be compared to a warehouse or stockpile of "arguments" to be used in demonstrations. The "arguments" are the component parts of the syllogistic reasoning that it is the very purpose of theology to construct. The *loci* are therefore the principles—in the broadest sense of this term—of theology, inasmuch as they make it possible to gain knowledge of the material for theological argumentation—they contain in storage the arguments that are the components of a reasoning process.

In the last analysis, the reasoning process or argumentation does not derive its force from the content of its individual parts (the premises of the syllogism) but from a formal characteristic of these premises—namely, that they are revealed. For Cano the value of a particular item of theological knowledge depends on the witnesses for it (does it come from a human being or does it come from God?), and he is therefore quite logical in giving the name *loci* to the various sources of theological knowledge (scripture, tradition, and so on).[1]

Cano's position here is also consistent with the division of theology into positive and speculative. The task of positive theology is to find the elements that serve as points of departure for argumentation; the task of speculative theology is to construct argumentation.[2] It is already possible to perceive in this conception of a theological *locus* a dangerous extrinsicism. For in fact the theological synthesis, the insight into the meaning that results from the systematization and the reciprocal relationship between the data, is the work of the art of logic that has an origin different from that of the Christian fact itself and is the logic developed by the Scholastic Aristotelian tradition. Scripture and tradition provide the "material," but the "understanding" has its seat elsewhere.

The second point to be kept in mind in Cano's position is the description of history as a *locus* that is "foreign" to theology and therefore different from its "specific principles." History, like "natural reason" and the "authority of the philosophers," is a "foreign" *locus* and therefore a subordinate tool of knowledge, because, unlike the specific principles that Cano lists, it is naturally knowable.[3]

With this distinction Cano separates the knowledge of faith from human history. History becomes a very useful storehouse of apologetical demonstrations, but Christian knowledge as such follows a law of its own that is characterized by assent to an external authority. It is no accident therefore that though Christian historiography gradually took over

---

1. I am here repeating what is said in A. Lang's study, *Die loci theologici des Melchior Cano und die Methode des dogmatischen Beweises* (Munich, 1925; reprinted: Hildesheim, 1974); on Cano see also the lucid remarks of M.-D. Chenu, "Les lieux théologiques chez Melchior Cano," in *Le déplacement de la théologie* (Paris, 1977), pp. 45–50.

2. John Major (1469–1550) was perhaps the first to make this distinction in his commentary on the *Sentences* (1509); see Y. Congar in *DTC*, 15/1:426–27.

3. Cano therefore reduces history in fact to a series of arguments that are to provide an extrinsic confirmation of Catholic dogma; see *De locis theologicis*, XI, cap. 4.

some fruitful elements of the critical method, it too has looked at the history of the Church primarily from an apologetical point of view.[4] Christian revelation (but how ambiguous the category of "revelation" has become in the modern period!) is thus anchored in ahistorical categories presumed to carry their own intrinsic guarantee of truth and irrefutably confirmed by an external demonstration of the "fact." Cano's theory was a structure destined to crumble, but it would be defended, propped up, and repeatedly overhauled as late as the first half of the present century.[5]

There was, indeed, a historical parenthesis rich in promise when the men who started the faculty of Catholic theology in Tübingen became the proponents of a strongly historical vision of Christianity. One of them, J. S. Drey, could write that just as "the scientific consciousness of a nation is simply the ideal and highest expression of what lies hidden within the nation and functions as its spiritual life," so it should be possible and fruitful to view the history of theology as "parallel to general history" and, with the help of this juxtaposition, "to understand how they condition each other."[6] But this vision was destined to be replaced, in the neo-scholastic reaction, by a rigid conception hostile to the modern sensitivity to history, which it suspected of relativism.[7] The inevitable acceptance of the historico-critical method, especially in biblical exegesis, was thus delayed by the well-known shower of negative declarations about the Mosaic authorship of the Pentateuch, the "historical" character of the biblical story of the origin of the world and humankind, Aramaic Matthew, and so on.[8] All this was a rearguard action that was

4. Men like Mabillon or Muratori thus formed an independent line of thinkers that had no place in the theological syntheses. Until the nineteenth century "histories of the Church" were in very large measure shaped by theological prejudgments. A representative instance: the 21-volume *Della Istoria Ecclesiastica*, which Giuseppe Agostino Orsi (1692–1761) began in 1746 in order to give the "Roman" view in response to the *Histoire ecclésiastique* (20 vols.; 1691–1720) of "Gallican" Claude Fleury.

5. See, among others, A. Dulles, *A History of Apologetics* (New York, 1971); H. Bouillard, "De l'apologétique à la théologie fondamentale," in his *Les quatre fleuves*. Vol. 1, *Dieu connu en Jésus-Christ* (Paris, 1973), pp. 57–70; J. Flury, *Um die Redlichkeit des Glaubens. Studien zur deutschen katholischen Fundamentaltheologie* (Fribourg, 1979); P. Eicher, *Offenbarung. Prinzip neuzeitlicher Theologie* (Munich, 1977); G. Ruggieri, "Per una storia dell'apologia in epoca moderna. Note bibliografiche e metodologiche," *Cristianesimo nella storia*, 4 (1983) 33–58; idem, "L'apologia cattolica in epoca moderna," to appear in *Enciclopedia di teologia fondamentale*, G. Ruggieri, ed. (Turin: Marietti).

6. J. S. Drey, *Revision des gegenwärtigen Zustandes der Theologie* (1812; reprinted: Darmstadt, 1971), pp. 3f. On the relationship between Christian revelation and history in Drey and Mohler, see R. J. Cornelissen, *Offenbarung und Geschichte. Die Frage der Vermittlung* (Essen, 1972), pp. 11–69.

7. See R. Aubert in A. Fliche and V. Martin, eds., *Storia della chiesa*, 21/1:292–349; B. Welte, "Zum Strukturwandel der katholischen Theologie im 19. Jahrhundert," in his *Auf der Spur des Ewigen* (Freiburg/Basel/Vienna, 1965), pp. 380–409; G. A. McCool, *Catholic Theology in the Nineteenth Century. The Quest for a Unitary Method* (New York, 1977).

8. See DS 3394ff.; 3512ff.; 3561ff.; these are only three examples, though important ones, from among many; see E. Poulat, *Histoire, dogme et critique dans la crise moderniste* (Tournai/Paris, 1962) (and the review in *RHE*, 61 [1966] 222–32).

essentially ended by the encyclical *Divino afflante Spiritu* of Pius XII (1943). In the early part of our century, however, it still prevented a calm assessment of the real issue in the so-called Modernist crisis: on the one hand, the recognition of the historical character of Christianity and, on the other, a religious anthropology that would do greater justice to the findings of historical consciousness.[9]

It is chiefly the generation after the Modernist crisis that must be credited with preparing the ground for a calmer and more productive vision.[10] A number of factors combined to give rise to a new and different appreciation of history: the rediscovery of patristic thought and the resultant breakdown of the claims made by the neo-scholastic approach; the consciousness of an irreversible crisis in relationships between church and society, which could be reestablished only on a new foundation; the impact of the ecumenical and liturgical movements; the crisis in Western civilization itself, which imposed a serious examination of conscience on all; and so on.

Signs of the Times

In this context the pontificate of John XXIII brought the turning point that had long been in preparation. The turn to a recognition of history was accompanied by a novel phraseology. I refer to the gospel phrase "signs of the times," which Pope Roncalli made part of everyday Catholic language. In the apostolic constitution *Humanae salutis* (Dec. 25, 1961) in which he convoked the Second Vatican Council he said: "As we make our own the recommendation of Jesus that we learn how to discern 'the signs of the times' (Matt 16:4), we seem to see amid so much darkness not a few indications that give hope for the future of the Church and the human race." The council was to use the same phrase four times, but the idea is also encountered elsewhere.[11]

To understand the meaning of this new phrase we must bear in mind that it expresses a changed attitude of the Church toward history. Since the end of the eighteenth century it had become customary among Catholics, with rare exceptions, to pass a wholly negative judgment on modern history.[12] The Syllabus of Pius XI was not the first document to

9. This was the point M. Blondel was trying to make in his *Histoire et Dogme. Les lacunes philosophiques de l'exégèse moderne* (Paris, 1904), which appeared originally in the journal *La Quinzaine*; now in *Les premiers écrits de Maurice Blondel* (Paris, 1956), pp. 149–345; Engl. trans., *The Letter on Apologetics and History and Dogma* (New York, 1965).

10. See G. Alberigo, "Cristianesimo come storia e teologia confessante," in M.-D. Chenu, *Le Saulchoir. Una scuola di teologia* (Casale Monferrato, 1982), pp. vii–xxx.

11. See GS 4; PO 9; AA 14; UR 4.

12. See G. Miccoli, "Chiesa e società in Italia tra Ottocento e Novecento: il mito della 'cristianità,'" in *Chiese nelle società* (Turin, 1980), pp. 151–245; G. Alberigo, "Dalla bastone alla misericordia. Il magistero nel cattolicesimo contemporaneo (1830–1980)," *Cristianesimo nella storia*, 2 (1981) 487–521.

give systematic expression to this view. It is also found in the introduction to the dogmatic constitution on faith that was issued by Vatican I; post-tridentine history is there described as a progressive corruption of human beings due to the Protestant denial of the principle of authority. Even earlier, Pope Gregory XVI (1831–46), in his encyclical *Mirari vos* of August 15, 1832, had found himself forced by the conspiracy of the wicked to abandon leniency and kindness, for the only suitable course henceforth was to "curb with the rod" (*virga compescere*).

It is against this background that we must locate the quite different vision of history that John XXIII expresses in the idea of "the signs of the times," thereby completely reversing the attitude of Gregory XVI. Thus in his opening address to Vatican II Pope Roncalli says:

Nowadays . . . the Spouse of Christ prefers to apply the medicine of mercy rather than the medicine of severity; she believes that she will meet today's needs by showing the grounds for her teaching rather than by repeating condemnations. It is not that there are no false doctrines, opinions, and dangerous ideas to be guarded against and warded off; but these are in such clear contrast to the right norm of honesty and have produced such deadly fruits that men and women on their own seem inclined to condemn them.

Here history is being left to correct its own errors, and the Church concerns itself solely with bringing out the positive character of the gospel message. The condemnation of history that was so common in the magisterium of the Restoration, and is emerging again today, is itself branded (in the opening discourse) as lacking in discretion and moderation:

In the daily exercise of our pastoral ministry we are offended at times by having to listen to the views of those who, although full of zeal, have no great sense of discretion and moderation. They see the modern age as nothing but disasters and calamities; they keep repeating that our age, as compared with past ages, is getting steadily worse. . . .

But we must disagree with these prophets of doom who are always predicting disaster, as though the destruction of the world were imminent.

In the present course of human events, when society seems to be entering into a new order, we must see rather the hidden plan of divine providence that through the ages has been using the works of human beings—usually without their intending it—to achieve its purposes.

A double misunderstanding often keeps people from grasping what was happening in the consciousness of Catholics generally and was revealed in Pope John's phrase "signs of the times," and in related gestures. The first misunderstanding shows in the attempt to play down the importance of the Council by insinuating that John XXIII did not fully realize what he had set in motion when he convoked it. But the publication of the several drafts of the opening discourse and a comparison of Roncalli's various statements on the Christian view of history should henceforth suffice to dispel some of the myths and clichés on this subject.[13]

The second misunderstanding is manifest in the effort to empty the phrase "signs of the times" of its meaning by relating it not to concrete experience and specific attitudes but to a possible theology and theory of history.[14] But in this connection Yves Congar has rightly observed:

This category does indeed need more careful definition in order to take into account its biblical, christological, and eschatological dimensions. What is of greater interest, however, is the intention implicit in the language used. The aim is a full recognition of the *historicity* of the world and of the Church itself which, though distinct from the world, is nonetheless bound up with it. Movements in the world must have their echo in the Church, at least to the extent that they raise problems.[15]

For the Church, then, to take note of the signs of the times is to understand that time itself with its decisive events, which bring a collective awareness wherein humanity becomes conscious of the road it is traveling, furnishes the Church with "the signs of present expectation of the Messiah who has come, the signs that the gospel is consistent with the hopes of human beings."[16]

What was, and is, at issue, then, is the abandonment of a *deductivist*

13. See G. Alberigo and A. Melloni, "L'allocuzione *Gaudet Mater Ecclesia* di Giovanni XXIII, 11 ottobre 1982," in *Fede Tradizione Profezia. Studi su Giovanni XXIII e sul Vaticano II* (Brescia, 1984), pp. 185–283). Alberigo has also analyzed the same address from the viewpoint that concerns us here: "Cristianesimo e Storia nel Vaticano II," *Cristianesimo nella storia*, 5 (1984) 577–92, esp. 583–85; he regards the opening address as from beginning to end a single, unbroken reflection on history as conditioning Christianity and on the unparalleled importance of this fact for the Council.

14. This is the approach taken not only in articles such as that of P. Valadier, "Signes des temps, signes de Dieu?," *Etudes*, 335 (1971) 261–79, but also in the book of C. Boff, *Segni dei tempi* (Rome, 1983). Furthermore, it is not an exaggeration to say that the phrase used by John XXIII expresses a "Catholic" sensitivity that is less concerned with biblical and theological qualifications. In the Protestant tradition, on the other hand, the expression has been marked, especially in the nineteenth century, by a strong eschatological orientation; see W. Kahle, "Die Zeichen der Zeit," *ZRGG*, 24 (1972) 289–315. A bibliography on the signs of the times is given in G. Alberigo, "Cristianesimo e Storia" (n. 13, above), pp. 589–90; and K. Füssel, "Die Zeichen der Zeit als locus theologicus. Ein Beitrag zur theologischen Erkenntnislehre," *FZPT*, 30 (1983) 259–74. It must not be forgotten, however, that more justice is done to the signs of the times, as the sense of the words indicates, by a concrete and specific interpretation of the religious meaning of history than by hermeneutical disquisitions on the phrase as such. I may cite A. Neher, *L'existence juive* (Paris, 1962), as an outstanding example of a theology of the signs of the times. Again, John XXIII himself has left us an effective example of a prophetic reading of the signs of the times in his *Pacem in terris* with its new appraisal of the problem of war in the atomic age, its recognition of the movement for the emancipation of women, its insight into the role of new nations, and so on.

15. "Bloc-Notes sur le Concile," *ICI*, Nov. 15, 1964.

16. M.-D. Chenu, "Les signes des temps," *NRT*, 97 (1965) 35. This short essay offers basic reflections on the subject; the author then developed them along various lines in other publications.

outlook according to which a few principles yield conclusions valid for human activity in every age, and its replacement by an *inductive* mindset that reads in and educes from facts the signs of a consistency between the gospel that is believed and proclaimed and the desires of human beings. As thus understood, the "signs of the times" do not constitute a theological category but a call for the positive acknowledgment of history as an authentic "place" wherein the imminent presence of the kingdom may be perceived. The phrase is linguistically incompatible with a fixed theology ("a theology of conclusions")[17] and calls for a consonant theology of its own;[18] its meaning cannot be adequately captured by second-level reflection or a theological theory, because it expresses first and foremost an attitude of faith, a concrete disposition of mind for which history is not an accident or an extraneous fact but is constitutive of the salvation that Christians hope for and proclaim.

The Aggiornamento Effected by the Council

In his opening address John XXIII urged the Council not simply to repeat the teaching of the Fathers of the Church and of the theologians ancient and modern, and not to confine themselves to safeguarding the doctrinal treasure of the Church. The need, he said, was rather that "this certain and immutable doctrine, to which we must faithfully adhere, should be examined and explained (*pervestigetur et exponatur*) in a way that meets the needs of our time (*ea ratione . . . quam tempora postulant nostra*)."[19] He gave as the justification for this necessary updating not only the well-known distinction between the deposit of faith and the way in which the truths of the deposit are enunciated, but also the "primarily pastoral function" of the Church's teaching office.

17. There is a short, clear introduction to the problem and a basic bibliography in J. Dubois, "Conclusion théologique," *Catholicisme*, 2:1452–55.

18. This theology must be regarded as still in the making. See above all those contemporary christologies (W. Kasper, E. Schillebeeckx,) in which the greater clarity gained through historico-critical research makes possible reflection that no longer follows the deductive pattern. In particular, Schillebeeckx (see, among other books, *Christ. The Experience of Jesus as Lord* [New York, 1980]), and J. B. Metz (*Faith in History and Society: Toward a Practical Fundamental Theology* [New York, 1980]) have constructed models for theological reflection along these new lines. The basic contribution in this area, however, continues to be the "theology of liberation"; for an overview see R. Gibellini, ed., *Frontiers of Theology in Latin America* (Maryknoll, N.Y., 1979).

19. See J. W. O'Malley, "Reform, Historical Consciousness, and Vatican II's Aggiornamento," *TS*, 32 (1971) 573–601. O'Malley stresses the point that this approach is the direct opposite of the one expressed by Giles of Viterbo (1469–1532) in his opening address to the Fifth Lateran Council: "Men must be changed by religion, not religion by men" (*Homines per sacra immutari fas est, non sacra per homines*). On aggiornamento, see especially C. Butler, "The Aggiornamento of Vatican II," in *Vatican II: An Interfaith Appraisal*, J. H. Miller, ed. (Notre Dame, Ind., 1966), pp. 3–13.

The "pastoral role" of the Church was here being defined as the ability to connect the truths of the Gospels with the demands of history. This ability must find expression in a double movement. On the one hand, the expression and presentation of truth must be geared to the needs of one's own times. On the other, the accommodation of expression arises in turn from a deeper grasp of the message, not from its watering down. Updating (*aggiornamento*) was therefore to take the form not of an adaptation but of a deeper penetration and fidelity—the very source of the ability to meet the needs created by history.

It is with this kind of updating in mind that the work of Vatican II is to be assessed: the link it established between tradition and present-day history, and its successful rejection of theological schemas that would prevent the making of this connection. The first need was to vacate the prison of the neo-scholastic framework that for over a century had provided a fortress within which the Church could settle down and take cover from the errors of the modern age. Acceptance of the idea that the modern age, even though an age of revolutions, showed not only signs of corruption but real "signs of the times" meant laying aside a theological weaponry intended for hostile action. It was no accident that the great dispute over the schema on the sources of revelation in the first session of the Council was also, and above all, a dispute over the validity of recent theology and its claim to be a satisfactory mediation. Thus in a well-known intervention Cardinal Frings claimed:

The schema prepared by commissions still under the control of the Roman Curia does not take account of the entire Catholic tradition in its presentation of the Church's teaching, but only of a small segment, the tradition of the last hundred years. Almost nothing is said of the Greek tradition and very little of the ancient Latin tradition, although both are extremely rich. This limitation is clear from the notes accompanying the schema and from the sources cited in them. In Chapter IV, for example, there are six pages of notes, but in the six pages there are only two brief citations from a Greek father. And the references to the Latin fathers and the Middle Ages are not much more numerous; the six pages are almost entirely filled with references to the last hundred years. . . . The same pattern is to be found in all the chapters of the constitution. Is such a procedure to be called right, universal, ecumenical, and catholic—in Greek: *katholon*, that is, embracing everything and keeping everything in view?[20]

The recognition of history and the location of faith not alongside history or in opposition to it had to mean, therefore, a renewal of historical memory, not a mere adaptation. And, as a matter of fact, where the conciliar texts are more successful in recapturing ecclesial tradition, they also open the way more fully for contact with the men and women of today. This is true of the "Constitution on the Sacred Liturgy" in which

---

20. *Acta synodalia*, I, part IV, 218–19; on the relationship between Vatican II and tradition, see A. Dulles, "Das II. Vatikanum und die Wiedergewinnung der Tradition," in *Glaube im Prozess, Christsein nach dem II. Vatikanum*. E. Klinger and K. Wittstadt, eds. (Freiburg, 2nd ed., 1984), pp. 546–62.

the revival of the traditional motif of the Church—that is, the entire ecclesial body—as the subject of liturgical actions (§ 26), implied the rejection of clerical exclusivism and opened the way to an active participation of all Christians in the celebration. This had the inevitable result, which we have seen and are still seeing, of increased interaction between liturgy and lived experience, rite and immediate history, memory of the foundational events and involvement in the present.

The recognition of history as an indispensable *locus* and the accompanying abandonment of all the artificial *loci* in which the experience of faith might take shelter are thus to be seen not only and not principally in the Council's *explicit* statements about history and the connection between faith and history. The recognition is to be seen much more in the introduction and formulation of elements that, as it were, *structurally* require such recognition. Thus, despite regrettable delays and hostile attitudes,[21] the liturgical reform made possible by the conciliar constitution, and especially the introduction of the vernacular, is now necessitating a continual exchange with cultures and their problems and with the subjects of history.

Similarly, it is certainly important that the "Dogmatic Constitution on Divine Revelation" should have moved beyond the neo-Scholastic vision, shaped by controversy, of revelation as consisting primarily of "truths" communicated to human beings and that it should have asserted instead that the economy of revelation "is realized by deeds and words that are intrinsically connected with one another" (§ 2), thus locating God's communication with human beings in history and its events. But it is even more important that the constitution approves the efforts of the biblical movement and puts Scripture at the center of the Church's life, thus requiring believers to pay heed to the essentially historical plan of salvation.

Another fact that is heavy with implications is that the constitution reckons among the factors in the development of tradition not only the magisterium but also the contemplation and study of believers, as well as their "profound understanding arising from experience of spiritual things" (*intima spiritualium rerum quam experiuntur intelligentia*) (§ 8). This reference to experience introduces a central theme from the Modernist controversy and acknowledges the fruitful dynamism of the life of faith, while rooting it in turn in the dynamism of the transmission of the Gospel.

All the *dynamic* elements emphasized in the various conciliar documents are likewise important for an understanding of the connection between faith and history that Vatican II established. The first that calls for mention here is the very structure of the "Dogmatic Constitution on the Church," in which consideration of the hierarchic and institutional

---

21. See the appraisal given by the Liturgical Commission of the Italian Episcopal Conference (CEI), "Il rinnovamento liturgico in Italia," *Il Regno–Documenti*, 28 (1983) 589–95.

dimension is subordinated to reflection on the Church as a mystery (chap. 1) and to the privileged place given to the biblical image of people of God (chap. 2). This dynamic approach leads as far as the subtle and sophisticated distinction between the one Church of Christ and the Catholic Church in which the Church of Christ "subsists" (§ 8). Membership in the Church is then described primarily in terms of a spiritual dimension (*Spiritum Christi habentes*: § 14), so that the institutional aspect is located in the dynamic and ultimately inscrutable context of the Spirit's action in history.

A second point at which this dynamic vision bears fruit is in the pluralistic view that dominates the "Decree on the Missionary Activity of the Church." Various reasons are given for the pluralism. On the one hand, because we live in the economy of the incarnation, pluralism flows from the diversity of cultures that the Gospel reaches. In this context the human riches of the various cultural traditions are looked upon as a "sustenance" that the word of God draws from the soil in which it is sown (§ 22). On the other hand, the diversity of theologies is explained by the diversity of the particular churches, which with their rich traditions are all part of a single ecclesial communion (ibid.). The "Constitution on the Church" in its turn defines the pluralism created by the particular churches as a pluralism of disciplines, theologies, liturgical usages, and spiritualities (LG 23).

Here again we find ourselves in the presence no longer of an explicitly and ultimately abstract proclamation of the centrality of history but of "institutional" formulations that require a very concrete and effective respect for history precisely in regard to those implications of it that are most unsettling for a body that lives in and by unity as its essential foundation. In fact, diversity, plurality, irreducibility to a universal formula are among the specific characteristics of the historical dimension of things. For Christianity, then, history and the pluralism it brings with it are not simply the reverse side of the modern way of life or a simple accommodation to the bourgeois spirit of tolerance; they are part of its very nature and are rooted in its Trinitarian origin and its eucharistic dimension. It is no accident that the pluralism and dynamic character of Christianity emerge whenever these two aspects, the Trinitarian and the eucharistic, are made clear.

A third point to be mentioned in assessing the connection that Vatican II establishes between faith and history is the novel approach taken in the constitution *Gaudium et spes* or "Pastoral Constitution on the Church in the Modern World," as it is known. Here, for the first time in its history, the Church bases a solemn document on an analysis of the historical situation in order to elicit directives from it. Moreover, the approach is taken in the conviction that when the Church enters into "communion" with the various cultures, both the Church and the cultures are "enriched" (§ 58). The various contents of this document can be the subject of debate, but the method adopted is undeniably novel and is one of those *structural* factors that have vast implications for the historical situation of faith.

Alberigo has collected the principal explicit statements of Vatican II regarding history.[22] But as his analysis and my own brief references show, an understanding of the connection between faith and history still requires a study that goes beyond the phase of the "commentaries" that abounded in the first decade after the Council. There is need of analyzing the published and unpublished sources (especially those concerned with the work of the commissions) and tracing the path followed by the Catholic Church during the Council in making its own the attitude of friendliness and critical wisdom that Pope Roncalli proposed to the faithful as he called to mind the aspirations and sufferings that had marked the great ecclesial movements of the first half of our century. The interpretive hypothesis I have been seeking to set forth in a purely summary fashion is that during those years certain attitudes were formed that despite inevitable setbacks and corrections have created for the coming decades an irreversibly friendly view of history and an increasingly deeper rooting of Christian experience in the *common* fortunes of men and women. In this sense Vatican II put an end to the long period of hostility that in varying degrees and with varying results characterized relationships between church and society since the French Revolution.

The Fear of Untying the Knot

I said, a few lines back, that during the years of Vatican II the Church developed an attitude that cannot be reversed. In saying this I took the conscious risk of making a statement that has nothing to do with history, that is, with the subject of my discussion. For in history nothing is irreversible. For this reason I limited the scope of my statement by specifying a period of time: the decades ahead. Despite this qualification, my intention is nonetheless to express my conviction that as far as the connection between faith and history is concerned, the Council tied a knot and that we cannot help untying it in one manner or another. The knot is the interlacing of experience that is particular and peculiar to a few people with a common lot. The common lot is history in the most commonplace sense of the word: relationships of the ordinary, everyday kind, the encounter and clash of interests, subjection to languages and

22. "Cristianesimo e Storia" (n. 13, above). Alberigo divides the statements of Vatican II under four headings: (1) references to the historical situation; (2) statements on the way in which Christians and the Church are involved in history; (3) statements on the way in which historical conditions are also a criterion decisive for faith; (4) passages in which the Council recognizes and stresses an organic connection between history and human salvation.

laws, fixed modes of production, the balance between powers of various kinds, the collective imagination, and so on. The particular experience, which is one of many particular experiences that are not reducible to a common denominator, is in this case Christian religious experience with its complex symbolic, communal, and personal dimensions. The knot ties Christian experience to universal experience according to a strict rule that the "Constitution of the Church" expresses in sacramental terms: "The Church in Christ is a kind of sacrament, or sign and instrument, of intimate union with God and of the unity of the entire human race" (§ 1).[23]

In this definition the life of the Church is related to life generally by means of what might be called its "symbolic" function.[24] That is: the destiny of the human race (union with God and unity among human beings) is prefigured in its full form in the Church, and the prefiguration is at the same time the source of the active power needed for attaining that destiny of communion and reconciliation (the Church is therefore sign and sacrament). But this amounts to saying that the Church's existence is wholly relative to the history of humankind and that Christianity is the common life of human beings in a transfigured form, because in the midst of this common life the future that the God of Jesus Christ has given to it in the form of a hidden desire now makes its appearance. It is not by chance that the sacrament that is the Church finds its climactic expression in the celebration of the Eucharist in which the eschatological stage of history is prefigured as communion, that is, as an experience of the brotherhood and sisterhood that is bestowed on human beings by the action of Jesus in giving himself for the brethren.

When seen in this light, the Church does not belong to itself, for it is simply a sign and sacrament of the common life.[25] That is, there is no

23. See the analysis of this sacramental conception of the Church in W. Kasper, "Die Kirche als universales Sakrament des Heils," in *Glaube im Prozess* (n. 20, above), pp. 221–39; the author distances himself somewhat from Rahner's view and points out that the apocalyptic reference acts as a corrective for a vision that emphasizes the continuity between the salvation announced in the sacrament and the salvation already present in history (pp. 226–30). In other words, the central problem is how to think of the "difference" between history and faith. My own concluding reflections will be meant as a contribution to resolution of this problem.

24. In using "symbol," "symbolic dimension," and similar terms, I have in mind the basic constitution of human reality, which *of itself* refers to something distinct from it; "symbolic dimension" implies that *in* (and not *alongside* or *despite*) every presence an absence is concealed. The absent can manifest itself to those who follow a certain course and learn to see more deeply, without therefore abandoning the signifier for the signified. For the theological aspect of the matter, I refer the reader to K. Rahner, "The Theology of the Symbol," in his *Theological Investigations* (Baltimore, 1966), 5:221–52; F. Mayr, "Symbol," *LTK*, 9:1205–8; and J. Splett, "Symbol," *SacMundi*, 6:199–201. For philosophical reflections on the subject, see, among others, V. Melchiorre, *L'immaginazione simbolica* (Bologna, 1972).

25. In saying that ecclesial life is a sign and sacrament of common life my meaning is not that common life is what is signified; the signified that is represented in the sacraments is the act by which God accepts the world in Jesus Christ. But a sacrament mediates pre-

specific "matter" for the Church's life: the matter in this as in every sacrament is taken from the matter of common life. The Church exists only *within* history, *within* society, *within* the common life, not only in the sense that it is surrounded by these things but in the much more profound sense that it exists only as a "symbolization" of history, society, and the common life. This means that the problems the Church faces are problems of history and the common life of human beings.

It follows from this that no separation is possible between "the history of salvation" and "the history of the world." Above all, however, this consciousness of the real situation must be the basis for developing an entire hermeneutic of human existence as such, without the limitations of sacral categories (that is, categories that distinguish two societies, one sacred, the other profane). The "turn" taken by Pope Roncalli and the Second Vatican Council consists in fact, as I pointed out earlier, in a new practical direction. But the turn must also be grasped in a more reflective consciousness that will allow a consolidation of the new direction, and will *recognize* it and give it a universally acknowledged validity.

Further light can be shed on this need by looking at two obvious problems that are proving increasingly important for an understanding of the role of Christianity in history.

The first is connected with a fact that is becoming ever clearer: Christians seem destined to become numerically more and more of a minority. We cannot, of course, exclude the possibility that countries as large as China or India may be converted. But, as far as we can now see, the possibility is a remote one, and the rate of growth of non-Christian peoples is much greater than that of Christian peoples. The problem that then arises is how to understand the positive role of Christianity and its catholicity in a history that is "foreign" to it.

The second problem is connected with the first and arises because of the role—which is by no means finished but on the contrary is even increasing—of the great non-Christian religions. Vatican II, however, was already aware of this problem and in its "Declaration on the Relation between the Church and the Non-Christian Religions" it officially adopted a positive view of the great religions of the human race, instead of the old attitude of hostility. Here again, the action of the Council made necessary a subsequent revaluation of the relationship of the "particular" experience of Christians to the "particular" experiences of other believers and to the religious experience *common* to all. The unique historical role of Christianity can no longer be identified with a historical "absoluteness" in the literal sense of the term, that is, with a state of being "loosed from" (*ab-soluta*) or "free from," as a result of which Christian uniqueness must seek the disappearance or absorption of the other religious "particularities."

---

cisely *between* God and the world; it is the world insofar as the world is eschatologically accepted in the reconciliation accomplished by Jesus of Nazareth.

Mention of these two problems throws light on the direction to be taken by a hermeneutic that is respectful of the "symbolic" place of faith within history: it must be the hermeneutic of a renewed catholicity that excludes any desire for, any anticipation of, the disappearance or absorption of what is different from it. I believe that such a hermeneutic is only now being developed and that the postconciliar Church is still torn between the fear of untying the knot and a courageous attempt to go forth to a new land. For the moment I shall simply give examples of the fear.

A first expression of this fear is the great return (whether ephemeral or longlasting, I do not know) to political Catholicism and consequently to the conception of the Church as a society.[26] In this conception the Church is seen precisely as a society that is distinct from the state and that, in virtue of its supernatural end and its possession of revealed truth, is able both to make up for the defects of civil society, which is dependent solely on its own natural resources, and to guide it in all matters that imply a subordination of natural to supernatural ends. Historically this conception has taken varied and complex concrete forms that range from an acceptance of democratic pluralism and the consequent role of Christianity as one political force among others, to more authoritarian visions of the Church or again to "popular" visions in which the Church incarnates the deepest consciousness of the people and is their most qualified representative in conflicts with the state.

In order for this kind of historical embodiment of the faith to express itself, the Church must have not only the Gospel but also, as a link connecting the Gospel with ethical and political praxis, a theory of the human person and of society (the so-called social teaching of the Church, which the Council carefully avoided mentioning, at least in this context). In this teaching, the truth of the Gospel is made to yield a body of universal truths about human beings and society.

The return to political Catholicism has moreover been made easier by the contradictions in Western societies. These contradictions, especially in view of the consolidation of our technological culture, seem to call for a "complement of soul," a new religious recasting of the values on which the shared life of civil society rests. But this return also tends to delay development of the consciousness inaugurated by the Council in its new attitude to history.

Political Catholicism tends in fact to make faith an "organically dominant" element in society and history, with the result that they remain incomplete parts, destined never to be more than minors.

By contrast, the relationship between faith and history as conceived by analogy with the sacraments presupposes that our common human history possesses a greater dignity. The attitude of ecclesial faith to this history is, then, at once more respectful and more demanding. Faith

26. See the essay of D. Menozzi in the present book (chap. 16, below).

does not substitute itself for history or take over key functions in it, but symbolically leads it to its own truth in the same fashion and manner in which the world and history were brought to their own truth in the cross of Jesus of Nazareth. The crucified Jesus is not an "organically dominant" element in the development of history; he is the presence, behind the course of history, of the God who by embracing the cross restores to its proper place a history that had gone astray from the Father ever since its origin in the loving action of God who gave it being, an action that is nothing other than unqualified love, unqualified acceptance, and immense forebearance (*makrothymia*; 2 Pet. 3:9).

If I may use a metaphor based on contemporary linguistics, I might say that in the cross human history is the "lay subject" of the action of God who, when seized by history, renounces the use of his own power, precisely because he is God, and not despite the fact that he is God (see John 18:36), and who in this very foolishness shows himself to be true wisdom and, in this very weakness, truly strong (1 Cor. 1:18–25). Inspired by this vision the Council (in LG 8) sees the Church as related to history after the manner of the Christ who emptied himself (Phil. 2:6–7) and the Christ who became poor (2 Cor. 8–9). In other words it sees the Church's attitude to history as one of humility and self-sacrifice.

The problem I have raised—which is not simply the problem of prophecy or of faith-inspired experience, but of *recognition*—implies that the direction taken by the Council in speaking of the manner of the Church's presence in the midst of humanity should serve as a hermeneutic both of the meaning of history as revealed to us by the cross and of the relationship between Gospel and history as inaugurated on the cross. When seen from this standpoint, attempts to shape the presence of the faith in political terms express simply an uneasiness and a fear of turning the logic of the cross into a logic that effectively governs the entire historical form to be taken by the Church.[27]

A second form taken by the fear of establishing the kind of relationship between faith and history that takes history seriously may be exemplified by the reaction to the so-called theologies of liberation. I think that if we are to grasp the real meaning of the reaction, the problem must be placed in a much broader context than it usually is. In a movement of which the Council showed itself clearly aware, both in *Lumen gentium* and in *Ad gentes* (but also in all the other documents that speak of the particular churches, for example, the documents on the Eastern churches and on ecumenism), the development of the history of the Church is requiring an end to theological uniformity. The theological pluralism that the Council proclaims is not to be understood as operating at the intellectual level, or at least not at this level alone; the mean-

---

27. For a further development of these reflections on political Catholicism, see my essay, "La necessità dell'inutile: Sul rapporto tra fatto cristiano e politica," in the collective work, *La necessità dell'inutile. Fede e politica* (Turin, 1982), pp. 7–43.

ing is not, for example, that revealed truth can be given many complementary interpretations. Such a statement is quite accurate, but it is
insufficient. The Council in fact describes theological pluralism as flowing first of all from the plurality of particular churches (see, e.g., LG 23).
In other words, theological pluralism is the result of the divergent
courses followed by the various churches in their times and places.

The problem is becoming acute today because among the churches of
the Latin tradition the Latin American churches, sharing as they do the
tragic poverty of their peoples, are developing hermeneutics and theologies that ignore the theological mediations already systematized by the
West. Their originality includes even an unprejudiced use of the Marxist
analysis of social conflicts.[28] This use evidently reflects a naiveté similar
to the naiveté that has always marked comparable cultural syntheses in
the past. For an example we need only recall the difficulties, which persisted for centuries, in reaching a balance in christological and Trinitarian doctrine as various patristic theologies tried to use terms and categories from Hellenistic philosophy.

The attitude taken by some ecclesiastical circles, among them the Congregation for the Doctrine of the Faith, that wish to banish the Latin
American theologies; they deny the very possibility that the kind of activity that has in fact occurred over and over again in the history of the
Church can occur in certain cultures and certain philosophies, namely,
American theologies; they deny the very possibiliy that the kind of activity that has in fact occurred over and over again in the history of the
Church can occur in certain cultures and certain philosophies, namely,
the transfer of particular elements of a philosophy or worldview to a
different context that possesses a different kind of unity and is therefore
able to integrate these elements into itself.[29] The claim is made:

28. Even though a more diligent analysis might show the need of describing the cultural novelty in different terms. As a matter of fact, the "Marxism" of the Latin American
theologies does not seem reducible to any one of the forms of Marxism presently to be
found in European political life, but no careful study has yet been made of this point. Reference might be made to José Carlos Mariátegui (1894–1930), but also the "Marxism"
found in so many exponents of the Latin American story. In my opinion, the real novelty
of the "Marxism" of the Latin American theologians is their unique recovery and inclusion
of a popular approach to religion within the Latin American ecclesial experience. But this is
only a hypothesis and needs verification.

29. Here, perhaps, we see the real root of the fear. The claimed role of Marxist analysis
in the theologies of liberation not only raises the question of their specific consistency; it
also introduces a novelty to which the Church and the western Latin theologies can only
react with bewilderment. For Marxism, like liberalism, is one of the principal historical
enemies against which the "social teaching" of the Church was developed, in the atmosphere created by the nineteenth-century restoration, as a replacement and a contrary
mediation. To claim, then, that a different cultural mediation is valid implies a disturbance
of a balance that other places and other churches regard as essential to their very existence
(for example, the churches living under the governments of Eastern Europe). If these
observations are correct, the problem in the final analysis is whether churches that follow a
theological line of their own (and therefore use different cultural mediations) have a right
to exist. On the ideological character of the Church's "social teaching," see M.-D. Chenu,

The thought of Marx is such a global vision of reality that all data received from observation and analysis are brought together in a philosophical and ideological structure, which predetermines the significance and importance to be attached to them. The ideological principles come prior to the study of the social reality and are presupposed in it. Thus no separation of the parts of this epistemologically unique complex is possible. If one tries to take only one part, say, the analysis, one ends up having to accept the entire ideology.

The group speaking here has arrogated to itself the right to determine which interpretations of reality a particular church must avoid in its own approach to experience, and this as a matter of principle and apart from what has in fact occurred or may occur. It is worth recalling the diametrically opposed teaching of John XXIII in *Pacem in terris*, § 159, where he maintained that even historical movements cannot be legitimately identified with the teachings from which they took their origin and from which they still draw their inspiration:

This is so because the teachings, once they are drawn up and defined, remain always the same, while the movements, working in constantly evolving historical situations, cannot but be influenced by these latter and cannot avoid, therefore, being subject to changes, even of a profound nature.

The positions taken by some today deny this historical law according to which a historical group (and much more—for Christians at least—a particular church) can develop an original experiential unity that differs from the unity of the separate contexts from which it derives the elements used in constructing this experiential unity.[30]

These considerations also suggest that when fears have been overcome, the effective reassertion of the individuality of the particular churches will, despite tensions and delays, bring not only a plurality of styles and approaches to reality but also the end of a universalist and deductive relationship between faith and history.

The Analogy of History

Such fears are often supported by hermeneutical prejudices derived from theologies that played an important role in the past but now need

---

La dottrina sociale della chiesa. Origine et sviluppo (1891–1971) (Brescia, 1977); see also my remarks in "Ecclesiologia e dottrina sociale della chiesa," *Il Regno–Documenti*, 26 (1981) 683–87.

30. It is noteworthy that the passage cited just above from the Instruction of the Congregation for the Doctrine of the Faith on Certain Aspects of the Theology of Liberation is followed directly by a citation from Paul VI's apostolic letter *Octogesima adveniens*, § 34. I say "noteworthy" because it was this Letter of Paul VI that began the restrictive interpretation of John XXIII's statement in *Pacem in terris*.—The translation of the instruction is the Vatican translation as reproduced in *Origins. NC Documentary Service*, 14 (1984) 199. The citation of *Pacem in terris* is from the America Press translation as reproduced in J. Gremil-

to be rethought in the new historical context into which the council has brought the Church. For example: in the distrustful reluctance to accept new theologico-cultural syntheses there is often at work a model of the relationship between nature and grace, gospel and ethics, reason and revelation that was developed in other historical contexts and in response to questions different from those raised by the present situation. Those, for example, who would wish to take the nature-grace model or, better, the various kinds of nature-grace relationships that were developed in the post-tridentine era and simply apply them to the contemporary discussion of the problems of liberation and reconciliation, would end up confusing radically different contexts and problematics. In fact, the dispute between Catholics and Protestants on the salvation of the individual or, within Catholicism, the controversy among the various schools (Augustinian, Thomist, Molinist) on the same subject may not be identified with the contemporary problem, which is at once historical and collective, of the liberation of a people or a culture or an oppressed social class. Again, those who would take the model or, better, the various models developed by the writers of treatises on morality, even those of recent vintage and those of a personalist kind, and apply them to the ethical problems raised by new cultures, would simply be bypassing the real challenge to the Christian conscience, namely, the fact that ethics as such has today taken forms that presuppose a new global confrontation between the evangelical dimension of the Christian message and the ethics developed within a specific historical praxis.[31] Again, those who would take the contrast between reason and revelation as developed against the Deists and regard it as an adequate answer to the present call for a new understanding of the relationship between human history and the reign of God, would simply go on talking to someone who is no longer there.

It is obviously not possible in this essay to develop a theololgical hermeneutic of the relationship between faith and history that would do justice to the gains made at the Council. Such a hermeneutic would require in fact a rethinking even of trinitarian theology (because there is need of a serious rethinking of the "sin" of history in a way that is not unconnected with the divine self-communication), a rethinking of christology and pneumatology (because it is not possible to be satisfied with devalued statements about the complementarity of the christological and pneumatological aspects of salvation), a rethinking of the theology of creation (which is still developed in a way that is too unrelated to the mystery of the Trinity), and so on.

---

lion, ed., *The Gospel of Peace and Justice. Catholic Social Teaching since Pope John* (Maryknoll, N.Y., 1976), p. 236.

31. For a fuller explanation of these thoughts I refer the reader to my essay, "Riflessioni teologiche in margine alla crisi della soggettività borghese," in *La compagnia della fede. Linee di teologia fondamentale* (Turin, 1980), pp. 143–65.

What I should like to do instead, by way of a conclusion to this essay, is to offer a brief reflection on the relationship between human history and the Christian fact. I use the expression "Christian fact" here as equivalent to "revelation"; this latter term carries such a burden of history that it now seems less satisfactory for expressing the sum total of contents and aspects that are the object of Christian faith.[32]

The solid core of the new attitude of faith toward history is that it no longer looks upon history as a field of independent apologetical proofs of truths and no longer seeks to deduce practical attitudes from doctrines, but, on the contrary, it seeks to read God's call in history itself. The history of which I am speaking is the common history to which I referred earlier. It is never given in its purity but is always already thought, experienced, and interpreted before the application of theories and philosophies of history. Faith itself is a particular historical form, being a unification of experience that comes when human beings lay as the foundation of their existence the fact of Jesus of Nazareth as transmitted by other human witnesses. The "Christian fact" is itself a piece of particular history, both personal and collective, that comes into being when the faith, of an individual or a group, enables the emergence of a horizon, a living context visible to others, possessing characteristics that range from an objective message to attitudes of affective devotion, from rites to doctrines, from specific values to institutions of many kinds. The message, the attitudes, the rites and doctrines, the values and institutions, and all the other things characteristic of the Christian fact, are not

---

32. During the first Christian millennium and even beyond it the word "revelation" referred not to Christian doctrine but to its source; the word was essentially a synonym of "inspiration" (see Y. Congar, *Tradition and Traditions: An Historical and a Theological Essay* [New York, 1968], pp. 125–39). Only in a second phrase, perhaps in Suárez, did "revelation" come to mean the objective content of God's self-manifestation. But in this shift, post-tridentine theology separated the action of God from the experience of believers. Furthermore, the first documents of the ecclesiastical magisterium that use "revelation" for the object of faith go back only to the nineteenth century; see H. Bouillard, "Le concept de révélation de Vatican I à Vatican II," in the collective work, *Révélation de Dieu et langage des hommes* (Paris, 1972), pp. 35–49. In its new meaning the word "revelation" became the opposite of reason and, with its connotation of suprarational knowledge, was used as a weapon especially against modern rationalism. In Protestant theology, on the other hand, and in the framework of German idealism (see W. Pannenberg, in W. Pannenberg et al., *Revelation as History* [New York, 1968], pp. 3ff.), revelation became synonymous with the self-communication of the absolute, without reference to any medium of communication distinct from the absolute itself. The concept of revelation then went on to mean, especially in contemporary theology, the Christian fact in its entirety, in its aspect of manifestation of God to human beings (see P. Eicher, *Offenbarung. Prinzip neuzeitlicher Theologie* [Munich, 1977]). One of the strongest challenges to the use of the category of revelation comes from F. G. Downing, *Has Christianity a Revelation?* (London, 1964), and, in summary, idem, "Revelation in the New Testament and among its Expounders," in *Studia Evangelica*, (Berlin, 1964), 3:183–86. Apart from all this discussion, one simple fact should show clearly why revelation tends to be an ambiguous term: in its modern Catholic usage it can easily prescind from faith and thereby falsify the relationship between the Christian fact and history, by looking at it from an abstract and objectivist viewpoint.

erratic masses, but show countless analogies with other messages, rites, institutions, and so on.

The analogy has always been asserted in the Christian tradition, though with different emphases and nuances. Here again it is impossible for me even to list the various conceptions of it.[33] I shall instead take my cue from a conception of analogy found in the British theological tradition and shall offer some thoughts that may be helpful in understanding the nonextrinsic connection between Christian fact and common history.[34]

The emphasis in this conception of analogy is on the mysteriousness of reality as a quality not limited to Christian reality but intrinsic to existence as such. If we presuppose the unity of all reality, then even nature is mysterious. This conception was developed against the Deists, who (it was claimed) did not realize that their objections against Christianity are the very ones that can be urged against the natural order of things. For there is in fact an analogy between all the parts of reality, and the structure of the reality that is naturally accessible to human beings raises the same basic problems as does revealed reality.

Alongside this conception of analogy that was developed chiefly on negative lines there exists another, more positive one by which John Henry Newman set great store; it says that human attitudes evolve by a process that is basically analogical, inasmuch as we always move from things better known to us to knowledge and certainty about things less well known to us. Probability is the guide we follow in our lives, and it is to be contrasted not with certainty but with demonstrative proof. Certainty can in fact be reached either by way of demonstration or by way of convergent probabilities.

I have only sketched very roughly (because the precise form of the relationship between probability and certainty differs from author to author) the basic idea of this original conception of analogy that is peculiar

---

33. A summary of the problems and a useful bibliography are provided in E. Przywara, "Analogia entis" and "Analogia fidei," *LTK*, 1:468–76. It becomes clear that even in the *analogia fidei* the movement of analogical knowledge is no longer seen as a movement from positive Christian experience to "natural" reality, but always stops within the relationships between the different aspects of the Christian fact, or else serves to shed light on the Christian fact in its "difference" from "nature." Even W. Pannenberg, though attentive to an "indirect" revelation through history, confines himself to using analogy in a sense that reflects essentially the movement from the more known to the less known; see his programatic essay, "Redemptive Event and History," in his *Basic Questions of Theology* (Philadelphia, 1970, 1:15–80). A different view is developed by E. Jüngel in his *Gott als Geheimnis der Welt* (Tübingen, 3rd ed., 1978); for an initial appraisal of his thinking on analogy I refer the reader to W. Breuning, "Je grössere Unähnlichkeit," in J. Brantschen and P. Selvatico, eds., *Unterwegs zur Einheit (Festschrift H. Stirnimann)* (Freiburg, 1980), pp. 373–85.

34. For variations in this idea of analogy, between J. Butler, on the one side, and Keble and Newman, on the other, see W. de Smet, "L'influence de Butler sur la théorie de la foi chez Newman," *ETL*, 39 (1963) 30–49. But even the analysis in I. T. Ramsey, *Religious Language* (London, 1957), presupposes Butler's conception of analogy.

to the British tradition, beginning especially with Joseph Butler (1692–
1752). My purpose is not to offer it once again for the reader's acceptance, but to turn to my own account an emphasis in it that seems to me
to be important and fruitful. The point to which I refer is the rooting of
mystery in nature itself. God is not alone in being mysterious; "nature"
too is mysterious. The Christian fact shows a logic of "its own" in the
world and in history, but in its very "singularity" this logic is in harmony with the "other logics" of history. Mystery is part of history and
has not been introduced into it in a "second phase." Thus, the Christian
fact on its positive side is called upon not only to take advantage of the
analogy of the real for a better knowledge of God and mystery (this is
the "classic" emphasis in the doctrine of analogy) but also to put the
analogy of faith at the service of a better understanding of the riddle of
history. The symbol that is the Christian fact is a particular manifestation
of the mystery of history itself.

In describing the relationship between faith and history, however,
Christians too often remain prisoners of the anti-Deist contrast in which
the problem was the justification of diversity within the Christian religion. With this as their point of departure, western theologies have
often been controlled by the problem of the difference between faith and
history, and have confused Christian "particularity" with a radical
separation from common historical experience. By contrast, the biblical
attitude to history, which has fortunately been renewed in Catholic
theology of the present century and was proclaimed with prophetic insight by John XXIII and the Council, presupposes a basic unity of mystery and history. This unity plays a part, first of all, in reading history
itself, the difficulties it raises, and its endangered future. The faith of the
prophets and the "faith" of Jesus Christ are a proclamation of the place
of God in history.

The proclamation achieves its supreme verbal clarity in the Beatitudes:
God is the future of those who have no future; absence (of the satisfaction of hunger, of riches, joy, justice) is not emptiness but is enriched by
the visitation of God. Then, on the cross, verbal clarity becomes clarity
of gesture; mute evidence of the act by which God makes his own the
extreme form of historical lostness: the death of the innocent. The cross
is a symbol of history because in it God reveals and enacts the hidden
truth of history, namely, that history is a history of unity, reconciliation,
the welcoming of what is far off, the liberation of what is lost to human
beings. The Christian fact therefore continues to propose this symbol in
the often defective multiplicity of its own mediations, thus asserting history to be a presence, and therefore reading in history itself the signs of
divine visitation. Thus the very "particularity" of the Christian fact reveals its "catholicity," to the extent that it situates itself *within* other particularities and within common human experience, makes known the
analogy of history, adjusts its own breathing, so to speak, to the breath-

ing of history, and by this adjustment makes it possible for the panting of human beings to be transformed by the deep and regular breathing of God.

This link between faith and history is not primarily a theoretical fact or a theological explanation; it is an active gesture of reconciliation, a concrete sharing of lots, a real act of companionship after the manner of Jesus of Nazareth (LG 8). For Jesus, being rich, became poor and sat down at table with the lost, with those who were "different," thus revealing how close they were to the reign of the Father and showing the analogy that existed between their lives and certain privileged gestures of the symbol that he was in his person (the humility of the tax collector's prayer: Luke 18:9–14; the greater gratitude of the man who was free in relation to observance of the law: Luke 17:11–19). Then those things in history that are "different" from faith become a common responsibility on a journey toward final unity on which nothing will be lost, because God in vast forebearance puts up with these differences and wills that they be reasons not for condemnation but for conversion (see 2 Pet. 3:9).

This reading of the analogies of history in light of the Christian fact can never be done hastily, for, as in the Sunday Eucharist, we are dealing with an expectation of him who is risen and with a symbolic anticipation of what has yet to make itself known. From one point of view, faith is always ahead of history, just as a symbol lets desire go on ahead. The representation of eschatological reconciliation in the Sunday celebration is a remembrance of a gesture that history has not yet made its own. But all this refers not to the *res* but to the *sacramentum*, that is, the movement of faith ahead of history is an advance at the sacramental level, the level of sign, for the fruit comes only through an ongoing ripening, and the sign is only a pledge. That is why the celebration ends with an invitation to go forth at the very moment when the rite, the symbol, has been completed. The reading of the analogy and its symbolic celebration are thus an invitation to a daily sharing of Christ's own sentiments, of the Father's own vast patience, and of the concern of the shepherd who goes looking for what has not yet entered the warm security of the fold.

In the final analysis, the problem of the relationship between faith and history is the problem of their unity, a unity of reconciliation between the desire contained in history and the present condition of history. There is no question of a relationship between two things complete in themselves, or of a relationship between two complementary and organic elements of a single whole (these are the confusions that are the source of the various kinds of integralism: of hostility or the claim to be the dominant partner). The relationship is rather that between symbol and life, and the existence of the connection is wholly dependent not on claims but on witness and the ability to reveal the analogy, in imitation of the testimony of Christ who reveals the Father's acceptance at the very moment when the world rejects him, and in the powerlessness of

God that is more powerful than the great and mighty of history. The relationship between Christian fact and history is therefore symbolized by the voice of a man who on the moonlit night of the day of the Lord, October 11, 1962, succeeded in crossing the institutional distance that had banished him to a balconied window high up in the darkness of an old palace; he went down among men and women, within their hearing, brought his face close to theirs, and spoke of children waiting to be fondled.

Enzo Bianchi

7. The Centrality of the Word of God

After centuries in exile the word of God once more occupies its central place in the life of the Catholic Church. The fact is beyond denying. One might even speak of a *rediscovery* of the word of God by the Catholic faithful who for centuries did not experience or practice a direct contact with the word of God and did not even have occasion to appreciate the value of that word for the life of faith. It is true, of course, that the Catholic Church had always lived by the word of God. But inasmuch as habitual familiarity with the scriptures was reserved to clerics and specialists, the general situation was in fact one in which the centrality of the word was eclipsed, dimmed, as it were, by ecclesiastical traditions and a system of doctrinal and disciplinary mediations that intervened between the consciousness of the faithful and the sacred scriptures, which served only in a formal sense as the criterion for the validity or invalidity of the life of the Church.

After being preceded and prepared for by the liturgical, ecumenical, and biblical movements, the Second Vatican Council as a matter of fact set free the word of God and declared an end to the exile of the sacred scriptures. It did so, perhaps, to a degree that exceeded the understanding and intentions of the council fathers. I am increasingly convinced that of all the areas of conciliar reception this restoration of the word to the people of God is the most epiphanic. Whatever failure of fulfillment, whatever inadequacies the twenty years since the Council may show, it must be admitted that the renewed centrality of the word of God can hardly be denied,[1] nor can it be diminished by the forces that are trying to forget the Council or reinterpret it in a reductionist or impoverishing way.

Now that it has been installed once more at the center of the Church's

1. Many students of the reception of Vatican II now regard the rediscovery of God's word as the most fruitful outcome of the Council; I shall mention only a few authoritative examples: M. Card. Pellegrino, "Il dopo Concilio nella Chiesa italiana," *Vita e pensiero*, 1 (1979) 20; G. Hourdin, *Pour le Concile* (Paris, 1970), pp. 117–24; C. M. Card. Martini, "Crisi della Chiesa e Parola di Dio," *Il Giorno*, Jan. 2, 1984, p. 4; R. Card. Etchegaray, "Un survol de l'oeuvre conciliaire," in *Le Concile: 20 ans de notre histoire* (Paris, 1982), pp. 57–58.

life, the word of God ceaselessly renews a process that had for a long
time come to a standstill and ceased to operate: the process in which
God passes judgment on life, history, and the Church itself as the community of saints and sinners making its pilgrim way toward the
kingdom.

The ecclesiastical hierarchy has lost its exaggerated fear of putting the
scriptures in the hands of the faithful and instead now eagerly recom-
mends their use. The result has been a notable extension of the room
given to the word, as well as a new openness of the faithful to it, an
openness that at times becomes a hungry demand for it. The word has
thus been rediscovered as vital, dynamic, and efficacious, capable of
nourishing faith, inspiring life, and standing in judgment over the attitudes of Christians to history and their fellow human beings. In the daily life of the basic communities of Latin America, in the lives of Christians who belong to the traditional historical communities of the West,
and even in the present pope's exercise of his teaching office, reference
to the sacred scriptures seems to have become continuous and indispensable.[2] This is a real turnabout in relation to the period before the
Council when access to sacred history was possible, at best, only to the
better off among the faithful and when popes and bishops in their
teaching rarely had direct recourse to the Bible or, if they did, used it as a
prop and proof rather than as an authoritative source of inspiration.

The present essay has for its purpose to sketch the Church's reception
of the centrality of the word as forcefully asserted in the dogmatic constitution Dei Verbum on divine revelation. I know, however, that reception is a long-term process, and I realize that I myself belong to the postconciliar generation; I would like, therefore, to attempt a rereading of
the essential elements on which this reception depends and, with that as
a basis, of the trends that have appeared. Of necessity, then, this will be
a critical reading.

The Council and the Centrality of the Word of God

In November 1962 the Council had shown a noteworthy unanimity in
approving the preparatory text on the sacred liturgy as a basis for discussion. Suddenly and unexpectedly, however, the presentation of the text
on revelation showed that the Council was entering a difficult and painful critical period that caused a rift to appear among the council fathers.

2. However one may judge the exegetical and spiritual quality of what he says, it is
certainly a novelty to find the present pope, in the exercise of his teaching office, giving a
running commentary on biblical texts in his Wednesday audiences and supplying exegetical notes that take the biblical "letter" into account (notes that are sometimes quite
lengthy, although this is hardly in keeping with the literary genre of apostolic exhortations). See his *Dives in misericordia* and the more recent *Reconciliatio et poenitentia*.

At the same time, however, the debate on revelation established a method for drawing up the conciliar documents and gave direction not only to the *letter* but also to the *spirit* of the Council.

Although the liturgical movement of preceding decades had evidently influenced the body of bishops, it became clear that the biblical movement had exerted much less influence and that, despite its fruitfulness and wealth of new insights, it had remained within the world of biblical scholars.

The main body of the conciliar fathers had had no real experience of the word of God, and their interventions were by no means inspired by the Bible even when they incorporated a formal recourse to it. At most, some of the fathers—very few indeed—showed signs of having reached a level of biblical exegesis that enabled them to accept impulses from observers from other Christian churches. Even these council fathers, however, were unable to make carefully balanced and substantive statements that took into account above all the experience and biblical tradition of the patristic and medieval periods. I think that, twenty-five years after the beginning of that debate, I can empathize with the toil, the tensions, the pains that had to be endured in producing the final document.

Although *Dei Verbum* seems to be the most vigorous of the conciliar documents in its wording and structure, it is nonetheless timid and uncertain in comparison with what it might have said on the basis of the great tradition of the Church. This document, which forms such an organic whole, should have been a point of departure, not a point of arrival, for a new ecclesial understanding of the word of God and of its central place in the entire life of those who believe in the Lord.

The decision made a few days after the opening of the Council was certainly an important one, namely, to enthrone the Gospel at the beginning of each general meeting, as had been done at the Council of Ephesus, the Ferrara-Florence gathering, and Vatican I. It was important because it meant submitting the assembly to the primacy and rule of the word. It was a visible sign that the word would pass judgment on the Council and all its participants, even if some of them seem to have regarded the ritual as merely symbolic. It would have been appropriate had this gesture been accompanied by the word in the form of a homily, as at the Council of Trent, because this would assuredly have shown the word to be an *event* governing the conciliar debate, providing guidelines, and training the fathers to a new awareness of the Bible; but this did not happen and was not even suggested.

When the preparatory schema "The Sources of Revelation" with its classic Roman approach to the question was proposed, many of the fathers reacted very negatively and rejected it in its entirety as being unsuited for discussion. November 20, 1962, thus brought into the open the split between the majority and a tenaciously militant minority. According to the regulations directing the Council, however, the schema had to be discussed and could not be set aside, because its opponents did not have the needed two-thirds majority. But John XXIII took a prophetic, courageous, and liberating step: he intervened personally to support the rejection and ordered that a new draft of the schema be drawn up by a mixed commission comprising not only members of the theological commission that had produced the original schema but also members of the recently established Secretariat for Unity.

This manifestation of opposed tendencies was clearly echoed by John XXIII when, shortly after the end of the first session, he said in a letter to the council fathers (Jan. 6, 1963):

Continuing fidelity to the integrity of Catholic teaching . . . is certainly a great source of security as well as meritorious and honorable, but it does not by itself fulfill the command the Lord gave when he said: "Go and teach all nations," and when "he bade each one to take thought for his neighbor."

The pope was here saying that the Catholic Church had to take into account the other churches and the needs of all human beings.

The schema on revelation then began a very wearisome journey, the most wearisome of all at the Council; there would be four more redactions, until it was finally suggested that the schema be put aside for good. But in his address at the end of the second session (Dec. 4, 1963), the new pope, Paul VI, dispelled fears on this point by stating the necessity of an adequate response by the Council to the problem of revelation. I shall not here follow the text through all its changes,[3] but shall point out some key difficulties that made their presence felt in the final text: they led to some positive gains but also brought to light some uncertainties and inadequacies that would influence the reception of the document and therefore the post-conciliar period as well. I regard such a discussion as all the more necessary because during these postconciliar years *Dei Verbum* unfortunately remained, of all the conciliar texts, one of the least known and least analyzed and commented on.[4]

Scripture and Tradition

References to this relationship as discussed at the Council have generally been quite superficial: commentators have been satisfied to recall

3. An extensive and intelligent documentation on the development of *Dei Verbum* is given in U. Betti, "Cronistoria della Costituzione dogmatica *Dei Verbum*, in the commentary, *La costituzione dogmatica sulla divina Rivelazione* (Turin, 1966), pp. 11–50, and in B. D. Dupuy, "Historique de la Constitution," in *Vatican II. La Révélation divine* (Paris, 1968), 1:61–117.

4. Except for the commentaries listed in the preceding note, I know of no others possessing theological value; the situation is thus different from that of *Lumen gentium* and *Gaudium et spes*. See, however, the publication of the Italian Biblical Society, *Dei Verbum. Atti della XX settimana biblica* (Brescia, 1970), which contains many essays not directly relating to the constitution.

that the Council rejected the idea of two sources of revelation, scripture
and tradition, and that on the positive side it proclaimed:

There exist a close connection and communication between sacred tradition and
sacred scripture. For both of them, flowing from the same divine wellspring, in a
certain way merge into a unity and tend toward the same end. . . . Therefore
both sacred tradition and sacred scripture are to be accepted and venerated with
the same sense of devotion and reverence [DV 9].

This statement is indeed very important, especially in view of the
effort made not to contradict the councils of Trent and Vatican I but "to
follow in the footsteps *(inhaerens vestigiis)"* of these councils (DV 1). It is
also true, however, that there was no in-depth resolution of the problem
of the relationship between scripture and tradition, and that the very
concept of tradition was not explained and set forth with sufficient
clarity.[5] On the one hand, the council fathers did not reach the point of
saying clearly that scripture alone is the book containing the word of
God and that scripture alone is *inspired,* whereas tradition enjoys only
the *assistance* of the Holy Spirit. On the other hand, they did not manage
to give a satisfactory description of tradition. They referred a number of
times to sacred tradition, showing themselves almost obsessed with setting it alongside sacred scripture, but they did not engage in any profound rethinking of the whole concept as it is attested especially among
the Eastern fathers and in the Orthodox churches. As a result, they did
not succeed in distinguishing traditions from tradition.

Because of the impoverished state of the theology of tradition,[6] the
council fathers, fearful of diminishing the role of tradition, did not even
mention its great function as in the fullest sense a *doxological hermeneutic*
of scripture, as an *epiclesis pronounced over the "letter"* of the Bible, and as
being historically attested also by the *sensus fidelium.*

Unless there is an awareness of tradition that will prevent an emptying out of the concepts either of scripture or of the Church, the appeal for "reading the Bible in the Church" can become an empty
formula, reserved for polemical use against a contemporary exegetico-
critical reading and calling for conformity to the Church's magisterium.
As we shall see, the failure of *Dei Verbum* to explain tradition would in
fact weigh heavily on the approach to scripture in the following years.
The reading of the scriptures would lack deeper and more spiritual

5. The same judgment is expressed by G. Dossetti, Cardinal Lercaro's *peritus* at the
Council, in his "Per una valutazione globale del magistero del Vaticano II" (manuscript;
Bologna, 1966), pp. 9–12.
6. The theological debate on tradition had been going on for some years, and Y. M.-J.
Congar had made a valuable contribution in his *Tradition and Traditions: An Historical and a
Theological Essay* (New York, 1966; French original: Paris, 1960–63). The council fathers,
however, do not seem to have paid much attention to theological research on the subject.
See also J. Geiselmann, "Die Tradition," in *Fragen der Theologie heute* (Einsiedeln, 1960),
69–108; see also *Mysterium salutis* (Einsiedeln, 1965), 1:497–621.

moorings and a more conscious and vital theological context. The result would be interventions of authorities that were more or less timely and more or less characterized by discernment with regard to theological research and to the attitudes that Catholics should adopt toward the Bible.

Word of God and Life of the Church

The centrality of the word of God contained in the scriptures is attested not only by the relationship established between it and tradition and by the express admission that the teaching office of the Church is in the service of the word (DV 10), but also and above all by chapter 6 of the constitution, which speaks of sacred scripture in the life of the Church. At the same time, however, this chapter is also one of the texts that shows most clearly the shift in perspective that occurred during the work of the Council. The preparatory text said concisely that "the heavenly treasure of the sacred books which the Holy Spirit with supreme love and generosity has given to human beings through the Church has never been hidden away in the Church." With an eye on objections it also claimed that "from the beginning the Church has guarded the divine words with the greatest reverence and care, defended them against every false interpretation, used them especially in sacred preaching, and never ceased to set them daily before all in its liturgy."[7]

The text was unsatisfactory, and with great labor the commission produced a redaction that was chronologically the third (textus emendatus); it showed a great advance with regard to the positive place of scripture in the life of the Church.[8] There is a strong statement here that "the Church has always venerated the sacred scriptures as it does the very body of the Lord, never ceasing to take the bread of life from both the table of God's word and the table of Christ's body and to give it to the faithful."

A sizable number of fathers objected, however, to this parallel between scripture and eucharist. Their objection drew a weak response from the commission, which defended the parallel "as based on scripture itself (see the discourse on the bread of life in John 6) and as customary in tradition (see also the Imitation of Christ)."[9] But the fathers of the minority, including those of the coetus internationalis, kept up their attack on these expressions, claiming that the text excessively likened (nimis assimilare) the table of the word to the table of the Eucharist; they ex-

7. Sacrosanctum Oecumenicum Concilium Vaticanum Secundum, Schemata constitutionum et decretorum, Series prima (Vatican City, 1962): Schema constitutionis dogmaticae de fontibus revelationis, cap. V, § 24 (p. 19).

8. See Schema constitutionis dogmaticae De divina revelatione (Vatican City, 1963), cap. VI, § 21.

9. Schema constitutionis dogmaticae De divina revelatione (Vatican City, 1964), Relationes de singulis numeris, cap. VI, § 21.

pressed their fear that the Eucharistic presence would be reduced to a symbolic presence, and they asked that the parallel be omitted.[10] Unfortunately, these fathers not only did not see that with the omission an idea regarded as important in the ancient and medieval church would be dropped; they also showed that they themselves believed the Lord to be only symbolically present when the bread of the word is broken in the Church, and thus they once again emphasized the sacrament at the expense of the word of God.

Despite this opposition, the parallel was kept in the only slightly altered final text,[11] which makes it clear that there is but a single bread of life on which the Church and the faithful are fed when they approach the table of the word and the Eucharist.[12] The Church fully embodies its essence and achieves its epiphany in the liturgy, in which scripture and bread reveal their mystery and are transformed into the word and body of the risen Christ.

On the other hand, this relationship is the only one that properly expresses the intrinsic unity of word and sacrament, two mutually inclusive realities that alone are capable of perpetuating the saving event that was accomplished and brought to fulfillment in the Lord Jesus Christ. Moreover, the parallel goes back to the Fathers of the Church—Ignatius of Antioch, John Chrysostom, Jerome, Augustine—and was customary as late as the medieval Cistercians and Victorines, through whom it made its way into the *Imitation of Christ*. Nor should it be forgotten that from Origen onward the same theological and symbolical language used in speaking of the incarnation of the Word was always used also of scripture and the Eucharist.

This passage of *Dei Verbum* is thus extremely important and pregnant with consequences,[13] because scripture, as celebrated and prayed in the Church as God's own word by the power of the Holy Spirit, is here

---

10. *De divina revelatione. Modi a patribus conciliaribus propositi et a commissione doctrinali examinati* (Vatican City, 1965), cap. VI, § 21: "Many of the fathers think the text excessively assimilates the table of God's word and the body of Christ, since the latter may in consequence be reduced to a mere symbol, especially in view of some contemporary theories on the eucharistic presence."

11. The expression "Divinas Scripturas *velut* ipsum Corpus Dominicum semper venerata est Ecclesia" became "Divinas Scripturas *sicut et* Corpus. . . ," thus lessening the force of the image (italics added). See n. 10, above, and DV 21.

12. This reference to the table of the word and the Eucharist was to have been included in *Sacrosanctum Concilium*, § 48, but even at that earlier point the interventions of some fathers who opposed the parallel and the relationship intimidated the conciliar commission on the liturgy. As a result, the final text of the liturgy constitution only expresses a wish that the faithful "should be instructed by God's word and be refreshed at the table of the Lord's body," and says nothing of the connection between the two. The idea of the table of the word appears in § 51, but unconnected with the table of the Eucharist. The image of the twofold table would, however, be used later on; see PO 18, AG 6, and PC 6.

13. See the commentaries on this chapter of DV: C. M. Martini, "La Sacra Scrittura nella vita della Chiesa," in *La Costituzione Dogmatica sulla Divina Rivelazione* (Turin, 1966), pp. 265–305; A. Grillmeier, "La sainte Ecriture dans la vie de l'Eglise," in *La Révélation Divine*

given the quality of a sacrament (and no longer simply of a sacramental, as used to be said). That is, it is a grace-event in which God encounters the community and the faithful, strengthening their communion with the Trinity and showing himself to be the God who speaks and who reveals and makes himself known.

Significantly, § 21 ends by saying that therefore "these words are perfectly applicable to sacred Scripture: 'For the word of God is living and efficient' (Heb. 4:12) and is 'able to build up and give the inheritance among all the sanctified' (Acts 20:32)." From this statement it follows that the central place of the word of God is fixed and specified for the four areas making up the life of the Church: "in the sacred books" that are read in the liturgy, "the Father who is in heaven meets His children . . . and speaks with them," while these same books "make the voice of the Holy Spirit resound" (§ 21); "all the preaching of the Church must be nourished and ruled by the sacred Scriptures" (ibid.); theology "rests on the written word of God . . . as its primary and perpetual foundation," and its soul must be the study of the word (§ 24); and finally the daily life of the faithful should be charactreized by the diligent reading of the scriptures (§ 25). The word is thus located within the life of the Church where it exercises its full primacy and dominion, making every ministry a service of the word and turning every Christian into a servant of the word (see Luke 1:2; Acts 20:24).

It was these strong statements that made Karl Barth say, in addition to the specific and precise criticisms he, as an Evangelical, had of *Dei Verbum*, "If there was ever a reform council, it was Vatican II!" Jerome's words, cited in the constitution (§ 25), could not fail to become part of the consciousness of God's people: "Ignorance of the scripture is ignorance of Christ!"

The Word of God and History

The third positive gain is the relationship established between scripture and history. The connection is an essential one that, when properly understood, opens the way to, and grounds, recognition of history not simply as the scene or setting of revelation but as itself revelatory and therefore playing a constitutive part in salvation. It is the place where faith and the Church must live and recognize God to be at work. This recognition of history as something into which both revelation and the life of the Church are integrated is adequately attested in other documents of the Council. The fact, however, that this recognition is systematically present in *Dei Verbum* is important, because it can be fruitful in further ways. Unfortunately, it is one more point that seems to me to be rarely prominent and emphasized in commentaries on the conciliar texts; for this reason, some observations are in order.[14]

In the preparatory schema the historical aspect of revelation was simply mentioned as an apologetical argument that narrowly reflected Vatican I, where history was defined as a sum total of events external to revelation itself: "divine facts, especially miracles and prophecies . . . [which] manifestly display the omnipotence and infinite knowledge of God, . . . are the most certain signs of the divine revelation."[15] In this approach only words are revelatory, as is clear from these statements of the schema: "This revelation . . . has been communicated chiefly through *preaching* and received through *hearing*. . . . During his life Christ made the mysteries of the kingdom of heaven known *orally*, and after his resurrection he commanded his disciples to *preach* them to every creature. . . . Therefore in fact the apostles *preach* in his name."[16]

Even more negative in their attitude to history were some passages in the preparatory schema *De deposito fidei pure custodiendo*, which was likewise rejected without having been discussed. This schema said: "External, public revelation by which the object of Christian faith has been divinely communicated . . . *is the act of speaking (est locutio)* in which God with supreme kindness gave witness to himself, the mysteries of salvation, and the truths connected with these mysteries." A few lines further on, it added: "Although it must be acknowledged that revelation has been given to us in the *history, whether prophesied or narrated*, of human salvation, yet it is not at all to be thought that revelation is constituted by mere events."[17]

In this vision of things history is the scene of revelation and can, at best, serve only as a proof of the word of God; it acquires a density, so to speak, only when it is prophesied or narrated, and it is thus reduced to the status of something accidental in the economy of revelation. The point of departure was unpromising, yet in the definitive text, which was reached only after a laborious journey, *words and events* are closely connected and consistently interrelated on the grounds that together

14. Attention is rarely paid to the relationship between history and revelation as found specifically in DV. See, e.g., L. Alonso Schökel, "Carattere storico della Rivelazione," in *Dei Verbum. Atti della XX settimana biblica* (Brescia, 1970), pp. 31–56, and I. de la Potterie, "La vérité de l'Ecriture et l'histoire du salut d'après la *Dei Verbum*," NRT, 88 (1966) 149–69. On the relationship between Christianity and history in Vatican II, see G. Alberigo, "Cristianesimo e storia," *Cristianesimo nella storia*, 5 (1984) 577–92; M.-D. Chenu, "La Chiesa nella storia: fondamento e norme dell'interpretazione del Concilio," *Idoc Dossier*, 1 (1966) 19.

15. See Vatican I, dogmatic constitution *Dei Filius*, chap. 2; Latin text in *Conciliorum Oecumenicorum Decreta* (Bologna, 3rd ed., 1973), p. 807; English translation from J. Neuner and J. Dupuis, *The Christian Faith in the Doctrinal Documents of the Catholic Church* (Staten Island, N.Y., 1982), no. 119 (p. 42).

16. *Schema constitutionis dogmatica De fontibus revelationis*, § 2, italics added.

17. See *Schemata Constitutionum et Decretorum* (n. 7, above): *De deposito fidei pure custodiendo*, cap. IV, §§ 23–62; *De revelatione publica et de fide catholica*, §§ 17 and 18, italics added.

and inseparably they make up the whole plan of salvation and the whole economy of revelation. In fact, the word of God was not spoken outside time and history, in some mythical "time," or outside a culturally determined place; consequently, it is not a set of abstract, atemporal truths or universal ethical precepts. Rather it always has reference to a specific historical context; its roots are in history; it is determined by history and intrinsically correlative to history. History too, therefore, is a revelation of God's plan of salvation for all humankind![18]

On the other hand, the whole of scripture, from Genesis to the Apocalypse, bears witness that the word (dabar-logos) of God is a word-event. Consequently, dicere Dei est facere (the speaking of God is a doing or acting), but also facere Dei est dicere (the doing or acting of God is a speaking).

Right at the beginning, the constitution Dei Verbum states that the Council makes its own the words of John the apostle: "That . . . which we have heard, which we have seen with our eyes, which we have looked upon and touched with our hands, concerning the word of life," which is Christ, "we proclaim also to you" (see 1 John 1:2–3). It goes on then to say that "this plan of revelation is realized by deeds and words having an inner unity: the deeds wrought by God in the history of salvation manifest and confirm the teaching and realities signified by the words, while the words proclaim the deeds and clarify the mystery contained in them" (DV 2, italics added). The events of history thus contain a mystery that is God's saving plan and its accomplishment brought to completion in Christ, who is both revealer and revelation, being as he is the Word made flesh and therefore an event in history.

This unity of word and history, which had been suspect in classical Roman theology, is constantly attested in Dei Verbum. The document emphasizes the point that Jesus Christ "perfected revelation by fulfilling it through his whole work of making himself present and manifesting himself: through his words and deeds" (§ 4), and that the apostles "handed on what they had received from the lips of Christ, from living with him, and from what he did" (§ 7). What the Church received from the apostles it therefore passed on to all generations "in teaching, life, and worship." It is this that allows tradition to develop in the course of history:

There is a growth in the understanding of the realities and the words which have been handed down. This happens through the contemplation and study made by believers . . . through the intimate understanding of spiritual things they experience . . . As the centuries succeed one another, the Church constantly moves forward toward the fullness of divine truth until the words of God reach their complete fulfillment in her [§ 8].

This acknowledgment of history cannot but have many and wide-ranging consequences for the faith and life of the Church. If revelation is

18. For the radical and widely criticized position of W. Pannenberg, see his Revelation as History (New York, 1968).

historical in the full sense of the term, then theology too must be historical; it is compelled to make history and events part of its object and, without allowing itself to be reduced to a historical science, it must positively recognize history as a hermeneutical locus for discerning, proclaiming, and narrating the presence of God. The area it covers in its reflection must therefore include Christian experience, that is, the Christian fact as rooted in and conditioned by the evolution of the world and by the vicissitudes of human life and history. As the Church continues its pilgrim journey toward the kingdom, it is aware that history is still revelatory. It is true that nothing can be added to the fullness of revelation that came to us in Christ, but it is also true that this fullness includes an advance toward the whole truth (see John 16:13) and a participation, neither fearful nor crusading, in "whatever happens."

Once the Church is thus situated in history, it ceases to be a fortress and can no longer live in accordance with a logic of hostility toward those human beings who do not share the faith. It must rather think of itself as the fulfillment of the mystery of Christ in historical form and therefore put itself at the service of the race, scrutinizing *the signs of the times* and *the signs of places*, showing the prophetic dimension of lived experience, and waiting faithfully on earth for the Lord's return.[19]

As far as the interpretation of scripture is concerned, this much must be said: inasmuch as scripture itself came into existence within a people who had experienced God through meaningful historical events, the interpretation of scripture must likewise be historical. The word of God was given to human beings in human words (DV 12–13) and took flesh without evading the conditions imposed upon it by a particular historical period and a particular culture. Its interpretation, therefore, calls for the methods used in the understanding of any and all human texts. On this point *Dei Verbum* must be said to have remained silent rather than to have spoken; as the passage of time has made clear, it simply gave legitimacy, with some ambiguities, to a now quite dated technical approach to the Gospels (§ 19) and to scripture as a whole (§ 12). At the same time, however, it is being recognized that *Dei Verbum* freed biblical scholarship from onerous working conditions by authorizing, as needed for a correct interpretation, the methods used in all historical study and criticism.[20]

Unfortunately, the hermeneutical problem was not set forth in a satisfactory and rounded way. As a result, although *Dei Verbum* did affirm the right to use the historical method, it did not supply the directives needed for achieving the kind of actualization that turns the scriptures into the word of God when they are proclaimed, heard, and meditated

19. For a situating of faith in history and on the signs of the times, see M.-D. Chenu, *L'Evangile dans le temps* (Paris, 1964); idem, "Les signes des temps," *NRT*, 97 (1965) 29–39 (a foundational essay developed by the author in other publications); J.-P. Jossua, "Discerner les signes des temps," *Vie spirituelle*, 114 (1966) 546–69.

20. See J. Dupont, "Storicità dei Vangeli e metodo storico nella *Dei Verbum*," in *A vent'anni dal Concilio* (Palermo, 1983), pp. 51–75.

on in the Christian community. This lack of firm criteria would likewise not fail to influence the approach to the scriptures in the postconciliar period, for an authentically ecclesial interpretation of scripture is possible only through the interplay of hermeneutical methods, the experience of believers, and the principle that the scriptures form a single whole (*scriptura sui ipsius interpres*). In an address to the Italian Biblical Society on September 25, 1970, Paul VI would try to fill the void by offering directives especially to exegetes. His address, however, did not outline a method that would shed light, in the Spirit, on the letter of scripture and on its actualization in the Christian community that lives in the midst of humanity.

Yet the connection between word and history is clear not only from the passages of *Dei Verbum* already cited, but also from the way in which the Old and New Testaments are presented in chapters 4 and 5 of the constitution. These chapters refer frequently to a "plan" and an "economy" of salvation that embrace the whole human race and that, after being revealed to the people of Israel, were brought to their fulfillment in Jesus Christ.

Allow me in this context simply to express regret at a passage in § 15 that shows how the idea of revelation as historical is more easily applicable to the Old Testament than to the New. The passage says of the Old Testament that "these books, though they also contain some things which are incomplete and temporary (*imperfecta et temporalia*), nevertheless show us true divine pedagogy." But, no less than the law and prophets of the Old Testament, the apostolic exhortations of the New also contain "things that are incomplete and temporary." Only in Christ, in his life and his word, is everything complete and definitive; the same cannot be said of the life of the Church any more than it could of the life of Israel. Furthermore, although § 16 asserts the unity of the two Testaments, the statement is so formulated that it risks playing down the authority of the Old Testament, which unfortunately is still not understood and is given little importance in the life of the Church.

As I end this first part of my essay, I can only say that the centrality of the word, with all its dynamism and efficacy, was accepted by the Council, especially in *Dei Verbum*. I have thought it necessary to emphasize the positive gains made at the Council, to show the uncertainties, and to point out the unresolved problems that awaited some further mediation and fruitful approach. I turn now to an interpretation of the road traveled during the twenty years since the Council.

The Centrality of the Word in the Postconciliar Period

A complete and accurate summary of what the end of the exile of the word has meant during these twenty years would require thorough re-

search in the different areas in which the Christian reality has been experienced and applied to the many and varied milieus in which believers
and others live their lives.

I intend to focus on only a few of the dynamics that have come to
light. I am conscious that I am giving a very general interpretation to
certain tendencies that have been emerging in what may be called
"Western" Christianity. I shall be dealing in particular with the approach to and the function of the word of God in the liturgical and
catechetical activities and the life of faith of three groups or movements:
traditional historical communities (parishes and their associations), *charismatic groups* (recent ecclesial movements and monastic centers of spirituality), and *liberation movements* and the basic communities they have
inspired. In limiting myself to these groups and movements I shall
admittedly be restricting myself generally to Europe and the Americas,
but it is not possible for me here to identify the fruits produced by the
centrality of the word in Asia and Africa. These are essentially missionary areas, still much indebted to and therefore, apart from a few sporad-
ic undertakings, dependent on the other areas.

A further point to be made is that the Bible is now being read by nonbelievers as well as believers. "Scripture has ceased to be a restricted
book. It is no longer the private property of the Christian community. It
circulates freely in contemporary culture, and is no longer subject to the
control of the churches."[21] The Bible exerts its influence on the masses
through the media and not through agencies of the churches; the importance of this phenomenon is not to be underestimated, but it is not
possible here even to try to formulate it.

The Approach to and Use of the Word in
Traditional Historical Communities

This sector certainly contains the widest and most fully organized part
of the people of God, and the one to whom the Council intended to en-
trust the implementation of reform and the carrying out of its inspirations. The introduction of the national languages into the liturgy, the
enactment of the new liturgical *ordo*, and the publication of a festal and
ferial lectionary that, even if necessarily anthological, makes possible a
contact with practically the whole of scripture—all these steps wrought a
profound change in the relationship of the faithful to the Bible.

The most obvious result has been the "reappearance" of the liturgy of
the word, which had in fact been nonexistent before the Council: it had
been reduced to a hortatory homily on morality that was almost never
based on the biblical texts. The word of God has been given back to the
people who, as they listen to it, encounter the Lord and enter into com-

21. J. Audinet, "The Banquet of Scripture: The Bible and Adult Catechesis," *Concilium*,
70 (1971) 130; see also P. Gritti, in *Bible et techniques de masse* (Paris, 1970), p. 193.

munion with him. This is without qualification the greatest fruit of the Council, even if we are still far from being able to gauge its effects and consequences for faith and Christian practice. Even "Sunday Christians" are now able to hear the entire Gospel and the most revelatory parts of the Old and New Testaments, which had previously played only a marginal role in the liturgy. In this way the entire people of God is gradually being compelled to give their prayer, their devotion, and their life a biblical dimension, whereas previously they had access, at best, only to "sacred history," as it used to be called, in the handbooks of devotion that flourished especially at the end of the nineteenth century and the beginning of the twentieth.

This restoration of the word of God to the people—even were it only a restoration of the "letter" (the *gramma* or *graphē*)—is very important and cannot fail to produce effects.

When we look at matters from this point of view, we can see how of all the conciliar texts *Sacrosanctum Concilium* and *Dei Verbum* have been the most fruitful, the ones endowed with the greatest virtualities, and the ones most fully received, notwithstanding the obstacles and the objective difficulties encountered in the course of the reform. "Within" the people of God there has emerged a powerful liturgical and biblical revival that has borne much, relatively ripe fruit; it has put an end to liturgical fossilization and the clericalization of the sacred texts. Every Christian now understands the Mass to be a single act of worship comprising a liturgy of the word and a liturgy of the sacrament that are necessarily and intrinsically interconnected. The discovery of the word has even been so potent and vigorous that many parishes and many religious communities regard reflection on the biblical texts during the week or on the vigil of Sunday as a necessary communal preparation for the festal homily. All this allows us to say that, at least virtually, room has been made for the centrality and rule of the word in the life of the Church.

All this is visible and positive. There are also, however, inadequacies and shadows that keep the conciliar guidelines from being followed to the full.

When the liturgical reform became law, many publishers undertook (and others are still undertaking) to provide preachers with tools and aids for their homilies.[22] The fact is, of course, that the introduction of the lectionary caught the majority unprepared as far as the Bible was concerned, but it is also a fact that use of these various handbooks, these "sermon materials," bypasses direct contact with the scriptures and excuses ministers of the word from study and an effort at personal insight

22. In this context I should mention some undertakings that are of great interest because they present tools for preaching rather than materials for sermons: *Assemblées du Seigneur* (Paris: Cerf), which is also published in Italian: *La Parola per l'assemblea festiva* (Brescia: Queriniana); *Servizio della Parola* (Brescia: Queriniana); G. Becquet, *Lectures d'Evangile pour les dimanches et les fêtes A, B, C* (Paris, 1971–75).

into the scriptures. As a result, they have entered upon a path that can be described as one of "biblical consumerism." This cannot be of real, fruitful help to priests, because these aids to preaching, though prepared by specialists or pastoral experts, can hardly inspire a proclamation of God's word that is adapted to a particular context and a particular moment; this kind of proclamation depends on the experience of the community to which it is addressed. The danger is that the real purpose of the reading of the Bible—namely, to allow it to make a critical appeal to the life and experience of the celebrating community—will be missed and that the dynamism and efficacy of the word will be blunted. On the other hand, participants in the liturgy remain passive listeners: only rarely do they find themselves involved in a homily carried on as a dialogue. This contributes in a notable degree to lessening the impact of the word of God on liturgical preaching.[23]

Authentic biblical preaching has continued to be rare in traditional Christian communities. Despite an initial enthusiasm on the part of the faithful, to which the clergy has not been able to respond adequately, there has been a retrogression to a catechetical, if not moralistic, type of preaching. The real need is for both ministers and faithful to acquire a biblical mentality; otherwise a gap between the word of God as embodied in history and in the daily life of believers becomes inevitable, and an actualization of the scriptures on the basis both of history and the life of the community becomes impossible. The word of God has formally become central in the liturgical life of the Church, but we are still far from allowing the word to judge and inspire. This is because the prevailing conception of the word of God does not include a sense of history, and its proponents lack a hermeneutical awareness that can restore scripture to its primatial place and enable it to exert its efficacy in the present moment.[24]

In addition to the liturgical area, the traditional historical communities have other areas that are open to the word of God—for example, schools of theology, courses in scripture, and meetings of various kinds that have biblical texts for their focus and whose participants are to be found among the activists of the various Catholic parochial associations, as well as among catechists and pastoral workers.

In these cases, the approach to scripture is primarily catecheticocultural and has been attended thus far by new national catechisms showing a clearly biblical orientation. Many of the laity have been involved in these undertakings, and this has promoted the growth of a call for and an interest in the Bible, with notable results especially in the

23. See G. Orlandoni, L'omelia: monologo o dialogo? La predicazione alla luce della sociologia della communicazione (Rome, 1977); B. Maggioni, "Per un'interpretazione della Scrittura a scopo di predicazione," Communio (Italian ed.), 29 (1977) 58–69; O. Du Roy, "Crise de la prédication," in Crise du biblisme, chance de la Bible? (Paris, 1973), pp. 74–93.

24. See the Italian Episopal Conference's appraisal of the implementation of the liturgical reform: "Il rinnovamento liturgico in Italia," Il Regno–Documenti, 19 (1983) 589–95.

catechesis of children. The level of encounter with the Bible, however, is distinctively cultural; it is at the level of an introduction to the scriptures rather than of direct contact with the texts and therefore cannot yield a firm hermeneutical or interpretive orientation. Such an approach does not effect a contact between the historical reality attested by the Bible and the present life of Christians in the world. It does not give the biblical texts the power to involve and transform; and it risks making the scriptures once again a repository of truths, of ideas chosen with a view to pastoral programs.

This lack of contact between the historical situation of believers and the history of God's people in the old and new covenants has ended, here and there, in weariness and disaffection; the heyday of schools of scripture studies or theology for the laity is perhaps now past, as a result of the impasse created.[25] In this context we cannot fail to take note of the remark made by the secretariat of the French Episcopal Conference:

We are confronted today with two facts pointing in opposite directions: the institutional decision, never before expressed in such clear terms, that all the faithful should read the Bible; and the fact that this desire does not yet have at its disposal adequate hermeneutical tools for making this reading fruitful.[26]

The restoration of contact with the word of God is nonetheless a factor in the renewal of the historical communities. Even though the Bible has not become familiar even to all priests, to say nothing of all the faithful, thie renewed contact seems to be an acquired experience. The more the word is heard, the more the presence of the Lord makes itself felt as unexpected and provocative.[27]

Ecclesial Movements and Centers of Spirituality

The reality and international spread of contemporary movements in the Church is such that it forces us to inquire into the centrality of the word of God in their life and spirituality, though I realize that there are great differences and sometimes a distance not unmarked by tension among them.[28] What these movements have in common is a spon-

25. A crisis in the area of reading of the Bible began in the 1970s, especially in French-speaking countries, and found expression in a lively debate; see the collective work, *Crise du biblisme, chance de la Bible?* (Paris, 1973); A. Paul, "Pour la Bible: une anti-exégèse," *Cahiers universitaires catholiques* (1973–74), 7–10; F. Refoulé, "L'exégèse en question," *Supplément à la Vie spirituelle*, 111 (1974), 391–423; P. Grelot, "L'exégèse biblique au carrefour," *NRT*, 108 (1976) 416–34, 481–511; P. Dreyfus, "Exégèse en Sorbonne, exégèse en Eglise," *RB*, 82 (1975) 321–59; idem, "L'actualisation à l'intérieur de la Bible," *RB*, 83 (1976) 161–202; idem, "L'actualisation de l'écriture," *RB*, 86 (1979) 5–58, 161–93, 321–84.

26. See *Bulletin du secrétariat de la Conférence Episcopale Française*, 9 (April 1977).

27. See M. Card. Pellegrino, *Il Post-Concilio in Italia* (Milan, 1979), pp. 30–31; J. Bajot, *Le risque de la Bible* (Paris, 1974), p. 7.

28. See J. Le Du, *L'Evangile dans les groupes* (Paris, 1974).

taneous birth and foundation; a charismatic organization; an existence as structures and spaces that are, as it were, parallel to the historical communities and to the local churches, from which they keep a certain distance; a zeal and an enthusiastic sense of belonging that is keenly felt by the members; and finally an ecclesial status that is acknowledged more at the papal level than by local bishops.

In some cases, the inspiration that gave rise to the movements was the rediscovery of the word of God; in others it was the need of prayer; in the case of *Communione e Liberazione* groups, it was the need of once again giving the Christian faith an effective, visible presence in society. Scripture is usually approached by way of Bible study groups. The meetings of these groups are characterized by the interaction of the participants, all of whom share a common method of reading the scriptures that is determined by the spirituality proper to the group.[29] More than elsewhere, there has been a shift here from "the Bible of the experts" to "the Bible of the group," which lays hold of its content through common study, sharing, revision of life, and prayer. The approach to the Bible varies, therefore, from group to group: it is more kerygmatic and methodical in neocatechumenal groups, more fragmented and spiritual among the Focolari, more prayerful and spontaneous among the charismatics, less trenchant, more hesitant, and with little of the conventional about it in *Communione e Liberazione* groups.

All these groups seek to affirm and understand the sacramentality of the word and the unity of the Old and New Testaments. They realize the need of eliminating as far as possible all cultural and ideological filters in reading the Bible. They wish to give the Bible once again the unqualified primacy that inspires an evangelical radicalism to be realized in their lives. The word of God is thus seen as a message from a living God who lays direct claim to the life of the individual and the group. The Bible is a book that must be heeded and from which strength must be derived for facing difficulties on the way. Neocatechumenal groups, in particular, make a great effort to give primacy to the word, and are very faithful in maintaining direct contact with the scriptures, which they do not simply listen to and pray over but also preach.[30]

We must not, however, overlook the fact that, although these movements realize the inadequacy of the isolated critical method of the experts, they too readily have recourse to other methods of reading (it is difficult to draw up an exact list of them) and forget the need of a historical reading, without which any hasty appeal to the spirit reflects a failure to grasp the mystery of the incarnation. Distrust of serious research

29. See R. Fabris, "L'uso della Bibbia nelle communità cristiane," in *Chiesa in Italia 1975–1978* (Brescia, 1978), pp. 61–69.

30. For an analysis of the neocatechumenal movement, see G. Zevini, "Il cammino neocatecumenale," in *Movimenti ecclesiali contemporanei* (Rome, 1982), pp. 231–67, with a bibliography; idem, "The Christian Initiation of Adults into the Neo-Catechumenal Community," *Concilium*, 122 (1979) 65–75.

and study can beget a certain dilettantism, subjectivist interpretations, and a cultivation of spontaneity in reading that can lead to fundamentalism and a spiritualism cut off from social reality. Unless an effort is made to take the biblical context into account, it is difficult, almost impossible, to establish a link between scripture and present history, between the hearing of the word and historical involvement.

Apparently more successful (the success may be rare but it is not to be neglected) is the experiment undertaken by monastic centers of spirituality. Some of these centers are older ones that have been revitalized; others are more recent foundations, especially in Europe.[31] Here the practice of *lectio divina* has been restored. Its aim is to make the scriptures a daily food, so that the Bible, read, meditated, prayed, and contemplated by community and individuals, becomes the basis of the spiritual life and the inspiration for activities carried on among externs.[32] These communities give a great deal of room to the word in their liturgy, which does not consist solely of the Mass but is also celebrated in other forms, from the liturgy of the hours to vigils and liturgies of the word in the true and proper sense. Those reading the Bible in these centers are usually able to handle the tools of historical criticism in an adequate way. They are attentive to the great patristic tradition of the Church. They pay heed to stimuli arising from comparisons with the Hebrew tradition and those of other Christian churches.

In these centers the word of God, together with the Eucharist, becomes the basis of life; it gives the community its form; it shows itself able to put Christian experience on new foundations; it brings about a return to the sources of Christianity. Guests, who are usually quite numerous, are not drawn away from their local churches but are urged and encouraged to develop a mature and responsible sense of the Church and to work among their fellow human beings without detaching themselves from history but rather giving an account of the hope that is in them. This reading of scripture, which I would describe as doxological, seems very promising and has found an important measure of acceptance among Christian militants. It must, however, be on guard to avoid the dangers of elitism and a limited kind of actualization that is not open to the experience of ordinary believers and human beings generally.

Liberation Movements and Basic Communities

In the years immediately after the Council a very vital and interesting communal movement made its appearance. Especially in Italy and

31. I am thinking, for Italy, of the communities of Bose, Monteveglio, Camaldoli, Spello, and others, and, for France, of Boquen in the 1970s and of monasteries and centers such as La Tourette, La Sainte-Baume, and others today.

32. See E. Bianchi, *Pregare la Parola* (Turin, 1974) (French translation: *Prier la Parole* [Bellefontaine, 1983]); M. Magrassi, *La Bibbia pregata* (Milan, 1975).

France, it led to the rise of what were called "spontaneous ecclesial groups," which made the word of God their focus of attention and tried to set Christian life on new foundations outside the framework of the traditional parishes.[33] They lasted but a short time. Some of them finally succumbed to the logic at work in the effort at spontaneity that had given them birth. Around 1970 others ended up in the "basic communities" or the "Christians for Socialism" that appeared in Europe in connection with the liberation theologies and liberation movements in Latin America. In these groups the word of God was truly central, and they bore witness that the approach to scripture was the very reason for the formation of the community. Reading, serious study, meditation, and actualization restored to the word its prophetic power and made it able to shed light on the lives of believers and their relationship to social reality and history. Father M.-D. Chenu, who was always alert to the relationship between gospel and history in the past and in the present, could say that scripture thus read was "the preeminent theological *locus* of the moment."[34]

The phenomenon was thus a promising one but, as I noted, developments, including a lack of understanding on the part of the hierarchy, led to dissent, contestation, and eventually marginalization in the Church.

Now that years have passed it is easy to see that these groups were absorbed by the "Christians for Socialism" movement within the far wider sphere of the basic communities. The latter still exist; they are showing signs of weariness in Europe, but they are alive and have a definite ecclesial status in Latin America, where they are connected with liberation movements.[35]

The phenomenon of the basic communities is not easy to analyze, having grown complex and many-sided as a result of development or of the varied situations in which the communities exist (Europe, Latin America). Nonetheless the use made of the Bible and the ways of approaching and actualizing it are uniform enough to allow some remarks on the central place of the word in these communities.[36]

33. See E. Bianchi, "Un incontro di gruppi ecclesiali," *Testimonianze*, 120 (1969) 909–20. Analyses of the ecclesial group phenomenon usually pass over that early period, but there were in fact a number of dynamic undertakings in Italy and France at that time.

34. Cited by J.-P. Jossua, "Dalla teologia al teologo," in *L'avvenire della Chiesa* (Brescia, 1970), p. 78; see also E. Bianchi, "Una valutazione globale del fenomeno dei gruppi ecclesiali," *Testimonianze*, 130 (1970) 903–27.

35. On the spirituality of the Latin American liberation movements, see L. Boff, *Testigo de Dios en el corazón del mundo* (Madrid, 1977); G. Gutiérrez, *A Theology of Liberation* (Maryknoll, N.Y., 1973); idem, "The Poor in the Church," *Concilium*, 104 (1974) 11–16; C. Boff, *Teologia e practica. Teologia do político e suas mediaçôes* (Petrópolis, 1978); S. Galilea, *Spiritualità della liberazione* (Brescia, 1974); and *Concilium*, 104 and 106 (1974), in their entirety.

36. See E. Perrenchio, *Bibbia e communità di base in Italia* (Rome, 1980), with an extensive bibliography and documentation; B. Besret, *Les communautés de base* (Paris, 1973); Alonso Antonio, *Comunidades eclesiales de base* (Salamanca, 1970), and the collective work, *Centralità della Parola di Dio per il movimento che nasce dalla base* (Turin, 1976).

The horizon within which the word is read is the social situation that calls for the deliverance of the oppressed and an end to every form of enslavement. These ends are to be achieved through a revolution in which the Bible proves to be a source of inspiration and capable of exercising a liberating power in behalf of the poor. The politico-social involvement of Christians takes shape in a choice between social classes and plays an important role in an authentic approach to the scriptures, which are thereby wrested from monopolization by the clergy and academic experts. The word is thus read within a people who at last "makes it its own" by acquiring the abilities and tools needed for a communal reading purified of all the mystificatory dross that had emptied the word of its original message and subversive power.

Contact with the Bible, when effected by the people and almost exclusively in a communal context, tends to be in the form of an authenticating comparision between present-day history and the history of a people whom God set free and entrusted with the Gospel. Study of the Bible becomes a search for a way to achieve the human deliverance and advancement that was once given to Israel and the early Christian communities, and must be made a reality again today. The Gospel is thus resituated in history; the history of salvation is identified with the road traveled by the poor and the oppressed classes and peoples; and the word of God successfully inspires these Christians to militancy. For these reasons, the reading of the Bible is the only religious factor that unites the basic communities.

As for the manner of reading, the communities do not reject certain methodological tools, such as a materialistic reading that, more than other kinds, allows an encounter with the liberating events attested in the scriptures and with the messianic praxis of Jesus of Nazareth.[37] It is not accidental that a privileged place is given to the Book of Exodus, the message of the preexilic prophets, and the Pauline texts that give evidence of the life and atmosphere of the first Christian communities prior to institutionalization. Precisely because the *Sitz im Leben* or sociological context of the basic communities is not a vague, neutral mingling of classes but a choice of arena, the reading of the Bible becomes a political reading and deliberately avoids an intellectual and spiritual approach to the texts so that it may yield an orthopraxis of liberation and real solidarity with the poor, the marginalized, and the exploited.

Apart from some excesses, it must be acknowledged that by means of this reading the basic communities attempt to promote a lively communal and often popular participation. They go beyond an intimately personal and individualistic approach to the Bible. They attempt above all to induce the practice of listening to the scriptures and linking present history with the history of salvation. In this way the word of God ac-

37. The prototype of a materialist reading is F. Belo, *A Materialist Reading of the Gospel of Mark* (Maryknoll, N.Y., 1981), followed by M. Clevenot, *Materialist Approaches to the Bible* (Maryknoll, N.Y., 1985).

quires the capacity to transform human beings and the world, and is able to exercise a prophetic judgment on life and history. It must not be forgotten that these communities are in a privileged position to effect a fruitful confrontation with the word of God because they are being formed by individuals who are ardently involved in social issues and in history, and are able to interpret the difficulties and aspirations of the modern world. The word is understood to the extent that it is put into practice (in opere intelligens); the basic communities are making a real effort at this kind of understanding.

These are the positive values that must be acknowledged. I must also, however, point out some dangers and confusions. The chief of these is the temptation to instrumentalize the word of God by turning it into a prop for a predetermined position, instead of allowing it to exercise a critical judgment on the whole life of believers. When the demand is made for an "epistemological break" in which Christian values received from tradition must be subjected to a class analysis and at times to a rigidly Marxist analysis, then faith loses its priority and the word of God is no longer the criterion for discerning the signs of the times. Instead, an ideology sheds its light on the scriptures to interpret them along certain lines.[38]

This approach thus represents a neo-Marcionist choice of some biblical texts and rejection of others, the criterion being the liberation of the oppressed. In this case the word no longer judges the community, but the community judges the word.

The letter of the scriptures is thus in danger of being interpreted reductively and ideologically.[39] Not enough heed is paid to the fact that the liturgy and prayer are the authentic and truly fruitful context for the word and that only in union with the Church as a whole can a full understanding of the scriptures be achieved. The neglect of the great patristic tradition, the elimination of the Church's tradition on the ground that it carries the mark of Western bourgeois culture, the will to move beyond the Sitz im Leben of the biblical text and replace it with a Sitz im Kampf,[40] that is, to relate the text to the struggles that have gone on in the course of history: all this betrays a profound ideologization and the presence of the temptation for the interpreters to believe themselves the first and only ones to have an authentic understanding of the scriptures. Actualization then becomes a hasty process prejudiced by an impatient effort to infer a political praxis from scriptural texts. Meanwhile, unfortunately, the interpreter avoids all the other passages that should

---

38. See also E. Bianchi, "Bilancio dei dieci anni di post Concilio," Il Regno, 5 (1976) 123.

39. Critical remarks, with which I agree, can be found in G. Barbaglio, "Il primato della Bibbia: quale lettura ermeneutica?" in Il Concilio davanti a noi (Brescia, 1980) pp. 68–69; R. Fabris, "L'uso della Bibbia nella communità cristiana," Servizio della Parola, 103 (1978) 12–20; G. Zevini, "Attualizzazione della Parola di Dio nelle communità e nelle gruppi ecclesiali," in Attualizzazione della Parola di Dio (Bologna, 1983), pp. 205–32.

40. See G. Franzoni, "La nostra lettura biblica: una proposta per una predicazione diversa," Com–Nuovi Tempi 34 (1978) 9.

be considered, as well as the difficulties inherent in the hermeneutical process,[41] and produces a quick and facile adjustment of the word of God to information of a sociological, anthropological, and psychological kind.

Is not all this a threat to the central place of God's word in the life of these communities?

Conclusion

Allowing for the circumstances and difficulties I have mentioned here, it cannot be denied that thanks to the energies released by the conciliar event, the word of God has regained its central place in the life of the Church. The recovery seems, moreover, to be irreversible, even if it will prove fruitful only in varying degrees.

Much remains to be done to bring together, on the one hand, an approach to the word that is serious, not timid, and capable of using the hermeneutical tools dominant in the linguistic and historical sciences, and, on the other, the Church's liturgy, the reception of the great ecclesial tradition, and, above all, present-day history, which finds Christians in solidarity with other human beings on the road to liberation and peace.

Exegesis at the Sorbonne and exegesis in the Church, prayerful reading and ordinary history: these must still be brought together in a harmonious way among the people of God. But the word of God is no longer in chains and is already giving Christian life and Christian praxis in the world a new countenance.

41. There are enlightening pages on the hermeneutical process in A. Rizzi, "Teologia della liberazione. Spunti correttivi," *Rivista di teologia morale*, 18 (1973) 190–96.

René Girault

8. The Reception of Ecumenism

As late as the middle of the twentieth century the Catholic Church had not yet taken any official part in the ecumenical movement. The condemnation of incipient ecumenism in 1928 (encyclical *Mortalium animos*) had indeed been replaced in 1949 by a small degree of openness in the instruction (*Ecclesia Catholica*) of the Holy Office. Meanwhile, ecumenical undertakings of many kinds, inspired by the great pioneers of unity, were beginning to appear almost everywhere in the Church. In 1948, nonetheless, the Catholic Church declined the invitation to take part in the first assembly of the World Council of Churches in Amsterdam and had refused even to send observers. The invitation to attend the second assembly at Evanston in 1955 met with the same response.

As late as the eve of the Council some well-known theologians and some bishops were still denouncing Abbé Couturier's proposed formula of prayer for unity as ambiguous and dangerous.[1] Then there is the telling incident related by Pastor Boegner. Shortly after John XXIII had announced the Council, a Catholic theologian who was studying the problem of ecumenism told him with utter conviction: "I pray God that there may be nothing said at the Council about unity. That is the worst thing that could happen."[2]

Then came the revolution at the Council, the extent of which can be gauged from two statements of Karl Barth. In 1948, when the Catholic Church refused to join the World Council, the great Reformed theologian said with fierce irony: "The only attitude we can adopt toward Catholicism is one of mission and evangelization, not of union."[3] In 1963, however, shortly after the first session of the Council, he did not hesitate to write:

---

1. In 1960 Father R. Rouquette in a bulletin in *Etudes*; in the same year Bishop Charrière in instructions to his diocese; in 1960 Father Charles Boyer in Rome. See my article, "La prière pour l'unité de l'abbé Couturier," *Unité chrétienne*, 66 (May 1982) 21–22.
2. Marc Boegner, *The Long Road to Unity. Memories and Anticipations* (London, 1970), pp. 287–88.
3. Cited by H. Roux, *De la désunion vers la communion* (Paris, 1978), p. 199.

How would things look if Rome (without ceasing to be Rome) were one day simply to overtake us and place us in the shadows, so far as renewing the Church through the Word and Spirit of the Gospel is concerned? . . . It could very well be possible that we others might find more to learn from the Roman Church than the Roman Church for its part would have to learn from us.[4]

Starting at the top and joining countless currents at the base, a wave of ecumenism, the direction of whose flood waters could not be foreseen, began to sweep through the Church as undoubtedly one of the most powerful forces in the conciliar aggiornamento. Is it possible to say, a generation later, that the history of the two following decades lived up to the hopes felt at the outset?

It is a dangerous undertaking to pass judgment on a history that is still going on; it is even more risky to try to anticipate in a short sketch what a very lengthy and still unwritten study will some day have to say. Etienne Fouilloux needed a thousand pages and lengthy research to deal only with the past, and even then he restricted himself to the French-speaking European world![5]

The best I can hope to do, therefore, is to suggest a few tentative landmarks, while giving prominence in many cases to the French milieu. After recalling the outlines of the conciliar message on ecumenism with the superior insight a little distance has given us, I shall explore three linked phases that shed light on one another: the period immediately after the Council, the end of the first postconciliar decade, and, finally, the last years of the second decade.

What Kind of Ecumenism Did the Council Propose for the Church?

Even before rereading the decree I must emphasize the point that the Council in its entirety sent a strong ecumenical message. The presence of a hundred or so observers from about thirty Christian churches compelled the bishops to recognize the existence of the other churches and was itself an exemplary gesture. Several major dynamic ideas with vast resonances were launched as a result of a few very simple words or phrases that entered the collective consciousness of the Church either as negative norms ("triumphalism," with the contrasting image of a church that is poor and a servant) or, more often, as calls to action, for example, "signs of the times" (the Church lives within a history in which the Spirit always has something new in store) and aggiornamento (the necessity of evangelical renewal). Two fruitful ideas in particular made their way:

4. K. Barth, "Thoughts on the Second Vatican Council," *EcumRev*, 15 (1963) 364–65.
5. E. Fouilloux, *Les Catholiques et l'unité chrétienne du XIXe au XXe siècle. Itinéraires européens d'expression française* (Paris, 1982).

(1) the Church needed to be renewed in depth and, (2) it would be helped in this renewal by dialogue with the other Christian churches as they seek unity. Ecumenism stood at the crossroads where the two ideas met.

Document after document added details to the picture. Now, a generation later, the essential points stand out more clearly.

In the first session, a basic choice was made on November 20, 1962, when a preparatory draft that spoke of scripture and tradition as two distinct sources of revelation was rejected. There is but a single source, namely, scripture as read in the light of the Church's tradition. It has been suggested that the day this vote was taken was the symbolic end of the Counter-Reformation.[6]

In 1964 another important choice was made when the constitution on the Church brought structures up to date. The document speaks of the people of God before speaking of the hierarchy, and makes it clear that the Church sees itself as linked in a very close way with all the baptized of the other churches. It also makes this very important theological point: without at all denying its conviction that it is authentically the Church willed by Christ, the Catholic Church, after an important discussion and an important rejection, agrees through its bishops that in the concrete order it is not exclusively the Church willed by Christ.[7] In that same year the decree on ecumenism, with all the needed distinctions, stressed the values that exist in the various Christian churches. After centuries of an "all or nothing" theology, it was now possible to move beyond the idea of unity that had frustrated incipient ecumenism in the Church: the idea of unity as possible only through a "return."

Aggiornamento, attention to the signs of the times, distrust of triumphalism, the humble admission that the Church is not purely and simply coextensive with the mystery it expresses: all these discoveries were beads strung on a single theological thread. The end result was the admission in the decree *Unitatis redintegratio* (1964) of the need of a *continual reformation* "in moral conduct . . . in church discipline, . . . even in the way that church teaching has been formulated—to be carefully distinguished from the deposit of faith itself." The decree added that this renewal has notable ecumenical importance (§ 6).

6. See R. Rouquette's bulletin in *Etudes*, Jan. 1963, p. 104. Y. Congar has written that "it is to this action that Vatican II owes its greatest ecumenical influence" (in his *Le Concile Vatican II. Son Eglise, Peuple de Dieu et Corps du Christ* [Paris, 1984], p. 58).—The translation used here for the "Decree on Ecumenism" is from A. Flannery, ed., *Vatican II: The Conciliar and Postconciliar Documents* (Collegeville, 1975).

7. See LG 8 and the well-known substitution of *subsistit* for *est* in the Latin text. The Church that Christ willed is (authentically) found in the Catholic Church, but the Church as Body of Christ is not strictly coextensive with the Catholic Church. See Congar, *Concile*, p. 160: "There is no strict—that is, exclusive—identity between the Church as Body of Christ and the Catholic Church. At bottom Vatican II acknowledges that non-Catholic Christians are members of the Mystical Body and not simply *ordinati ad*, 'ordered to,' it." See the same thought in his *Essais oecuméniques. Les hommes, les mouvements, les idées* (Paris, 1984), pp. 215ff.

At the very end of the decree, a final behest deliberately emphasizes a point that crowns the whole and opens the way into the future:

This sacred council firmly hopes that the initiatives of the sons of the Catholic Church, joined with those of the separated brethren, will go forward, without obstructing the ways of divine Providence, and without prejudging the future inspirations of the Holy Spirit [§ 24].

Sufficient heed has not always been given to the final words of this passage. Not only does the Council solemnly sanction the entrance of the Catholic Church into the ecumenical movement and emphasize the needed effort at internal reform; it also anticipates that the Spirit will lead the Church into new situations. This vision is the framework within which we should locate the other novel elements in the decree: the nuanced judgments on the various churches; the remarks on the concrete practice of ecumenism; the encouragement given to joint prayer and action; the caution to be shown in *communicatio in sacris*; the advice on presenting doctrine as a "hierarchy of truths"; and so on.

The world of ecumenism immediately and instinctively grasped all of this. All that was left was to put it into practice.

The Period Immediately Following the Council: Ecumenism Set Free

The end of the Council brought a time of great ecumenical euphoria. In a memorable ceremony of farewell at St. Paul's outside the Walls, Pope Paul VI expressed his profound thanks to the observers for their help in the work of the Council and told them how saddened he was at their departure: "We have gotten to know you a little better. . . . We have recognized certain failings. . . . Our ecumenical council has taken steps in your direction in many ways. . . . We have begun to love each other once again." Finally, after reminding them that the Catholic Church is conscious of not having betrayed the deposit of faith but has found in it "treasures of truth and life . . . that it would be an infidelity to give up," he ended on a bold note: "Keep in mind that the truth rules over all of us and sets us free, and also that truth is close, very close, to love."[8]

The green light had been given. At every level, from the Secretariat for Christian Unity, which had been established in 1964 and given a place among the other Vatican commissions, to the least of the small groups meeting in the far corners of the world, which now felt confirmed in their mission, ecumenism had become one of the tasks of the Church.

Spontaneous refusals of the task were rare and came, quite naturally,

8. Paul VI, Address of Farewell to the Observers (Dec. 4, 1965), in *TPS*, 11 (1966) 36–40.

from those who rejected the Council in its entirety (for example, the movement started by Archbishop Lefebvre or the movement of Georges de Nantes with its revealing name "The Catholic Counter-Reformation of the Twentieth Century"). It can be said that the Catholic world as a whole quite readily accepted ecumenism as it did all the other "novelties" of the Council. As time went on, the level of consciousness and the degree of commitment varied widely from place to place. In the years immediately after the Council I had the opportunity of visiting a number of countries on different continents. Of course, there can be no question of categorizing these countries, but what a difference there was between the "calm" reigning in some countries and the drastic changes, excessive at times, in others! But let us look here at the broad scene between these two extremes.

Undertakings at the Top

At the highest levels of Church life exemplary initiatives and gestures came in rapid succession. Need I list them all?

In relation to the Orthodox churches there were the important meetings of Pope Paul VI and Patriarch Athenagoras I in Jerusalem in 1964 and in Istanbul and Rome in 1967. Meanwhile, in 1965, the two churches solemnly lifted the mutual excommunications of 1054.

There were also top-level meetings with Anglicans. Even before the Council Dr. Fisher, archbishop of Canterbury, had taken the first step by coming to Rome to meet with Pope John XXIII. In 1966, Dr. Ramsey, successor to Dr. Fisher, likewise came to Rome to visit Pope Paul VI, who put his fisherman's ring on the archbishop's finger as a symbolic acknowledgment of his episcopal ministry.

In 1969 Paul VI took advantage of a journey to Geneva to visit the World Council of Churches and hail it as a "marvelous movement of Christians."[9] But long before this visit a quasi-institutional collaboration between Rome and the World Council had already begun: as early as 1965 a Joint Working Group with members from the World Council and the Catholic Church had been established "to determine the principles that should govern collaboration and to establish the methods to be followed." In its second report (1967) the group reviewed all that had been accomplished in six areas: faith and worship (Week of Prayer, the theme of which would henceforth be decided in common), unity and mission (common witness, work with non-Christians), the laity and unity (many meetings and collaborative undertakings), service of humanity (especially for justice and peace), translation of the Bible (about a hundred projects!), and special problems (proselytism, mixed marriages, regional and national councils of Christians).

9. *DC*, July 6, 1969, p. 625.

The year 1968 saw three important undertakings. First, the joint establishment of a unique institution, responsibility for which was shared by
Rome and the World Council: the Joint Commission on Society, Development, and Peace (SODEPAX). The members were appointed for
three years and had the modest task of channeling information to the
two founding institutions. But as early as the first meeting of SODEPAX
at Beirut in the very year of its foundation the goal became more ambi-
tious: to make Christians aware of situations of injustice, to work for a
better world, and to motivate ecumenical groups to share in the quest
for a new society.[10]

At the same time that this link was established between Rome (represented by the Pontifical Commission for Justice and Peace) and Geneva
(Justice and Service), a new collaboration was begun between the Faith
and Order Commission of the World Council and the Roman Secretariat
for Christian Unity, inasmuch as Catholic theologians now became full
members of the commission. There would soon be about twelve of them
(a tenth of the entire membership) taking part in the work and attending
the important meetings; a Catholic would even become vice-president of
Faith and Order.

The same year, 1968, saw a third event that should be regarded as
even more important than the first two: Catholic participation in the
fourth assembly of the World Council at Uppsala. The Catholic Church
had not been present at Amsterdam in 1948 or Evanston in 1955; it had
made a timid appearance at New Delhi in 1961 in the person of five
observers. Now it came forward and stood frontstage, inasmuch as a
Jesuit, Roberto Tucci, was invited to give one of the main addresses. He
spoke only in his own name, but his appointment by the Secretariat for
Unity lent importance to his remarks. In fact, he asked the most crucial
question of all: If the Catholic Church, having engaged in many forms of
collaboration with the World Council, were to go a step further and ask
for membership, would it be accepted?[11] The question was exploratory
and looked to a still remote future, but it had a striking effect on opinion
within the Council.

At the top level of the Church giant steps had been taken. What was
going on meanwhile at other levels?

Undertakings at Other Levels

As I mentioned earlier, a wide variety of ecumenical activities was to
be seen at levels other than the topmost. A survey of the extent to which
the Week of Prayer for Unity had taken hold a few years after the Coun-

10. *Inf. Serv.* (Bulletin of the Secretariat for Christian Unity), 31 (1976) 15.
11. Tucci's address, "The Ecumenical Movement, the World Council of Churches and
the Roman Catholic Church," is in *The Uppsala Report 1958*, N. Goodall, ed. (Geneva,
1968), pp. 323–33.

cil will provide us with a reference point. In Europe, North America, and some Asian countries (Japan, for example) the celebration of the week was well organized and spreading. The spread was less visible in the developing countries (in South America, for example, or central and southern Africa), which had a different set of priorities.[12]

Let me take France as a concrete example. Here the ground had been prepared by the activity of pioneers (Mgr. Dumont, Abbé Couturier, Père Yves Congar, and others) and by the establishment of ecumenical centers ("Istina" in Paris, "Unité chrétienne" and "Saint-Irénée" in Lyons). Official institutions now came into existence: an episcopal commission and a permanent secretariat were established even before the end of the Council. They were supplemented by joint committees for dialogue (with Protestants in 1968, Anglicans in 1970, and the Orthodox in 1980; but regular meetings had already been held long before the committees were officially appointed). Most dioceses had a delegate for handling ecumenical matters, as required by the instruction *Ecclesia catholica* of 1949, and these delegates had been meeting every two years since the opening of the Council. Beginning in 1968 the national secretariat officially organized these meetings.

Meanwhile, the Instituts Catholiques of France had been setting up their ecumenical departments: the chair of ecumenism at Lyons as early as 1965; the Institute of Advanced Ecumenical Studies (ISEO) in Paris in 1968.

Young adults began gathering at Taizé under the banner of ecumenism, and many Catholics attended. In ecumenism as in other areas, the young, despite their seeming naivety, are like radar detectors of what is on the way. Their gathering at Taizé in 1966, where they were accompanied by people in authority from all the churches, was a remarkable event, and it set alarm bells ringing. Listen to what they had to say. The atmosphere of the meeting was evangelical, fraternal, and enthusiastic. After sharing the word, the young asked that they might share the Eucharist as well. The Catholic authorities and, even more, the Orthodox told them that such a gesture, which the churches regarded as premature at that stage of dividedness, was not possible. The young yielded but they also drew up a final statement expressing their disappointment and their hopes:

We are disturbed and disappointed at the prospect of an ecumenism which is becoming too institutional and losing its dynamic character of pressing on towards the unity which we already believe is not too far distant.

We are ready to accept the slow pace and the shortcomings of our Churches as we are their bold moves, but . . . we are waiting for their authorities to give real support to the efforts of youth to achieve visible unity. . . .

Bound together by a true communion and living a common prayer, we are distressed that we cannot share the bread of the Eucharist . . . and we are wait-

12. *Inf. Serv.*, 18 (1972) 13–20.

ing for the authorities of our Churches and their theologians to think again and give us a definite answer.[13]

At Taizé, as in many other places, the young have shown that they fully accept the Council's ecumenical statements, but they read them as calling for continual progress.

Another stimulus to ecumenism has come from couples in mixed marriages, who daily experience both the mystery of unity and the tragedy of separation, and whom the various churches are beginning to care for in a joint pastoral effort. A journal, *Foyers mixtes*, devoted entirely to them, was started in France in 1969.

To sum up: a few years after the Council the ecumenism that the Council called for was in full swing. Its antennae were out, and there was already a feeling of impatience. Would things settle down after all the initial bubbling?

Ten Years after the Council: Quickenings and Hesitations

Observers attempting to take stock of the situation ten years after the Council generally used contrasting terms to indicate that, on the one hand, progress had continued and even increased and that, on the other, questions had arisen and early problems had made their appearance. Mgr. Moeller spoke of "lights and shadows" at a plenary meeting of the Roman Secretariat in 1974. An international symposium in 1976 spoke of "expansion and impasse." It was as if there were some hesitation about maintaining the accelerated rhythm that had marked the beginnings. Because not everyone was prepared to follow? Because too many major problems remained unresolved? Did the Holy Spirit want the Church to keep to a steady cruising speed?

A symposium was held in Rome in November 1974, under the sponsorship of the Pontifical University of St. Anselm and the Institute for Ecumenical Study in Strasbourg (the latter established by the Lutheran World Federation). Its subject was the impact of the decree on ecumenism ten years later, and it provides a worthwhile point of reference.[14] Some fairly clear ideas emerge from the addresses and dialogues: the Council marked a "Copernican revolution" in relations between the Catholic Church and the other churches; there has been a profusion of undertakings (bilateral conversations, formation of spontaneous groups, and so on); some impasses were becoming visible; dialogue in-

13. Boegner, *Long Road*, p. 368 (except for the sentence "We are ready . . . our Churches, but," which I have translated from the author's original text).

14. See G. Békés and V. Vajta, *Unitatis redintegratio 1964–1974. The Impact of the Decree on Ecumenism* (Studia anselmiana 71; Rome, 1977).

duced each church to seek a better definition of its own identity; the establishment of new forms of communion aroused desire for a shared eucharistic communion; finally, a number of Christians deliberately set aside interest in ecumenical questions and devoted themselves instead to the problems of the world, and especially of the Third World.

One report also uses a new vocabulary, which I shall be emphasizing shortly: the vocabulary of conversion or *metanoia*. This had already cropped up here and there, being based on the exhortation of the conciliar decree to conversion of heart (§ 7). Here, however, it is given a new reference: it is applied no longer to individual conversion but to the transformation of the community, that is, to a renewal of structures that will meet the needs of our day and contribute more effectively to ecumenical progress.[15]

It can be said that ten years after the Council this symposium had a very clear insight into what was taking shape.

Let us therefore inquire in some detail into what was going on around 1975.

The Main Bilateral Conversations

The great novelty ten years after the Council was the emergence, one might almost say the proliferation, of bilateral conversations. At the risk of boring the reader I think it necessary to run through the impressive list. All of the churches are involved to some degree, but the Catholic Church is a participant in the majority of them.

The Dombes Group, which originated in the private initiative of Abbé Couturier and brings about forty Catholics and Protestants together each year in the first week of September, started in 1937 under the patronage of Cardinal Gerlier. It did its work in silence; the general public began to hear of it only in 1971 when it published an agreement on the Eucharist. This was followed in 1972 by points of agreement on the ministry and in 1976 by reflections and theses on the episcopal ministry.[16]

15. Ibid., p. 161.
16. On the Dombes Group, see the special issue of *Unité des chrétiens*, April 1974. The theses of the group are published by the Taizé Press and distributed by Editions du Seuil, Paris:
Vers une même foi eucharistique. Accord entre catholiques et protestants (1972). Engl. trans.: "Towards a Common Eucharistic Faith. Agreement between Roman Catholics and Protestants," in *Modern Eucharistic Agreement* (London, 1973), pp. 51–78.
Pour une réconciliation des ministères. Elements d'accord entre catholiques et protestants (1973). Engl. trans.: "Towards a Reconciliation of Ministries," in *Modern Ecumenical Documents of Ministry* (London, 1975), pp. 89–107.
Le ministère épiscopal. Réflexions et propositions sur le ministère de vigilance et d'unité dans l'Eglise particulière (1976).
A fourth document, *L'Esprit Saint, l'Eglise et les sacrements*, followed in 1979. The group's work is presently focused on the ministry of unity in the universal Church.

In this period, however, it was mainly "official" groups that produced statements. The establishment of a Joint Preparatory Commission of the Catholic Church and the Anglican Communion had been decided on in 1966 at the time of Archbishop Ramsey's visit to Rome. In 1970 this group developed into the "Anglican-Roman Catholic International Commission" (ARCIC). The first ARCIC statement appeared in 1971; it was known as the Windsor Statement and dealt with the Eucharist. A second document (the Canterbury Statement) on ministry and ordination followed in 1973; a third (the Venice Statement) on authority in the Church appeared in 1976.[17]

A similar and likewise very fruitful dialogue was begun with the Lutheran World Federation in 1967. It led in 1972 to the Malta Report on the Gospel and the Church; in 1978 a final report on the Eucharist; and in 1981 a report on ministry in the Church.[18] In the area of Catholic-Lutheran dialogue mention must also be made of the very extensive conversations held between the two churches in the United States.[19]

A group bringing together representatives of the Secretariat for Christian Unity and the World Alliance of Reformed Churches was established in 1970. In 1977 it published a report, "The Presence of Christ in Church and World."[20]

A very intense dialogue with the Orthodox churches was inaugurated by Pope Paul VI and Patriarch Athenagoras I in 1964, as I noted earlier. In 1975 there was an agreement in principle that a real theological dialogue should take place, and in 1979 a joint commission was established. In 1982 the commission published a document, the Munich report, "The Mystery of the Church and of the Eucharist in the Light of the Mystery of the Holy Trinity."[21]

17. The whole set of documents, including a second Windsor Statement of 1981, was published as a "Final Report" of this first commission. It may be found in H. Meyer and L. Vischer, eds., *Growth in Agreement. Reports and Agreed Statements of Ecumenical Conversations on a World Level* (Ecumenical Documents 2; New York/Ramsay, N.J., 1984), pp. 61–129.

18. *Growth in Agreement*, pp. 167–275. Meanwhile, in 1980, the joint commission published *Ways to Community*, which emphasized the necessary stages and the means of achieving them.

19. The successive documents produced by these conversations (and published by Augsburg Publishing House in Minneapolis) are: I. *Status of the Nicene Creed as Dogma of the Church* (1965); II. *One Baptism for the Remission of Sins* (1966); III. *The Eucharist as Sacrifice* (1967); IV. *Eucharist and Ministry* (1970); V. *Papal Primacy and the Universal Church* (1974); VI. *Teaching Authority and the Infallibility of the Church* (1978); VII. *Justification by Faith* (1981); VIII. *Mary and the Saints* (1984).

20. *Growth in Agreement*, pp. 433–63.

21. *Inf. Serv.*, 48 (1982) 12–29. The documents exchanged between Rome (John XXIII, Paul VI) and Constantinople (Patriarch Athenagoras I) from 1958 to 1970 were published in *Tomos Agapis. Vatican-Phanar* (Rome/Istanbul, 1971). For Paul VI and Athenagoras, see T. F. Stransky and J. B. Sheerin, eds., *Doing the Truth in Charity. Statements of Pope Paul VI, Popes John Paul I, John Paul II, and the Secretariat for Promoting Christian Unity, 1964–1980* (Ecumenical Documents 1; New York/Ramsay, N.J., 1982), pp. 178–97.

The Catholic Church has begun conversations with other churches as well: with the World Methodist Council in 1966, with some Pentecostal churches in 1971, and with the Evangelicals (Disciples of Christ) in 1977.[22] These have not yet produced statements of major importance.

The Catholic Church and the World Council of Churches

In 1975, the year I have taken as my point of reference, dialogue with the World Council of Churches was intensifying. The report of the Joint Working Group emphasized three priorities: church unity (with the collaboration of Faith and Order), common witness (dialogue on this subject had led to a 1970 study entitled "Common Witness and Proselytism" and would lead to another, "Common Witness," in 1981[23]), and, finally, collaboration on social issues (the area on which SODEPAX concentrated its efforts).

The World Council's fifth assembly at Nairobi also took place in 1975. This time the Catholic Church was represented by sixteen observers. At the end of an address on the theme of unity as found in the Orthodox conception of "conciliar fellowship," Father Cyrille Argenti offered the gathering a grandiose vision of the future:

May I express the wish, or rather the prayer, that through the participation in the World Council by all the Christian Churches (in particular by the very ancient and venerable Church of Rome, our elder sister, and all the holy churches in communion with her) . . . if not the 5th or 6th Assembly of the World Council of Churches, then at least the Nth Assembly will be recognized by the whole Christian people as the 8th Ecumenical Council of the One, Holy, Catholic, and Apostolic Church of Christ.[24]

Under the influence of this vision, a motion of the assembly on the "desirability" of the entry of the Catholic Church into the World Council was revised to say that the assembly "impatiently awaits" this entry. The motion passed unanimously. Mgr. Moeller, undersecretary of the Roman Secretariat, took the platform to say in an emotional speech how deeply moved he was by this unanimous vote. Was this indirect answer to the question Father Tucci had asked at Uppsala, seven years earlier, a sign that the Catholic Church would soon become a member of the World Council? Some began to think so.

---

22. For the documents produced by these three conversations, see *Growth in Agreement*, pp. 307–87, 421–31, and 153–66, respectively. On all the conversations and agreements down to 1982, see J.-E. Dessaux, *Dialogues théologiques et accords oecuméniques* (Paris, 1982).

23. *Inf. Serv.*, 14 (1971) 18–23, and *Diakonia*, 18 (1983) 278–94, respectively.

24. Cyrille Argenti, "Christian Unity," *EcumRev*, 28 (1976) 34.

In the Dioceses

Still in 1975, a Roman document remarkable for its openness was issued on ecumenical collaboration at the local level. It served to link the Roman center with the Church at the grassroots level throughout the five continents. Far from being a restrictive warning, it gave approval to a new phenomenon, "councils of churches" and "Christian councils." These are local institutions embracing a country or a whole region, under the egis of the authorities of the churches involved. They seek to engender agreement on collaborative efforts and even on concerted pastoral action. The Catholic Church approved these new forms of ecumenical progress, which were then beginning to appear in nineteen countries.[25]

In 1975 a Catholic Synod for the whole of Switzerland, using a seemingly very negative formulation, but one that in fact opened up new perspectives, allowed that a Catholic who in specific and exceptional circumstances receives communion at a Protestant Lord's Supper is not thereby excluded from Catholic communion.[26]

All things considered, ecumenism was spreading and consolidating, and it seemed permissible to entertain great hopes for it.

A few indications of what was going on in France will show how the latter was in tune with the worldwide situation.

In 1972, after long thought and much consultation, Bishop Elchinger of Strasbourg, a diocese in which Catholic-Protestant mixed marriages are very numerous, published a ruling that admitted the possibility, in well-defined circumstances, of even reciprocal eucharistic hospitality.[27]

In 1974 the biennial meeting of ecumenical leaders, held that year for the first time in the great conference hall at Chantilly, became interconfessional. All the Catholic diocesan delegates met for four days with their Protestant counterparts and with leaders from the Orthodox and Anglican churches.[28]

In 1975 the Joint Catholic-Protestant Commission issued a statement, "The Ecumenical Celebration of Baptism," which quickly became the standard reference on the subject.[29]

25. "Ecumenical Collaboration at the Regional, National and Local Levels" (Feb. 22, 1975), in Stransky and Sheerin, *Doing the Truth*, pp. 89–114. The nineteen countries were: Denmark, Sweden, The Netherlands, Switzerland, Belize (British Honduras), Samoa, Fiji, New Hebrides, Solomon Islands, Papua–New Guinea, Tonga, West Germany, Botswana, St. Vincent (British Antilles), Sudan, Uganda, Finland, Guyana, Trinidad and Tobago.

26. *DC*, June 1, 1975. The next year the German synod held at Würzburg took a similar line: "Because unity in faith is still lacking, the synod cannot presently approve a Catholic's taking part in the Lord's Supper. It is not impossible, however, that Catholics following their own conscience may find in their particular situation reasons that make their participation in the Lord's Supper spiritually necessary" (*Gemeinsame Synode der Bistümer in der Bundesrepublik Deutschland. Offizielle Gesamtausgabe* 1 [Freiburg, 1976], pp. 214–15).

27. *DC*, Feb. 18, 1973.

28. See *Unité des chrétiens*, July 1974.

29. *DC*, April 6, 1975.

In 1978, at the annual meeting of the French episcopacy, held in Lourdes that year, the bishops spent an afternoon and the following morning discussing ecumenical pastoral care.[30]

Given this very positive overall picture, what hesitations could have been felt?

Hesitations

In his report to the plenary session of the Secretariat for Christian Unity in 1974, Mgr. Moeller had mentioned certain "gloomy points" before going to speak of "brighter" ones. He said that in his opinion it was legitimate to talk of "a slowing down," a "standstill," and a gap between two extremes: on the one side, an "official" ecumenism that seemed "too slow," "too congealed," and, on the other, at the grass roots, currents that seemed to be "running wild." He made his own a thought of Dr. Visser t'Hooft: the central problem was to "put together again these two aspects of ecumenism: the official one and the grassroots one."[31]

Tensions were felt in two areas especially: pastoral care of mixed marriages, and calls for eucharistic hospitality. With regard to mixed marriages, a directory for applying the decree on ecumenism recalled the openings made at the Council, but it also emphasized restrictions. A non-Catholic marriage partner may no longer have to sign a "guarantee" as to the baptism and Catholic upbringing of the couple's children (this was the happy effect of the conciliar "Declaration on Religious Freedom"), but the Catholic partner must promise to do "what he or she can" to achieve the same result.[32] At the same time, § 55 of the directory takes a very firm stand on what the conciliar decree says about *communicatio in sacris* (§ 8). A series of Roman documents repeat the same point.[33]

The Church at large responded in divergent ways to these rules. In some dioceses there was hardly any problem. I am thinking of one country in far-off Asia where a Catholic bishop, on the one side, and the neighboring Protestant leader, on the other, told me in similar terms, a

30. See *Unité des chrétiens*, April 1979.

31. *Inf. Serv.*, 23 (1974) 6–13.

32. See, however, the excellent way in which the bishops of France reconciled this provison with freedom of conscience in their 1970 statement: "We know that the promise required of the Catholic partner in our marriage—namely, that he or she 'do all that depends on them to see to it that the children are baptized and raised in the Catholic Church'—must be carried out in the concrete circumstances of our family. This means that, in sincere dialogue and with respect for the reasons and religious convictions of each of us, we must jointly come to a decision that we can both accept in conscience" (*DC*, Dec. 20, 1970, p. 1131).

33. Clarification from the Secretariat (*DC*, Sept. 15, 1968); Note from the Secretariat (*DC*, Nov. 3, 1968); Declaration of the Secretariat (*DC*, Feb. 1, 1970); Instruction of the Secretariat (*DC*, Aug. 6–20, 1972); Note from the Secretariat (*DC*, Dec. 2, 1973).

few days apart, that mixed marriages were not a problem for them, because there were no mixed marriages. Tradition decreed that when an engaged couple belonged to different churches, they should agree on the one in which they would live their Christian lives together (with the less convinced partner yielding to the other). In other places, however, where dialogue and fellowship among Catholics and Protestants were quite advanced, these reminders were keenly felt and resented. Some individuals engaged in "wildcat" gestures, others became very angry, and leaders who wanted to remain in contact with their people found themselves in a bind.

In addition, unusual acts of eucharistic receptivity to Protestants disturbed the Orthodox Church, for in its view eucharistic sharing is not to be thought of except among members of the same Church.

One last shadow: the possibility of Catholic membership in the World Council seemed to be growing more remote after the hopeful period between Uppsala and Nairobi.

Did all this mean the beginning of a retreat? By no means. In 1978 the new pope, John Paul II, immediately said that the entry of the Catholic Church into the ecumenical movement could not be reversed and that the Church must bring to completion what it had undertaken. And had not Paul VI said at the end of his pontificate that ecumenism was the most mysterious and important undertaking of his papal ministry?[34]

Twenty Years after the Council: A New Age of Ecumenism

It is always rash to describe one's own times as a "new age." Yet Cardinal Willebrands did not hesitate to make that very idea the theme of an address in which he described the present years as a new critical moment in the ecumenical movement and as "a transition towards a stage of decision."[35]

Before asking what precisely this new age holds for us, let us first continue to observe the progress of ecumenism.

The Ecumenical Wave

To the attentive eye each year brings a multitude of small steps at every level, all of them moving in the same direction. I can only give some examples of this trend.

34. DC, Feb. 6, 1977, p. 141.
35. Cardinal Willebrands, "Called to Unity and Wholeness," Communio, 10 (1983) 117–18 (address at a conference in Baltimore).

Nothing was said of ecumenism in the 1917 Code of Canon Law. It does make an appearance, however, in the new code of 1983: "It is within the special competence of the entire college of bishops and of the Apostolic See to promote and direct the participation of Catholics in the ecumenical movement" (canon 755, § 1).

The International Eucharistic Congress held at Lourdes in 1981 continued an aggiornamento begun at previous congresses and showed great concern for its ecumenical impact. The theological statement that served as a basis for the celebration expounded a doctrine of the Eucharist that drew upon the best ecumenical advances in this area and in particular upon the agreement reached by the Dombes Group ten years before.[36] One entire day at the congress was taken up with a round table (the participants including couples in mixed marriages and Protestant pastors),[37] an ecumenical celebration in the vast underground basilica (with participation of Orthodox, Protestants, and Anglicans), and an address by Cardinal Willebrands.

Several days earlier, a symposium at Toulouse, "Responsibility, Sharing, Eucharist," had included Protestants from the various churches as full participants.[38]

At Pentecost 1982, the charismatic renewal celebrated a large-scale congress in Strasbourg; some twenty thousand Christians from the various churches and from twenty-four different countries participated. The event showed, as does an analysis of the charismatic base groups, that renewal provides one of the new venues of ecumenical encounter.

In 1983 the Sixth Assembly of the World Council at Vancouver saw a hitherto unmatched number of Catholics in attendance: observers, hosts, guests, experts, accredited visitors. Some months later the "official report" appeared with the signatures of a Protestant pastor and a Catholic priest.[39]

In 1984, an Ecumenism Pavilion was opened at Lourdes, the great center of international pilgrimage with its four million visitors annually. The purpose of the pavilion is "to offer pilgrims desiring it the opportunity of continuing their pilgrimage, in the direction set out in the Lourdes message on conversion to the demands of the Gospel, by reflecting on the problem of the disunity and unity of the separated churches."[40]

How many more particulars might be added to these symbolic glean-

36. Jésus-Christ, pain rompu pour un monde nouveau (Paris, 1980).

37. See "Eucharistie et oecuménisme," in Un peuple qui parle. Les tables rondes du 42ᵉ Congrès eucharistique international (Paris, 1982), pp. 147–70.

38. On the Lourdes congress and the Toulouse symposium, see the special issue of DC, Aug. 9, 1981.

39. Rassemblés pour la vie (Rapport officiel de la sixième assemblée du Conseil Oecuménique des Eglises), J.-M. Chappuis and R. Beaupère, eds. (Geneva and Paris, 1984).

40. Unité des chrétiens, July 1984, p. 30.

ings?[41] I would have to speak, for example, of the ecumenical dimension of meetings of young people in which many Catholics are always present; such gatherings continue at Taizé and are proliferating throughout the world. Or of the ecumenical impulse that animates the Focolari Movement. I would have to mention the ecumenical openness of monasteries and abbeys, and their irreplaceable contribution to the spiritual side of unity. I would have to call attention to the ecumenical centers being established in all countries.[42] The Centre Saint-Irénée in Lyons, for example, plays an important role in the participation of the Catholic Church in the pastoral care of mixed marriages[43] and in ecumenical journeys throughout the world (sponsored by CLEO: Culture, Loisirs et Oecuménisme).

As water slowly makes its way into the soil, so ecumenism is at last infiltrating the entire Church, either visibly or in secret.

Let me offer two proofs. First, a survey. In 1981–82 the Center for Ecumenical Studies in Strasbourg conducted a worldwide survey on ecumenism at the local level. The survey led to two conferences, one in Strasbourg (1981), the other in Indonesia (1982). The final report inevitably emphasized the diversity of situations throughout the world and took note of the slow rate of progress. On the other hand, it is remarkable that the survey shows no difference between the attitude of Catholics and that of Christians from the other churches. The Catholic Church has been the most recent to enter fully into the ecumenical scene, but it has made up for its late start. The survey also mentions a latent ecumenism that is ready to show itself in response to the slightest appeal; the coming of a zealous priest or pastor makes it emerge as though by magic in places where previously there seemed to be nothing at all. There is also evidence that some of the resistance to ecumenism is due simply to the fear of change. New towns and cities, unaffected by the difficulty that very stable societies have in changing, are the easiest places in which to promote an ecumenical consciousness.[44]

My other proof will bring a smile to more than one reader, but I do not regard it as irrelevant. Books on the recent appearances of the Blessed Virgin at Medjugorje in Yugoslavia mention statements she has made that encourage ecumenism.[45] This is certainly something quite novel in reports of this kind. Without anticipating the judgment of the Church on the appearances, let me construct a very simple argument. Either the message is really a message from heaven; if so, ecumenism has received

41. Many details are given in the Jan. 1982 issue of *Unité des chrétiens*, which is devoted to "L'oecuménisme à la base."

42. See "An International Directory of Ecumenical Research and Publications," in *Bulletin du Centre Romain "Centro pro Unione"*, 20 (1982), with additions in no. 24 (1983).

43. See the periodical *Foyers mixtes*, which is written by and for couples in mixed marriages.

44. "L'oecuménisme au plan local," in *Positions luthériennes*, Jan.-March 1983.

45. E.g., R. Laurentin and L. Rupcic, *La Vierge apparaît-elle à Medjugorje?* (Paris, 1984), p. 136.

its best possible encouragement. Or the appearances are simply a projection of the psyche of sensitive, fervent children; if so, they vividly illustrate the extent to which ecumenical concern has now imbedded itself in the collective consciousness of the Christian people, so that the young visionaries breathe it as they do the air around them.

Bilateral and Multilateral Dialogues

It has been estimated that in the 1980s the Catholic Church is a participant in about sixty bilateral conversations out of the hundred or so in which the various churches are involved at the international or national level.

I shall not repeat what I said earlier about the range of conversations that are continuing and expanding.[46] I do, however, wish to call attention to two of them that have reached an especially advanced stage: the conversations with the Anglican communion and with the Lutheran World Federation.

Progress in relationships between the Catholic Church and the Anglican communion has been exemplary. What a distance we have traveled since the first chance encounter, unnoticed at the time, of Lord Halifax and Abbé Portal in 1889–90 and their attempt at dialogue on which they were quickly brought to their senses! Thirty years later, in 1921–25, the Malines conversations kindled new hopes, but the resultant report on the idea of "the Anglican Church united not absorbed," which had dominated the dialogue, was for practical purposes rejected. Yet in 1977, when Pope Paul VI welcomed Dr. Coggan, the archbishop of Canterbury, he accepted the very formula that was once rejected: "These words of hope, 'the Anglican Church united not absorbed,' are no longer a mere dream."[47]

In 1981, after ARCIC had studied the Eucharist, the ordained ministry, and authority in the Church, it was able to claim in its final report that there was "substantial agreement" on points that had previously divided the two churches. The last page of the report shows an awareness of the difficulties that must still be overcome, but it also puts its finger on the level where further progress will be made: theological dialogue must now be prolonged by everyday life and must yield place to practical initiatives (the reference seems to be to the authorities of the two churches) and to a more visible experience of communion.[48]

46. In the dialogue with the Orthodox, the meetings in Patmos and Rhodes in 1980 and at Munich in 1982 were followed by one in Crete in 1984. Conversations with the World Alliance of Reformed Churches slackened somewhat, but a new meeting took place in January 1984. Finally, there was a first meeting with the Baptist churches in Berlin in July 1984 (see *Inf. Serv.*, 55 [1984] 67–68. A third meeting between Catholics and Evangelicals took place at the Abbey of Landevennec in France.

47. *Doing the Truth in Charity*, p. 262.

48. *Growth in Agreement*, pp. 62 and 129.

In the following year the dialogue entered a new phase when Pope John Paul II visited the Archbishop of Canterbury. From the statements made by both parties to the conscious symbolism of gestures and celebrations (the Canterbury book of the gospels placed at the center of the cathedral choir; the bishop of Rome and the bishop of Canterbury praying side by side on the spot where Thomas Becket was murdered for his faith; shared proclamation of the baptismal creed; etc.) and the final statement—everything converged to yield a single meaning.

In their final joint statement the two bishops established a new international commission that would try to resolve the major difficulties still remaining and would recommend the practical measures needed for eventually restoring full communion. They said that in the progress made and the difficulties encountered they saw "a renewed challenge to abandon ourselves completely to the truth of the Gospel."[49]

An intense theological dialogue with the Lutheran churches is likewise continuing. The joint study commission met in Rome from February 27 to March 3, 1984, for what was the tenth and last in the series of meetings begun in 1973. There was mutual agreement that dialogue should continue in a third series of meetings. Most importantly, the atmosphere that permeates this theological dialogue is one of rapprochement to which the Catholic Church has committed itself in a spectacular way. John XXIII struck the right note in 1959 when he said: "We shall not put history on trial . . . we all share responsibility."[50] In 1970 Cardinal Willebrands addressed the Lutheran World Federation at Evian and could say that Catholics had not always had a proper appreciation of Martin Luther and had not always correctly explained his theology. As a result, neither truth nor love had been properly served. He took as an example the question of justification, which had been Luther's main concern, and said that on this subject Luther could serve as "our common teacher."[51]

In 1980 came the 450th anniversary of the Augsburg Confession, which became the confession of faith of the Lutheran churches after it had failed to serve its original purpose of being a document all Christians could accept as a basic statement of common faith. A new edition of the text was published in France with an afterword from Bishop Le Bourgeois, then president of the episcopal commission for Christian unity. The bishop spoke of the suggestion that the Catholic Church recognize the Augsburg Confession, and gave the reasons why this seemed unfeasible; he went on, however, to propose a common reading of the text.[52]

49. "Common Declaration of Pope John Paul II and the Archbishop of Canterbury" (Canterbury, May 29, 1982), in One in Christ, 18 (1982) 261.
50. John XXIII, "Address to the Parish Priests of Rome"; see Daniel-Rops, "Ces Chrétiens nos frères," in his L'Eglise des Révolutions (Paris, 1965) 3:703.
51. Cardinal Willebrands, "Sent into the World," Lutheran World, 17 (1970) 341–53.
52. La Confession d'Augsbourg (Paris and Geneva, 1979), pp. 135–36.

Still another anniversary came in 1983, the 500th anniversary of Luther's birth. This occasion, and a number of Catholic books whose publication and wide circulation was an event in its own right, provided many Catholics with an opportunity for a fresh look at the father of the Reformation.[53] A statement, "Martin Luther—Witness to Jesus Christ," by the Joint Roman Catholic–Lutheran Commission acknowledged, on the one hand, that Luther's message had been somewhat oversimplified and distorted in the Lutheran tradition and, on the other, that Vatican II had met the main challenges of the reformer.[54]

In a letter in *Semaine religieuse* of Marseilles, Cardinal Etchegaray, new president of the episcopal commission for Christian unity, placed the event in its proper perspective. He wrote in his usual lively style: "Luther has been celebrated as much by Catholics as by Protestants. Pope Leo X, Cajetan, and many others must be turning over in their graves as though the Church had reversed its course!" He said that Luther had unfortunately "thrown away inalienable treasures of the undivided Church," but he did not hesitate to preface this remark with another: "Luther was a Christian straight out of the gospel. His purpose was to have the Church return to the only struggle that is truly its own: to make God's word transparent to a church that is loaded down with excess baggage."[55]

Some weeks later, Pope John Paul took a new step forward by visiting a Lutheran church in Rome.[56]

Are we not moving toward a possible extension of the term "sister churches," which is currently applied to Catholics and Orthodox? Pope Paul VI had already used it of the Anglican Church.[57] Father Congar has asked whether it could not be extended to the Lutheran churches as well.[58]

Bilateral conversations might have a negative effect by suggesting that a narrow approach to dialogue is being taken. This is offset, however, by the existence of many multilateral conversations promoted by Faith and Order. The Catholic Church, as we have seen, has been an active partner in them since 1968.

53. In 1983 alone the following appeared in France: Y. Congar, *Martin Luther, sa foi, sa reforme*; the French translation of P. Manns, *Martin Luther. An Illustrated Biography* (New York, 1982); J. Delumeau, *Le cas Luther; Luther aujourd'hui*, H.-R. Boudin and A. Houssiau, eds. (= *Cahiers de le Revue théologique de Louvain*, 11). See also the "Dossier Luther" in *Unité des chrétiens*, Oct. 1983, and in *Unité chrétienne*, Nov. 1983.

54. "Martin Luther—Witness to Jesus Christ," *One in Christ*, 19 (1983) 291–97.

55. *Eglise à Marseille*, Nov. 6, 1983.

56. *Inf. Serv.*, 52 (1973); the pope's homily is on pp. 94–95. The Lutherans realized the importance of this event; Eduard Lohse, speaking for the Evangelical Church of Germany, wrote that the visit was one of the high points of the anniversary year (*SOEPI*, April 6, 1984, p. 14).

57. Paul VI, "Address at the Canonization of the Forty English Martyrs," in *Doing the Truth in Charity*, pp. 257–58.

58. See Y. Congar, *Diversity and Communion* (Mystic, Conn., 1985), pp. 91–92.

An important step was taken in 1982 in the Lima report, "Baptism, Eucharist, Ministry" *(BEM)*, published by the Commission on Faith and Order of the World Council of Churches.[59]

This document is a statement not of agreement but of convergence. It is evidence of a new attitude at work in an ongoing effort at reunion, which, as the report notes, is unparalleled in Christian history. The text is now offered for "reception" by the churches, that is, for their careful study to determine whether in their judgment it correctly expresses the faith of the apostolic Church. But the document also has an ecumenical purpose: the churches are asked whether consideration of the differences and even contradictions between the theologies and practices of the various churches (differences very openly set forth in the text) may not be for each church the occasion for self-criticism and a salutary examination of conscience.

The Catholic Church is giving serious consideration to the request, in the formulation of which theologians appointed by it played a part, and is officially consulting all the episcopal conferences before giving its answer at the appointed time (which was extended to the end of 1985). Studies have begun to appear in which Catholics express their views on aspects of the *metanoia* to which *BEM* urges their Church. Has anything like this ever been seen before?

At this point, I must hasten to add that not everything has yet been said about the general situation. The facts I have set down are beyond any doubt by far the most important ones; there are others, however, which must also be made known.

Tensions and Intransigence

When we turn to relationships between the Catholic Church and the World Council of Churches, we cannot but note a lessening of the hope that the Catholic Church would soon become a member of the Council. It was clear at the Vancouver Assembly that the hope was weakening.[60] Furthermore, SODEPAX, which had seemed so promising an agency for collaboration, came to an end in 1980, a year before the appointed term of its third mandated period. The impression given was of a failure for which the establishment of a joint commission for consultation on social

59. Commission on Faith and Order, *Baptism, Eucharist, Ministry* (Lima, Peru, 1982), in *Growth in Agreement*, pp. 465–503.

60. See the letter of Philip Potter to Cardinal Willebrands in which he says he knows this attitude does not fully reflect the wishes of the World Council. He insists that there is rather a desire for increased collaboration and that in fact "simple collaboration" is an inadequate description of the relationships of "fraternal solidarity" that are in place (*DC*, Jan. 15, 1984, p. 103). In *Lumière et Vie*, no. 162, which is entirely devoted to the World Council, see the remarks of René Beaupère who urges the entry of the Catholic Church into the Council, and the viewpoint expressed by Pastor Conrad Reiser.

thought and action was but a poor compensation.[61] Very plausible explanations were given (the organization had been simply experimental;
reservations had not been unilateral; there were difficulties resulting
from factors on both sides), yet ecumenical circles could not but feel a
certain disenchantment. Was this not the first seeming setback on a journey that had hitherto been smooth? But we must not overdramatize the
event.

More important is talk of blockages in the conversations. Take the
concrete case of dialogue with the Anglican communion. "Elucidations"
published in 1979 and 1981 to justify positions taken in the earlier
ARCIC statements had already shown that further progress would be
difficult. When the final report, which brought together all the agreed
statements (including the most recent one on authority), was published
after twelve years of work, Cardinal Ratzinger, the new prefect of the
Congregation for the Doctrine of the Faith, sent a letter to the Catholic
episcopal conferences, together with observations of the congregation
on the text of the final report; these were offered as the congregation's
contribution to the ongoing dialogue.[62] This last statement was susceptible of divergent interpretations. The most optimistic reading of it was
that this was an entirely new way of proceeding in which two Roman
agencies were combining their charisms (vigilance in the case of the congregation; initiative and dialogue in the case of the Secretariat for Christian Unity) and also broadening the base of their study through collegial
dialogue with the episcopal conferences. Another, more wary, reading
found reason to be alarmed at certain positions taken (for example, the
denial that "substantial agreement" had been reached) and at the overall
tone, which seemed to suggest a definitive judgment rather than participation in a dialogue.

It is of interest, however, to see how the situation developed. A year
after the publication (March 1982) of the final report and the congregation's observations, Cardinal Ratzinger, writing in his own name, published an article on the Anglican-Catholic dialogue in an English ecumenical journal; two months later, two Catholic members of ARCIC
replied.[63] A careful reading of the three articles shows where the crux of
the difficulty is located and what a laborious journey will be required to
advance further.

The cardinal puts his finger on real difficulties (especially the different
structure of authority in the two churches; the connection between

61. See the explanations given in the report of the Joint Working Group of the Catholic
Church and the World Council, which is included in the official report of the sixth assembly: *Rassemblés pour la vie*, 39, pp. 166–69.
62. Congregation for the Doctrine of the Faith, "Some Observations on the Final Report of the Anglican–Roman Catholic International Commission," *TPS*, 27 (1982) 257–67.
63. Cardinal Ratzinger in *Insight*, 1 (March 1983) 2–11; Edward Yarnold, S.J., a little later in the same journal; and Jean Tillard, "Dialogue with Cardinal Ratzinger. (1) Tradition
and Authority," and "(2) Christian Communion," in *The Tablet*, Jan. 7 and 14, 1984, 15–17
and 39–40. French translation of all three in *DC*, Sept. 2, 1984.

scripture and tradition; the relationship between the universal Church and local churches), but he also insists that the declaration issued by his congregation be read as positive in character. He stresses the point that in ARCIC we see a maturation of theological thought after ten years of work: "Recourse to scripture and tradition has brought to light the common foundations of diverging confessional developments and so opened up that perspective in which apparently irreconcilable elements can be fused together into the wholeness of the one truth." This he calls the "hermeneutics of unity."

The authors of the two responses carry on the dialogue in the same calm tone as they clear up what they regard as misunderstandings perhaps caused by the exceptional conciseness of the ARCIC statements. One of them reminds us that the hermeneutical method for dealing with unity urges a distinction between the essential truth of a doctrine and the historically conditioned form in which the truth has been defined. This hermeneutics of unity, he says, "will lead us to read the statements of each side in the context of an entire tradition and with a deeper understanding of scripture." In a divided Christendom threatened by unilateralism and imbalance, this means (he continues) that "the hermeneutics of unity will have to take into account the statements of the faith of the other churches in order to discern the essential truth in a teaching of a given church." Divergent formulas may well complement each other: "Neither of the two churches has to surrender its tradition; each must share the insights of the other."

Polemics are not entirely absent from the three articles, but the tone is nonetheless new. It seems that the major underlying problem is the historicity of the Church, which was one of the Council's great insights. The theological outlook inherited from an inferior kind of Scholasticism spontaneously rejects the idea of historicity in this context because it confuses it with doctrinal liberalism.[64] Cardinal Ratzinger allows historicity its place. But the whole idea is so new that general acceptance of it will come only very slowly. Meanwhile, dialogue between those who accept it and those who do not is necessarily a dialogue of the deaf.

It must also be said that two types of minds are in conflict in all the churches and that intransigence and cries of alarm have made their

64. This "historicity," which if accepted can play a very important role in ecumenism, was emphasized (the more notably for being so unexpected) in a passage of the declaration *Mysterium Ecclesiae*, which the Congregation for the Doctrine of the Faith issued on June 24, 1973. The purpose of the declaration was to "explain a number of truths concerning the mystery of the Church which are at present being either denied or endangered." Four consequences of the "historical condition" of revelation are listed: dependence on semantic variations; incompleteness of expression, calling for subsequent improvements; limitation of the scope of statements to the extent that they are responses to questions or to errors; use of changeable conceptions of a given era. Conclusion: "It can sometimes happen that these truths may be enunciated by the sacred magisterium in terms that bear traces of such conceptions." The declaration is in *TPS*, 18 (1973–74) 145–57.

appearance among all the dialoguing partners, leading to all kinds of interaction.

Many of our Orthodox brethren agree that our churches are sister churches and nothing fundamental is keeping them from unity. Yet, even among the Orthodox, voices are raised in opposition to ecumenism. At a conference in 1980 the metropolitan of Patras rejected "dialogue of love" as equivocal and reminded his flock that Orthodox law prohibits them from joining in prayer with the heterodox.[65] The holy monks of Mount Athos use the same language.[66]

In the churches of the Reformation progress in dialogue has likewise elicited warnings. The publication of the Lima report (BEM) has at times met with distrust. The journal of the theological faculty at Montpellier devoted a series of articles to it, with such titles as: "Non possumus . . .," "Compromises and Ambiguities," "Uneasiness and Rejection."[67] At times the Catholic Church is even suspected of secretly intending to use ecumenism to consolidate its own power.[68]

But in many cases sudden changes of direction and retreats into an inherited identity occur within a commitment to dialogue that is too long-standing and deep to be reversed. Relationships between the Catholic Church and the Reformed churches in France are a good illustration of this truth. On the one hand, there are signs of new difficulties, and warnings are heard; on the other, the agencies for encounter at all levels that were patiently established years ago, the prayer groups, dia-

---

65. Address of Metropolitan Nikodemos of Patras, "Les conditions nécessaires du dialogue entre l'Eglise orthodoxe d'Orient et l'Eglise d'Occident," DC, Nov. 1, 1981, p. 991, note 3. It is to be noted, however, that at the end of this text in its Greek form (in Ekklesia, Jan. 1 and Feb. 1, 1981) there is a note summarizing a number of very positive remarks made by Metropolitan Damaskinos of Tranoupolis. The latter's views are expressed in an address, "L'unité dans la diversité: Le point de vue orthodoxe," DC, May 2, 1982; far from condemning common prayer, he goes so far as to ask whether we have the right to refuse communion to each other!

66. See, for example, the interview given by a delegation from the Holy Mountain and, in particular, their answer to a question about ecumenical dialogue with the Catholic Church, in Episkepsis, Dec. 15, 1981, pp. 10f. To this should be added the corrective commentaries of Orthodox believers living in the West and participating in the dialogue—Father Boris Bobrinksoy and Madame Elisabeth Behr-Sigel—which appeared in Service Orthodoxe de Presse for March 1982. When Metropolitan Damaskinos was enthroned at Zurich on Nov. 21, 1982, as the first Orthodox metropolitan of Switzerland, the group of representatives and higoumeni from the twenty monasteries of Mount Athos reminded him that his mission is especially "to bear witness to the Orthodox faith among Christians of other confessions which are separated from the Church of Christ, so that they may become aware of their errors and return to the one, holy, catholic, and apostolic Church of Christ, that is, to Orthodoxy" (Episkepsis, Dec. 1, 1982, p. 8).

67. See Etudes théologiques et religieuses, 2 (1983). At the same period, Positions luthériennes, Oct.-Dec. 1983, published very positive articles as well as critical remarks.

68. See Document sur l'oecuménisme: Un raidissement du dialogue en Italie, approved by the synod of Waldensian and Methodist churches at Torre Pellice in August 1982; text in SOEPI, Oct. 8, 1982.

logue groups, groups for Bible study, or for concerted action, all continue on their own way undisturbed.

In 1983, for example, the French Catholic episcopal commission was
worried about a possible spread of eucharistic hospitality between
Catholics and Protestants at a time when, paradoxically, there were
growing trends within the Reformed Church to reject ordination for pastors and to widen the gap between the two churches, which the ecumenical movement was endeavoring to close. The result was a note published by the commission in March of that year reminding Catholics of
current discipline and its connection with the faith they lived and professed (the note was incorrectly taken as symptomatic of a hardening of
positions when in fact it was simply a reminder of current pastoral principles and even made allowance for something new: the possibility in
exceptional cases that a Catholic's conscience would allow him or her to
participate in the Lord's Supper).[69] Two months later, the National
Synod of the Reformed Church, the first of a series of three on the subject of "ministry," confirmed Catholic apprehensions by following a
trend that would lead, a year later, to the withdrawal of the word
"ordination" and its replacement by "recognition of ministry."[70]

In April of that same year, however, between the two events just
mentioned, all the ecumenical leaders, Catholic and Protestant, held
their triennial meeting at Chantilly on the subject of the urgent need of
ecumenism. They were very conscious of the new problems, even de-
voting an unscheduled evening session to them, but the meeting was
carried on in an atmosphere of fraternity.[71] The ecumenical wave is carrying all of us forward.[72]

Well then? How are we to describe the position of the Catholic Church
in the current ecumenical situation in which such complex factors are at
work? Let me try to pull the various threads together.

What the Future Seems to Hold

Three simple observations will help shed light on my analysis:

1. In contrast with the situation in the preceding generation, the contemporary situation is characterized by the fact that ecumenism has

69. Note on "L'hospitalité eucharistique avec les chrétiens des Eglises issues de la Réforme en France," addressed by the Episcopal Commission for Unity to Catholic priests
and faithful (DC, April 3, 1983).

70. See, in Information-Evangélisation, 1 (1982), the set of "Etudes et propositions con-
cernant la consécration-ordination et le rôle des ministres," which very forthrightly show
the existence of radical currents opposing the ordination of ministers.

71. See Unité des chrétiens, July 1983.

72. As Father Beaupère was to say a little later on: "Dear pastor, I am not going to
break the ecumenical commitment we entered upon together, simply because I disagree
on one or other point with the pastors of the Reformed Church. You do not have the right
to abandon us simply because the thought and style of John Paul II or other Catholics are

moved from the level of *theological reflection* and of *local meetings* and *activities* to the level of an *existential movement* that involves *the entire Church* and *all the churches*. We have "taken ship"; a time of study must give way to a time of decision. Cardinal Willebrands emphasized this point when he expressed his agreement with the conclusion of the ARCIC final report:

They [the members of ARCIC] showed that the moment had come to pass to a crucial new phase of the dialogue . . . to pass from a time of research to a time of decision by their respective Churches. . . . They judged it could not any more be put off too long. To put off the decision would be to risk going around in circles and reducing the dynamism of the ecumenical movement to sterility.[73]

2. This movement is so swift that the churches are tempted to be afraid. They feel insecure to the extent that some degree of communion is already manifesting itself and that fellowship, dialogue, and common action are lowering the barriers that separate and are promoting osmosis and borrowings (very modest ones, perhaps, such as liturgical songs and prayers, but not the least important). Are we not protestantizing Catholicism, and vice versa? In this time between separation and unity, Lukas Vischer once wrote, "one feels homeless."[74]

This explains the instinctive tendency of church authorities and theologians to be cautious and preserve "identity."

3. All the churches are in this together. They find themselves in the same situation and ask the same questions. It must even be said that none of them can pass judgment on their situation entirely on their own or define the stance they are to take independently of the others. Dialogue has led them to question ambiguous traits in their long-standing identity, and they now realize, confusedly and without daring to admit it to themselves, that only together can they redefine this identity. This is a disturbing realization.

This is the situation—new in relation to the situation at the time of the Council—that the Catholic Church must accept when it inquires into its "reception" of the Council. It must indeed continue to absorb both the letter and the spirit of conciliar teaching, but it must also carry it further. In doing so, it will be strictly obeying the final recommendation of the

---

displeasing to you. I myself am not always in agreement with the pope, and you are doubtless not always in agreement with your presidents and synods. But this is not a reason for burning the bridges" (editorial in *Chrétiens en marche*, Bulletin oecuménique, Oct.-Dec. 1984).

73. "Called to Unity and Wholeness" (n. 35, above), p. 118. Lukas Vischer was of the same opinion: we must "pass over to actions and show the visible unity of the Church" ("Oecuménisme: rallentissement?," *Echo de Lausanne*, May 28, 1981; see *Episkepsis*, May 1, 1981, pp. 9f.). At Vancouver, in a press conference on August 5, 1982, Conrad Reiser told journalists inquiring about the future that we are in transition from "a time of programs and themes" to a time when the emphasis will be on "energetic action."

74. See *Episkepsis*, May 1, 1981, p. 10.

"Decree on Ecumenism," which asks (as I noted earlier) "that the initiatives of the sons of the Catholic Church, joined with those of the separated brethren, will go forward, without obstructing the ways of divine Providence, and without prejudging the future inspirations of the Holy Spirit" (§ 24). Care must be taken, of course, that we move forward "as a church." But it seems that this is precisely what we are doing, even though convulsive movements and tensions continue to appear. Is it conceivable that the journey should be perfectly smooth when we are dealing with an ecclesial body of some eight hundred million faithful interacting with an equal number of Christians in all the other churches and when the same mingling of openness and rejection is to be found on both sides?

I have no desire to turn a new word into a magical key, but I wonder whether the real issue for both sides is not the acceptance or refusal of the *ecclesial metanoia* they are beginning to talk about. Once the meaning of this "conversion' is explained with sufficient care, it frightens Christians less and less as they increasingly see it to be in full accord with the Council, just as the Council is in full accord with the Gospel. I must dwell on this point for a moment as I bring this essay to an end.

Use of *metanoia* in this context probably began in a 1972 statement of the Groupe de Dombes, which carefuly defined it as an ecclesial conversion as distinct from the individual conversions of Christians.[75] Over the years we have seen the word gradually winning favor in published documents, whether explicitly or beneath the surface of similar formulas and images. As I pointed out earlier, in the symposium held at San Anselmo in 1975 *metanoia* was mentioned as an essential element in ecumenism. The point made there was that the interior conversion called for in the "Decree on Ecumenism" required not only the conversion of individuals but also the transformation of the community and, if need be, the renewal of structures.[76]

This is in keeping with the teaching of the Council on the continual reformation of the Church as a human, earthly institution (UR 6). It is also in keeping with the example that the Council itself gave in inviting observers to contribute their questions.

The "passage" called for is a difficult one, for it requires that the Church convert what ought to be converted though surrendering nothing of its basic fidelity, and that it begin to do so by listening humbly to the valid questions of others. For a long time, the churches regarded it as self-evident that the questions they ask of each other were symmetrically opposed, so that one church could not accept the major questions of another without abdicating its own identity. We are beginning to realize that these reciprocal questions are not strictly exclusive and that each

75. Groupe des Dombes, *Pour une réconciliation des ministères* (n. 16, above), p. 26 (in the Engl. trans., p. 102). This was the second statement issued by the group. A few years later, a third document, *Le ministère épiscopal*, made the word *metanoia* part of its vocabulary.

76. Békés and Vajta, *Unitatis redintegratio, 1964–1974* (n. 14 above), pp. 160–61.

church can lend an ear to questions of the other that call for a *metanoia* without sacrificing its basic fidelity, which is expressed precisely in the radical questions it asks in its turn. The Catholic Church for its part is beginning to see, for example, that without sacrificing the unique role of the bishop of Rome it can and ought to listen to the challenge issued to it by all the other churches regarding certain age-old ways in which its Roman center exercises authority. This is the subject of an important book of Jean Tillard.[77]

In like manner, a church of the Reformation can and ought to listen to the questions asked of it by all the other churches regarding ministry and its link to apostolic succession, without thereby sacrificing their own message to the other churches about evangelical freedom in relation to the institutional and historical forms ministry has taken.[78] The reader should bear in mind here the remark made earlier about the churches *together* accepting the *metanoia* to which they challenge one another; otherwise the heroic *metanoia* of one will only confirm the serene triumphalism of another!

It is this kind of reciprocal listening to questions that has determined the procedure followed in the statements on the Eucharist, on ministry, and on authority, which have been the laborious fruit of the very promising major conversations Catholics have engaged in, especially those with Anglicans and Lutherans.

The same kind of listening is urged upon the churches in the Lima report. It can also be glimpsed at work beneath the surface of certain positions taken by those in charge of Roman ecumenism. I have reread the reports of the plenary sessions of the Roman Secretariat with this idea in mind and have been struck to find there the idea—though not the word itself—of an ecclesial *metanoia* and the spiritual sacrifice that it requires.

As early as 1969, a statement on dialogue signed by Cardinal Willebrands and Archbishop Hamer asked that Catholics "become aware of the changes in behavior and thinking that seem to be required." The authors referred to St. Augustine's saying that we must "seek in order to find, and find in order to seek still further."[79]

At the plenary meeting of 1974 Cardinal Willebrands emphasized the utter novelty of the situation in which the Catholic Church finds itself as it dialogues with other churches as equal partners. This, he said, requires a spiritual conversion, and he applied the words of Philippians 2:7 to the Church: "He emptied himself."[80] Mgr. Moeller made the same point the following year, citing what Philip Potter had said in an intervention at the Roman synod: "Dialogue is a form of existence, the

77. J. Tillard, *The Bishop of Rome* (Wilmington, Del., 1983).

78. On this difficult question I refer the reader to the discussion in my book *L'oecuménisme: où vont les Eglises?* (Paris, 1983), pp. 168–89.

79. *Inf. Serv.*, 11 (1970) 5–10.

80. Ibid., 23 (1974) 2–6.

form of the incarnate Lord as a servant living among human beings, being open and vulnerable to them. It is the way of the Cross." At that same meeting Cardinal Willebrands (citing Lukas Vischer) had already expressed a similar thought:

The Spirit alone can lead the churches from their present division into unity. . . . But what does that mean if the churches do not really start moving and changing? . . . To call upon the Spirit is a radically dangerous and even explosive thing.[81]

At the plenary meeting of 1978 Cardinal Willebrands refuted the objections of those who wanted theological dialogue stopped, and showed that the real reason for the reluctance was a fear at the idea of challenging ourselves on the basis of questions asked by others and having to be converted:

When we declare that a truth, a liturgical rite, a moral rule ought to be maintained, is it easy in every case to say whether this necessity is of divine law or ecclesiastical law? And is there a better medium through which to see more clearly than our ecumenical encounter, where we can profit from the observations and reflections of other Christians?

On some very important issues, he added, we are presently gaining renewed understanding and revised interpretations: the ministry of Peter, the meaning of presidency at the Eucharist, sacramentality, the teaching office, marriage, the status of the Uniates, and secular ecumenism.[82]

At the 1981 meeting Cardinal Willebrands made the same point with regard to the signs of "reconfessionalization" that are being seen in the ecumenical movement. He focused his attention especially on doctrinal issues. It is necessary, he said to strip the mask from some subtle temptations—for example, that of identifying the objective content of the faith with its exposition or its perception, with one or other theology, one or other type of piety, one or other religious sensibility; or that of identifying the truth of faith, on which agreement is necessary, with the formulation or formulations made of it in the course of history. He referred in this context to "historicity" as described in the declaration *Mysterium Ecclesiae*, and applied the ideas expounded in that document to the agreed statements of ARCIC. In his view, this is the first time in its history that the Church has been faced with texts of this kind. The Christian world is watching us. How will the Church respond to this new situation? What is at issue, he said, is the credibility of our ecumenical movement and our commitment to it:

81. Ibid., 27 (1975) p. 11 (citing a statement of Phillip Potter at the 1974 Synod of Bishops) and p. 3 (citing Lukas Vischer's report to the Central Committee of the World Council in Berlin, Aug. 1974).
82. Ibid., 39 (1979) 2–5.

[The new generation] often speaks of its dissatisfaction with the ecumenical movement. Is this not partly because in their haste they have the impression that it consists of a game of technocrats where commissions succeed commissions without really changing anything?[83]

I have cited Cardinal Willebrands at length because of the importance of the "place" from which he speaks: the heart of the Catholic communion. It is here that the most decisive signs are given of the basic direction being taken by the Catholic Church. Here, too, is the most important point at which any *metanoia* of the Catholic Church must be implemented (because the authority of the bishop of Rome is the target of converging challenges from all the other churches). It is the place, finally, where we have a right to hope that watchfulness and initiative will be harmoniously combined with an authentic reception of the Council.

A collection can also be made of small hopeful signs that other churches are likewise accepting the idea of a *metanoia*. Good example is contagious.[84]

Commenting (in 1982) on a wide range of ecumenical experiences, a Catholic theologian was able to sum up as follows:

[In 1970] I distinguished three major phases in the ecumenical movement: first, a period of *conversion of heart*, paving the way for an ecumenism of love; then a *conversion of minds* that makes doctrinal dialogue possible; and finally a period, which I saw in the offing, of *confessional conversion* that would some day lead to a reconciliation among the Churches.

He went on to say:

Today I see more clearly the form this third, inevitably lengthy, period is taking: that of a *conversion to a progressive symbiosis*. We used to live under the "sign" of separation; we are trying now to live in a new fellowship and under the "sign" of communion wherever this is possible.[85]

83. Ibid., 47 (1981) 115–16.
84. In the world of the Reformation churches, for example, Hébert Roux said back at the time of the Council: "Faced as we now are with a Catholicism that challenges itself and allows itself to be challenged, we too must allow ourselves to be challenged" (*Le Concile et le dialogue oecuménique* [Paris, 1964], p. 165). Similarly, the former director of Faith and Order, William Lazareth, in "Exposé sur l'oecuménisme à la 7ᵉ assemblée de la Fédération luthérienne mondiale à Budapest," *SOEPI*, Aug. 14, 1984, p. 4: "The Roman Catholics are today purifying their obedience to the totality of the apostolic faith. Are we Lutherans, as evangelical catholics, capable of regaining our catholic participation in the totality of the apostolic order?" As for the Orthodox world, in a memorable address to the ecumenical leaders of France, Olivier Clément expressly urged all the churches to *metanoia*, and he included his own church in the exhortation. In this context he emphasized especially certain inconsistencies between "saying" and "doing" that elicit a compensatory "aggressive triumphalism." See "L'oecuménisme et l'acceuil au Christ qui vient," *Unité des chrétiens*, July 1983, p. 27; the address was published in *DC*, Jan. 15, 1984.
85. B. Sesboüé, "Relecture et prospective," *Unité des chrétiens*, Jan. 1982, p. 25.

The present stage of the ecumenical journey to which the Council irreversibly committed the Catholic Church[86] is gradually becoming clearer. Some Catholics are admittedly not ready to accept the possibility and consequences of *metanoia* (which they often misunderstand: it is meant to be nothing else than a manifestation of authentic fidelity, not trickery or betrayal).[87] It is remarkable, on the other hand, that Christians, once they get a clear explanation of the situation, *accept it as though they had been waiting for it.* Not all problems are resolved, of course, but at least everything is clear.

Against the background of this basic conviction and the hope it engenders, it is easier to see how the disparate pieces of the ecumenical puzzle fit into place; this includes the countless difficulties that it would take a whole book to discuss.

Under the heading, for example, of reasons for impatience, there are the timidity shown by the new Code of Canon Law in its ecumenical advances, the danger of vigilantism, the instinctive shrinking from possible progress in eucharistic sharing.

Under the heading of ecumenical imagination (or lack of it), there is the hesitation felt at what have been called models for unity, from "pluralistic unity" to "reconciled diversity," from "types of churches" to "conciliar fellowship."

Under the heading of ecclesial "strategy" there is the situation of the Catholic Church relative to the other major churches and the World Council, namely, its delayed but massive entrance into the ecumenical movement, which has to some extent deprived the Council of its leading role and given the impression that the Catholic Church wants to take over the reins.[88]

Under the heading of the connection between ecumenism and the world there is the difficulty of achieving a balance between a doctrinal ecumenism and a secular ecumenism. The former flourishes, for practical purposes, only in the "developed" Western countries, whereas the developing nations give priority to the tasks of service to the world.[89]

86. The irreversibility is frequently emphasized by John Paul II. See, e.g., his address to the plenary meeting of the Roman Secretariat, Feb. 8, 1980, which Fr. Duprey formally cited at Vancouver (*DC*, Jan. 15, 1984, p. 107, note 1). See also the address to the World Council on June 12, 1984 (*DC*, July 15, 1984, p. 107).

87. See, e.g., Paul Toinet, *L'oecuménisme entre vie et mort* (Paris, 1981); see pp. 154f. on "The ambiguities in the theme of 'confessional conversion.'" The author's observations might have been useful, had they not been undermined by his aggressive polemics.

88. Some months after the vote on the conciliar "Decree on Ecumenism," Lukas Vischer was of the opinion that two interpretations might be given of the document: either the Catholic Church was going to take the other churches seriously and look upon them as equal partners in dialogue; or, in opening itself to dialogue, it would seek to take charge and ultimately in one way or another ask the non-Roman churches to unite themselves to it. See his report to the Central Committee of the World Council at Enugu, Nigeria, in January 1965; cited in A. Wenger, *Vatican II, chronique de la 3ᵉ session* (Paris, 1965), p. 315, note. Has the doubt been fully resolved?

89. On this point, see the analysis of J. Tillard, "L'Assemblée de Vancouver. L'oecuménisme à un carrefour," *Irén*, 56 (1983) 361–70.

Let me say by way of conclusion that at a deeper level, beneath all the upheavals and hesitations, the Catholic Church as a whole is clearly continuing to "receive" the ecumenical orientation given by the Council. As Father Congar has put it in a sentence in which every word counts, "without losing its Roman center or its papal head, the Catholic Church has become a demanding but open partner in the *quest* of unity."[90] Like all the other churches, it is now on the threshold of decisions that will condition the building of unity.

Let me end this essay by relating a personal experience. I am writing these final lines just after returning from the Third European Ecumenical Meeting,[91] held at Riva del Garda and Trent in the very Catholic Trentino region of northern Italy. Some eighty participants from twenty-five countries (that is, almost all of Europe) met there to discuss our common creed and our common Christian witness. The final day of the meeting was a memorable one. On Sunday morning—saddened only by the impossibility of sharing the eucharist—the Catholics who had acted as our hosts in about twenty small parishes had the experience (almost all of them for the first time in their lives) of coming together with Christians from other churches. I witnessed once again the joyous outburst of that latent ecumenism that is ever ready to manifest itself, as I mentioned earlier. In the afternoon a celebration of the word brought us together in the very cathedral where the Council of Trent had met and put its seal on the break between the Catholic Church and the churches of the Reformation. On this day it was filled with a crowd that was looking for unity. Before we all exchanged almost endless signs of peace, we proclaimed together, in the languages of each of us, the fourth-century creed that is "the source of our hope."

The living icons of unity being restored thus continue to multiply. In 1967 I was an entranced witness to the meeting of Pope Paul VI and Patriarch Athenagoras I in the ancient church in the Phanar at Constantinople. I saw them embrace while the crowd shouted *"Axios!"*—"It is fitting!" On this image another has now been superimposed: that of Cardinal Hume and Pastor Appel standing side by side in the pulpit of the cathedral of Trent and together giving the final blessing to all. Old Europe, in which the Church broke apart and which then brought division to all the continents, was here making a modest but nonetheless striking gesture toward the restoration of unity.

The Catholic Church of Trent, whose bishop welcomed us, received this gesture and received with it the ecumenical call of the Council. The latent ecumenism to be found everywhere in the Church asks only to be awakened.

90. Y. Congar, *Concile* (n. 6, above), p. 60.
91. These triennial meetings bring together the Council of European Episcopal Conferences, which is Catholic, and the Conference of European Churches, which includes the Orthodox, Protestant, Anglican, and Old Catholic churches from some twenty-five countries. The first meeting was held at Chantilly, France, in 1978, the second at Logumkloster, Denmark, in 1981. The two presidents are at present Cardinal Hume and Pastor Appel.

III. THEMES TAKEN FURTHER
IN THE RECEPTION

Gustavo Gutiérrez

9. The Church and the Poor: A Latin American Perspective

The Second Vatican Council is undoubtedly the most important event in the history of the Catholic Church for several centuries. In making this claim I am thinking not only of its documents but also of the spirit that permeates them and of the impulse given them by John XXIII and Paul VI. All these together make up the conciliar event.

Twenty years later, some Catholics have the impression that all this is a stage we have left behind and that we must now face new challenges. It is true, of course, that new situations have indeed arisen and that these must be regarded as having their own special facets; nonetheless we are faced, in Vatican II, with a complex event that cannot be dealt with in summary judgments. Yves Congar was correct in saying that Vatican II "embodied a tremendous dynamic, but only with time will it reveal its full contribution."[1] We might almost say, therefore, that the real postconciliar period is only now beginning, inasmuch as we are entering upon a stage of greater clarity about the enormous contribution of the Council but also of its limitations.

Much that happened in the Church during those twenty years had its origins in the preconciliar period, but this did not, and could not, hold back the postconciliar process, for Vatican II provided first and foremost an orientation for understanding it in the light of God's word and for entering into the postconciliar movement in a fruitful and critical way. The new discussion of the Council that is now beginning will help to clarify this meaning and to define positions.

My task in these pages will be to reflect on the "reception" of Vatican II in Latin America in relation to the theme of "the poor."[2] Reception, involving as it does a struggle against inevitable forms of inertia, is made

1. Y. Congar, *Le Concile Vatican II. Son Eglise, Peuple de Dieu et Corps du Christ* (Paris, 1984), p. 67. Earlier, citing Newman, Congar reminds us that every council has been followed by a more or less critical period (ibid., p. 6).

2. I use "reception" in the sense explained by Y. Congar in his "La réception comme réalité ecclésiologique," *RSPT* 56 (1972) 369–403.

up (as every authentic acceptance must be) of both fidelity and creativity. Reception supposes a certain otherness; in this case the otherness is to be seen in the difference between the historical context of the Church in Latin America and the European world in which the universalist vision of the Council originated.

Some years ago, Karl Rahner offered a theological interpretation of the Council in the context of an understanding of the history of the Church. His thesis was that Vatican II began the Church's "discovery and official realization of itself as *world Church*." This event, according to the great German theologian, is itself located in the third period of the Church's history, in which for the first time "the Church's living space is from the very outset the whole world,"[3] not simply the European world. This or that detail, or the significance of a particular argument, may be open to discussion, but the power of Rahner's vision is undeniable; it provides an imaginative and stimulating perspective in which to understand the present moment in the Church's life.

If we take the universal Church as our point of reference, I think it possible to say that for the Church of Latin America (and of other continents as well) the Council was a summons to adulthood; that is, it was a call to that Church to accept its own being and, as such and on that basis, to bear witness to the Gospel. The greater part of the experience and thinking of Latin American Christians during the years since then can be regarded as a response to the Council's call. The episcopal conferences at Medellín and Puebla were an expression of this experience and reflection, and at the same time a new stimulus to them. In the opening years of the postconciliar period the Latin American Church was reaching adulthood; for this reason it felt itself to be in full communion with the universal Church.[4] The essence of its reception of the Council is to be seen in this maturation, this movement toward adulthood.

We may not forget, however, that this reception has clearly and necessarily been mediated by an acceptance of the conciliar demand that we heed the signs of the times. In the case of the Latin American Church this has meant facing up to the inhuman situation of poverty and oppression in which the vast majority of Latin Americans live, and being responsive to their longing for deliverance. But the Church cannot do this in an authentic way unless it applies the message of the reign of God to the situation and to the yearning of the people.

When we put the matter in these terms, we are inevitably reminded of the intuitions that made John XXIII summon the Council. The period of maturation, with its internal fluctuations and resistance from without, that is now beginning for the Latin American Church is not to be understood apart either from the intentions of John XXIII or from the accept-

3. K. Rahner, *Concern for the Church* (New York, 1981), pp. 78 and 83.

4. See Cardinal Landázuri's closing address at Medellín, in *Between Honesty and Hope. Documents from and about the Church in Latin America*, issued by the Peruvian Bishops' Commission for Social Action (Maryknoll, N.Y., 1970), pp. 221–27.

ance and development of these intentions by those who labored at the Council.

In the first part of this essay, therefore, I shall try to read the conciliar event in all its complexity from the viewpoint of the acceptance given to the Council in the life of the Latin American Church. In the second part, I shall suggest some characteristics of this church that is beginning to see itself as adult.

John XXIII and the Council

As time passes and the conciliar event comes into better perspective, the stature of John XXIII also increases. Not everything has yet been said about his reasons for calling the Council or about the tasks he meant Vatican II to carry out. In any case, it is clear that we must turn back upstream to Pope John XXIII if we want to understand my theme, the reception of the Council in Latin America. For this reason, I shall discuss the matter of relationships between John XXIII and Vatican II not in itself but in the framework of this theme.

To Look Far Ahead

In the very first statement that John XXIII made about the Council he mentions a point that was one of his firmest convictions: we, as a church, must be attentive to the signs of the times if we want to proclaim the Gospel of Jesus Christ. This first need is accompanied by another: we must find an adequate expression for this message so that it will be understood by the people of our time. At bottom, the pope's great concern—expressed at the beginning of his announcement of a council—was how to say "thy kingdom come" in the "age of renewal" in which we are living.[5]

In subsequent statements John XXIII would explain his concern in greater detail. A treatment of the subject calls for a method; the pope realizes this and therefore says that "the leap forward" that the Council is to make in matters doctrinal presupposes that the Church's teaching is "studied and expounded according to the research methods and literary forms of modern thought."[6] The same document goes on to recall the classic distinction between the "substance of the deposit of faith" and the "way of presenting" the truths contained in it. The method thus indicated proved very fruitful both for the Council and for many magiste-

5. John XXIII, "Announcement of the Council," in F. Anderson, ed., Council Daybook, Vatican II, Sessions 1 and 2 (Washington, 1965), pp. 1–2.
6. John XXIII, "Opening Address at the First Session of Vatican II (October 11, 1962)," ibid., p. 27.

rial documents (those of Medellín and Puebla among them) in subsequent years.[7] It was also consonant with the pope's main concern: the preaching of the Gospel in our time.

The same need made the pope energetically repulse those who thought the Church had nothing to learn from history and who therefore remained focused on the past. He called them "prophets of doom who are always predicting disaster, as though the destruction of the world were imminent."[8] As is well known, the pope was referring to churchmen and, in his capacity as supreme shepherd, calling them to order. His words were an effort, on the very day when the Council opened, to place this event in its proper perspective.

This opening address, like another given just a month before, made clear to the universal Church what Cardinal Lercaro later called the "institutional solitude" of Pope John during the period of preparation for the Council.[9] As the cardinal observed, these two addresses showed the distance between the outlook of John XXIII and the preparatory schemata delivered to the Council. They undoubtedly provided a basis for the almost complete rejection of the schemata (except for the one on the liturgy) by the conciliar assembly in its first session. It was nonetheless not easy for the Council to grasp the pope's vision fully. John XXIII's "prophecy embedded in fidelity" (to use the description of A. and G. Alberigo) anticipated insights we today still find challenging.

A fine passage in the *Journal of a Soul* shows the broad perspective Pope Roncalli felt it necessary to adopt. He refused to settle for a single family or native land or country or limited goal, but sought instead a broader horizon. He wrote in this regard: "The whole world is my family. This sense of belonging to everyone must give character and vigor to my mind, my heart, and my actions."[10]

This universalist outlook was a matter of profound conviction with him. Thus shortly before his death he dictated to Cardinal Cicognani the following statement in which he sums up his vision of things and looks prophetically to the future:

7. In his book *Il nuovo Popolo di Dio* (Brescia, 1971), J. Ratzinger says that this distinction enabled the Council to "move beyond a narrow way of doing theology that might be defined, a little abusively, as 'encyclical theology,' toward broader theological horizons. By 'encyclical theology' is meant a kind of theology in which tradition seemed to be gradually identified with the most recent statements of the papal magisterium. Many theological works before and even during the Council could be seen as efforts to reduce theology to a record—and perhaps a systematization—of magisterial statements" (pp. 310–11). (The German original of Ratzinger's book, *Das neue Volk Gottes*, was published in Düsseldorf in 1969.)

8. John XXIII, "Opening Address at the First Session of Vatican II," in Anderson, *Council Daybook*, p. 26.

9. Giacomo Cardinal Lercaro, "Suggestions for Historical Research," in G. Lercaro and G. De Rosa, *John XXIII: Simpleton or Saint?* (Chicago, 1967), p. 13.

10. Notes on his retreat at the Vatican, end of 1959, in *Journal of a Soul* (New York, 1965, p. 299.

Today more than ever, certainly more than in previous centuries, we are called to serve man as such, and not merely Catholics; to defend above all and everywhere the rights of the human person, and not merely those of the Catholic Church. Today's world, the needs made plain in the last fifty years, and a deeper understanding of doctrine have brought us to a new situation, as I said in my opening speech to the Council. It is not that the Gospel has changed: it is that we have begun to understand it better. Those who have lived as long as I have were faced with new tasks in the social order at the start of the century; those who, like me, were twenty years in the East and eight in France, were able to compare different cultures and traditions, and know that the moment has come to discern the signs of the times, to seize the opportunity and to look far ahead.[11]

This is a programatic statement, and for this reason I have cited it in its entirety. It should help us to be present to the immediate situation and at the same time "to look far ahead" as we speak of the reception of Vatican II in Latin America.

The Council and the New Self-Awareness of the Church

I think it may be said that in the framework established by his fundamental insight (attentiveness to the signs of the times), John XXIII set down three major themes for the Council in various addresses given before the bishops began their work: (1) openness to the modern world; (2) unity among Christians; and (3) the church of the poor. For reasons that are readily understandable, the Council was more alert to the first two than to the third.

All three themes presupposed what Paul VI, in full continuity with his predecessor, called "a keen desire [of the Church] to come at last to a full understanding of her true nature . . . [a desire] forced upon her by very necessity and her obvious duty."[12] This new self-awareness—geared to the proclamation of the Gospel in the modern world—would lead to a renewal of the Church and enable it to respond to the great themes set forth by John XXIII and to the challenges they contained.

A Bridge to the Modern World

Of the three themes singled out by John XXIII, the necessity of dialogue with the world was the one that received the most extensive and profound treatment in the Council. It was this issue that accounted for the great turnabout toward the end of the first session and opened up

11. Statement of May 24, 1963, cited in P. Hebblethwaite, *Pope John XXIII, Shepherd of the Modern World* (Garden City, N.Y., 1985) pp. 498–99.
12. Paul VI, "Address at the Opening of the Second Session of Vatican II (September 29, 1963), in *TPS*, 9 (1963–64), 131. In his encyclical *Ecclesiam suam* (Aug. 6, 1964) Paul VI had said that the Church needed to "ponder the mystery of its own being" (*TPS*, 10 [1964–65] 255).

pathways along which the work of the Council would advance very fruitfully. I have in mind here not only the document eventually to be known as *Gaudium et spes* but the entire body of documents.

In "bridging the gulf between ourselves and contemporary society" (the words are those of Paul VI), the Council had to be aware not only of the limitations and defects of the world but also of its values, from which the Church has much to learn. The purpose of the awareness was that the Church might put itself at the service of the world. Paul VI would subsequently make this point in a formal and incisive way:

The world will surely realize that the Church looks upon it with profound understanding, with sincere admiration, and with the sincere intention not of mastering it but of serving it, not of despising it but of increasing its dignity, not of condemning it but of bringing it comfort and salvation.[13]

In this spirit the Council developed a truly impressive wealth and variety of theological approaches and pastoral guidelines. There can, of course, be no question of going into these in detail; I shall simply call attention to one question that is important for its immediate impact on the matter that concerns me in this essay. The world to which the Council opened itself was the world of modern science and technology; it was also the world of democracy and of the human rights and modern freedoms that have been claimed over the last two centuries, especially in Europe (which is not to underestimate the universal importance of the development).[14] This concentration at the Council also meant the inclusion of certain secular and democratic values (I use these terms in their broadest and most basic sense) in the reforms which the Council was striving to bring about within the Church itself.

The Church offers itself to this world as "the universal sacrament of salvation" (LG 48), that is, as the efficacious sign within human history of God's will to save all human beings and the whole human being. I need not dwell here on the novelty of the eschatological perspective that this description implies and that will set its impress on the life of the Church for a long time to come. It is in this perspective that the Latin American Church would subsequently think out its role in relation to the process of liberation.

The Ecumenical Perspective

Reconciliation with Christians of other confessions was another of John XXIII's major concerns. Like the question of openness to the world,

13. Paul VI, "Address at the Opening of the Second Session of Vatican II," *TPS*, 9 (1963–64) 137 and 139.

14. The ambivalence in the values of the modern world is indicated in some texts, but by and large the critical perspective is not developed. Little is said of the negative side of these values in present-day society: e.g., the causes of the poverty and marginalization of

this one was first treated with indifference by those in charge of preparation for the Council, and then enthusiastically received by the Council itself. Ecumenical dialogue was undoubtedly one of the richest and most striking fruits of Vatican II and of the early postconciliar period.

Once the presence of values for salvation was recognized in the other Christian confessions, there was an opening as well to Judaism and other religions. Here again there was question of building bridges and cultivating an attitude of service to persons in other spiritual families. All this had consequences for understanding the Church and its historical task; at bottom, however, it was a matter of humble respect for the saving action of the Lord.

Following the path opened up by the idea of the Church as universal sacrament of salvation, the Council met these challenges by a new approach to the classic question of the relationship between institution and community. Community was to be a basic theme in the ecclesiology of the Council, although this did not prevent the council fathers from following tradition and legitimately reaffirming the visibility of the Church.

The problem of ecumenism meant less to the Latin American Church than did that of openness to the world, although there were some exceptions. The other Christian confessions have a relatively limited presence in Latin America (especially in comparison with Europe, North America, and the other continents), and as a result ecumenism was of direct concern only to limited groups. On the other hand, the basic ecumenical attitude of openness and dialogue was heartily welcomed and helped reinforce the spirit of openness to the modern world. The consequences of an ecumenical attitude were to play a part in the Latin American conception of the Church and its mission.

It must be noted here that in both areas—ecumenism and openness to the world—the soil of the Church had been readied for several decades. In the years before the Council both themes had been developed in many pastoral experiments and in solid theological reflection. The experiments and the thinking were the response of some church circles, especially in Europe and North America, to the challenges that the separated brethren and modern society had embodied for centuries. These experiences, contacts, and reflections were very useful in paving the way for a fruitful reception of the insights of John XXIII.

Many of those who had been working along these lines were present at Vatican II and indeed played a central role in it. Their thinking, which they put at the service of the Council's work, provided the backbone, in these two areas, of what John XXIII said should be the "salient point" of the Council: not a "discussion of one or another article in the basic

---

the majority of the human race. As a result of historical circumstances, the prevailing tone at the Council was understandably optimistic.

teaching of the Church," but "a leap forward toward an understanding of doctrine and a formation of consciences"[15] in relation to new problems.

The third theme singled out by John XXIII—the Church of the poor—had not received a comparable development in the years before the Council. This fact, combined with the Council's very sketchy awareness of the problems of Third World countries, explains the quite limited mark left by this last insight of Pope John on the conciliar documents. The insight was nonetheless a full response to the challenges the Church of Latin America was experiencing and is experiencing today. It is worth our while, therefore, to devote a few pages to the subject and to the fate of the theme during the years of the Council. We will then be in a position to see more clearly the way in which the theme was subsequently taken over in the life and thinking of the Latin American Church.

The Church of the Poor and the Third World

The theme does not appear in the early statements of John XXIII on the Council. The question therefore arises: How did he come to speak of it in his message of September 11, 1962? The question deserves further study, being an important element in one of the problems that A. and G. Alberigo regard as still potentially contributive to a better knowledge of the pope. The problem in this case is "the inseparability of Roncalli's personal journey from the events of the pontificate of John XXIII."[16]

Poverty undoubtedly played an important part in the life of this holy man from his infancy to his final days. But this circumstance cannot by itself explain his speaking of a church of the poor, for it has a different theological character and scope. A sensitivity to poverty can help prepare the way but it cannot by itself bring a person to the kind of statement made by Pope John. Yet everything indicates that what he said on that day represented a profound conviction. Perhaps this was one of those insights peculiar to this man who "looked far ahead," although he himself was not able in every case to develop his insights in detail and draw all the conclusions from them.[17] Nor was it necessary that he should do so. Prophets are creative figures who, when inspired by the breath of the Spirit, bring new forces into play, but in many instances they cannot themselves foresee the long-range effects of their action. This, it seems to me, was the role of John XXIII, and it is why he continues to be relevant.[18]

15. John XXIII, "Address at the Opening of the Council," in Anderson, *Council Daybook*, p. 27.
16. See A. and G. Alberigo, *Giovanni XXIII, profezia nella fideltà* (Brescia, 1978), p. 105.
17. Ibid., p. 91.
18. I cannot but agree with what A. and G. Alberigo say at the end of their essay on

A Luminous Point

A month before the opening of the Council John XXIII raised the question of the Church of the poor in a surprising form. He reminds us that Christ is our light and that it is with Christ as its point of reference that the Church must serve human beings. With this as background he makes three important points: (1) the equality of all peoples in the exercise of their rights and duties; (2) the defense of the family; and (3) the obligation to reject individualism and accept responsibility for society. The pope then adds: "A further luminous point:[19] confronted with the underdeveloped countries, the Church presents herself as what she is, and wants to be, as the Church of all, and particularly, the Church of the poor." A few lines further on he speaks of "the miseries of social life that cry out for vengeance in the sight of God."[20] I should like to call attention to three ideas in this passage.

First, the pope links the Church and the poor countries. The wording used is important: in his encyclical *Mater et magistra* he had spoken of "developing countries"; here he drops this milder expression and speaks of "underdeveloped countries." He is talking, in other words, of the *real poverty* of the vast majority of the human race. This state of affairs challenges the Church to take new stock of itself. From the outset, then, the question of poverty is one the pope regards as having ecclesiological implications. The situation of wretchedness and injustice in which the poor live is not simply a matter for concern on the part of the Church or for measures to alleviate it. Rather it represents a challenge to that renewal of self-knowledge to which Paul VI would emphatically summon the Church a short time later. John XXIII thus cuts to the heart of the relationship between poverty and the Church apart from which any concern of the Church for the situation of the poor is likely to be considered provisional and, in the final analysis, extraneous to its mission and its real being. John XXIII avoids this danger because in this same message he situates himself in the perspective of liberation in Christ and of the nearness of God's reign (he refers in this context to Luke 21:20–33).

Secondly, the passage indicates the two poles of an important tension. It begins by saying that the Church is (and wants to be) the Church *of all*; this is a clear statement that the Church's task embraces the whole world. The reign of God embraces all; no one is excluded from it. The Christian community is an expression of divine love (its sacrament in history, to use the Council's words) and therefore reaches out to every

---

Pope John: "To study John is to have the exhilarating experience of writing the history of the future" (ibid., p. 108).

19. John XXIII liked the image of the "luminous point" for emphasizing the importance of an idea; see his announcement of the Council and his *Journal of a Soul*.

20. Radio message of Sept. 11, 1962, in Anderson, *Council Daybook*, pp. 18–21.

human being without exception. It is significant that the passage begins with this statement and thus provides a proper and fruitful setting for the other pole of the tension, namely, that the Church is (and wants to be) the Church *of the poor*. This particularism, this predilection (which obviously does not mean exclusiveness) is not opposed, in the pope's understanding of it, to universality, but rather gives the latter a demanding concrete form in history. The God proclaimed by Jesus Christ is a God whose call is universal and directed to every human being, but also a God who has a preferential love for the poor and the dispossessed. The dialectic of universality and particularity is a key to understanding the Christian message and the God who is revealed in it.

Finally, John XXIII presents the Church, thus viewed, as something that is in process of becoming. As I just pointed out, he twice says that the Church "is and wants to be." The situation is not cut and dried. The Church is not yet everything it ought to be; it has a journey to make through history. John XXIII shows the direction the journey must take, and without any triumphalism (to use a word much in favor during the years of the Council) acknowledges what remains to be done.

The passage I have been analyzing is a short one but every word in it counts. Its restraint and moderation must not make us overlook its generative power. The words, backed by the witness of that free spirit, John XXIII, marked the beginning of a movement, a process with advances and setbacks, that is still going on, because it has not yet deployed all its virtualities.

The Theme of the Council?

The first session of the Council brought a revolution in the ways the Church had been following until that time. As a result of the richly creative ferment of ideas whose proponents were trying to reflect faithfully the insights of John XXIII, numerous paths were opened up that transformed previously unshakeable patterns of thinking and acting. At the end of this first stage of the Council, Cardinal Lercaro, archbishop of Milan, gave a memorable address on the theme of the Church of the poor. It deserves a detailed analysis, but I shall limit myself to two points.

With a clarity and prophetic vision that still amaze us, Cardinal Lercaro said:

If we treat this subject of winning the poor for the Gospel as just another one of the many themes which must occupy the attention of the Council we shall not satisfy the most real and most profound exigencies of our day (including our great hope of furthering the unity of all Christendom)—indeed, we shall make it impossible for us to do so. . . . The Church herself is in truth the theme of the Council [especially insofar as] she is above all "the Church of the poor."[21]

21. Excerpts from Cardinal Lercaro's intervention are given in Paul Gauthier, *Christ, the Church and the Poor* (Westminster, Md., 1965), pp. 153–57. The words cited here are on p. 153.

The passage is very clear. The cardinal was here endeavoring to be faithful to the first two great themes set for the Council by John XXIII: the needs of our time and the unity of Christians. To achieve this goal, he says, the attention of the Council must be focused on the third of the pope's themes: the Church of the poor.

This was a valid reading of Pope John's intentions by one who was always very close to him. Would it be going too far to say that Cardinal Lercaro was expressing the mind of the pope himself? In any case, the archbishop of Bologna took his stand on solid and promising ground when he made the connection between poverty and the Church an important theme of the Council.

A second point emerges from Cardinal Lercaro's address. His outlook here is profoundly theological, not because he is insensitive to the social dimension of poverty, but because he is bent on placing the mystery of Christ at the center of the discussion. He says: "The Mystery of Christ in the Church is always, but particularly today, the Mystery of Christ in the poor, since the Church, as our Holy Father Pope John XXIII has said, is truly the Church of all, but is particularly 'the Church of the poor.' " He therefore thinks that the absence of this essential aspect of the Christian message is a serious defect in the provisional schemata presented to the Council.[22] The situation of the poor must be related not only to the social teaching of the Church but also and above all to the light of Christ and his reign. Given the archbishop's approach, it is not surprising that in his view the other two themes of John XXIII—Christian unity and openness to the world—required making the theme of the Church of the poor a central concern of the Council.

Some task forces were set up to deal with these ideas, and they were very active in the corridors of the Council. The results achieved, however, were quite modest when judged by the extent to which Cardinal Lercaro's outlook made its way into the documents. LG 8 seeks to include these concerns in a rich but brief christological statement.[23] Then there is the fine passage in AG 5, though it is even shorter, and a few allusions scattered through the other documents. I should like to call attention to two important points.

The two texts just mentioned carefully make Christ the focus of their treatment of poverty. Both refer to the evangelization of the poor, and *Lumen gentium* bases this mandate on the fact that the image of the Lord is to be seen in the poor. Puebla will take over this idea and give it beautiful and powerful expression.[24]

22. Cardinal Lercaro later took the same clear and profound theological approach to poverty in his "Preface" for *Eglise et pauvreté* (Paris, 1965), pp. 9–21.

23. In his study of the ecclesiology of *Lumen gentium*, A. Acerbi does not mention this idea of the Church of the poor: see *Due ecclesiologie. Ecclesiologia giuridica ed ecclesiologia di communione nella Lumen Gentium* (Bologna, 1975).

24. See the "Final Document" of Puebla, §§ 31–39, in J. Eagleson and P. Scharper, eds., *Puebla and Beyond. Documentation and Commentary* (Maryknoll, N.Y., 1979).

Both texts speak of poverty as a "way" that Christ followed and that the Church too must follow on its pilgrimage through history. Poverty is thus not a goal or an ideal but a means of giving authentically evangelical witness.

These two texts and a few others are valuable, but it is clear that they fall far short of realizing Cardinal Lercaro's proposal that the "Church of the poor" (a phrase not used in the documents of Vatican II) be made *the* theme of the Council. The ground had doubtless not been sufficiently prepared here, as it had in the other two areas singled out by John XXIII: Christian unity and openness to the world. As I mentioned earlier, the most active participants in Vatican II felt at ease in these two areas and had better theological tools for dealing with them.

The Council's observations did, however, provide room for experiments and thinking along the lines of the "Church of the poor."

A Poor, Missionary, and Paschal Church

With some exceptions, the participation of the Latin American Church in the Council was limited.[25] The Council, however, did have an impact on the Latin American Church as it did on the rest of the Church. Ordinary Christians felt this impact initially through liturgical reform, but as time went on they also became aware of the changed mentality resulting from Vatican II. The Council's main themes—dialogue with the world, ecumenism, greater participation of the laity in ecclesial structures and tasks, new theological perspectives—gradually became part of the life of the Church in Latin America.

The presence of the Council did not, however, become as powerful in Latin America as in Europe, nor did it follow the same rhythm. The difference in historical context explains this difference in intensity. Latin America had a greater distance to travel in coming to grips with the challenges of modern society as posed by the Council. It would be absurd to say that the challenges of Vatican II did not affect the Latin American Church, but they quickly took on a different complexion.

A churchman who clearly realized the situation was Bishop Manuel Larrain of Talca (Chile), undoubtedly one of the most outstanding members of the Latin American episcopate in our time. Don Manuel, then president of the Latin American Episcopal Council, CELAM (Don Hélder Câmara was vice president), got the idea, toward the end of the Council, of a meeting of the Latin American bishops that would take

25. The Brazilian and Chilean episcopates were perhaps the most active and best organized of the Latin American episcopates at the council. A few individual bishops did participate to a significant degree.

stock of our situation in the light of Vatican II. The meeting took place a few years later at Medellín.[26]

A Deafening Cry

Don Manuel's insight was not mistaken. The seeds of profound change were germinating in Latin America, though not everyone was able to see this as he did. It was not a question (or, at least, not only a question) of isolated facts or unconnected situations created by a few visionaries. Despite the anecdotal element in some descriptions of the process, the real meaning of what was happening was that an entire people was beginning to stand up and claim its right to life. A real *irruption of the poor* was taking place in Latin America and in the Church. Historical events often have modest and even ambivalent beginnings that call for discernment.[27]

The Council ended its work in December of 1965. That same year brought a crisis in the situation that had been developing for some time: a situation of increasingly intolerable poverty, a sharpening perception of the chief causes of this unjust state of affairs, a new assertion of the personality of the ancient indigenous races and cultures, a determination of the poor to organize, a restless search for nonviolent ways of dealing with the existing situation, and a hardening on the part of a social system that even used violence to defend its privileges.

It was a difficult time, overcast by brooding clouds that Don Manuel Larrain saw as a threat to peace in Latin America and the Third World. Shortly after the Council he wrote:

Wretched conditions, hunger, and the sickness hunger brings with it lead every year to as many deaths in the Third World as occurred in the four years of the Second World War. . . . The history of the world has never seen a crueler struggle. The tax in blood that the underdeveloped world is paying is a scandal that cries out to the heavenly Father.[28]

26. Don Manuel Larrain did not see the fruition of his plan; he died in an automobile accident in 1966. But his witness of fidelity to the Church, combined with evangelical boldness, was a major inspiration for the Church of Latin America and especially for Medellín.

27. Some who had not been present at the events or had not understood the ferment of those years later developed a simplistic—and erroneous—explanation in an attempt to comprehend what had happened. According to them, there was an initial phase in which minorities composed of students and intellectuals played the dominant role; only later, and in a break from the first stage, did interests and individuals linked to the people make their appearance. Some ecclesial circles possessed of more good will than historical discernment have repeated this explanation in an effort to interpret pastoral and theological developments. But that is not the way things really were. What we are experiencing today had its roots in those years; the poor were from the outset actively involved in various ways in the events of that time. But this presence intensified, of course, and created new problems. This is what happens in any historical development.

28. M. Larrain, *Desarrollo. Exito o fracaso en América Latina* (Santiago de Chile, 1965), p. 2.

All this affected the life of the Church and was a challenge to many Christians. How were they to receive the Council without taking into account the situation in which the vast majority of the Church's members were living in Latin America? What light did Vatican II supply for facing up to the new situation appearing in our midst? These were questions that could not be put off until the end of the Council. The impulse given and—why deny it?—the joy produced by the Council would soon fade away unless Christians had the courage to rethink, in light of the direction being taken at the Council, the increasingly serious state of affairs in Latin America during those same years.[29]

In the midst of this situation Paul VI's encyclical *Populorum progressio* came as a trumpet call to Latin America. It dealt with matters not discussed at the Council as it gave a critical description of the "world" (that is, the social and economic order) of which Latin American countries were a part. Themes whose absence in *Gaudium et spes* was regrettable from the viewpoint of the Third World were powerfully stated in the encyclical. This explains the influence of the document on Medellín and on the theological thinking about liberation that was developing in Latin America in those years.[30]

The encyclical was faithfully echoed in "A Letter to the Peoples of the Third World" (August 1967), a message from bishops of the underdeveloped countries (eighteen bishops, nine of them Brazilian, signed the letter). Following in the steps of John XXIII and Cardinal Lercaro, the document describes the challenge that the poverty of the greater part of the human race represents for the Church. In addition, it makes a statement that was to become a key point in the theology of liberation then being developed in Latin America: "From the viewpoint of doctrine, the Church knows that the gospel calls for the first and most radical revolution: conversion, the thoroughgoing transformation from sin to grace, from egotism to love, from haughtiness to humble service."[31]

These two documents—the encyclical and the bishops' letter—formed a bridge between Vatican II and Medellín.[32] In accordance with the vision of Bishop Larrain the Medellín Conference took as its theme "The

29. I remember Don Manuel's remark in Rome during the last session of the Council: "This has been a deeply moving experience, but unless we in Latin America are attentive to our own 'signs of the times,' the Council will pass our church by, and who knows what will happen then?"

30. What is said of "integral development" in §§ 14–21 of the encyclical was the inspiration for the idea of "integral liberation" or "total liberation," within which three levels or aspects of the one comprehensive process are distinguished; see G. Gutiérrez, *A Theology of Liberation* (Maryknoll, N.Y., 1973), pp. 36–37 and 176–78 (on the passage in *Populorum progressio*, see 171–72). The tripartite distinction is repeated in the "Final Document" of Puebla, §§ 321–29.

31. In *Between Honesty and Hope* (n. 4, above), p. 4. The theology of liberation often makes the point that sin is the ultimate root of social injustice and that only the gift of liberation in Christ can reach this root. See Gutiérrez, *A Theology*, passim.

32. Over a two-year period a series of fruitful, continent-wide meetings sponsored by the agencies of CELAM served as immediate preparation for Medellín. The meetings dis-

Transformation of Latin America in the Light of Vatican II." Rightly so, for a transformation was precisely what was needed; the real situation demanded nothing less. But what directives could the Council give for this necessary change?

At Medellín the Church was faced with a sign of the times—the yearning for liberation—which it described as "a deafening cry" arising from the poor ("Poverty," § 2). It wished therefore "that the Church in Latin America should be manifested, in an increasingly clear manner, as truly *poor, missionary and paschal*, separate from all temporal power and courageously committed to the liberation of each and every man" ("Youth," § 15; italics added).

The issue, then, was to understand the Church as the Council did: as a "universal sacrament of salvation" for the Latin American world. Something of what happened at the Council happened at Medellín as well, though on a more modest scale: the search for pastoral orientations produced some rich and interesting theological thinking.[33] I shall take the words just cited as my guiding thread in an effort to see what the Church's task is in Latin America.

Sacrament of Salvation in a Poor World

What is required of the Church if it is to be a universal sacrament of salvation in a world stamped by poverty and injustice?

This is the great question the Council puts to many Latin American Christians. Medellín was an effort to answer it, as was Puebla later on.

Poor with the Poor . . .

The first problem is to take a stand on the "inhuman wretchedness" ("Poverty," § 1) I mentioned earlier. The situation these two words describe has to be analyzed not only in its effects but also in its causes, so

---

cussed such subjects as priestly vocations, pastoral planning, the role of the Catholic universities, missionary activity, social action, and the permanent diaconate. Conciliar renewal provided the inspiration in all these areas. See H. Parada, *Crónica de Medellín* (Bogotá, 1975), and the issue of *Páginas* (Lima), Dec. 1983, on Medellín, with articles by J. Alvárez, R. Antoncich, and C. Romero.—The Medellín documents will be cited from: Latin American Episcopal Council, *The Church in the Present-Day Transformation of Latin America in the Light of the Council*, L. M. Colonnese, ed. (Bogotá, 1970), I. *Position Papers*, II. *Conclusions*. All the documents cited are in volume II.

33. It is worth noting, as a manifestation of a deeply ingrained mentality, that during the preparation for Medellín Cardinal Samoré—who played an important part in the Conference and later in other areas of Latin American life as well—wrote to CELAM: "For discussion of the *theological aspects* use might be made of someone from outside Latin America; but with regard to the *practical side*, to which the greater part of the available time would naturally be devoted, it is more appropriate that the choice be made from among the Latin American bishops" (cited in Parada, *Crónica*, p. 43; italics added).

that they can be eliminated.[34] The situation in which the reign of life must be proclaimed is one of conflict. Puebla therefore says that in Latin America we have opted for "a Church that is a sacrament of communion, a Church that, in a history marked by conflicts, contributes irreplaceable energies to promote the reconciliation and solidary unity of our peoples" (§ 1302).

This supposes, however, what the Council glimpsed: that the Church travel the "way of poverty" (AG 5). The Church must be what Medellín calls a "poor church"—that is, a church that in order to be a sacrament of salvation involves itself with the poor and with poverty: "The poverty of the Church is, in effect, a constant factor in the history of salvation" ("Poverty," § 5). This involvement will require a denunciation of "the unjust lack of this world's goods and the sin that begets it," and an ability to preach and live in "spiritual poverty, as an attitude of spiritual childhood and openness to the Lord" (ibid.).

This perspective gave rise in Latin America during those years to many commitments and experiments by local churches, Christian communities, and religious families that wanted to bear witness to liberation in Christ in the midst of the poor. The task was not an easy one. That is why Puebla would speak of the necessity of a "conversion" of individual Christians and of the Church as a whole: "We affirm the need for conversion on the part of the whole Church to a preferential option for the poor, an option aimed at their integral liberation" (§ 1134). The idea of a "preferential option for the poor" is stated six more times in the Puebla document. What the phrase calls for is a radical change of outlook, a change that cannot come about except by a gradual process. The pursuit of it brings advances but also pitfalls, enthusiasms and discouragements, successes and failures.

This preference for the poor must find expression in an authentic "solidarity with the poor . . . [which] means that we make ours their problems and their struggles, that we know how to speak with them" ("Poverty," § 10). The requirement of solidarity would put its seal on the practice of the Church in the years after Medellín. John Paul II would later repeat the same theme in a very powerful way, speaking of the Church's solidarity with the poor as "its mission, its service, a proof of its fidelity to Christ." Then, using an expression of John XXIII not heard for a long time in magisterial documents at this high level, the pope added that the purpose of this solidarity is "so that it [the Church] can truly be the 'church of the poor.' "[35]

From the beginning, however, it was also understood that preference for the poor must not lead to forgetfulness of another basic principle of

34. In this context Puebla § 1146 cites a statement of the Council: "Not only the effects but also the causes of various ills must be removed" (AA 8).

35. John Paul II, encyclical *Laborem exercens* (Sept. 14, 1981), § 8, in *TPS*, 26 (1981) 302. The pope has returned several times to the subject of "the Church of the poor"; see A. Barreiro, *Os pobres e o Reino. Do Evangelho a João Paulo II* (São Paulo, 1983).

the Gospel: the universality of Christian love. Consequently, after speaking of solidarity with the poor, Medellín went on to say that the Church must be "the humble servant of *all* our people" ("Poverty," 8; italics added).[36] Later on, Puebla repeated this point, drawing its inspiration from Medellín and the theology being developed in Latin America during those years.

. . . Because of Christ

The theme of the Church of the poor has a clearly christological dimension both at Medellín and in the pastoral practice and theological thinking the Medellín documents inspired. In other words, there is no question simply of being sensitive to the concrete situation of the poor who make up the vast majority in Latin America; the fundamental call is rather to faith in Christ, which is to give full meaning to everything. Medellín's statement on poverty makes this unmistakably clear. Of the many relevant passages in it I shall cite only one: "The poverty of so many brothers cries out for justice, solidarity, open witness, commitment, strength, and exertion *directed to* the fulfillment of the redeeming mission to which it [the Church] is committed by Christ" ("Poverty," § 7; italics added). The salvation that Christ brings and of which the Church is a sacrament within history is what gives meaning to the whole issue of "the Church of the poor."[37]

This christological outlook is also inspired by another statement of the Council. In LG 8 the Council says that the Church "recognizes in those who are poor and who suffer the image of her poor and suffering founder . . . and in them she strives to serve Christ." This identification of Christ with the poor (see Matt. 25: 31–46) is a principal theme in reflection on the Church of the poor. Puebla expresses the idea beautifully in a lengthy paragraph on the "suffering features" of Christ as seen in the many "very concrete faces" of the poor ("Final Document," §§ 31–39).

The Church of Latin America thus takes a *theological approach* in its treatment of the Church of the poor (in official teaching, pastoral practice, and theology). That is, in dealing with this theme the Church does not emphasize solely the social aspects of its mission, but relates the theme primarily to its own nature as sign of God's reign. This was, of course, the very heart of John XXIII's insight ("The Church is, and wants to be"), as developed by Cardinal Lercaro. It is important to call attention to this point because there is a tendency to see the whole issue as a "social problem" and to think that one has grasped the full significance

36. This idea is repeated several times in the same document (see no. 18) and in other documents of Medellín.

37. This idea was to be a constant element in the Latin American theology of liberation; see the writings of Leonardo Boff, Ronaldo Muñoz, Jon Sobrino, and my own contributions.

of poverty for the Church when one has established a secretariat for social concerns.

That is not how "the Church of the poor" is understood in Latin
America. The approach taken by the Church there manifests rather a
profound fidelity to John XXIII and to the imprint his ideas left on the
Council.[38]

The Mystery of Evangelization

Medellín said that the Church, in addition to being poor, must be *missionary*. The word sums up a comprehensive thrust of Vatican II and
what may even be called the principal inspiration at work in its various
documents. A missionary church is a church that looks outside itself in
service to the world and, in the final analysis, to the Lord of history, as
Gaudium et spes repeatedly says.

This missionary inspiration is well expressed in *Ad gentes*, which is
one of the most richly theological documents of the Council. In it mission is presented, in light of its Trinitarian foundation, not as one among
many activities of the Church but as a central characteristic of the Christian community as a whole. Medellín adopts the same perspective, but
in terms of a church that has existed peacefully, even if in its own special
manner, within a Christian culture and society.

Puebla repeats the call to mission that was uttered at Medellín and
speaks of "a missionary church that joyously proclaims to people today
that they are children of God in Christ; that commits itself to the liberation of the whole human being and all human beings . . . and that
in solidarity immerses itself in the apostolic activity of the universal
Church" (§ 1304).

In this context of mission I should like to emphasize two things that
have been characteristic of the Latin American Church.

The Poor Have the Gospel Preached to Them

This demanding theme, which is so very much a part of the Gospel,
played a part in Vatican II but, as we saw earlier, did not become a major
issue. It did, however, become a central concern at Medellín, where it
supplied the context for the preferential option for the poor that inspired
the principal documents of that conference.

38. In the beginning, the term "people's Church" or "Church of the people" was used
for "Church of the poor," this last being understood not as an alternative to the traditional
Church but as expressing the vocation of the entire Church; another description was
"Church born of the people" (Puebla, § 263). Today, however, the term "people's
Church" or "popular Church" should be firmly rejected (Puebla calls it "quite unfortunate," ibid.) because of its ambiguity and the singular interpretations given of it. Use of it
nowadays causes needless confusion.

Everyone is familiar with the biblical basis for this proclamation of the Gospel to the poor. The point to be emphasized here is that this ideal has characterized the life of the Latin American Church in recent years. Many experiments have been undertaken and many commitments made in an effort to proclaim the message to the most disinherited. In proceeding along this line, the Church has found itself in tune with the deep longing the poor of Latin America have for liberation.

All this has brought with it an extensive renewal in the Church's way of acting. The call to mission always entails a going out of its own world and an entering into a different world. This is what sizable sectors of the Latin American Church have experienced as they have embarked upon the evangelization of the poor and the oppressed: they have begun to discover *the world of the poor*. That world is far more alien to the Church than churchmen had been accustomed to think. It is a world that has deficiencies and limitations but also potentialities and riches. To be poor is to survive rather than live;[39] it is to be subject to exploitation and injustice; it is also, however, to possess a special way of feeling, thinking, loving, creating, suffering, and praying. The proclamation of the Gospel to the poor requires entering their world of wretchedness—and of hope.

The Church in Latin America has only entered upon this road. It has made a beginning, however, of what is one form of openness to the world as called for by the Council: in this case, openness to the world of poverty. The proclamation of the Gospel to the poor has also become a point of fruitful contact with Christians of other confessions and has thus opened new paths for ecumenical dialogue. The efforts made are only beginnings, but they are real, and the other churches of Latin America can repeat what the Church of Peru has said in light of its own experience:

This message of liberation has in recent years inspired the life of the Church in Peru, as it has numerous statements of the bishops, for it is a source of deeper spirituality. The Church has achieved an important presence, as sign of hope and salvation, in society as a whole and especially among the poorest and most marginalized.[40]

But this closeness to the poor brings new challenges to which no response is possible apart from a deepening Christian maturity in the Spirit.

The Evangelizing Potential of the Poor

Puebla, like Medellín, emphasized the importance for the Church of evangelizing the poor; this is a basic and abiding requirement of the Gospel. At the same time, however, the years that elapsed between the

39. See John Paul II, "Address to the Bishops of Peru" (Oct. 4, 1984).
40. Statement of the Peruvian Episcopal Conference on the theology of liberation, § 10 (Oct. 1984).

two conferences had made it possible to study the call to evangelization more thoroughly and discover new aspects of it.

They had been years of commitment "to defend the rights of the poor and oppressed according to the Gospel commandment" (Medellín, "Peace," § 22); years, too, in which Christian base communities were established as "the first and fundamental ecclesiastical nucleus, which . . . must make itself responsible for the richness and expansion of the faith" (Medellín, "Joint Pastoral Planning," § 10). These experiences "helped the Church to discover the evangelizing potential of the poor" (Puebla, § 1147).

The poor, the privileged (though not exclusive) addressees of the message of the kingdom, are also its *bearers*. One way in which they carry out this role is through the base-level ecclesial communities that Puebla hails as one of the most important developments in the life of the Latin American Church and as an embodiment of "the Church's preferential love for the common people" (§ 643). In these communities, moreover, the poor "are given a concrete opportunity to share in the task of the Church and to work committedly for the transformation of the world" (ibid.).

The base-level ecclesial communities are undoubtedly one of the most fruitful forces at work in the Latin American Church. They have their place in the broad channel cut out by Vatican II in its reflections on the people of God and its historical journey. They are a manifestation of the people of God as existing in the world of poverty but at the same time they are profoundly marked by Christian faith. They reveal the presence in the Church of the "nobodies" of history or, to use a term from Vatican II, of a "messianic people" (LG 9). They are, in other words, a people journeying through history and continually bringing about the messianic reversal: "The last shall be first."

A Paschal Service

When the Church proclaims the Gospel at the heart of the world of poverty it bears witness to *life* in the midst of *death*.

It must pay a price for doing this. Medellín had spoken of a "paschal church." Later on, after many painful experiences, Puebla spoke of "a servant church that prolongs down through the ages Christ, the Servant of Yahweh, by means of its various ministries and charisms" (§ 1303). The reference to the suffering servant (the document cites Isa. 42) shows that the Church is aware of the road it must travel in carrying out its mission of service.

To Set Free from Death

In the final analysis the poverty in which Latin America is living means premature and unjust death caused by hunger and sickness or by the repressive methods that the wealthy use to defend their privileges. "Death" means bodily death but it also includes cultural death caused by contempt for races and cultures, as well as death in other areas of human concern because of the refusal to acknowledge fully the dignity of women, especially women belonging to the exploited strata of society.

In this real world of death the Church must proclaim life, that is, it must announce the reign of life as an expression of God's love for every human being. This is the starting point for those who commit themselves to the liberation of the poor. In the Latin American situation, to liberate means to give life and to give it in its entirety, because the liberation Christ brings is integral liberation. It includes liberation from the ultimate root of every kind of injustice, namely, sin, but it also includes liberation from everything that keeps a man or woman from being fully human.

To give life, then, means giving bread to the poor, helping a people to organize, defending its rights, being concerned with the health of the most marginalized, preaching the Gospel, forgiving one's brothers and sisters, celebrating the Eucharist, praying, and giving one's own life. The Christians who are increasingly committing themselves to these tasks do not confuse the various levels or claim that they are interchangeable, so that someone may arbitrarily choose one or another. They are, however, conscious that the reign of life includes life in all its forms.

The service of the Church to the world, of which the Council had so much to say, takes the form in Latin America of witness to and proclamation of total liberation in Christ, not as something fully realizable within history but as something that even now breaks the bonds of selfishness and opens one to the gift of fellowship and communion. When Medellín spoke of the course of behavior and thinking upon which many Latin American Christians have embarked, it also gave it a solid theological basis: "It is the same [creator] God who in the fullness of time sends his Son in the flesh, so that he might come to liberate all men from the slavery to which sin has subjected them: hunger, misery, oppression, and ignorance, in a word, that injustice and hatred which have their origin in human selfishness" ("Justice," § 3).

Death as Witness to Life

Talk of liberation does not presuppose, as some seem to think, a facile and enthusiastic optimism. On the contrary, the language of liberation can arise only out of an experience of oppression and death; otherwise the very word would become meaningless.

Furthermore, as recent years have made clear beyond any doubt, few things in Latin America are more life-threatening than the attempt to defend the right to life. The road of commitment to the poorest and most oppressed is for many a road of imprisonment, torture, disappearance, exile, and death. Among those suffering this fate are many Christians, who are mistreated precisely because they bear witness to the Gospel by their effort at solidarity with the marginalized. Perhaps we lack as yet the perspective needed for an objective examination of this martyrdom of the Latin American Church, but one thing is certain: this church cannot be the same after so many of its children have given this kind of witness.[41]

The Church of the poor disturbs the great of this world, whatever their ideological framework, and attacks their interests. For this reason it encounters the Lord's cross as it pursues its way. To use the description of Medellín, this church is a "paschal church," a church that for this very reason cannot be "triumphalist" (as people were already saying at the time of the Council). The blood of those who attest their love of God by solidarity with the poor is proof that this encounter with death and the cross is taking place. But the "blood of Christians is the seed" of a new life and a new hope (as AG 5 and 24 remind us).

The blood of martyrs is always a source of new life for the Church. Ours is a church that through the suffering and death of so many of its members proclaims with new words the abiding message of the death of death and the definitive victory of the risen Christ. This is what Latin American Christians are experiencing in our time, and the experience is preparing them for receiving the gift of God's unmerited love and at the same time impelling them to accept their obligation to the poorest. Paschal suffering and joy is the part they have chosen, and no one shall take it from them.

Conclusion

It can be said, I think, that the Church in Latin America has made an important change of direction in light of the perspective opened up to it by the Council, which it has accepted in a mature and dynamic fashion. The change shows in the way it has taken into account what is for it *the* sign of the times, namely, the yearning of the poor and oppressed for liberty, justice, dignity: in the final analysis, life. The importance of the poor in the reign of God and therefore in the proclamation of the Gospel is the key realization behind the change the Latin American Church is now experiencing. Because of it, and only because of it, has it been possible for Medellín and Puebla (and the theology of liberation) to regard poverty as a "social problem." The preferential option for the poor is a theocentric option, for faith in the God of Jesus Christ is its first and most important motive.

41. See M. Lange and R. Iblacker, *Witnesses of Hope* (Maryknoll, N.Y., 1981), with its interesting preface by Karl Rahner on the meaning of martyrdom.

The result is that the Latin American Church, like the base-level ecclesial communities, the theologians of liberation, and Medellín, has made
its own the insight of John XXIII vis-à-vis the Church of the poor, and it
has tried to interpret the great themes of the Council in light of this insight. The statements made at Medellín and the program it laid out are
inexplicable without reference to the Council with all its complexity and
all its varied languages and problematics. There is no question, however, of a simple, mechanical application of Vatican II. Rather, the Latin
American Church is endeavoring in a profoundly mature way to be
faithful, with the Council, to the Lord of history and to a church that is
beginning to become truly universal, as Karl Rahner has said.[42]

Nothing could be further from my mind than to claim that the Latin
American Church is moving unanimously and victoriously along the
path of which I have been speaking. The many instances pointing to the
opposite are stubborn facts. It seems to me, nonetheless, that the period
since the Council has been one of rich and profound life for Latin American Christians with their sufferings and joys, their enthusiasms and
frustrations, their advances and their setbacks. It has been a favorable
time, a *kairos*, for proclaiming the God of life in a world of death.

But the time will prove really fruitful only if the Church has the courage and humility needed for becoming poor, missionary, and paschal.
The Latin American Church's reception of the Council will be found in
its response to this *kairos*, which remains more a possibility than an
established fact.

42. It is sometimes said that the spirit of the Council is more important than its documents. There is a good deal of truth in this, but on the other hand it is not legitimate to
separate spirit and documents utterly. Flight from the letter that kills can lead to a disincar-
nate spiritualism that lacks any foothold in history and any connection with the concrete
challenges the Council was facing (and the limits it found imposed on it). The spirit of the
Council is embodied in its documents and reveals in them the task it sets for our time.

Pierre Toulat

10. Peace: Between the Good News and the Lesser Evil

"The coming ecumenical council will stir up and encourage thoughts and resolutions of peace in all human beings of good will." Thus said John XXIII in the apostolic constitution by which he convoked the Second Vatican Council.[1] He himself was evidently concerned for peace and would later give striking expression to this concern in his Encyclical *Pacem in terris* (April 1963). Meanwhile, the fathers of the Council echoed it. In a message to all of humankind they made their own two points emphasized by the pope: peace among nations, and the requirements of social justice.[2] The Council would speak of peace, and John XXIII had set the tone.

The concern for peace that the pope expressed so forthrightly was not to be found in the preparatory texts. Yet from the very first days of the Council, due to the efforts of several bishops, Dom Hélder Câmara among them, the theme of peace did make its appearance.[3] It ultimately became the subject of chapter 5 of the "Constitution on the Church in the Modern World" (Dec. 7, 1965); the chapter was given the title, "Fostering of Peace and Establishment of a Community of Nations."[4]

1. Bull of convocation *Humanae salutis*, Dec. 25, 1961, in *AAS* 54 (1962). Same theme, with reference to the Council, on May 16, 1962, in *Discorsi, messaggi, colloqui del santo padre Giovanni XXIII* (= *DMC*, 4:805–7; June 21, 1962 (*DMC*, 4:391–96); Sept. 9, 1962 (*DMC*, 4:512–18); Oct. 11 at the opening of the Council (*AAS*, 54 [1962] 786–96); and Feb. 2, 1963 (*DMC*, 5:105–11).

2. "Message of the Fathers of the Council (October 20, 1962)," in *TPS*, 8 (1962–63) 302–3.

3. *DC*, no. 1390, cited by A. Wenger, *Vatican II*. Vol. 1, *The First Session* (Westminster, Md., 1966), p. 125.

4. GS 77–82 and 83–91. All the citations that follow in the text (with section numbers in parentheses) are from this section of the constitution; translation from A. Flannery, ed., *Vatican II: The Conciliar and Postconciliar Documents* (Collegeville, Minn., 1975).

Gains Made by the Council

The question that chiefly occupied the attention of the Council was that of "every kind of weapon produced by modern science" (§ 79). The expression is typical, in that we will look in vain for the words "atomic" and "nuclear" in the conciliar documents, even though these weapons were the primary focus of the discussion. The Council's description says that science, by reason of its applications to armaments, is a decisive cause of the dangerous situation in which the human race finds itself.

There is no unqualified condemnation of any and every kind of war. The Council does indeed say: "It is our clear duty to spare no effort in order to work for the moment when all war will be completely outlawed by international agreement" (§ 82). The statement echoes, in more detailed but also more neutral terms, the urgent cry that Paul VI uttered at the United Nations a few days before the conciliar text was adopted: "War never again!"

At the present time, however, as long as there is no universal authority capable of ensuring the security of all nations, heads of state cannot reject all war without qualification, because they undoubtedly still have the right of *legitimate self-defense*.

In this matter of self-defense the Council nonetheless makes several clear points:

- "It is one thing to wage a war of self-defense; it is quite another to impose domination on another nation" (§ 79). "Self-defense is not conquest."
- "The possession of war potential does not justify the use of force for political or military objectives. Nor does the mere fact that war has unfortunately broken out mean that all is fair between the warring parties" (§ 79). Self-defense, though legitimate, does not justify any and every kind of "strike."

For these reasons, the Council clearly and unequivocally condemns the following:

- The *extermination* of a people, nation, or ethnic minority (genocide and ethnocide): "These actions must be condemned as frightful crimes" (§ 79).
- *Total war*, which would make unrestricted use of the scientific weapons already stockpiled by the major powers and thus lead to "the almost complete reciprocal slaughter of one side by the other" (§ 80).
- Every act of war directed to the indiscriminate destruction of whole cities or vast areas with their inhabitants." Such acts are "a crime against God and man, which merits firm and unequivocal condemnation" (§ 80).

(Nuclear) *deterrence* is the subject of a qualified judgment. For one thing, the Council observes that, paradoxically, the possession of nuclear weapons serves to make potential enemies think twice. For another, it notes that "many people look upon this [the stockpiling of arms] as the most effective way known at the present time for maintaining some sort of peace among nations" (§ 81). It is clear of course from the context that the actual use of these weapons is condemnable and condemned; their use would end in "barbarities far surpassing those of former ages" (§ 79). But nothing is said expressly about the manufacture or possession of nuclear weapons. In addition, neither the problem nor the vocabulary of threat as distinct from use appears clearly.

When all is said and done, the conciliar text passes no categorical judgment on deterrence as a strategy. The judgment reached is marked by perplexity, as is clear from the transitional phrase used: "whatever one may think of this form of deterrent" (§ 81). In any case, the Council does not make its own John XXIII's judgment that "nuclear weapons should be banned."[5]

The *arms race* merits a strong denunciation. It is "one of the greatest curses on the human race." It results in a "so-called balance of power" that "is no sure and genuine path to achieving" peace. "The harm it inflicts on the poor is more than can be endured" (§ 81).

For these reasons, "all must work to put an end to the arms race and make a real beginning of disarmament, not unilaterally indeed but at an equal rate on all sides, on the basis of agreements and backed up by genuine and effective guarantees" (§ 82).

The question of *nonviolence* is only touched on in passing, in the form of approval of those who renounce violent means "to vindicate their rights" (§ 78). Conscientious objection, for its part, is mentioned in connection with agreements entered into between nations in order to render military actions less inhuman. Like wounded soldiers and prisoners of war, conscientious objectors should be treated humanely: "It seems just that laws should make humane provision for the case of conscientious objectors who refuse to carry arms, provided they accept some other form of community service" (§ 79).

Many questions are not discussed in the conciliar document: for example, ideological wars and wars of independence, or terrorism. On the other hand, the text does say that the work for peace includes the transformation of relationships between rich nations and poor nations, and of the structures involving both. Finally, it emphasizes the precariousness of the situation. It therefore urges that we "profit by the respite we now enjoy, to take stock of our responsibilities and find ways of resolving controversies in a manner worthy of human beings" (§ 81).

5. *Pacem in terris*, § 112. Translation from J. Gremillion, ed., *The Gospel of Peace and Justice: Catholic Social Teaching Since Pope John* (Maryknoll, N.Y., 1976). The schema for *Gaudium et spes* that was presented in the third session suggested that the Council call for the removal and destruction of nuclear weapons; see A. Wenger, *Vatican II. 3ᵉ session*

Has the "message" of the Council been received? How much of it have Catholics retained? To what extent has it been a point of reference, a sign, a catalyst? What change has it wrought in the activities of Christians and in the pastoral practice of the Church? In this area it is difficult to distinguish clearly between the response of a living faith to events and what comes from the Council as its own special message. We can nonetheless discern the influence of the Council by studying some important statements made at different points during the twenty years since the Council ended.[6]

The 1960s or the Period Immediately Following the Council

The dominant event of the 1960s was the achievement of independence by countries that had until then been colonies. The Bandung Conference of 1955, at which representatives of twenty-seven countries had condemned colonialism and the arms race, still had a considerable impact on the countries of the Third World. This ongoing influence marked the years immediately after the Council.

Development, the New Name for Peace

The Council spoke of peace and the organization of a community of nations. This message was given and received as an invitation to link peace with what Paul VI would later call "international social justice."

Three successive events served as signs of this close connection between justice and peace.

First, there was the recognition of human rights in the encyclical *Pacem in terris*, published during the Council (in April 1963). The fact that a document dealing with peace should include human rights, point out their importance, and set down the demands these rights make was enough to show that justice in its various aspects is closely connected with peace.

(Paris, 1965), p. 441. On the overall position of the Council, see H. de Riedmatten, "L'enseignement du Concile sur la guerre et la paix," *Etudes*, Feb. 1966.

6. The study that follows deals with documents published by episcopal conferences. It does not review, except incidentally, the pontifical teaching of the period. Nor, finally, does it bring in books and articles on moral theology, which included works by Frs. Dubarle, de Riedmatten, Bosc, René Coste, Jacques Jullien (now archbishop of Rennes), Joseph Comblin, and Christian Mellon. These omissions point up the first limitation of this article, which might have been subtitled, "Landmarks in Episcopal Documents (1962–1984)." A further limitation is shown by the fact that at least in the first period the bishops were not only transmitters of the conciliar message on peace but also its recipients.

Then, hardly a year after the end of the Council, the Pontifical Commission *Justitia et Pax*, for which the conciliar document had called,[7] was established, on January 6, 1967. The very name chosen was symbolic. In terms of syntax, it expresses a juxtaposition, interrelationship, or concomitance of two terms. The biblical passage from which the name was derived says a good deal more: that the one prepares for the other, peace being the fruit of justice and justice a condition for and effect of peace. Moreover, the *motu proprio* establishing the commission was basically concerned with "justice" as an objective.

Finally, the act of changing the name for peace showed an insight into the connection between peace and justice. The encyclical *Populorum progressio* (March 1967) made its own a statement of the Pax Christi movement: "Development is the new name for peace." The statement went too far, as was realized later on, but it was to have a fruitful, lasting, and concrete influence.

Peace as development was the concept most clearly understood in the Catholic community and beyond. Peace was henceforth rebaptized "development" and, for practical purposes, identified with it. The emphasis was certainly rendered explicable by the historical context but also, and perhaps even more, by the contact between the bishops of North and South over a three-year period at the Council. There they were able to convince one another that unless justice is done to the poor it is difficult to talk of peace. They would eventually say, in *Gaudium et spes*, that peace "is the fruit of that right ordering of things with which the divine founder has invested human society and which must be actualized by man thirsting after an ever more perfect reign of justice."[8] The document goes on to urge Christians actively to alleviate "the immensity of the hardships which still afflict a large section of humanity."[9]

Many declarations and resolutions of the postconciliar period show that the message of peace-justice or peace-development had "made its way" into the Christian community. It was repeated, for example, by assemblies of bishops,[10] in the first documents issued by the European National Commissions for Justice and Peace,[11] and in the resolutions of the third World Congress for the Apostolate of the Laity.[12] Development

7. GS 90.
8. Ibid., 78.
9. Ibid., 90.
10. See, among others, the first statement of the French episcopate after the Council, Oct. 27, 1966 (*DC*, no. 1479), the message of the Synod of Bishops in Rome, Oct. 28, 1967 (*DC*, no. 1505), the final statement of the Kampala Symposium, July 31, 1969 (*DC*, no. 1548). See also the ecumenical message in behalf of peace that was sent to General de Gaulle, Dec. 20, 1967 (*DC*, no. 1508).
11. Texts in *DC*, no. 1553. See the report of the French Commission for Justice and Peace on "France's Policy of Helping the Developing Countries" (an appraisal in the light of *Populorum progressio*), in *Projet*, 31 (Jan. 1969).
12. Rome, Oct. 1967 (*DC*, no. 1508).

and peace, sometimes identified, sometimes distinguished but linked, seemed to be *"the* problem of the present time."[13]

The Struggle for Justice

As a matter of fact, out in the field development meant conflicts. Local churches came to acknowledge what they had long overlooked: Yes, in the end, development is synonymous with peace, but during the time when it is being promoted it brings tensions to light and also engenders them. The general conference of the Latin American episcopate at Medellín in 1968 understood this. "Peace," the second of the final documents, opens with these words: "If 'development is the new name for peace,' Latin American under-development, with its own characteristics in the different countries, is an unjust situation which promotes tensions that conspire against peace."[14]

These tensions are so many threats to peace. One threat is "internal colonialism," that is, the state of tension caused by inequalities between social classes and by the nonsatisfaction of the legitimate desires of less favored classes. Another threat is "external neocolonialism," that is, the dependence of the Latin American countries on foreign powers that act as their center of gravity. Still another threat is the "exacerbated nationalism" of some Latin American countries, which leads them to arm themselves to an excessive and unreasonable degree.

In such a situation, "order" has only the outward appearances of peace. Oppression allays suspicion. It makes people think that peace and order are being maintained, but in fact it is a continual incitement to revolts and wars. Force can establish a static peace. Authentic peace, however, supposes a struggle, a capacity for inventiveness, and an ongoing conquest of selfishness and injustice, both individual and collective.

The struggle can turn violent. The bishops at Medellín therefore set down some principles to govern action. Christians, they said, are people of peace; the Gospel makes this part of their manner of life. But they are not pacifists: they can fight. They have clear insight, moreover, into the forms of violence. By violence is usually meant actions performed under the impulse of anger and rebellion. But there is also "institutionalized violence." This distinction brings to light a new kind of violence, that exerted by established situations defended by dominant groups who possess power and have no ear for the needs of the poor. The poor are finally unable to endure any longer being thus pushed aside. They be-

13. Kampala Symposium, July 31, 1969 (*DC,* no. 1548).
14. Second General Conference of the Latin American Bishops, *The Church in the Present-Day Transformation of Latin America in the Light of the Council,* M. Colonnese, ed. (Bogotá, 1970), 2:71.

come conscious of their aspirations and rights, gather their strength, and are tempted to violence. Institutional violence provokes acts of violence by the oppressed, whom the "forces of order" then repress to the point of brutality. The result, to use the image of Dom Hélder Câmara, is "the spiral of violence."

Basing themselves on *Populorum progressio* (§ 31) and not on the conciliar document, which does not mention the point, the bishops recognize that revolutionary insurrection can be legitimate.

They add, however, that revolution usually begets new injustices. That is why, all things considered, they desire that "the dynamism of the awakened and organized community be put to the service of justice and peace" ("Peace," § 19).

In Latin America, the struggle for "justice in the world" (Synod of Bishops, 1971) not only went on in a climate of violence but was made more difficult by the doctrine of national security, which inspired a repressive system that sought justification in the concept of "permanent war." The third general conference of the Latin American episcopate (Puebla, 1979) would later put Christians on guard against this ideology, though many of the bishops had long since been denouncing it.[15] It was in this climate of thought and in this experiential context that peace movements developed with "liberation" and "nonviolence" as their guiding ideals. These two terms, though little used in the conciliar documents, became for the ecclesial communities of Latin America a sign that these documents were present and at work in a special situation of which they showed an awareness and provided an analysis.

Independence by Warfare

The Vietnam war was a world event. The United States alone was directly involved in it, but public opinion and political organizations in the various countries were actively mobilized as the war expanded.

About a year after their country began to participate actively in the war,[16] the bishops of the United States undertook to reflect on the conflict. Divergent positions emerged. Cardinal Spellman's was the best known,[17] but it was not the most representative. The statement prepared in 1966 by a commission under the presidency of Cardinal Shehan of

15. See the "Final Document" of the Puebla Conference, §§ 49, 314, 547–49, 1262, in J. Eagleson and P. Scharper, eds., *Puebla and Beyond: Documentation and Commentary* (Maryknoll, N.Y. 1979).

16. June 28, 1965: American paratroopers take part in the Vietnam fighting for the first time; Aug. 21–22, 1965: first air attack and barrage north of the 17th parallel; etc. (headlines from *Le Monde*).

17. Several interventions of Cardinal Spellman received wide-ranging attention: the circular letter of Dec. 2, 1965, signed by ten bishops, urging a *non placet* vote on chapter 5 of *Gaudium et spes* (*DC*, no. 1465); his statement to the American soldiers in Vietnam on Dec. 24, 1966, and the reactions of the French bishops (*DC*, no. 1487).

Baltimore expressed a more carefully weighed point of view.[18] With the conciliar documents as point of reference, the statement justified the presence of the United States in Vietnam as aid to a nation struggling against an oppressor. But the justification was not unqualified. As Cardinal Shehan had already said in a pastoral letter, "All is not permissible in even a presumably just war of self-defense. . . . Assuming that our cause in Vietnam is just, our duties to mankind as a whole forbid us to indulge in passions of hatred and aggression."

In these two statements the Vietnam war was seen as being, on the part of the United States, an intervention of the strong in defense of the weak. There was yet no thought of the right of the weak, or the supposedly weak, to become independent. The perspective was still that of defense and protection, although the stakes extended beyond the borders of the country being "protected."

The problem of independence was taken up a few years later (1974) in a statement from a different context, that of South Africa.[19] After ten years of war there, Bishop Vieira Pinto, in Mozambique, endeavored to set forth a Christian position on decolonization. He specified the reasons that move a people to resist a foreign power: injustices, but, above all, the aspiration for and natural right of self-determination, in which human beings are regarded no longer as objects but as subjects of their own development. Self-development is a sign of advancing self-awareness and "a forward step in the process whereby human beings achieve liberation and communion in Jesus Christ." Unless the right to self-determination and independence is acknowledged and respected, there can be no lasting peace.

Do these reasons make war legitimate? Referring to the short sentence in which the Council said we must "undertake a completely fresh reappraisal of war" (GS 80), the bishop told the warring parties that "recourse to arms in order to avenge serious violations of justice is never an appropriate means or one worthy of human beings. War is an evil and a source of evils." In the present state of international relationships, war is still a last resort, once all other possibilities of peaceful settlement have been exhausted: but it is the last resort, never the first.

A reappraisal of war also brings an assertion of the inviolable principles of justice. Thus in peace as in war a sacred respect for human life must be an inviolable principle of action. No human being has the right to decide on life or death for others. God alone is master. The duty of not killing remains even in the midst of armed conflict. Legitimate defense is not an authorization to kill; ends do not justify means. The bishop had in mind here the slaughter of innocent people, prisoners of war, and ci-

18. Pastoral letter of Cardinal Shehan of Baltimore, "Peace and Patriotism" (July 3, 1966), in *Catholic Mind*, Sept. 1966, p. 4; statement of the commission (Nov. 18, 1966), in *Pastoral Letters of the United States Catholic Bishops*, H. J. Nolan, ed. (Washington, D.C., 1983–84, 4 vols.), 3:74–77.

19. Homily of the bishop of Nampula, Jan. 1, 1974 (*DC*, no. 1653).

vilians convicted of complicity with the enemy. "To set up military operations and guerilla actions without taking measures to safeguard the
innocent is to commit crimes and thus to make a war overtly criminal,
even if by hypothesis it is a war of legitimate self-defense." The same
holds for inhuman treatment and torture.

This statement touched on a particular situation: in a war of subversion the distinction between civilians and combatants disappears. In this
kind of conflict civilian populations are a very important factor. And
they make the problem of war even more complex.

This homily was written for January 1, 1974, but the bishop was unable to deliver it (should we see in this a sign of the difficulty the Church
has in speaking out on this kind of war?). It showed a concern to set
limits on violence and war (a traditional concern of the Church), but
above all an effort to attain clarity on the meaning of a people's struggle
for political independence.

A New Kind of Patriotism

The war in Vietnam confronted the bishops of the United States with a
new problem: conscientious objection.[20] To avoid fighting in Vietnam
young men either left the country or risked imprisonment.

Not all instances of refusal of military service were to be explained
(said the bishops) as some tended to explain it, namely, by moral or
physical cowardice, though this could be the reason in some cases. It
would be unjust to level such a blanket charge against those young men
"who are clearly willing to suffer social ostracism and even prison terms
because of their opposition to a particular war. One must conclude that
for many of our youthful protesters, the motives spring honestly from
principled opposition to a given war as pointless or immoral." At any
rate, this kind of opposition is not the result solely of subjective considerations. Conscientious objection can also be based on the Gospel message and the teachings of the Church.

Conscientious objection is not simply a refusal. It is, say the bishops, a
new form of patriotism. The young, urged by a new spirit of devotion to
the human race, are eager to assist their brothers and sisters. Their attitude is a reassuring sign of a sense of individual responsibility. There is
a decline in uncritical conformism "to patterns, some of which included
strong moral elements, to be sure, but also included political, social,
cultural, and like controls not necessarily in conformity with the mind
and heart of the Church." Here we see a breach being made in the wall
of "exaggerated nationalism," and an emphasis being placed on "princi-

20. Statement of the United States bishops, "Human Life in Our Day" (Nov. 15, 1968),
in *Pastoral Letters* (n. 18, above) 3:164–94. The citations in the text are from §§ 144, 147, 148,
151, 152, and 147, successively.

ples of nonviolent political and civic action in both the domestic and international spheres."

Given this perspective, what legal solution is to be recommended for dealing with conscientious objectors? The bishops suggest that the law no longer take account solely of those whose conscientious objection is based on a total rejection of the use of military force. The time has come to pay heed likewise to "those whose reasons of conscience are more personal and specific" that is, to "selective conscientious objectors." These individuals do not reject all war but they do refuse to "serve in wars which they consider unjust or in branches of service (e.g., strategic nuclear forces) which would subject them to the performance of actions contrary to deeply held moral convictions about indiscriminate killing."

In calling for this modification of the law the bishops look upon themselves as "witnesses to a spiritual tradition that accepts enlightened conscience, even when honestly mistaken, as the immediate arbiter of moral decisions."

Conscientious objection, after being only diffidently touched on at the Council, was thus accepted as a position with a solid Christian basis. The bishops' stand, taken as it was while the war was still going on, was a testimony that was influential beyond its immediate field of application.

The 1970s

The 1970s were a decade filled with conflicts: repression, coups d'état, domestic wars, wars between nations. Europe itself was not spared. The same period saw the first oil crisis with all its consequences; it also saw negotiations for arms limitation.

The Bomb and Nonviolence

In France (to speak only of this one European country) the 1970s were characterized by a pastoral orientation formulated after the events of May 1968. The bishops said:

We appear to be uninvolved with the causes of tomorrow's wars, and our consciences are oblivious of them: the arms race, the increasingly inequitable distribution of wealth, the wretched conditions of the Third World, the rebellions that these conditions cause.[21]

21. Statement of the Plenary Assembly of the French Episcopate, Nov. 2–9, 1968 (DC, no. 1529).

They urged Christians to resist these two plagues not by fruitless denunciations or purely individual efforts but by taking an active part in social and political organizations that work for peace.

This period saw positions being taken on the atom bomb and the arms trade, while it also brought the rapid expansion of the practice of nonviolence.[22]

The decision of the French government in April 1958 to build an atomic bomb elicited various reactions, among them that of Pax Christi, which in that same year published a study, "The Atom: For or Against Human Beings?" In 1959 and again in 1961, Archbishop Guerry of Cambrai signed the French Federation petition against atomic weapons. He was the only bishop to do so, and the silence of the episcopate frightened him.[23] On March 15, 1964, Bishop Guilhem of Laval published a statement on "the atomic danger."

During the 1970s the bishops spoke out individually on the question of the bomb. The only collective interventions were the Pax Christi statement and the statement issued jointly by the Commission for Justice and Peace and the Protestant Federation.[24]

In L'Express for June 25, 1973, Bishop Boillon of Verdun spoke his mind on the atomic tests conducted by the French government:

(1) The bomb is for use against cities, and that is how it is presented. It enables us to threaten to wipe out an entire city and thus deter the enemy. The Council formally prohibits this kind of action as immoral. (2) One or other of two courses is open: Either we will use the atomic bomb against those who do not have it and thus be striking at an unarmed people, or we will use it against those who have it, and then we obviously risk being annihilated within twenty-four hours by an attack in reprisal. (3) We are on the way to alienating the hearts of the Pacific peoples. This will not contribute to the image of France or to the general cause of peace. (4) We are also spending considerable sums of money at a time when people are going hungry all over the world.[25]

The statement issued by Bishop Riobé of Orléans on July 10, 1973, started a controversy that has still not been forgotten.[26] In fact, he said only what his confrere of Verdun had said: "No to nuclear weapons!" He formulated his arguments with brevity:

No political or economic interest of any nation can justify the use of the atomic bomb. To claim that it is a means of deterrence is to suppose that one intends to

22. On this period, see P. Toulat, ed., Des évêques face au problème des armes (Paris, 1973), and idem, "L'Eglise en France et les problèmes de la paix," in Documents Episcopat, April 1984, J. Klein, ed.

23. See G. M. Garrone, Le secret d'une vie engagée: Mgr Emile Guerry d'après ses carnets intimes (Paris, 1971), pp. 193–96.

24. Pax Christi communiqué of June 9, 1973, published in Le Journal de la Paix for June 1973, and in DC, no. 1635.—Communiqué of the Justice and Peace Commission and the Protestant Federation (June 18, 1973), in DC, no. 1635.

25. Short letter in L'Express, reprinted in DC, no. 1637.

26. See Des évêques (n. 22 above), pp. 119–27.

use it if attacked. No one has the right to support such a project. How great France would show itself if it said to the world: "I have the ability to conduct nuclear tests and stockpile atomic bombs, but for the sake of peace I will not do so!" We must believe in the power of moral values, the power of nonviolence. All citizens of France who want a peaceful future owe it to themselves to show in an effective way their strong disapproval of any planned atomic escalation.[27]

The nonviolence of which Bishop Riobé was speaking was at this time gaining in popularity. Even though the Vatican II position on the subject had been cautious, it was sign enough for many Christians who were already responding to the witness of men like Gandhi, Lanza del Vasto, and Martin Luther King, Jr., the Nobel Peace Prize winner (1964) who had been assassinated in Memphis on April 4, 1968, at the age of thirty-nine. During these same years books were appearing that determined the spiritual and political course of nonviolence in France.[28] Various actions and even spectacular phenomena, whether occasional or on-going—the Mururoa expedition; the struggle of the farmers of Larzac—revealed the face of nonviolence to a general public that continued to have reservations. The trend was aided by the cooperation of the bishop of Orléans, who discovered the spiritual resources of the movement from contacts with upholders of nonviolence to whom he lent his public support on occasions when they had to answer for their conduct in court.

Local Churches and Problems of Defense

Something further happened after the Roman Synod of Bishops in October 1971. Cardinal Gouyon, delegated by the French Episcopal Conference to be national president of Pax Christi, asked his colleagues this question: "The popes and the Council have denounced the arms race, but have the local churches done their duty in this area?"[29]

As a matter of fact, something did emerge, because after the synod the episcopal conference gave a working group the task of reflecting on one of the most notable aspects of the arms race in France: the arms trade. The ecumenical statement published on this subject in April 1973 was no longer a simple cry of alarm, but a study, a "statement of thinking." In it pastors, exercising their ministry of watchfulness (Ezekiel 3), were

27. Communiqué of July 10, 1973 (DC, no. 1637). See the similar remarks of Cardinal Guyot in Des évêques, p. 142.
28. This period saw the publication of J.-M. Muller, L'Evangile de la non-violence (Paris, 1967); idem, Stratégie de l'action non-violente (Paris, 1972); J. J. Lanza del Vasto, Techniques de la non-violence (Paris, 1971); J. Toulat, La bombe ou la vie (Paris, 1970). It also saw the launching of two periodicals: Alternatives non-violentes (end of 1973) and Non-violence politique (Feb. 1978, published by the Mouvement pour une alternative non-violente), and the publication by Pax Christi of the little book, Les objecteurs de conscience aujourd'hui (Paris, 1975).
29. Cardinal Gouyon, Rome (Oct. 22, 1971; DC, no. 1597), and speech at the plenary assembly of the French episcopate, Nov. 1971 (DC, no. 1601).

addressing the Christians of their country with something more than a reminder of principles.[30]

But, interesting though this ecumenical statement was as an exercise of pastoral responsibility by a local church, it did not directly face the problems of national defense and nuclear deterrence. Nor did the Christian Cadres movement, which twice published documents on the arms trade (1968 and 1977). The Pax Christi movement did tackle the subject in its publications, but in ways determined by particular events. The most outstanding document, however, was one published in September 1973 by a national team of groups of Christian officers under the title "Thoughts on Defense."[31]

The specific subject of the document is the Christian attitude to defense. The problems of defense are discussed on the basis of the idea of the common good, which is the purpose—"at once heritage and promise"—of defense. Defense is necessary to the extent that the common good is threatened. The importance of the military component in defense is relative: "sometimes vital, often secondary, never isolated." The document studies the different responses to threats and then examines the attitudes of individuals to the main problems posed to conscience by the activation of military defense. It is here that the question of nuclear weapons arises. The document refers the reader to *Gaudium et spes* (§ 81), where it is acknowledged that the stockpiling of weapons can deter potential enemies. It is a "lesser evil," which (the document says) Christians have the right to reject, "provided they calculate carefully the risks attached to their choice and do not simply yield to the desire to have a 'good conscience.' They can also not reject this lesser evil, but they may not accept it as a permanent solution."

This document was to remain for years the only statement of Christian thinking on the problems of defense.

The 1980s

In 1978 and 1982 the United Nations assembly held two extraordinary sessions on disarmament. Wars were continuing while negotiations on arms control were getting bogged down. There was also talk of limited nuclear war as possible and winnable. Nuclear weapons were installed in Europe or would be at the end of 1983. In many European countries great marches were held in vigorous protest against a future that would

30. Standing Committee of the French Episcopate and Committee of the Protestant Federation of France, "Note de réflexion sur le commerce des armes" (April 13, 1973), in *DC*, no. 1631.

31. Réflexions sur la défense," published by the military vicariate and reprinted in *Revue de la défense nationale* for Oct. 1973 (*DC*, no. 1640).

be patterned by recourse to nuclear deterrence (the protest was ambiguous as well, by reason of partisan views mingled with it).

The Bishops and Peace

In this turbulent setting the churches began to move. In many countries of the Americas and Europe, associations, movements, and communities took an active part in peace demonstrations. As a rule, Catholic bishops did not "march" in these exciting events, which were described, usually with a pejorative intention, as "pacifist." In Europe the bishops of the Netherlands were the only ones to mention them (in their statement of May 1983). They recognized that the peace movements (they single out Pax Christi and the I. K. V.) have played an important part in increasing pressure for disarmament.[32]

Two political interventions of 1982 deserve to be pointed out.

In June of that year, the presidents of the German and French episcopal conferences issued an unprecedented joint statement on peace. It was the first such statement since the end of the Second World War. The action throws light on the solid reconciliation that had been effected between the two countries as well as their current cooperation. The subjects discussed were contemporary tensions and conflicts, peace policy (which is more than a policy of military security), the threats coming from inequalities between rich and poor countries, and disarmament, which cannot be unilateral because this would be dangerous for peace and for the autonomy and freedom of our peoples.[33]

On July 2, 1982, fifteen days after the publication of the joint statement, a delegation of church leaders, Catholic and Protestant, presented the president of the French Republic with a mutually agreed "viewpoint" (agreed to within limits) in connection with the second United Nations session on disarmament.[34] The text warned against the proliferation of nuclear weapons, noted with interest the message being sent by popular peace demonstrations, suggested possible steps the French government might take, mentioned the uneasiness the Pacific peoples felt at continuing nuclear test, pointed out the contradictions in the arms trade, and spoke of the desirability of having public opinion play a part in the development of disarmament policies.

The novelty of these two interventions was to the tenor of the messages, expressing as they did positions hitherto only implicit on the problems of defense. These positions would take clearer form as events unfolded.

32. Pastoral letter of the Netherlands Bishops, May, 1983 (DC, no. 1863).
33. "Faire la paix," a joint statement of the French and German episcopates, June 15, 1982 (DC, no. 1863).
34. "Le désarmament: Point de vue d'Eglises chrétiennes de France," in DC, no. 1835.

The most important of these events was the NATO decision to authorize the United States to locate 464 Cruise missiles and 108 Pershing rockets in Europe, beginning in December 1983. The decision was taken at the very time when conversations were being held in Geneva (from November 30, 1981, onward) on the limitation of intermediate nuclear missiles, and others (from June 29, 1982, onward) on reduction in the number of strategic weapons. The episcopal conferences of the United States, Europe, and Japan could not but feel concern. In fact, however, the pastoral letter that the United States bishops published at this time was not inspired by the debate on missiles in Europe but rather by the danger in technological advances that were making a "limited" nuclear war seem feasible.

In any case, this letter on the "challenge of peace," which had been in the works since 1979 and was published in 1982, had a decisive impact.[35]

The United States bishops, "citizens of the nation that was first to produce atomic weapons, which has been the only one to use them," and pastors of a local church belonging to a world power, were here calling upon their colleagues in the European churches, who for the most part had had nothing to say about the problems of nuclear deterrence.

The step here taken was an unusual one in the Catholic Church. The novelty was that a regional pastoral document should be made public to the United States and the world. The action gave many individuals, groups, and even governments, an opportunity to respond. Inasmuch as the way in which others are addressed is sometimes as important as the message being conveyed to them, the bishops' action was interpreted as reflecting a desire to get many people thinking. The letter was based on serious inquiry, and its principal sources were available to the public. It supposed and looked for discussion. It was a trusting sign given to those willing to speak their piece.

War and Threats of War

The chief emphasis in the letter of the United States bishops is on the rejection of even limited nuclear war. The very idea of such a war must be set aside. It is not morally justifiable. Appealing to "just war" theory the bishops show that in a nuclear war there would be a disproportion between expected gains and the destructive means used: the principle of proportionality would not be observed. Nor would the principle of discrimination, because civilian populations would inevitably be attacked.

---

35. "The Challenge of Peace: God's Promise and Our Response" (May 3, 1983), in *Pastoral Letters* (n. 18, above), 4:493–581; the citation in the next paragraph of the text is from no. 4 (p. 494). See also the address on "The German, French, and United States Pastorals on War and Peace," which Cardinal Bernardin delivered at Louvain, Feb. 1, 1984, in *Origins*, 13 (1983–84) 605–8; and B. Quelquejeu, "La lettre des évêques américains et son accueil en France," *Le Supplément*, 148 (March 1984).

The impossibility of satisfactorily applying these traditional principles demands the outlawing of any nuclear conflict, even if limited or in reprisal. The United States bishops thus made the position of the Council more explicit, but they passed over the problem of the means that might be used for military defense.

One by one, the European episcopal conferences published their own letters and statements. The immediate background for these documents was the balance of nuclear forces in Europe as concretized and symbolized by the rockets now in place or to be put in place. Each country was led to speak out on the subject, including France, even though it was not affected by the NATO decision. The position taken by the churches was influenced by the geostrategic situation and the political position of their own countries. This explains the details and special emphases of the different documents.

There was unanimous agreement on war: atomic but also, as the French statement made explicit, bacteriological and chemical. The statement of the French episcopate reflected the tone of all: "War has become madness. It cannot be a humanly worthy way of settling conflicts, especially once the nuclear threshold is crossed."[36] This statement echoed the teaching of the Council but also made it more specific. On other points, too, the various pastoral letters and statements, taken as a body, added noteworthy complements to the conciliar teaching.

Unlike the Council, these documents spoke of threats and even named the enemy. Two main threats, not just one, were pointed out: the threat from totalitarian systems to the freedom of nations, and the threat of a possible catastrophic war as a result of spiraling rearmament.[37] The United States bishops emphasized the nuclear danger; the French bishops, warned by the historical experience of nearby countries to their east, highlighted the danger from totalitarianism.[38] The former, of course, had no illusions about the Soviet system, nor did the latter about the danger and provisional nature of recourse to nuclear deterrence.

Which was the greater of the two threats? In a talk to delegates of the United States and European episcopates at a meeting in Rome, January 18–19, 1983,[39] Cardinal Casaroli said that both dangers had to be carefully evaluated and that all must commit themselves "wholly and with good will" to warding off both. Morality demanded this response. The goal, however, was still distant. Meanwhile there was no choice but to stick to "the only practical means available to us, and one that has at least proved to be effective": adequate deterrence (which today and in

36. Statement of the French Episcopal Conference, "Gagner la paix," Nov. 8, 1983 (Paris, 1984), p. 11.
37. Statement of the German Episcopal Conference, "La justice crée la paix," April 18, 1983, in the edition published by the Swiss Episcopal Conference, p. 46.
38. "Gagner la paix," p. 16.
39. Report of the meeting in DC, no. 1856 (July 24, 1983); see also DC, no. 1846.

practice meant nuclear deterrence). On this point there was a kind of consensus in East and West, "despite all the problems and dangers that reliance on this means brings with it and which, of course, everyone knows: the cost; the atmosphere of suspicion and distrust that is created; the danger that one may take advantage of the existence of such weapons to use them either deliberately or in a less than completely pre-meditated way." Casaroli's position made clear the direction favored by the Holy See, and the United States bishops were invited to reconsider some of their statements.

The emphasis on the totalitarian threat elicited reactions from Catholics. They did not deny the reality and dangers of Soviet imperialism, but they did object to the limitations of an outlook that failed to recognize other dangers. The explanation was, in their view, too simplistic. In addition, it gave short shrift to the attitude the Gospel bids us adopt toward our enemies; on this point the German bishops offered some timely and realistic reflections.[40]

Nuclear Deterrence

A number of United States bishops took a radical position on deterrence and condemned the manufacture of nuclear weapons outright and without qualification.[41] The pastoral letter of the episcopal conference mentions the position of some bishops and Catholics who during the drafting of the letter asked the conference to issue a prophetic challenge to the community of believers. The bishops acknowledge the intellectual basis of this argument and the religious sensibility that gives it its force.[42] And if in the end they do not adopt this position and rally instead to the official position expressed by John Paul II, at least they do raise the question in terms reflecting the state of conscience of many Christians around the world:

May a nation threaten what it may never do? May it possess what it may never use? . . . The danger of the situation is clear; but how to prevent the use of nuclear weapons, how to assess deterrence, and how to delineate moral responsibility in the nuclear age are less clearly seen or stated.[43]

40. Reactions on this point in France came especially from movements and groups connected with the Mission Ouvrière (*SNOP* Nov. 30, 1983). The Mission de France voiced its position in a statement entitled "Apprendre à bâtir la paix" and published in *Lettre aux communautés*, 107 (July-Aug. 1984); the statement was signed by Jean Remond, auxiliary bishop of the Mission de France. See also "La lutte pour la paix," a statement of the Protestant Federation of France, issued at La Rochelle, Nov. 11–13, 1983 (*DC*, no. 1864).

41. Thus Archbishop Hunthausen of Seattle (1981) in *Origins*, 11 (1981–82) 111–13, and Archbishop John Quinn of San Francisco (pastoral letter of Oct. 4, 1981), in ibid., pp. 284–87.

42. "The Challenge of Peace" (n. 35 above), no. 197 (p. 546).

43. Ibid., nos. 137–38 (p. 529). In a statement published April 18, 1983, on the French

Two answers have been given to this last question. In summarizing their pastoral letter the United States bishops assert that we do not have the right to do or even plan what is morally wrong, not even to save our lives or the lives of those we love. The French bishops, on the other hand, distinguish between threat and use, and allow the threat while recognizing that there would be a problem if the moment came for acting on it.[44]

Despite the difference here, there is agreement among the bishops on two points that some Christians regard as incompatible. On the one hand, no episcopate opts for making the present system of deterrence permanent; the bishops see and describe it as unstable, provisional, and even scandalous.[45] On the other hand, in view of the world situation, they adopt a position that may be summarized as "a strictly conditional moral acceptance of nuclear deterrence."[46] This position was influenced by that of John Paul II himself, who said in his address to the United Nations in June 1982: "In current conditions 'deterrence' based on balance, certainly not as an end in itself but as a step on the way toward a progressive disarmament, may still be judged morally acceptable."[47]

This short sentence was cited in all the episcopal statements, except those of the Japanese and Austrian bishops.[48] It served as a rallying point despite the differences of emphasis in their respective positions. That is why one journalist claimed that in the final analysis the various pastoral letters were "episcopal variations on the prescribed theme." Prescribed? Suggested? Adopted by consensus? In any case, the report of the Roman meeting of representatives from the episcopal conferences, on January 18–19, 1983, did bring out the specific and determining influence of the centrally adopted point of view.

To sum up, the thinking of the Catholic Church on nuclear deterrence has taken clearer form twenty years after the Council. It makes explicit a distinction that is only implicit in the conciliar documents between the manufacture or possession of nuclear weapons, their actual use, the

nuclear deterrent force, the French Commission for Justice and Peace made this question its own (*Lettre d'information*, no. 12, 3rd quarter of 1983).

44. "Gagner la paix" (n. 36, above), pp. 24–27.

45. See, e.g., "Gagner la paix": "a limit-situation from which we must remove ourselves as quickly as possible because it is so risky" (p. 23); "a logic inspired by distress" (p. 24); "a dangerous narrow ridge . . . to avoid the abyss we must as quickly as possible distance ourselves from this logic of the absurd" (p. 27); etc. The Dutch bishops used the expression "to set free": i.e., from the system and very idea of deterrence (*DC*, no. 1863, p. 1117).

46. The words are those of the United States bishops ("The Challenge of Peace," § 186, p. 543), but they accurately sum up the position of the other episcopates.

47. Cited in "The Challenge of Peace," § 173 (p. 539). See J.-M. Muller, "La petite phrase de Jean Paul II," *Le Monde*, May 7, 1983.

48. Letter of the Japanese bishops, July 9, 1983 (*DC*, no. 1863). The letter of the Austrian bishops, April 14, 1983, was not published in France.

threat to use them, and even the intention or plan of carrying out the threat.[49] We are better informed about the complex problems of deterrence and have a better understanding of geostrategic situations.[50] At bottom, however, the moral position taken has not changed: nuclear deterrence remains, despite its dangers, a lesser evil and a morally acceptable recourse in our world that is so full of dangers for the human race. Christians continue to ask, however, whether such a position is an adequate reflection of the Gospel message.[51]

Nonviolent Approaches

As we saw, the Council spoke of nonviolence only briefly and in passing. The documents of the United States and French episcopates make statements that go much further, even if the proponents of nonviolence have expressed reservations about them.

The United States bishops connect nonviolence with the age-old effort of the Church to restrain violence and limit wars (the acknowledgment of war as legitimate has its limitation as a proviso). They describe nonviolence as resistance to injustice but also a form of popular defense. They acknowledge its limitations but find them acceptable when measured against the almost certain effects of a major war. For reasons both practical and spiritual, nonviolence must be seriously considered as a possible course of action. This is why the bishops recommend that funds

49. See C. Muller, *Chrétiens devant la guerre et la paix* (Paris, 1984), p. 161: "The difficulty from the ethical standpoint arises from the traditional view that the *intention* to commit a crime is already a serious sin. The bishops get around or solve this difficulty by avoiding the question of intention and speaking only of a *threat*. But it then becomes important to see that the threat they are legitimizing is a purely *verbal* threat, unaccompanied by any real intention of ever carrying it out."

50. This can be clearly seen—for France—in the various articles of Gérard Defois in *Le Matin*, March 24, 1983; *Le Monde*, July 9, 1983; *Etudes*, Dec. 1983; *Le Supplément*, 148 (March 1984); and *Etudes*, June 1985.

51. See, e.g., the articles of Jacques Gaillot, bishop of Evreux, and Jacques Maury, president of the Protestant Federation, in *Le Monde* for Nov. 12, 1983, and of Louis Boffet, bishop of Montpellier, in *Bulletin diocésain*, 38 (Nov. 19, 1983), after the publication of "Gagner la paix"; or the articles in *Témoignage chrétien* and the publications of the movements for nonviolence. In his book *Vous avez dit "pacifisme"?* (Paris, 1984), J.-M. Muller discusses the reasons for this dissatisfaction (see esp. pp. 27–47). See also, at an earlier period, the report delivered to SODEPAX at a conference on peace at Baden in April 1970: the authors point out "the inability of the churches to answer the question of the morality of possessing nuclear weapons," and they conclude: "We ourselves are very much tempted to come to a decision and reject the strategy of deterrence as a vicious, pessimistic, and inhuman approach to the resolution of a worldwide conflict" (report of 100 pages, printed by the Centre oecuménique, Geneva). In February 1985, the French Commission for Justice and Peace and the Social, Economic, and International Commission of the Protestant Federation published a statement on these various points: *Construire la paix* (Paris, 1985, and *DC*, no., 1890).

and university programs be devoted to the study of it. The churches
themselves are urged to take the initiative in this area.

The French bishops see nonviolence as a narrow but nonetheless us-
able way of escaping the dilemma of "war or capitulation." They have
two reservations: on the one hand, nonviolence cannot be the policy of
states, because the leaders of states have the duty of defending their
country (the implication is: defending it by military means). On the
other hand, the techniques of nonviolence, although having their value,
are not so convincing as to make armed defense outmoded. In the short
and middle term, then, nonviolence seems to be a risky alternative. But
are not the nonviolent right in the long term? The bishops therefore urge
that the voices of the nonviolent be heard, and the role and effectiveness
of nonviolent techniques be carefully studied. In their own way the nonviolent are realists because they are betting on the possibilities of transformation to be found in the contemporary situation. The nonviolent are
the pioneers of the future.

Conclusions

What conclusions does this brief survey allow us to draw about the
reception of the conciliar message on peace?

1. That message served, and still serves, as a basis and justification
for positions taken by bishops and Christian organizations. It is a point
of reference.

But the message has been, and is bound to be, developed and completed through contact with challenging events. Questions have been
aired, and new problems have been taken into account.

As a matter of fact, the responses of Christians in the area of peace
draw upon other sources, some more political, others more evangelical.
These would come to light were we to analyze not only episcopal statements but the words and actions of a multitude of Christians throughout
the world.

2. The local churches in the various countries have spoken out on
the problems of peace. In the process the messages have been made
more specific, because the emphases are not the same in the different
churches. These scattered statements fulfill the wish expressed by Paul
VI when, after acknowledging that it was "difficult [for him] to speak a
single message," he asked the Christian communities to accept their responsibility "in the special situations of their own countries." But the
role of the pope as model and overseer is no less decisive, as we saw in
the position taken on nuclear deterrence.

3. In its own way the Church shares in the building of peace. It takes
the risk of delivering its own special message. In doing so, it seems torn

between, on the one hand, a concern to share the human family's groping search for solutions that, for lack of anything better, are a lesser evil,
and, on the other, the desire to proclaim the good news of peace in a
way that is credible and acceptable.

Adrien Nocent

11. The Local Church as Realization of the Church of Christ and Subject of the Eucharist

Survey of the Issues

The existence of local or particular churches raised problems that the mind-set and theology of the pre–Vatican II period hardly prepared the Church to face. True enough, a return to the sources—the Bible, the church fathers, and the liturgy—had long since given rise to a widespread theological renewal. On the other hand, the development of a theology of the local churches with the concrete conclusions it entails required that churchmen first accept the necessity of not ignoring a series of difficult and tricky problems that a timorous prudence too often preferred to leave untouched.

If scholars were to understand the local Church and be able to see it as the "sacrament" of the universal Church, they could not avoid considering the person of the bishop and at least venturing to study his precise position in the Church and the sacramentality peculiar to his office. Furthermore, in recognizing and rediscovering the sacramentality of the episcopal office, they automatically rediscovered the true character of the *ordo episcoporum*, which was familar to the earliest documents and mentioned as obvious in, for example, the *Apostolic Tradition* of Hippolytus of Rome.[1] But when faced with a reality so difficult to ignore, minds that were focused on papal primacy and Vatican I found the situation difficult and felt uneasy, as though they were on the brink of heresy and schism. We need only page through the *Acta synodalia Concilii Vaticani secundi* to realize how bitter the debates were and how dramatic a tone the council fathers sometimes adopted in their speeches.[2]

---

1. Hippolytus of Rome, *La Tradition apostolique de saint Hippolyte. Essai de reconstitution*, B. Botte, ed. (Münster, 1963), chap. 2, *De episcopis*, pp. 5–11. The term *corpus episcoporum* does not appear in the *Apostolic Tradition*, but everything that is said about episcopal consecration shows its existence.

2. *Acta Synodalia Sacrosancti Concilii Oecumenici Vaticani II*. Vol. 3, *Periodus Tertia*, Pars I,

In his subsequent address at the proclamation of *Lumen gentium*, Pope Paul VI would acknowledge that this had been a difficult time for the Council.[3] In addition, he had taken a step without parallel in any other conciliar document by introducing the famous *nota praevia* into the section of *Lumen gentium* that deals with collegiality. In it he explained how collegiality is to be understood and stressed the place of the pope. His intention was to have readers interpret the declaration on collegiality not as a contradiction or denial of Vatican I but rather as a necessary complement to its teaching.[4]

The rediscovery of the bishop was at the same time a rediscovery of the true nature of his delegate, the presbyter or priest. The Council seems to say rather little of priests but in fact its theology of the bishop brings out as never before the true meaning of the presbyteral office and the incorporation of the individual priest into a *presbyterium*. In his *Apostolic Tradition* (§ 215) Hippolytus calls attention to the importance of the *presbyterium*: when the priests present lay hands on the head of a newly ordained priest, they are not conferring the sacrament on him (as Hippolytus is careful to note) but rather signifying that he now belongs to the *presbyterium*.[5] Being the delegate of the bishop the priest makes a parish a true local Church, linked to the diocesan Church.[6]

As they continued to study the nature of the local Church, the theologians and fathers of Vatican II were to find that this Church would be imperfect as long as the diaconate had not been revived, not as a transitional stage on the way to priesthood or as a purely liturgical office, but as a ministry that is an essential part of the sacrament of orders, and as a social and ecclesial function in the community.[7] The *Apostolic Tradition* of Hippolytus rightly connected the deacon with the bishop as his direct delegate, and not with the priest, and it envisaged him in all his relationships with the community.[8]

But does what has thus far been said yield a true and correct picture of

---

Sessio Publica IV, Congregatio Generalis LXXX, Caput II: "De constitutione hierarchica ecclesiae, et in specie De episcopatu" (Vatican City, 1973), pp. 211–70.

3. Paul VI, "Address at the Close of the Third Session of Vatican II (Nov. 21, 1964)," in *TPS*, 10 (1964–65) 132ff.

4. This *note* on the theological status of the constitution on the church and on the meaning of collegiality in particular was read by the secretary general of the Council during the 125th plenary meeting on Nov. 16, 1964.

5. *La Tradition apostolique*, chap. 8, p. 25.

6. *Sacrosanctum Concilium*, § 22. See the instruction *Eucharisticum Mysterium* of the Sacred Congregation of Rites (May 25, 1967), pp. 16–27, esp. p. 26: "It is fitting that the sense of ecclesial community, fostered and expressed especially by the shared celebration of Mass on Sunday, should be carefully developed. This applies to assemblies with the bishop, above all in the cathedral church, and to the parish assembly, whose pastor takes the place of the bishop" (*DOL*, 179 no. 1255). And see the passage cited in n. 16, below.

7. LG 29.

8. *La Tradition apostolique*, chap. 8, pp. 23–25. I shall say nothing more about the deacon in this essay.

the local Church? Is the local Church a church solely of clerics? No. The Second Vatican Council recognized that this church is the people of God and priestly in its entirety. All members of the people of God possess a priesthood given in baptism and are truly able, each according to his or her place in the Church, to offer covenantal sacrifice.[9] It is the merit of *Lumen gentium* that after the groping efforts of *Mediator Dei* and its silences, or at least the restrictive interpretations given of it, [10] it clarifies the nature of the priesthood of the faithful: this is a real priesthood, a real participation in the priesthood of Christ, though essentially different from the priesthood of the ordained.[11]

Now at last the Council had rediscovered the face the Church presents to us in the letters of Ignatius of Antioch[12] and, for example, in the *Teaching of the Apostles.*[13]

The constitution *Sacrosanctum Concilium* on the liturgy had paved the way in great measure for this complete vision of the Church that is fully communicated in *Lumen gentium.* Three important passages in the liturgy constitution had already made it possible for the Christian world to have a better understanding of the Church. *Sacrosanctum Concilium* teaches:

Liturgical services (*actiones liturgicae*) are not private functions, but are celebrations belonging to the Church, which is the "sacrament of unity," namely, the holy people united and ordered under their bishops. Therefore liturgical services involve the whole Body of the Church; they manifest it and have effects upon it.[14]

9. LG 10.
10. The reader will recall how difficult it was to achieve clarity on the priesthood of the faithful. L. Cerfaux, in his "Regale sacerdotium," *RSPT*, 28 (1939) 5–37, interpreted the passage in 1 Peter on the kingly priesthood as speaking analogically. On the other hand, P. Dabin, *Le sacerdoce royal des fidèles dans les livres saints* (Paris, 1941), concluded that the expression "royal priesthood" signified a true priesthood and that it was possible to distinguish levels within this one true priesthood. His theology anticipated that of *Lumen gentium.* He expressed his views in a more penetrating way in his book *Le sacerdoce royal des fidèles dans la tradition ancienne et moderne* (Paris, 1950). G. Thils, "Le pouvoir cultuel du baptisé," *ETL,* 15 (1938) 683–89, also anticipated the future theology of *Lumen gentium. Mediator Dei* showed great reserve toward the priesthood of the faithful and allowed them only the power to offer their spiritual sacrifices through the hands of the priest, who alone offered the real sacrifice; see *AAS,* 39 (1947) 538–39.
On this subject, see S. Marsili, "Chiesa-Liturgia prima del Vaticano II," in idem, ed., *Anámnesis. Introduzione storicoteologica alla liturgia* (Turin, 1974), 1:107; "Liturgia e sacerdozio commune" (ibid., 127–29); and "Sacerdozio spirituale e sacrificio spirituale" (ibid., 130–36). Although the "Constitution on the Sacred Liturgy" deals several times with the active participation of the faithful, it does not use the term "priesthood of the faithful." Only in *Lumen gentium* does the Council give a precise definition.
11. LG 10.
12. Many passages in these letters describe the Church; for example (in Funk's edition): *Ad Romanos,* Praef. (Funk, 1:252); *Ad Philad.,* Praef. (1:264); 1, 1 (1:264); 4 (1:266); 5, 2 (1:300); *Ad Magn.,* 6, 1 (1:231); *Ad Smyrn.,* 8, 1 (1:282); *Ad Eph.,* 5, 1 (1:216); 6, 1 (1:218); *Ad Trall.,* 2, 3 (1:242).
13. *Didascalia et Constitutiones Apostolorum* (ed. Funk), II, 26 (104–5); II, 57–58 (158–70).
14. *Sacrosanctum Concilium,* § 26 (*DOL,* 1, no. 26).

The theme of the manifestation of the universal Church by the local Church was repeated further on:

The preeminent manifestation of the Church is present in the full, active partic-ipation of all God's holy people in these liturgical celebrations, especially in the same Eucharist, in a single prayer, at one altar at which the bishop presides, sur-rounded by his college of priests and by his ministers.[15]

The eucharistic celebration is the supreme manifestation of the uni-versal Church in the local Church. Moreover, this manifestation is not limited to the diocesan Church with the bishop personally presiding at the celebration; it also takes place at the level of the parishes, for these too in some manner represent the visible Church established through-out the world.[16]

This theology of the local Church is based on a further essential point: the presence of Christ in his Church. Here again the constitution *Sacro-sanctum Concilium* reminded us of the full scope of a truth that had been interpreted as referring solely to the eucharistic presence; the latter, although the supreme mode of Christ's real presence, is not in fact its only mode.[17]

Oddly enough, the conciliar discussion of these points in *Sacrosanctum Concilium* brought no major difficulties to light. The same was no longer true when the points were reexamined for inclusion in the constitution *Lumen gentium*.

At the time when the conciliar debates were still going on, Mgr. Phil-ips, a professor at the University of Louvain, described two tendencies found in the theological thinking of the council fathers. They are tenden-cies that in fact still exist in the Church:

[The one] is more concerned with fidelity to traditional statements, the other with the spread of the message to the people of our time. [The first] moves easily in the world of abstract and changeless ideas, but risks being locked into that world and mistaking concepts for the mystery that transcends them. . . . The second type of theologian . . . is convinced that his vision of the truth is not identifiable in all its forms with the truth itself. . . . He has a keener sense of history and, while he regards the definitions sanctioned by the Church as ir-reformable, he also believes them capable of being understood more fully and stated more clearly.[18]

Mgr. Philips realized that the decision of theologians to follow the one or the other tendency "is influenced by their temperament, their educa-tion, their main concerns, the particular office they may have, and the historical or local context in which they are called to work."

I must add, however, that at an ecumenical council, and today when

15. Ibid., § 41 (*DOL*, 1, no. 41).
16. Ibid., 42.
17. Ibid., 7.
18. Cited in *L'Eglise: Constitution Lumen Gentium. Texte et commentaires* (Paris, 1966), pp. 29–30.

Vatican II is behind us, these tendencies have to be transcended. Vatican II attempted to combine the two mentalities so clearly sketched by Mgr. Philips, while trying not to leave out the wealth of ideas that emerged in the explanations and debates. But we must also recognize that the Council did not succeed in conveying a global vision of the local Church and that some passages seem to lack editorial unity because the writers were trying too hard to combine unintegrated elements and elements interpreted according to opposing tendencies. At the end of the sometimes dramatic discussions on the famous chapter 3, unanimity was reached only with difficulty, and Paul VI could say in his address on the proclamation of the constitution:

We can declare that in God's providential plans a brilliant hour has shone upon us: an hour, We say, whose past approach was gradual, whose brilliance shines forth today, whose salvific power will surely enrich the future life of the Church with a new growth in doctrine, with increased powers, with better-suited means and instruments.[19]

The Statements of Vatican II about the Local Church, and Their Reception

Our effort here must be to see whether these hopes of Paul VI have been fulfilled in the contemporary Church.

The task is not an easy one. It is too soon for an overall appraisal of the situation; in addition, geographical locations, mentalities, and political circumstances all affect the way in which the doctrine—which I shall present in broad terms—has been received. What Mgr. Philips said of the theologians at the Second Vatican Council remains valid in assessing the reception in various milieus of the conciliar teaching on the local Church.

In making my own assessment I intend to pay heed to the variety of situations and achievements. I cannot, however, fail to emphasize some less fortunate aspects of the postconciliar period.

Theological Stimuli after the Council

Various authoritative theological statements have had for their purpose to shed light on points that are indispensable for understanding the theology of the local Church. I shall limit myself to a few of them.

In 1965 Pope Paul VI issued his encyclical *Mysterium fidei* in which he intended to emphasize the traditional faith of the Church in the real eucharistic presence. But while highlighting this presence he also made

19. Address cited in n. 3, above, pp. 133–34.

some valuable points about the different types of presence of Christ that are listed in section 7 of *Sacrosanctum Concilium*. Readers might interpret these presences, except for the eucharistic presence, as being presences only by analogy. The pope says, however, that "this [eucharistic] presence is called the *real presence* not to exclude the other kinds as though they were not real, but because it is real par excellence."[20]

This statement authorizes us to recognize real presences other than the eucharistic and to maintain that the real eucharistic presence does not somehow negate the reality of other kinds of presence. The eucharistic presence is indeed a presence par excellence because of its mode: here the very matter is transformed, and the presence lasts as long as the species remain. The same is not true of the other kinds of presence; in baptism, for example, the water undergoes no change, and the presence of Christ is limited to the moment of the sacramental action.

Catechetical instruction on the presence of Christ in, for example, the proclamation of the word is important; it is important in particular for the local Church that does the proclaiming and that fulfills its own being in the proclamation and in the divine office. The constitution on the liturgy mentions the office specifically: "Christ is always present in his Church. . . . He is present, lastly, when the Church prays and sings [the psalms]."[21]

This very interesting theology of Pope Paul VI has, however, hardly been received at all, and I know of no official document that repeats it. The most recent typical edition of the lectionary for Mass has a new preface, but it makes no reference to the theology of Paul VI. One has the impression, moreover, that there is a desire to avoid entering upon a path not recognized as "traditional." This important element in the theology of the local Church has therefore not yet been clearly grasped; instead, a kind of theological "fear" has had a paralyzing effect on the reception of this new message.

The instruction *Eucharisticum Mysterium* of 1967 provided a very valuable catechesis on the local Church. After stating that the eucharist is the center of all ecclesial life,[22] the instruction goes on to say that it is also the center of the local Church.[23]

Section 7 of the instruction synthesizes the teaching of *Lumen gentium* and other conciliar texts on the local Church. The emphasis is chiefly on the presence of Christ, which makes the community the Church. There is no emphasis on the fact that the local Church thus brought into being by Christ's presence is catholic and apostolic in relation to the one

20. Encyclical *Mysterium fidei* (Sept. 3, 1965), 39 (*DOL*, 176, no. 1183); Latin text in *AAS*, 57 (1965) 764. There is an excellent commentary by Marsili, "La liturgia, presenza di Cristo," in *Anámnesis* (n. 10, above), 1:92–96.

21. *Sacrosanctum Concilium*, § 7 (*DOL*, 1, no. 7).

22. Instruction *Eucharisticum Mysterium* (May 25, 1967), § 6. The document is translated in *DOL*, 179, nos. 1230–96.

23. Ibid., 7.

Church. A narrow reading of the text suggests that the controlling vision is still universalist and centralist, and that local celebrations manifest only parts and groups within the catholic and apostolic Church, these parts and groups having consistency only from a sociological view-point.[24] However—and this is to be carefully noted—the text does say that in its eucharistic celebrations each community enjoys the presence of Christ in its midst and that consequently the Eucharist forms and gathers the catholic and apostolic Church of God.

Another point to be emphasized is a very positive indication of the reception of the Vatican II teaching on the local Church, but at the same time it is somewhat ambiguous.

I refer to the fact that *Eucharisticum Mysterium* cites the fine passage in the liturgy constitution (§ 41) that speaks of the Church as Ignatius of Antioch and the early documents speak of it.[25] The instruction thus recognizes that the celebrations of the local Church around its bishop are the highest manifestation of the Church. But then, at the very end of the sentence, the instruction introduces some new words by speaking of "the preeminent manifestation of the *hierarchically constituted*" Church.[26] Two interpretations of the passage are now possible: these celebrations are the highest possible earthly manifestation of the Church's real nature; or there is another possible manifestation, this one being of the universal Church under the jurisdiction of the pope. There would thus be a contrast between, on the one hand, the hierarchically constituted local Church and, on the other, the universal Church under the guidance of the Roman pontiff, this latter being a superior manifestation. I do not think, however, that this is what the instruction means. The words "hierarchically constituted" seem to be intended simply as an echo of the famous *nota praevia* in chapter 3 of *Lumen gentium*, which recalls the bond uniting the bishops to the person of Peter. In any case, the instruction has already given clear expression to its thought in § 7:

Through the Eucharist "the Church continually lives and grows. This Church of Christ is truly present in all lawful, local congregations of the faithful, which, united with their bishops, are themselves called Churches in the New Testament. . . . Any community at the altar, under the sacred ministry of the bishop," or of a priest who takes his place, "stands out clearly as a symbol of that charity and 'unity of the Mystical body without which there can be no salvation.' In these communities, though frequently small or poor and living in isolation, Christ is present and the power of his presence gathers together the . . . Church."[27]

Another document, this time on the liturgy of the hours and the local Church, shows that the Council's teaching has been received, at least

---

24. See the excellent article by E. Lanne, "Chiesa locale," *Dizionario del Concilio Ecumenico Vaticano Secundo*, pp. 796–826, esp. p. 814.

25. *Eucharisticum Mysterium*, § 42.

26. Ibid. (*DOL*, 179, no. 1271).

27. Ibid. (The long quotation that occupies most of this passage is from LG 26, and the short quotation in the passage from LG is from St. Thomas, *Summa theologiae*, III, 73, 3.)

officially. The "General Instruction of the Liturgy of the Hours" speaks as follows in § 20: "This liturgy stands out most strikingly as an ecclesial celebration when, through the bishop surrounded by his priests and ministers, the local Church celebrates it. For 'in the local Church the one, holy, catholic, and apostolic Church is truly present and at work.'"[28] Especially to be noted here is the reference to the presence and activity of the holy, catholic, and apostolic Church.

The same "General Instruction" puts a heavy emphasis on the character of this local church whose activity depends on the priesthood of the entire ecclesial body:

Christ's priesthood is also shared by the whole Body of the Church, so that the baptized are consecrated as a spiritual temple and holy priesthood through the rebirth of baptism and the anointing of the Holy Spirit and are empowered to offer the worship of the New Covenant, a worship that derives not from our own powers but from Christ's merit and gift.[29]

The origin of this church and its unity is explained in the next section of the "General Instruction": "The unity of the Church at prayer is brought about by the Holy Spirit, who is the same in Christ, in the whole Church, and in every baptized person."

Theological studies published after the Council show that the teaching of Vatican II on the local Church as well as on the Eucharist that forms it has not been neglected.

Even before the Council theologians like Karl Rahner had thought it necessary to study the bond between episcopate and papal primacy. In *The Episcopate and the Primacy*, which he co-authored with Joseph Ratzinger, we find him saying that the Church in the full reality of its being becomes an actual "event" only in the local celebration of the Eucharist.[30] He would later develop this line of thought in several essays.[31]

Yves Congar in turn wrote in 1967:

The complete subject (*pleroma*) of liturgical action is the *ecclesia*, even when, from the standpoint of the required "powers," the ordained priest acts by himself. . . . But the ultimate and transcendent subject of liturgical action is Christ who through his Holy Spirit gives unity and life to his body, which he has made to be wholly priestly and which he has structured, within this common priesthood, as flock and shepherd, people and leader, community and president.[32]

28. Translation in DOL, 426, no. 3450. (The citation in this passage is from *Christus Dominus*.)

29. Ibid., 7 (DOL, 479, no. 3437).

30. K. Rahner and J. Ratzinger, *The Episcopate and the Primacy* (New York, 1962), pp. 20–30 (esp. pp. 24–26).

31. K. Rahner, *The Church and the Sacraments* (New York, 1963); idem, "The New Image of the Church" and "The Presence of the Lord in the Christian Community at Worship," in his *Theological Investigations* (New York, 1973), 10:3–29 and 71–83.

32. In J.-P. Jossua and Y. Congar, eds., *La Liturgie après Vatican II* (Paris, 1967), p. 282.

There could not be a better theological summary of the local Church in its liturgical activity.

I cannot but show my respect and affection by citing a man who was my esteemed colleague for twenty-four years at the Liturgical Institute in Rome and whose theology of liturgy has in my opinion rarely been matched for its depth. Father Marsili writes as follows (he is referring in part to the theology of K. Rahner, which he has rethought in a personal way):

Once the identity of "body of Jesus—body of Christ (church)" and "temple" has been established, it becomes clear that this "church" is a community at the local level, both because, being the "body of Christ," it is the locus of true worship and because it is a community that exists in a place. We know, too, that all this comes about in the sacramental celebration of the Eucharist, which by effecting the unity of the "bread—body of Jesus" forms the community that is the "body of Christ–Church." But in what sense does the Eucharist, in forming the Church, constitute it at the local level?[33]

At this point Father Marsili repeats Rahner's answer to which I referred above.[34]

Burkhard Neunheuser, another (now retired) professor at the Liturgical Institute in Rome, has tried to determine which communities merit the title "local church." He lists seven forms the particular Church can take. (1) The community celebration of the faithful with the bishop in the cathedral church. (2) The parish. (3) Small groups gathered to celebrate under the presidency of a priest who has authority from the bishop: "small, nonclerical, religious communities," "particular groups," and "meetings or congresses aimed at fostering the Christian life or the apostolate or at promoting religious studies" (Neunheuser derives this list from the instruction *Eucharisticum Mysterium*.)[35] (4) Monastic communities or canonically established communities that celebrate a non-eucharistic worship, especially the liturgy of the hours, under the presidency of a spiritual leader approved or appointed by the bishop. (5) The liturgy of the hours when celebrated morning and evening by the community consisting of husband and wife and their family (Neunheuser here cites *Sacrosanctum Concilium*, § 100, which encourages this kind of community to pray as a church and in the name of the Church). (6) Spontaneously formed groups of Christians who, even without a priest being present, pray the Church's prayer, as a church, and in whose midst the Lord is present. (7) Every Christian, priest or layperson, who prays the Church's prayer perhaps in solitude but who in praying intends to remain united with the praying people of God.[36]

33. S. Marsili, "Il culto locale forma la Chiesa locale," in *Anámnesis*, 1:120–22.
34. See n. 30, above.
35. *Eucharisticum Mysterium*, §§ 26, 27, and 30, respectively (*DOL*, 179, nos. 1255, 1256, 1259).
36. B. Neunheuser, "La liturgia della Chiesa come culto del Corpo di Cristo," in *Miscel-*

Other writings have of course appeared since the ones I have cited; they cannot be said, however, to represent an advance in the theology of the local Church. And yet not everything possible has been said on the subject; in particular, we lack catechetical materials directed to those of the faithful who are not specialists and are almost completely lacking in understanding of the local Church and its spiritual riches.

Concrete Results of the Council and Their Impact on the Faithful and on Their Vision of the Church

In this section I shall find myself compelled to be negative at times. Thus there can be no doubt that we badly lack catechetical instruction on various points that are indispensable for an understanding of the local Church. On the other hand, various institutions that owe their origin to the Council and really ought to enlighten the faithful regarding the nature of the local Church often in fact eclipse the rediscovered local Church because, once again, they are not the object of adequate catechetical instruction.

Let me begin with this second point. The synods of bishops and the episcopal conferences that ought to be means of calling attention to the local churches, expounding the theology embodied in them, and giving them vitality, are in fact more likely to inculcate in the faithful once more a pyramidal view of the Church. For those of the faithful who are poorly instructed or not instructed at all, synods of bishops and episcopal conferences are representative of the catholic and apostolic Church rather than of the local Church in its eucharistic celebration. These institutions do not necessarily suggest to the faithful of the Latin rite a vision of a renewed church. To theologians, of course, and perhaps to some of the clergy they are elements of a specifically contemporary ecclesiology. But as far as the simple faithful are concerned, these very visible institutions, which ought to be expressions of the local Church, are likely on the contrary to hide it because they do not make sufficiently clear their reference to the local Church as the ecclesiological focal point of the proclamation of the word, the celebration of the sacraments, and common prayer. The faithful continue to have the impression that a synod or a meeting of the episcopal conference are supreme manifestations of the Church's catholicity and apostolicity, whereas in fact they show forth the link between the one Church and the local Churches. The synod of bishops can be seen as simply a tool of central authority.

Yves Congar wrote long ago that "henceforth it [the doctrine of collegiality] will surely act as a corrective to an ecclesiology based solely on the papal monarchy and will relate the episcopate to the apostolicity of

lanea S. Marsili (Turin/Leumann, 1981), sections 4: "Chiesa locale e Chiesa universale" (pp. 36–39) and 5: "Forme diverse di attuazione della Chiesa locale" (pp. 40–47).

the Church in a way that will be of interest to the Orthodox."[37] Unfortunately, however, it cannot be said that the doctrine has affected the outlook of the majority of the faithful. It must even be admitted that the new synod of bishops, for example, which must of course be in close communion with the pope if its existence is to be legitimate, has not yet developed fully the various relationships that situate it properly within the Church.

In saying this, I am not blaming anyone. It takes time for such a set of subtle relationships to develop in a balanced way. For, even if we restrict ourselves to the sphere of power or authority, we know it is impossible to construct a set of laws that can anticipate and regulate all possible cases. Let me explain. The apostles were given power to establish and feed the flock; to this end they received full, supreme, and universal authority because they needed it if they were to carry out their mission. On the other hand, Peter had his own mission of establishing and leading the Church that Christ had entrusted to him, and to this end he was given full, supreme, and universal authority. In virtue, then, of episcopal consecration the *corpus episcoporum* has received a full, supreme, and universal authority, but Peter, being obliged as head of the college to feed the flock and strengthen his brethren, likewise needs full, supreme, and universal authority.

Does this mean confrontation or contradiction? No, but some people may see a real opposition in this situation, and in fact this interpretation of it has existed in the past and is still to be found in some degree today, at least in the form of tendencies: a kind of Gallicanism or a kind of papalism. In both forms the one or the other member of the opposed pair is eliminated. But, if the *mission* of the pope and the *mission* of the bishops as a college are not contradictory—and they evidently are not—then neither is there contradiction between the *power* or *authority* of the two. There must consequently be a modus vivendi that laws alone cannot determine. A balance established by the Spirit in mutual service and fraternal communion can, however, bring the two parties beyond a simple coexistence and into a collaboration based on mutual respect, though the supremacy of Peter must of course be preserved. Do churchmen patiently achieve an understanding of this? Can the faithful understand it if no one enlightens them and explains the necessary nuances?

Let me end with some more concrete cases. In reading what I say, the reader should set aside any bias and see my remarks as inspired not by a spirit of rebellion or assertiveness but simply by a desire to shed a little light.

When we turn to the conciliar documents we find that they recognize and teach that the typical form of eucharistic celebration is that of the local community with its bishop. Rome does not enter the picture, ex-

37. Cited in *L'Eglise. Texte et commentaires*, written by a team of priests and laypersons (Paris, 1966), p. 325.

cept when there is question of regulating the details of liturgical reform. Even in this latter case, the anticipated intervention—summed up in the words "Holy See"—must be properly interpreted. It is of the juridical order and has nothing to do with a theology of apostolicity or catholicity. Nonetheless many bishops prefer to have recourse to the Holy See (that is, to the Sacred Congregation for Divine Worship or other agencies), even when they clearly have the right to make decisions on their own. This was often the case in the past, and it is still the case with the liturgy. The bishops perhaps find it convenient to act in this way. The easier course is to have Rome back them up, for example, in difficulties with a priest, than it is to accept what may be the odium resulting from a painful decision. But this easy way out, this fear of responsibility, could be eliminated if a theology of the bishop and the local Church were introduced, assimilated, and lived by. Perhaps too—and this has sometimes happened—Rome would refuse to intervene in cases in which the head of the local Church can act on his own.

There are other, more touchy cases, but they too must be mentioned. I have in mind concrete facts showing that the ecclesiological centrality of the local Church has not yet been accepted.

No one could be more desirous than I of maintaining the unqualified primacy of the pope in the Church. It is also important that this primacy be manifested. I think it legitimate, however, to ask not whether certain ways of acting are valid or legitimate or are an acquired right of the pope, but whether they are opportune from a catechetical viewpoint.

Thus the Holy Father has consecrated many diocesan bishops at Rome. He has ordained a good number of diocesan priests there. He has confirmed many children and blessed many marriages.

There is absolutely no question of challenging what must be regarded as a right of the pope. On the other hand, we must ask what impression these papal actions make on the minds of the faithful.

The reader will remember that from as early as the time of Hippolytus of Rome neighboring bishops came to consecrate a new bishop in his future diocesan church. During the liturgy of the word and until his own consecration, the future bishop remained at the right of his consecrator; once he was consecrated, however, he presided over his first Eucharist as head of his church, together with his assembled diocese. It is in this context, moreover, that Hippolytus gives us the text of a eucharistic prayer that he offers as a model, though without making it obligatory; this prayer, after fairly radical changes, has become our present second eucharistic prayer.[38]

Hippolytus's entire ritual of episcopal consecration has been taken over into the new pontifical. Any reader of the document will realize how important a catechetical instruction on the bishop in his diocese this

38. *La Tradition apostolique*, chap. 2 (pp. 5–7), 4 (pp. 10–17), and 9 (pp. 28–29), on the freedom to improvise the eucharistic prayer.

liturgy provides. It is a lived catechesis that no discourse can replace. The liturgy is one that sheds light on the local Church without in the least diminishing the primacy of the pontifical see; on the contrary, it gives this primacy the full depth and prominence that it ought to have— and that it ceases to have as soon as it is not seen in its proper context.

A priest, for his part, is ordained to the service of his bishop in the local Church into which he is incardinated. Is it not fitting that his own bishop should ordain him? Recall again the ordination ceremony described in the *Apostolic Tradition* of Hippolytus and observe in particular the action of the *presbyterium* as it accepts the new priest as a member by imposing hands on him (the action in this case is not a sacrament).[39] I think it legitimate to mention the problem created here, namely, the difficulty of explaining in catechesis the meaning of a priest's not being ordained by his own bishop but incardinated into the latter's diocese. The ordination of foreign priests in Rome is a somewhat "Olympian" affair by reason of the large number of ordinands and the fairly strong triumphalist tone of the proceedings. But in addition may we not think that this type of celebration scarcely illustrates or teaches a theology of the Church barely twenty years old?

Why does the Roman Church regard the bishop as the primary minister of confirmation? Because it knows that the sacrament empowers confirmands to bear witness and appoints them to offer a worship that is obviously first and foremost the worship of the local Church. Here again catechesis becomes difficult and its character problematic.

The sacrament of marriage is a sign of the union of Christ (symbolized by the husband) and his Church (symbolized by the wife). Is it not obvious that the reference ought to be to the local Church and to the community to which the couple belongs? Christian initiation must be regarded as a highly artificial affair when it is celebrated in a milieu other than that in which the catechumens have been prepared for their incorporation into the Church as present in the local Church. So too, is it not artificial for two spouses to be united in a setting outside their own ecclesial community?

There is no need to be overly dramatic; the fact is that celebrations of the kind I am discussing illustrate a central doctrine, that of the supreme authority of the pope. At the same time, however, they are apt to undermine in the eyes of unprepared believers the theology of the bishop and the local Church. In the eyes of these faithful the local Church becomes simply one segment that is to be added to many others to make up the universal Church, which conversely is the result of adding local churches together; the bishop, for his part, has his authority from the pope and serves as the latter's vicar.

Such are the mistaken thoughts to which celebrations of that kind un-

---

39. Ibid., chap. 8 (pp. 24–25), on the *presbyterium* and the meaning of the imposition of hands by the *presbyterium* on the new priest.

wittingly give rise. In any accounting, they show a failure to understand and assimilate *Lumen gentium*. The failure is not surprising, inasmuch as this theology and its indispensable nuances require a long period of time for reception and experiential verification. There is, however, good reason to fear that such celebrations are obstacles to the concrete spread of this theology and to the development of the Church's life in accordance with its true structure. There is also reason to fear that they make ecumenical progress more difficult.

In *Lumen gentium* the Council makes an important statement when it calls the bishops the "vicars and legates of Christ."[40] But the uninformed faithful are scandalized if they are taught that the bishops exercise their power in the name of Christ; that they are not "to be regarded as vicars of the Roman Pontiff";[41] and that they receive their power from their episcopal consecration. That the bishops have a power of their own that is not derived from the power of another, a power that is connected with their function and not received by delegation, a habitual, direct power that is exercised without passing through another—all this has not yet been "received." It is only because of the difficulty the faithful have in assimilating this teaching that I have questioned celebrations that are likely to impede growth and are not calculated to give the faithful a true image either of the pope or the bishops or priests or the sacraments or the local Church.

It must also be said that the profound relationship between bishop and Eucharist is not yet adequately grasped in the West. The truth that the bishop is the high priest of the diocese and that he celebrates and presides over every eucharistic celebration, either in his own person or in the person of the priest who is his delegate, is one that has not yet become part of current thinking and of which the great majority of the faithful have not become aware.

This situation, however, has roots in the distant past. The reader need only turn to the periodical *Divinitas* and peruse the theology of the *Symposium theologicum de Ecclesia Christi Patribus Concilii Vaticani Secundi reverenter oblatum* that was held in Rome, at the Lateran, in 1962. Here the Church is seen "as a kind of deduction from or extension of its Roman head."[42] Fortunately, Vatican II did not follow this lead. At the same time, however, it must be said that Vatican II simply "impregnated theology, and left it the difficult task of giving birth"[43] (a statement that certainly applies to the doctrine of the local Church). It is possible to deceive ourselves by unreservedly extolling such institutions as the synod of bishops and the episcopal conferences. These are indeed the fruit of a

---

40. LG 27, trans. in A. Flannery, ed., *Vatican II: The Conciliar and Postconciliar Documents* (Collegeville, Minn., 1975), p. 382.

41. Ibid. (Flannery, p. 383).

42. *Divinitas*, 6 (1962) 461–85. See Y. Congar, *Le Concile Vatican II. Son Eglise, Peuple de Dieu et Corps du Christ* (Paris, 1984), p. 15.

43. Congar, *Le Concile*, p. 84.

new ecclesiology, but they have still to find their proper point of insertion. As long as this has not been achieved, they may play a role contrary to the one assigned them in theology and may obscure the local Church rather than give it its rightful place.

Much work needs still to be done in developing a catechesis for the faithful on the theological character of the local Church. An impatient creativity or an attitude of rebellious independence plays no part in a theology of the local Church and simply distorts its true image. The only true local Church is one that occupies its proper place in respect and love for the pastor of the universal Church, who likewise occupies his proper place.

IV. THEMES INSUFFICIENTLY RECEIVED

Lukas Vischer

12. The Reception of the Debate on Collegiality

On November 17, 1964, one of the liveliest debates at the Second Vatican Council was provisionally closed. The bishops now had to vote on the text of the third chapter of the constitution on the Church, which dealt with "the hierarchic structure of the Church and especially the episcopal office." An overwhelming majority (2,099 against 46) declared their agreement with the text proposed to them.

Argument and disagreement over the content and formulation of this chapter had been going on through three sessions. How is the episcopal office to be understood? What is the role of bishops in the Church? How is their authority related to that of the pope? These questions had become the focus of attention even in the first session. In the second and third they led to discussions that were to give the Council its special character. All who took part in the debate, no matter which side they took, were in agreement that their response to these questions would play a decisive role in the future of the Roman Catholic Church and indeed of the Christian churches generally.

The discussion centered on a key word "collegiality." To what extent can the pope and the bishops be said to form a college, as Peter and the other apostles did? And what consequences ensue if they are in fact understood as a college?

Why did this particular word become so important for the Second Vatican Council? The answer is obvious. For many bishops and theologians the concept of collegiality entailed a new vision of the Church. They were not primarily bent on turning the Church in a new direction. By its definition of the universal jurisdiction and infallibility of the pope, the First Vatican Council had emphasized the hierarchic apex of the Church. But must the emphasis remain there in the future as well? Or are there ways of moving beyond it?

The one-sidedness of the First Vatican Council had become clear. There had developed an irresistible desire once again to understand and actualize the Church to a greater extent as a *communio ecclesiarum*. The

Church ought not any longer be defined exclusively in terms of its apex. The importance of the local churches had to be brought out more fully, or at least there had to be less emphasis on the Roman centralization of the Church. The *ecclesia romana* needed to set aside something of its *romanitas* and make more room for the multiplicity of cultures and forms of expression. The understanding of authority in the Church needed to be changed. It could no longer be left exclusively in the hands of the pope and the Curia. Clarity was needed on how it could be exercised in a communal way.

The very convocation of the Second Vatican Council was already a breakthrough in this direction. It was by no means evident that another council should ever again be held after Vatican I, for the definitions of the latter had made further councils unnecessary in principle. Pope John XXIII had thus created a new situation by his unexpected decision. Bishops had assembled from all parts of the world to consult together. In thus gathering in Rome they experienced themselves as forming a college with a common task. What could be more natural under the circumstances than to project the same experience into the future? In such an atmosphere it was easy for the concept of "collegiality" to serve as a key word in discussing the proper view to be taken of the Church of the future.

The full meaning of "collegiality" can be grasped only against the background of Vatican I. The concept does not emerge with necessity from the biblical witness. Even during Vatican II New Testament scholars expressed doubts about whether the word *collegium* was appropriate for describing the fellowship of the apostles among themselves; the discussion at the Council was unable to remove the doubt. Nor did the tradition provide any extensive discussion of precisely this concept. On the other hand, if the definitions of Vatican I were taken as the point of departure, the relevance of the concept became immediately evident, for it served well to put the role of the bishop of Rome, as defined at Vatican I, into a new context.

In the beginning, the concept was used exclusively as a new description of the relationship between pope and bishops, but it soon began to be applied to a wider field. It quickly transcended its first meaning and became a symbol. What held in the area of hierarchic structure should, it was thought, hold also for the Church in its entirety. The relationship between bishops and priests, and even between priests and the members of the community, had to be rethought. The concept thus began to make its way into all areas of the Church's life. A church that takes collegiality seriously could not but prove to be in every way a more community-minded church. For several years after the Council the question of the consequences that the idea of collegiality and collegially exercised authority has for the Church was repeatedly raised from ever new points of view.

The Dynamics of Collegiality

What came of this entire debate? It undoubtedly had important consequences for the life of the Church; the face of the Catholic Church has
changed profoundly in the last two decades. I shall here call attention to
three aspects in particular:

1. The debate produced a new consciousness of the Church's mission
to every locality. The role of the individual bishops and consequently of
the local Church was enhanced as the Council sketched a new picture of
the bishop and his church. Far more than in earlier times, the individual
churches are today conscious of being responsible for the witness of the
Church in their localities.

An especially important step in this direction has been the development of the episcopal conferences. The conciliar decree on the pastoral
office of bishops expressly recommended that bishops of the same country or region should join together in permanent conferences:

Since episcopal conferences—many such have already been established in various countries—have produced outstanding examples of a more fruitful apostolate, this sacred Synod judges that it would be in the highest degree helpful if in
all parts of the world the bishops of each country or region would meet regularly, so that by sharing their wisdom and experience and exchanging views they
may jointly formulate a program for the common good of the Church.[1]

In the last two decades the episcopal conferences of many countries
have acquired an importance beyond what was anticipated in the conciliar decree. The Council emphasized chiefly the element of exchange and
simply said in general terms that the bishops should "exercise their pastoral office jointly in order to enhance the Church's beneficial influence
on all men, especially by devising forms of the apostolate and apostolic
methods suitably adapted to the circumstances of the times" (*Christus
Dominus*, § 38). In fact, however, individual episcopal conferences have
entered upon extensive undertakings. They have begun to exercise a
kind of teaching office. We need only think, for example, of the general
conferences of the Latin American episcopate at Medellín and Puebla, or
the declarations of the Brazilian episcopate on human rights, or the declaration of the bishops of the United States, "The Challenge of Peace:
God's Promise and our Response" (1983). These various statements
have made the voice of the Church heard in the countries in question;
they have even transcended their immediate context to become exem-
plars for the Church in other countries. The initiatives of the episcopal

---

1. Decree *Christus Dominus* on the pastoral office of bishops in the church, § 37. Citations of this and other conciliar documents are from A. Flannery, ed., *Vatican II: The Conciliar and Post-conciliar Documents* (Collegeville, Minn., 1975).

conferences have enabled the Church to exercise its teaching role at various levels.

The consequence of all this has been a deeper understanding and more vital manifestation of the universality of the Church. The vision of a *communio ecclesiarum* has in fact been realized concretely to some extent. The witness of the Church is heard through a multiplicity of voices, and the independence of the national and local churches has been manifested in a far greater measure than in earlier times. The universality of the ecclesial community finds expression today not only through its central authority but also through the witness of its parts.

2. The role of the pope in the Church has changed to a significant degree since the Second Vatican Council. His utterances come as definitive decisions to a far lesser degree than they did in earlier times. Widening circles in the Church increasingly regard them rather as a source of guidance in the process of opinion formation in the Church.

Admittedly, little has changed in principle. Now as in the past the bishop of Rome is able to exercise his unique fullness of authority and speak and act in irreformable ways. Isolated decisions are possible now as before. The encyclical *Humanae vitae* of 1968 made this clear.

In addition, the debate on collegiality has led in only a very limited degree to an effective participation of the college in the exercise of the papal office. The structural changes introduced after Vatican II have had no far-reaching consequences. At the Council there was also talk of establishing a senate of bishops alongside the pope; the Council was to be prolonged by a kind of permanent synod. One speaker explicitly linked this suggestion with collegiality and spoke of the projected synod as a *signum collegialitatis*. But the suggestion was not implemented in the way originally intended. Pope Paul VI forestalled a thorough discussion of the suggestion by issuing his *motu proprio Apostolica sollicitudo* on September 15, 1965. In this document he decided that a synod should indeed be established but that it should play only a consultative role. Several meetings of the synod have in fact taken place since the end of Vatican II and have undoubtedly dealt with important subjects and given new impetus in some areas. Discussions of evangelization in particular gave the episcopal conferences an opportunity for fruitful exchanges. The establishment of the synod has not, however, altered the exercise of the papal office in any profound way.

And yet a great deal has changed since Vatican II. The pope is trying today, far more than in earlier times, to appear as spokesman for the *communio ecclesiarum*. Now that individual bishops and episcopal conferences have a new perception of their responsibility in their own areas, the papal office has likewise acquired a new function: utterances and decisions of the pope must be able to interact fruitfully with the manifold voices now heard in the Church. In the exercise of his office he is dependent, not in principle but in fact, on the consent of the college. Exchanges between Rome and the individual particular churches have undoubtedly intensified in recent years.

It may be said that the special situation of the Council has continued to some extent in the life of the Church. The pope could in principle have authoritatively decided the questions controverted at the Council, but he saw his role as primarily that of enabling the process of opinion formation to go on in an orderly manner. His concern was that disagreements should not become excessive; he intervened, therefore, when he regarded initiatives as "overhasty," and tried to hold together forces that were pulling apart. So too in the years since the Council he has repeatedly acted as "moderator."

Since the Council the exercise of the papal office has also changed inasmuch as the pope can no longer take agreement for granted. In this respect, too, the situation at the Council has continued in the life of the Church. The Catholic Church is today an open forum of continuous lively debate. Papal utterances are openly and often critically discussed. Increasingly wider circles in the Catholic Church make it known that they can accept various papal statements only in part or not at all. They live in the expectation that even after a papal decision the process of opinion formation will continue and that the magisterium will eventually acquire new insights. They look upon it as their responsibility to play an active part in this process. There is undoubtedly an element of truth in the formula sometimes heard today: *"Roma locuta est, causa aperta est"* (Rome has spoken; the question is still open).

3. Finally, the debate on collegiality has also had an impact on the dialogue between the Catholic Church and the other churches. The discussions at the Council made the representatives of the other churches sit up and take notice. Did the new emphasis on the Church as a *communio ecclesiarum* mean that a door was being opened? Was the concept of a "college" helping to develop an understanding of the Church that would make possible a reciprocal rapprochement and perhaps even a unification? Was the great barrier erected by the First Vatican Council to be thrown down?

It is not surprising, therefore, that the dialogues carried on since the Second Vatican Council should have focused extensively on the question of collegiality. All realized, of course, that the debate at the Council was primarily an internal one; it was required if the internal structure of the Catholic Church was to be reorganized. The question after the Council was whether the concept of collegiality could be made fruitful for the fellowship of churches and the ecumenical movement. The conversations of recent years have pushed forward primarily in two directions.

They have attempted to show that a broad interpretation of the concept of "college" could, if need be, provide a basis for agreement among the churches. As a rule they have harked back to relationships between the churches in the first centuries. Just as the individual churches of that age formed a communion without preeminence or subordination, so must they be understood today as forming a *communio ecclesiarum*. The dialogues have thus attempted to detach the concept of college from its immediate setting in Vatican I and to interpret it, far more radically than Vatican II did, in light of the ecclesiology of the early Church.

The dialogues have at the same time been concerned with the question of the form the papal office must take if it is to be acceptable to the churches of other traditions. They have attempted to show that a primacy of one church is not antecedently excluded, provided it is consistently subordinated to the idea of the Church as a *communio*. A ministry devoted to the unity of the universal Church would be a meaningful one.

The debate on collegiality has thus had a reception of a special kind in conversations between the churches. It has stimulated joint reflection of a kind unthinkable before Vatican II. I say it is a reception of a special kind because the thinking inspired by the debate has gone far beyond the intentions expressed or even implied in the conciliar documents.

The Role of the Pope

Do these three points I have listed bring out everything there is to be said about the reception of the debate on collegiality? No, for it is obvious that what I have been discussing refers to only one line in the development that has taken place since Vatican II. A second line must be added to complete the picture. The preceding two decades have not brought only a deeper consciousness of the Church's universality, a new understanding of authority, and new prospects for the unity of the Church. They have also led to a new development of the papal office.

What is deserving of mention in this connection? Once again I shall make three points.

1. In the past two decades the papal office has acquired new importance not only in the Catholic Church but also in public consciousness. The pope is far more effectively present to the worldwide Church today than in earlier times, and this not only by reason of the authority attributed to him in Catholic teaching but also and above all because in growing measure he is actively taking on the role of a symbolic figure. It was always the case, of course, that the pope embodied in his person the mission and unity of the Church. In the past, however, he played this part in a static way, whereas today he exercises it actively. That is, he no longer merely claims to be shepherd of the flock, but tries to carry out his task in a concrete way by being as closely present as possible to the Church. The modern communications media have provided means of doing so that were not available before.

The change began with Pope John XXIII. He initiated a completely new style of leadership: the pope presented himself no longer as primarily an embodiment of authority but as a person whose spirituality represented the very heart of the Church's message. Precisely because he did not call attention first and foremost to his prerogatives, he acquired all the greater authority as a symbolic figure.

His successors have continued this development, each in his own manner. We may think here, for example, of the journeys of Pope Paul VI during his pontificate. The popes of the past left Rome only for a few days of rest at Castel Gandolfo, whereas Paul VI sought to underscore the universality of his mission by journeys to various parts of the world. The pope, who possesses universal jurisdiction, is also beginning to move about in the universal Church! Pope John Paul II has carried this practice even further by undertaking "pastoral" journeys to almost every area of the world.

Perhaps the most striking example of the pope's new role has been the two visits of Pope Paul VI and Pope John Paul II to the United Nations. The pope appeared there as spokesman for the whole Catholic Church, and even as representative of the Christian conscience as such, to the nations of the world.

This new way of bearing witness in the Church and before the public is certainly not opposed in principle to collegiality. By carrying out this new universal mission the popes continually enhance the importance of the episcopate as a whole. Nonetheless the new emphasis on the papal office at the international level does in fact repeatedly overshadow the role of the bishops. As a result of the new role that has devolved upon it, the center has acquired a new importance.

2. In order, however, to carry out this mission effectively, it is necessary to maintain as far as possible the traditional understanding of the papal office. It has become clear, of course, that the Church can no longer be "ruled" as it was in earlier times. Strict obedience can neither be expected nowadays nor enforced. In view, moreover, of the many different contexts that exist within the Church and in view of the spiritual situation generally, it has become extremely unlikely that the pope will exercise his teaching office by formulating infallible ex cathedra statements. Karl Rahner may well be right in his suggestion that the doctrine of infallibility has to some extent lost its relevance.

But the fact that the papal office is being exercised in a new way does not necessarily mean that the teachings of Vatican I can be altered. In fact, the new role of the pope in the Church and before the public makes these doctrines no less indispensable now than they were in the past. The personal charism of each pope undoubtedly plays a decisive role, but the influence of the papal office is also due to the authority tradition assigns to it. If the pope is to carry out his mission effectively, the office he possesses must have been given to him, and to him alone, by Christ. He must be independent of every other authority and be able to act on his own initiative. He must have direct authority over the entire Church. Thus the very thing on which some doubt was cast by the debate on collegiality must be emphasized once again by reason of the new role that has opened up for the pope.

It cannot come as a surprise, therefore, that during the last two decades the debate on collegiality has had to remain within narrow limits. The dynamic exercise of the papal office was not to be endangered. In many areas of teaching a multiplicity of views could indeed be allowed, but no doubt was to be cast on the prerogatives of the papal office. The discussions to which the publications of Hans Küng gave rise are the best illustration of this state of affairs.

The dynamic exercise of the papal office also required an administrative upgrading of the central authority in Rome. The Curia had to be reorganized in order to be effectively present to the entire Church. It had to be given an international character, something the Council had already said was desirable:

It is to be hoped that their [the congregations'] members, officials, and consultors, as well as the legates of the Roman Pontiff, may be chosen, as far as it is possible, on a more representative basis, so that the offices or central agencies of the Church may have a truly universal spirit [CD 10].

The wish of the Council has since been met in large measure. The Curia has become to a greater extent an instrument of the universal Church.

3. In the past two decades the papal office has also acquired a greater effectiveness in relation to the churches of the other traditions. The popes of earlier times avoided close contacts with representatives of other churches, but John XXIII introduced a new style. The popes are not only ready to receive representatives of other churches; they even seek meetings, conversations, and exchanges. Many of the journeys of Paul VI and John Paul II have had this as their partial or even their exclusive purpose. The papal office has taken on an active ecumenical role.

The expectation that guides the popes in this new ecumenical openness is that the importance of the papal office for the unity of the Church will gradually become clear in the ecumenical movement. Pope Paul VI repeatedly expressed this hope. He was aware, of course, that the papal office was the most serious obstacle to agreement among the churches, but he was also convinced that unity would come about through acceptance of it. When he visited the World Council of Churches in Geneva in 1969, he introduced himself by saying "My name is Peter." Pope John Paul II has voiced the same conviction less directly but no less clearly.

The response in the other churches has been ambivalent. On the one hand, there can be no doubt that in recent decades the pope and the papal office have become increasingly attractive to members of the other churches. It has become the accepted thing for leaders of the other churches to meet with the pope and even to submit to the demands of protocol. In the ecumenical movement since the mid-1960s there has even been something like a de facto recognition of the pope. This

emerged in an especially striking way at, for example, the death of Pope
Paul VI and the coronation of his two successors. At the burial of John
XXIII and the coronation of Paul VI almost no representatives of the
other churches were present. Sixteen years later the situation had
changed: representatives of almost all the churches gathered for the
ceremonies. On the surface, of course, this was no more than an act of
courtesy, but it also expressed the growing awareness that the ecumenical movement had no choice from now on but to "live with the papal office."

At the same time, however, the new development of the papal office
is also causing a growing uneasiness in churches of other traditions. The
readiness of the papacy for discussion and meetings has indeed created
a new atmosphere, but the manner in which the papal ministry is actively exercised does not offer any basis for real agreement. The expectation
that guides the popes in their ecumenical openness leads in a direction
different from the models elaborated in the dialogues. The popes hope
for unification under the egis of the papal office as this has developed in
recent decades and has, in the view of the popes, proven its value in
many respects. Must not the churches of other traditions come to realize, therefore, that the reception of the debate on collegiality, in the form
it has taken in the ecumenical movement, has created an illusion? That
the models developed in the dialogues are nothing but daydreams and
that the reports issued regarding them *cannot* at the present time be
accepted by the central authority of the Catholic Church?

Unresolved Tensions

How is this contradictory picture to be interpreted? Must it be said
that the reception of the debate on collegiality has been a failure? Have
the hopes that sustained Vatican II remained unfulfilled? Have they
been frustrated by other interests and considerations?

No, these would not be appropriate judgments on the situation. The
fact is that the contradictory picture that has emerged in the course of
reception was already latent in the debate at the Council itself.

The text finally adopted on November 17, 1964, represented a painful-
ly negotiated compromise. The new vision behind the concept of collegiality ran up against existing tradition and could not but be infiltrated
by it in the course of the discussion. The statements of Vatican I could
not be set aside but only reinterpreted. The new vision could develop
only once the declarations of Vatican I had been given explicit recognition. The reassertion of Vatican I was, as it were, the price that first had
to be paid. It is clear that the process of reception since Vatican II *could
not but be* codetermined by this explicit decision.

Many theologians believed that in the process of reception the new—

that is, the concept of the *collegium*—would play an explosive role; that the views defended by a minority with notable tenacity would gradually disappear, and the new vision of the Church would gradually take over. The normative element (they hoped) would prove to be not the compromise finally written into the document but that which was new in comparison with the existing tradition. They assumed that the existing tradition could not continue to prevail in the face of ongoing historical development. The forces at work in further development would show that the new element had to be taken as the hermeneutical key for interpreting the document.

This view was not accurate. The debate at Vatican II was not a debate between a tradition that was dying out and a vision to which the future belonged. The council fathers who resisted the idea of collegiality were not simply traditionalists afraid of novelties. They too had a vision of the Church. The debate was not simply between old and new but between two projects for the future. Both were echoed in the ensuing period; both have been operative in the process of reception.

On one side was the hope that the Council would consistently bring out the nature of the Church as a *communio ecclesiarum*; on the other, the conviction that a papal ministry renewed and dynamically exercised on the basis of Vatican I could give new effectiveness to the witness of the Catholic Church. One small incident will serve to bring out the mood of the second group. At the beginning of October 1965, Pope Paul VI visited the United Nations in New York. After his return Cardinal Ottaviani interpreted the papal journey in an emotional speech. A new age has dawned, he said; the pope has succeeded as never before in showing in a symbolic way that the Catholic Church is the soul of the human race (*anima humanitatis*). The Cardinal was summing up in a few words the vision he and his friends had of a revitalized papal office.

The compromise eventually reached at the Council could not dissipate the tension between the two plans for the future. Instead the two were set side by side, and it is therefore not surprising that the tension inevitably reappeared during the process of reception. No synthesis has as yet been effected.

The Interpretation of the Documents

The same tension can be seen at work in particular aspects of the idea of "collegiality." The text produced by the Council left room for divergent interpretations and developments even in more limited questions. Two examples will illustrate my point.

1. How should we speak of the unity of the Church? Should the emphasis be on the idea that the unity of the Church is ensured by the

office and person of the pope? Or may it be said that this unity is expressed by the college of bishops? Is unity made visible primarily by one man or by the communion of the college? Is unity still based on the monarchical principle, or is it to be looked for in the cooperation of powers?

Both views can appeal to the conciliar documents, and both have in fact been emphatically put forth in the process of reception.

There are good grounds for maintaining that Vatican II gave new emphasis to the importance of the pope for the unity of the Church. First of all, Vatican II followed "in the steps of the First Vatican Council" and explicitly repeated the statement, so important in the context of unity, from the Constitution *pastor aeternus*:

In order that the episcopate itself . . . might be one and undivided he [Jesus Christ] put Peter at the head of the other apostles, and in him he set up a lasting and visible source and foundation of the unity both of faith and of communion [LG 18].

This unique role of Peter and his successors is not restricted by the subsequent emphasis on the college but on the contrary is seen even more clearly to be indispensable. The emphasis on the college serves rather to bring out better the multiplicity in the Church. Precisely because of this multiplicity it is all the more important to keep in mind "the perpetual and visible source and foundation of . . . unity" (LG 23). Vatican II shows that precisely because the Catholic Church has a single head it can make room for multiplicity without disintegrating. Only because the college is linked with the successor of Peter does it become a symbol of unity:

This college, in so far as it is composed of many members, is the expression of the mutifariousness and universality of the People of God; and of the unity of the flock of Christ, in so far as it is assembled under one head [LG 22].

The same holds at the diocesan level. Vatican II heightened the importance of the episcopal office. It explicitly taught that "the fullness of the sacrament of Orders is conferred by episcopal consecration" (LG 21), thus deciding a question that until then had still been unresolved in the Catholic tradition. The resolution had a twofold consequence for the issue here under discussion. On the one hand, it laid the theological basis for a new consideration of the relationship between pope and bishops. On the other, it led to a strengthening of the position of bishops in relation to their priests. The relationship between pope and bishops is reflected at the diocesan level in the relationship between bishops and priests. "The priests, prudent cooperators of the episcopal college and its support and mouthpiece, called to the service of the People of God, constitute, together with their bishop, a single presbyteral college, dedicated it is true to a variety of distinct duties" (LG 28). Even more than in the past, the unity of the diocese is ensured by the office and person of the bishop.

But the conciliar texts are susceptible of another interpretation. The introduction of the idea of a *collegium* indicates that the unity of the Church can be represented only by the combined action of the members of the college. True enough, the declarations of Vatican I have been repeated and are valid now as in the past. But the necessity of supplementing them with considerations on the college shows that unity cannot be adequately ensured by the pope alone. As permanent and visible source of unity, the pope has an indispensable role in the college, but unity is given expression only by the college. To prove, therefore, that it abides in unity, the leadership of the Church must take collegial form at every level. But is it possible for this second interpretation to win out?

2. How is the role of the pope within the *communio ecclesiarum* to be understood? Is the emphasis to be on the pope as vicar of Christ and visible head of the *entire* Church (LG 18)? Or may it be said that he is only one, even if the most important, member of the college? Does he exercise his pastoral office directly over the entire Church? Or is his authority utterly inseparable from the accompanying authority of the bishops?

Here again two divergent tendencies are to be found today in the Catholic Church.

On the one hand, as I said earlier, there are those who lay heavy emphasis on the role of the pope as shepherd of the entire Church. He is not simply one bishop among others but the *episcopus universalis* who stands above all the other bishops.

On the other hand, since Vatican II there have been many attempts to approach the meaning of the papal office within the framework of the *communio ecclesiarum* and to interpret it restrictively. Even though the historical development since Vatican II has led rather to an enhancement of the papal role, the thesis has nonetheless been repeatedly proposed that the deepest insight at work in *Lumen gentium* leads in the opposite direction.[2] The doctrine of collegiality means (it is claimed) that the pope can exercise his special authority only in communion with the other bishops.

There are two reasons for urging this interpretation of the impulses at work in the Council. One is the anxiety that the *communio ecclesiarum* may not successfully develop as the Council wanted it to. More important, however, is the consideration that only such a revision of the Roman tradition can provide a basis for the unification of the churches.

Two opposed tendencies! The process of reception has thus far been determined primarily by the first, and it is unlikely that the picture will change in the near future.

2. J.-M. Tillard, *The Bishop of Rome* (Wilmington, Delaware, 1983), p. xii.

College and Council

The concept of collegiality and conciliarity are closely connected. As I pointed out at the beginning, the debate on collegiality became possible only because the convocation of Vatican II unexpectedly revived the conciliar tradition in the Roman Catholic Church. After the definitions of Vatican I there was good reason to think that councils were henceforth unnecessary. Once Vatican II was nonetheless convoked, it became necessary to explain what authority it had and what tasks it could carry out. How was this gathering of bishops from all over the world to be fitted into ecclesiology? What did it mean for it to be suddenly faced, as a college, with a common task? The debate on collegiality was an attempt to answer these questions. At the same time, it was an attempt to establish the conciliar tradition anew in the ecclesiology of the Roman Catholic Church.

Was it possible for this council to be simply an interlude in the history of the Roman Catholic Church? Would it not have to be rather a prelude to a new series of councils?

The hopes cultivated at the time went even further. Might not the next council be celebrated jointly by the churches that today are still separated? This notion was already being expressed after the convocation of Vatican II by Pope John XXIII. In fact, after the unexpected announcement of a council in January 1959 many thought that Vatican II itself might turn out to be an ecumenical council in the fullest sense of the word. But only the first steps toward such a council were taken. Representatives of other traditions were invited to be observers at the proceedings. Pope John XXIII made it clear, moreover, that although the Council was to effect an aggiornamento of the Roman Catholic Church, it must, in accomplishing this, listen to the voice of the other churches. The door to future dialogues must not be closed by precipitous definitions. The pope's desire that the Council have a primarily pastoral character was also very important in this regard. Given these circumstances, was not a joint council possible in the foreseeable future? Could the model so unexpectedly provided by Vatican II be developed further and extended to include all the Christian churches?

The idea of a "genuinely ecumenical council" was pursued especially in the World Council of Churches. Soon after the close of Vatican II a study examined the meaning that the conciliar tradition of the early Church might have for the ecumenical movement.[3] The assembly of the World Council at Uppsala in 1968 declared: "The members of the World Council of Churches, committed to each other, should work for the time when a genuinely universal council may once more speak for all Chris-

---

3. World Council of Churches, *Councils and the Ecumenical Movement* (Geneva, 1968).

tians, and lead the way into the future."[4] This declaration of intention was expanded in the years that followed. The assembly at Nairobi in 1975 undertook to describe the one Church as a "conciliar fellowship," that is, a community so closely united that it is capable, should the occasion arise, of celebrating a council together. The churches are still in a "preconciliar" state. The communion among them has not yet become so close that they are already able to hold a council today. But to the extent that they prepare themselves for the common goal of "conciliar fellowship," the bonds uniting them will become closer. The ecumenical movement is the way from a "preconciliar" state to "conciliar fellowship."

How much agreement must be achieved among the churches before it is possible to speak of a "conciliar fellowship"? The declarations of the World Council of Churches indicate that there must be room for great variety in the unified church that is the goal of the ecumenical movement. The churches must be able to recognize one another as churches of Jesus Christ. They must have become certain that all are based on the same apostolic tradition, that is, that they have achieved agreement on the content of the apostolic faith. They must recognize one another's baptisms and be in a position to celebrate the Eucharist together. They must be able to recognize one another's ministries and have reached sufficient agreement on their role in the Church that each can allow the others to represent them at a council. The present-day "preconciliar fellowship" of churches must focus its attention on creating all these conditions.

These considerations do not decide the question of the role to be played by the papal office in the conciliar fellowship. This role must rather first be clarified in the preconciliar fellowship of churches. One thing, however, is clear from the outset. The road from separation to unity will be more easily traveled to the extent that the "genuinely universal council" of the future is understood as a gathering that has its own authority and initiative. Each church will be able truly to contribute its own tradition only if it knows that it enjoys full recognition in the community of the churches. A conciliar fellowship must to some extent develop out of the churches themselves.

Has the process of reception of the debate on collegiality brought these hopes any closer to fulfillment?

It must be said in response that the process of reception has thus far led to only a very limited revival of the conciliar tradition in the Roman Catholic Church. If we prescind from the new possibilities of exchange and discussion that have been created at every level in the life of the Roman Catholic Church since Vatican II, it must be said that the debate on collegiality has not made room for new models of conciliar discussion and decision. In the Roman Catholic understanding of the matter, a gen-

4. *The Uppsala Report*, N. Goodall, ed. (Geneva 1968), p. 17.

uinely universal council is possible, now as in the past, only in strict sub-ordination to the authority of the pope. The ecumenical movement has thus had but limited results. The course of reception has not created a link between the debate on collegiality and ecumenical reflection on the goal of a "conciliar fellowship."

Immediately after the Council Karl Rahner was already predicting this outcome with his usual objectivity and astuteness. He wrote in 1966:

In practice, is not the initiative and the authority of the college reduced to a mere fiction, if the Pope is always "free" to repress its activities? Needless to say, this latter point is decisive in any ecumenical discussion about the primacy and the synodal structure of the Church.[5]

Especially important in this connection is the fact that after initial hesitation the Roman Catholic Church finally could not bring itself to become a member of the World Council of Churches. The question was actively considered for several years, but then dropped. The direction the process of reception was taking made it seem impossible that the Roman Catholic Church should join the other churches to form a "preconciliar fellowship."

What is to be Done?

Could the reception of the debate on collegiality have turned out differently? Could it have led to a breakthrough and made possible a joint conciliar future?

It is not really surprising that such a breakthrough did not emerge. The debate on collegiality was essentially an internal debate that had its roots in the most recent tradition of the Roman Catholic Church. It had become necessary because the one-sided declarations of Vatican I needed correction.

Is it reasonable to expect that an internal debate should be a decisive factor in resolving the issues that divide the churches? Can the compromise that was reached between divergent tendencies at Vatican II and expressed in chapter 3 of Lumen gentium be an answer to questions that are still controverted among the churches and still unsettled? Such an expectation would obviously be unrealistic. The tradition of Vatican I was presupposed in the debate at the Council and it is still presupposed in the process of reception.

The causes of the separation of the churches go further back and cannot be removed or transcended by a simple correction of Vatican I. They are to be found in the divergent theological and ecclesiological develop-

5. Rahner on Lumen gentium, chap. 3, art. 22, in H. Vorgrimler, ed., Commentary on the Documents of Vatican II (New York, 1967), 1:202.

ments in the East and the West. They are to be found in the development of the papacy that reached its climax at Vatican I. In order therefore to remove divisions and make possible a common conciliar future, it will be necessary to go back much further into the past and to reflect carefully together on the whole development of the papacy since the reform councils of the fifteenth century and since the Reformation and Counter-Reformation.

The real breakthrough in the ecumenical movement will come, therefore, not through reception of the debate on collegiality but only through a reception of the entire history of the conciliar idea in the church.

Eugenio Corecco

13. Aspects of the Reception of Vatican II in the Code of Canon Law

The response of commentators to the new Code of Canon Law during the first two years after its promulgation has been mostly positive.[1] The significance of this approval remains unclear, however, both because of the varied criteria used in evaluating the Code and because in individual authors positive and negative judgments are often heaped together without reference to any scale of values, so that they simply offset one

1. Among the many publications that have appeared since the promulgation of the Code, attention must be given to (a) the editions with commentary, in Spanish and Latin: *Codigo de Derecho Canónico*, under the direction of L. De Echeverria (Madrid, 1983); *Codigo de Derecho Canónico*, under the direction of P. Lombardia and J. I. Arrieta (Pamplona, 1983); (b) manuals: *Nuovo Derecho Canónico*, under the direction of L. De Echeverria (Madrid, 1983); H. Schwendewein, *Das neue Krichenrecht* (Graz, 1983); *Handbuch des katholischen Kirchenrechts*, J. Listl, H. Müller, and H. Schmitz, eds. (Regensburg, 1983); H. Heimerl and H. Pree, *Kirchenrecht. Allgemeine Normen und Eherecht* (Vienna/New York, 1983); M. Petroncelli, *Diritto Canonico* (Naples, 1983); G. Feliciani, *Le basi del nuovo diritto canonico* (Bologna, 1984); *Münsterischer Kommentar zum codex Iuris Canonici*, K. Lüdicke, ed. (Essen, 1984); (c) collections of essays: *Il nuovo codice di diritto canonico*, S. Ferrari, ed. (Bologna, 1983); *La nuova legislazione canonica* (Rome, 1983); *La normativa del nuovo codice*, E. Cappellini, ed. (Brescia, 1983); E. Cappellini and F. Coccopalmerio, *Temi pastorali del nuovo codice* (Brescia, 1983); F. Coccopalmerio, P. A. Bonnet, and N. Pavoni, *Perché un codice nella Chiesa?* (Bologna, 1984); *Dilexit Justitiam. Studia in honorem Aurelii card. Sabatani*, Z. Grocholewski and V. Carcel Ortì, eds. (Vatican City, 1984); (d) issues of periodicals: *AfkKR*, 152/1 (1983); *SCatt*, 112 (1984); (e) monographs: J. B. Beyer, *Dal Concilio al Codice (Il Codice del Vaticano II)* (Bologna, 1984); C. Cardia, *Il governo della Chiesa* (Bologna, 1984); V. Fagiolo, *Il Codice del Post-Concilio. Introduzione* (Rome, 1984); (f) acts of congresses: *Il nuovo codice di diritto canonico. Novità, motivazioni e significato.* Atti della Settimana di Studio del 26–30 aprile 1983, Pontificia Università Lateranense (Rome, 1983); *I diritti fondamentali del fedele e le garanzie costituzionali.* Atti del V Colloquio Giuridico della Pontificia Università Lateranense dell'8–10 febbraio 1984 (forthcoming); *Foi et Institution dans le CIC.* Actes de la XVIIe Session de Droit Canonique organisée par la Société Internationale de Droit Canonique et de la Législation Religieuse Comparée et par l'Institut Catholique de Paris, du 26–30 avril 1984 à Paris (forthcoming); *The New Code of Canon Law.* Acts of the 5th International Congress of Canon Law, organized by the Consociatio Internationalis Studio Iuris Canonico Promovendo and Saint Paul University of Ottawa, August 19–26, 1984 (forthcoming; already in print are two volumes of papers presented to the congress). For the history of the new Code, see F. D'Ostilio, *La storia del nuovo codice di diritto canonico* (Vatican City, 1983); J.

another. When tested by facts, therefore, the widespread acceptance may prove to be not unlike the special relief felt by those who believe they have been rescued from great peril.

When we turn to the specific question of the reception of the Council, the first thing to be kept in mind is that judgments on the Code reflect interpretations of the Council and the often differing degrees of importance assigned to its documents. In this context it is necessary to avoid any static reading of the conciliar documents and to attempt instead to grasp their deeper tendencies, which, it can be foreseen, will win the day in the future, even though the Council itself did not expressly state them with all desirable clarity.

One point of reference in this attempt, which is not without its risks, is to compare the documents with the doctrinal interpretations and developments already published whether by the universal and local magisteria or by theologians, whom canonists must keep in view even though they themselves possess an epistemological authority of their own. As far as the magisterium is concerned, it would be enough to take account of important documents like *Ecclesiam suam* and *Evangelii nuntiandi*, the documents issued by Medellín and Puebla, and the legislation, especially synodal, of the particular churches. The limited space at my disposal, however, allows me to make only occasional reference to all these sources.

A further point: in examining the reception of the Council in the Code a number of valuational standpoints are possible. I shall limit myself to two: epistemology and the incorporation of some of the most important contents of the conciliar documents (the assessment here is based on the reception, both material and formal, of these contents).[2]

The Epistemological Structure of the Code

1. The Council decreed (in *Optatam Totius*, § 16) that the mystery of the Church should be taken into account in the teaching of canon law. The logic of this principle requires that it have been applied first of all to the establishment of canonical norms. It should therefore have likewise been applied in a very strict way to the reform of the Code.

Gaudemet, "Collections canoniques et codifications," *RDC* 33 (1983) 82–109; R. Metz, "La nouvelle codfication du Droit de l'Eglise, ibid., 110–68.—The translation of the new Code is taken, unless otherwise stated, from *The Code of Canon Law. A Text and Commentary*, J. A. Coriden, T. J. Green, and D. E. Heintschel, eds. (New York, 1985).

2. Some other writings of mine complement the present article: "I presupposti culturali ed ecclesiologici del nuovo 'Codex,'" in *Il nuovo codice di diritto canonico*, S. Ferrari, ed. (n. 1, above), pp. 37–68 (German translation in *AfkKR*, 152/1 [1983] 3–30); "Theological Justifications of the Codification of the Latin Canon Law," in *The New Code of Canon Law*. Acts of the 5th International Congress (n. 1, above).

In a seemingly marginal way, and yet with the universal force proper to any methodological principle, the principle in question summed up the many-faceted desire of the Council for the dejuridicization of Church life. This desire had arisen as a reaction against the "institutional hegemony" under which the Church lived in the age when the idea of "Christendom" reigned[3] and which was consolidated in a notable measure by the codification of 1917.

The choice of codification as a tool is therefore a priori problematic, if not utterly inadequate. Although historically the concept of codification has been concretized in various ways,[4] the fact cannot be overlooked that from a methodological point of view codification refers to a gnoseological experience, that of the Enlightenment, which supplied a supposedly purely rational alternative to Christian culture, the latter being based on the indispensable part played by mystery in our knowledge of reality as a whole and thus on the priority of faith over reason.

Codification, a juridical tool developed on the basis of general theory as a way of making law rational, is thus more apt for expressing an institutional and societal view of the Church—and one on which the natural law shadow of the *societas perfecta* still rests—than for expressing the Church as a sacramental mystery. The problem arises ultimately from the fact that the philosophical notion of law that lies behind the modern idea and experience of codification is not applicable to canon law, because the formal definition of the latter cannot prescind from its theological dimension.[5] If we once admit the inescapably dictatorial nature of any methodological principle, then, as far as the risk of distorting the essence of ecclesial experience is concerned, there is no substantial difference between applying the method of Marxist analysis and applying the method of autonomous reason that is the mark of modern liberal rationalism.

When the Commission for the Revision of the Code of Canon Law opted for recodification, its members obviously could not fail to take into account the methodological directive of *Optatam Totius*, although they did not realize its full scope and implications. The resulting compromise has caused the Code to reproduce, and even magnify, the two divergent approaches to the Church that are found in the Council: the Church as *societas* and the Church as *communio*.[6] In fact, both the idea of law that

3. See G. Alberigo, "Egemonia istituzionale nella cristianità?," *Cristianesimo nella storia*, 5 (1984) 49–68.

4. See N. Irti, *L'Età della decodificazione* (Milan, 1979), pp. 3–39; R. Sacco, "Codificare: modo superato di legiferare?," *Rivista di Diritto Civile*, 29 (1983) 117–35.

5. See A. Rouco Varela, "Le statut ontologique et épistémologique du droit canonique," *RSPT*, 57 (1973) 203–26; E. Corecco, "'Ordinatio rationis' o 'Ordinatio fidei'? Appunti sulla definizione della legge canonica," *Strumento Internazionale per un Lavoro Canonico. Communio*, 36 (1977) 1–2 (French translation in *RCI Communio* 3 [1978] 22–39).

6. See A. Acerbi, *Due ecclesiologie: Ecclesiologia giuridica e ecclesiologia di communione nella "Lumen gentium"* (Bologna, 1975).

underlies the Code (as Sobanski has perceptively noted)[7] and the overall systematization reflect the continuation of this dualism in a very obvious way.

The reception, in the three central books of the Code, of the conciliar model of the Church as the people of God that shares in the three offices of Christ irreversibly shattered the unity of the rational epistemological principle that underlay the systematic approach, derived from Roman law, of the old Code. This same reception, however, did not lead the Commission to approach all the material in the Code in the epistemological light of faith. This remains true even if it must at the same time be acknowledged that the legislative material in its totality could not have been organized into a unitary system on the basis of the *tria munera* scheme. And, contrary to the impression often given, this was not primarily because of understandable technical difficulties. It was rather because of the theoretical weakness of the scheme itself and, above all, because the Commission did not attend in a sufficiently rigorous way to the fact that the participation of the faithful in the *munus regendi* is no less necessary theologically than their participation in the other two *munera*.

If the Commission was unable to emancipate itself completely from the existing juridical schema, it was because it found in the Council itself a cue permitting it to approach the Church as a society and to give a natural law justification for the existence of canon law. From this point of view, the ambiguity resides in the interpretation of LG 8, § 1. The primary intention there is not to assert the societal nature of the Church (an aspect that recurs in LG 14, § 2, which shows redactional confusion) but rather to explain the principle of an indissoluble unity between the invisible and visible dimensions of the Church by analogy with the mystery of the incarnation.[8] It is simply presupposed that the Church is also a society, but the Council did not intend to take a position on what precisely is meant by this.

The erroneous interpretation of the thrust of LG 8, § 1, which has long since found a place in theology,[9] and the lack of attention to the basic methodological directive in *Optatam Totius* had for result that the greater part of the books of the new Code were not plotted out under the guidance of a theological epistemology.

2. The adoption of the technique of "general norms" (an expression more characteristic of the method of abstract codification) caused the legislators to apply a strictly juridical criterion to the contents of Book I.

a) The principal subject of canonical regulations, namely, the believ-

---

7. "Rechtstheologische Überlegungen zum neuen kirchlichen Gesetzbuch," *TQ*, 163 (1983) 178–88.

8. See H. Müller, "De analogia Verbum Incarnatum inter et Ecclesiam (L.G. 8/a)," *Per*, 66 (1977) 499–512.

9. See, e.g., A. Rouco Varela, "Katholische Rechtstheologie heute. Versuch eines analytischen Überblickes," *AfkKR*, 145/1 (1976) 19.

er, is defined in Book I (as also in Book VII), not on the basis of his or her ecclesiological identity, but by the Roman law category of *persona physica*. The latter, however, is not only irrelevant from the theological point of view; it is even misleading both in itself and in relation to an understanding of *persona iuridica*.

This category is inadequate in itself because it suggests that in the canonical order the physical person exists prior to the Church, just as the human person exists prior to the state. Not only does this ambiguity emerge every time that natural law seems still to take precedence in the Code over divine positive law as the source of canonical regulation;[10] it also has ramifications whenever the new Code follows the line of the old and uses the category of "competence" to define the juridical situation of believers, instead of using the more conciliar category of "participation."[11]

The limiting clauses frequently occurring in the lists of the obligations and rights of the faithful reflect more than a mere preoccupation with external safeguards;[12] they seem to be dictated by the juridical category of "competence" that is at work in an almost subterranean way. But this approach does not seem to be as universally operative as has been claimed,[13] for in some fundamental norms the idea of participation dominates, whereas in the lists of obligations and rights the Code, unlike the *Lex ecclesiae fundamentalis (LEF)*, obviously gives priority to "obligation" over "right."[14] And in fact participation in the life of the Church can be described as primarily an obligation, once it is maintained that the believer as such does not exist prior to the Church but is called to it by divine vocation.

The second difficulty inherent in the definition of the faithful as physical persons is the ambiguity thereby indirectly introduced into the concept of juridic person. The factor that distinguishes believers from juridic persons in canon law is not natural physicality but sacramental structure. In accordance with what was affirmed in *Communicationes* (9 [1977] 240) the Code defines the Catholic Church and Apostolic See as moral persons (can. 113, § 1), because their existence does not depend on an act of the human will, but it describes as public or private juridic persons all the other collective entities that canon law or competent authority declares to be juridic subjects. This distinction should not have

10. As, e.g., in matrimonial law.

11. See R. Sobanski, "L'ecclésiologie du nouveau Code de Droit Canonique," in *New Code of Canon Law* (n. 1, above).

12. See H. Schnizer, "Individuelle und gemeinschaftliche Verwirklung der Grundrechte," in *I diritti fondamentali del cristiano nella Chiesa e nella società*. Atti del IV Congresso Internazionale di Diritto Canonico, Fribourg, Oct. 6–11, 1980, E. Corecco, A. Scola, and N. Herzog, eds. (Fribourg/Milan, 1981), pp. 419–48.

13. See Sobanski, "Rechtstheologische Überlegungen," pp. 186–88.

14. For example, in the list of the obligations and rights of the faithful (can. 208–223). See E. Corecco, "Il catalogo dei doveri-diritti dei fedeli nel nuovo CIC," in *Atti del V Colloquio Giuridico della Pontificia Università Lateranense* (n. 1, above).

been inferred from the fact of erection as such, but from the ecclesiological nature of the different entities in question. Thus even though the
particular Churches exist concretely only in consequence of being
erected by the Holy See (can. 373), nonetheless they exist prior to the
canonical organization of things insofar as they are necessary ecclesiological entities. If this were not the case, the implication of can. 113, § 1,
would be that only the universal Church (assuming that *catholica* means
"universal")—and not the particular churches—exists *ex ordinatione divina*. If, on the other hand, "Catholic Church" means "Church of
Christ" which is both universal and particular, then the particular
churches too should be defined as moral persons and not simply as juridic persons on the sole ground that their concrete existence must come
by an act of establishment.

It is therefore inaccurate to treat the particular churches in the same
way as all the other public juridic persons, as is evidently done in can.
1257, § 1 (but see also can. 1255), because there is a fundamental ecclesiological difference between these various entities.

The idea of making a terminological distinction between these entities
is a promising one, but it should have been carried out with greater
ecclesiological accuracy. The fact of having defined believers as physical
persons has prevented a clearer treatment of the material, because it has
kept the compilers from seeing that the status of necessary ecclesiological entities (the universal and particular churches, the Holy See, and
possibly other entities such as, for example, the college of bishops) as
juridic subjects flows from their sacramental nature (as it does in the
case of the faithful) and not from an arbitrary act of establishment as in
the case of other public and private juridic persons. All this should
obviously not cause us to forget that the moral personality of the Catholic Church and the Holy See, which are *ex institutione divina*, is only analogous to juridic personality as developed in the Roman juridical tradition.

b) The other canonical institution that by reason of its inclusion in the
book dealing with general norms is deprived of its theological meaning
to a much greater extent than in the old Code is the *potestas regiminis, seu
iurisdictionis*.

Stripped as it is of every reference to the conciliar idea of *sacra potestas*
and far removed from its appropriate constitutional context, the power
of governance is treated in the "general norms" as if it were essentially
different from the power of orders (can. 129ff.). This theological and systematic dualism, to which I shall return further on, is another manifestation of the fact that the power of governance (with the norms regulating
its exercise and its transmission by delegation) is seen as ultimately derived from the societal structure of the Church, in a way analogous to
statutory juridic power. Can. 129, § 1, emphasizes its divine origin, but
seems to do so as if this were a simple consequence of the fact that the
Church itself, as a society, is of divine origin.

When (as in title 8 of Book I) the power of jurisdiction is separated from the power of orders and unconnected with *sacra potestas*, it is not possible to bring out its theological connection with the three functions in which this power customarily finds expression: the function of establishing general norms (law and custom), the administrative function, and the judicial function. Because of the normative approach, the last named has been discussed in the completely different context of Book VII. If the Code in dealing with the power of jurisdiction had been concerned to bring out its theological and constitutional dimension, it would not have located the norms governing this power (even if it had dealt with them under "general norms" as in the 1917 Code) after those for laws and administrative acts. It should, if anything, have put them before these, because laws and administrative actions are functions in which the power of jurisdiction finds expression.

c) The result has been that in the new Code the norms for law and custom (to take only these two examples) have the same juridical and technical connotation they had in the preceding Code, and lack any ecclesiological dimension.

The norms governing law make no reference at all to the *sensus fidei*, in which the participation of all the faithful in the *munus regendi* of Christ and the Church finds expression, and therefore to the word of God. The *munus regendi* is treated, both in the opening canons (7–22) and in those dealing with the power of jurisdiction (135ff.), as though it were, as an instrument of governance, the prerogative solely of the hierarchy and its special participation in the *munus regendi* of Christ.

As far as custom is concerned, it must be noted that can. 23 recognizes the "community of the faithful" as its subject and that in accordance with tradition (and not canonical tradition alone) can. 27 repeats the principle that "custom is the best interpreter of laws." But even in this context the *sensus fidelium* does not emerge with sufficient explicitness to make it clear that the participation of the faithful in the establishment of custom is not reducible and attributable to the same social phenomenon in which all earthly customs originate.

It goes without saying that the participation of the faithful in the legislative function cannot be limited to the indirect form of interpretation through custom. It is also direct, both in the legislative phase (for example, when synodal procedures for which the Code itself provides are implemented) and in ensuring the survival of law through reception.[15]

d) The purely technical and positivistic approach to the norms for juridic acts also causes the Code to forget a fact basic for the development of the very idea of canon law: namely, that among the more constitutive (as well as more frequent) juridic acts of the Church must be

15. On the principle of reception, see, e.g., W. Krämer, *Konsens und Rezeption. Verfassungsprinzipien der Kirche im Basler Konziliarismus* (Münster, 1980), esp. pp. 318–36; G. Alberigo, "Wahl-Konsens-Rezeption," *Concilium*, 8 (1972) 477–83.

numbered the sacraments, whose binding juridic force has a value that is not simply social but also and above all soteriological. This approach has thus led to the absurdity of establishing (in can. 125 and 126) general rules for the validity or invalidity of juridic acts that are in principle not applicable to the sacraments.

3. The tribute that codification has paid to the societal and juridical principle is also to be seen with utter clarity in Books V (on temporal goods), VI (on sanctions), and VII (on processes).

The necessary role of *communio* in the possession and use of material goods shows up repeatedly in the conciliar texts and should have provided the keystone for Book V in its entirety. Instead, Book V has included among its fundamental norms the natural law parameters proper to a *societas perfecta*, the benchmarks here being the peremptory assertion of the Church's right to possess patrimonial goods (can. 1254, § 1) and its right to require of the faithful the contributions needed to meet its financial needs (can. 1260).

The patrimonial relationship between the faithful and the Church thus continues to be determined—though with fiscal variations—by similarity to the state model that provided the inspiration for the *ius publicum ecclesiasticum*. It is no accident, therefore, that precisely in this book of the code the Church is still seen (and this not simply by reason of terminology) as a hypostatized entity that, like the state, stands in a relationship of altereity with its subjects.[16]

In the final analysis, this overall epistemological structure is not impaired in Book V either by the definition of the purpose of ecclesiastical possessions, which is taken, more consciously than in the 1917 Code, from the early tradition of the Church (when the administration of the patrimony was structurally connected with the celebration of the eucharist), or by the reception of certain conciliar institutions, such as the diocesan and interdiocesan institutions of can. 1274, in which the communion structure of the presbyterate and the whole people of God takes concrete form in the patrimonial sphere. It may be asked whether the preferential option for the poor, which was formulated at the magisterial level in the Puebla document, could not have led the Commission to revive the early Church's idea that the poor are not only the beneficiaries of the Church's patrimony but its very owners, at least morally if not juridically.[17]

4. In Book VI, on sanctions, the concern to develop a juridical structure consistent with the general theory of penalties has likewise taken precedence over courageous reform in individual areas. Although the indispensable norms with reference to the sacrament of penance are not

16. See E. Corecco, "Dimettersi della Chiesa per ragioni fiscali," *Apollinaris*, 55 (1982) 467–87.

17. This idea endured in canon law until the seventeenth century; see W. Schwickerat, *Die Finanzwirtschaft der deutschen Bistümer* (Breslau, 1942), p. 79; J. Evelt, *Die Kirche und ihre Institute auf dem Gebiete des Vermögensrechtes* (Soest, 1845), pp. 4–6.

lacking, a more structural connection with this sacrament would have been helpful in understanding that not only excommunications *latae sententiae*, but also excommunications *ferendae sententiae*, which are imposed by a so-called *irrogatoria* judgment, do not in themselves correspond to the idea of penalty as found in the general theory of law. Excommunication is a de facto situation in which believers put themselves by anti-ecclesial behavior that can be officially observed by authorities and for which, in any case, juridical regulations specify certain juridical consequences. A statement of John Paul II provides valuable magisterial support[18] for this interpretation, which has been gaining increased acceptance.[19]

The nonpenal nature of the most important sanction exerts such an influence on lesser sanctions that it undermines the foundations of the entire epistemological structure of Book VI, which is still harnessed to the natural law categories of the restoration of justice (see can. 1341) and coercive power (can. 1311). The principle set down in can. 1314 and approved by the Synod of 1967, that *ferendae sententiae* penalties are to be preferred, is not enough to correct this approach to the subject. In fact, neither the Synod nor the Commission for the Revision of the Code of Canon Law derived the principle in can. 1314 from the logic of communion, with the intention of enabling church authorities to deal with the situation of the believer in difficulty by applying pastoral criteria unaccompanied by potentially harmful elements, formal and juridical. The concern that guided the formulation of the principle was rather to make the Church a more consistent image of a *societas perfecta* (sic!) in which the problems of juridical safeguards and equality before the law remain key points.[20]

Can. 1341 makes plain the futility of this approach,[21] but the expansive force of this canon in relation to the entire structure of Book VI is offset by its unfortunate location in the system of the Book. If it had been placed at the beginning, it might have made more explicit the supplementary nature of the entire penal apparatus.

This canon, which was inspired by the Council, as well as the principles governing imputability (can. 1321–1330) and the application of sanc-

18. See the pope's first address (Feb. 17, 1979) to the judges of the Roman Rota: "The penalty that is threatened by ecclesiastical authority (but that, in reality, is simply a recognition of a situation in which the subject has put himself or herself) is seen as a means of fostering communion" (*TPS*, 24 [1979] 220–21). For a comment, see Gerosa (next note), pp. 138 and 243.

19. On this question, see the doctoral dissertation of L. Gerosa, *La scomunica e una pena? Saggio per una fondazione teologica del diritto penale canonico* (Fribourg, 1984), esp. pp. 249–388.

20. See *Communicationes*, 2 (1969) 84–85.

21. "Only after he has ascertained that scandal cannot sufficiently be repaired, that justice cannot sufficiently be restored and that the accused cannot sufficiently be reformed by fraternal correction, rebuke and other ways of pastoral care is the ordinary then to provide for a judicial or administrative procedure to impose or to declare penalties."

tions (can. 1354–1363) and, even more decisively, the "general" norm in can. 1399, show how the penal law of the Church has in fact already been stripped, as far as its contents are concerned, of any real claim to follow the paradigms given in the doctrine of statutory penalties. It was all the more important, therefore, to drop the old formal and conceptual approach and thus show greater respect for the conciliar spirit behind the substantive material norms, and to cease trying to force all the material into schemata clearly dictated by a societal image of the Church.

5. The norms that begin Book VIII, on processes (can. 1400–1403), again reveal the same cultural and epistemological approach as in the Code of 1917.

Can. 1446 contains the directive that all the faithful (and bishops in particular) are to avoid recourse to lawsuits as a way of settling disputes. If this admonition, which is clearly conciliar in its inspiration, had not been interpreted reductively as a simple moral exhortation and had instead been allowed to exercise its full structural potential, it would have been possible to provide the whole body of norms dealing with processes with a more satisfactory ecclesiological setting.

This would have required, however, a theological rethinking of the nature of *potestas sacra* and its judicial function; instead, as we shall see, the entire Code takes a regressively positivist approach to this subject. The legislator has thus been deprived of the possibility of overcoming the dualism latent in the twofold requirement—both parts of which come from the Council—that canonical procedures be adapted to modern juridic sensitivities and that an ecclesiologically more profound image of the nature and function of canonical processes be conveyed.

To the extent that *sacra potestas* is a power of loosing and binding in reference to salvation, it can in fact operate, and has often operated in the past, even without having canonical processes available. The latter are technical superstructures that have probably become increasingly indispensable for dealing in a safer and juridically more equitable way with subjective situations in which the faithful find themselves as social bonds become increasingly more complicated even in the Church; nonetheless such processes are not constitutive for the existence and exercise of *sacra potestas*. Only when there is a statutory separation of powers do judicial procedures become an institutionally necessary and constitutive projection of the very existence of a judicial power that is separate and autonomous in relation to legislative and administrative powers. In the state the existence of judicial power is coextensive with the existence of procedures by which it finds expression.

From this point of view the removal of the canonization process from the Code and the failure to include in the Code the procedures for the examination of doctrine are symptomatic. The reason for saying this is not that these procedures cannot be regulated by special laws, but that because of their ecclesial importance and because they are procedures that have a formally more administrative than judicial character, they show clearly that in the canonical order there is no *potestas iudicialis* distinct and separate from the other two functions (the legislative and the administrative) of the power of jurisdiction. In all three functions a single *sacra potestas* operates, following the logic of communication that is specific not to the sacraments but to the word.

The jurisdictional function of *sacra potestas* is at work in these two procedures and takes on there a clearly magisterial quality. This explains why the document concluding these procedures (a document that is a decree, not a sentence) can be published only by him who possesses in its entirety the one undivided *sacra potestas*, namely, the supreme authority in the Church or, as the case may be, the bishop.

The other symptom of the dualism mentioned above is the fact that, in obedience to the requirements of the technique of codification, the new Code downgrades processes dealing with the constitutional state of persons (marriage, ordination, membership in the ecclesial communion, and the so-called penal process) to the level of simple "special" procedures. Even though these processes are a fundamental and indispensable part of the canonical order, they are grafted as simple appendices onto the ordinary procedures for dealing with litigation, procedures that the new Code continues to see as the keystone of the entire canonical judicial structure. This, despite the fact that these procedures are regarded by can. 1446 as simply supplementary, comparable to civil litigation processes that have for their purpose to settle disputes (private cases, cases dealing with patrimonies, benefices, etc.).

It can be maintained that the Church can accept the relevant civil processes as its own ordinary procedures for litigation (modifying them as need arises) and have the advantage of being able to take over as well any possible cultural and juridical connotations. It is unthinkable, on the other hand, that the Church can do away with procedures dealing with the constitutional state of the faithful. This impossibility is due to the fact that these procedures are directly related to participation in the Eucharist or to the fact that they show forth the special nature of canon law, which is guided by the principle that truth and material certainty take precedence over formal certainty (a principle that is alien not only to civil litigation but also to ordinary canonical litigation as now practiced).[22]

The fact that in ordinary litigation the sentence can also have a (constitutive or rescissory) definitive character (unlike sentences in processes dealing with the *status* of persons) is certainly not proof that in such litigation a *potestas iudicialis separata* (but not adequately distinct) from the other two functions (the legislative and the administrative) of jurisdiction is operative in a direct and constitutive way. The possible defini-

---

22. On the dispute that arose among Italian lay canon lawyers on this problem, see E. Corecco, "Valore dell'atto *contra legem*," in *La norma en el derecho canonico*, Actas del III Congreso Internacional de Derecho Canonico, Pamplona, Oct. 10–15, 1976 (Pamplona, 1979), 1:839–68.

tive character of a contentious process is nonetheless different from that of a process of canonization or an examination of doctrine. It is definitive, not because it determines the content, but only because canonical regulations decree that a final sentence has the force of turning its object into a *res iudicata*, regardless of the degree of material certainty attained in the examination of the case.

In contentious processes, as in those dealing with the state of persons, where the sentences are purely declaratory, *sacra potestas* (in its jurisdictional function) does not intervene directly but only indirectly in the act of passing sentence. It is directly operative only in the preliminary phase, that is, the action that initiates the procedures and appoints the judges.

In contentious procedures and procedures dealing with the state of persons, judges therefore do not exercise a *potestas iurisdictionalis iudiciaria*, which as *iudicialis* does not exist (once the difference between this and legislative or administrative actions becomes purely procedural); they only carry out a functional and technical task in relation to the *sacra potestas* of the bishop. It follows that the admission of laypersons to the office of judge poses no theological problem.

In light of this analysis it can be concluded that can. 1446 should at the very least have called for a different systematic arrangement of procedures. Instead of proposing as a paradigm ordinary contentious procedures as presently practiced, it would have made greater ecclesiological sense for the Code to propose as the typical kind of process that which deals with the constitutional states of persons (and the respective variants of these states), especially in view of the fact that because of marriage cases this kind of procedure is by far the most frequently occurring. The Code should have placed the "special" norms for canonical "civil" contentious procedures at the end, after the processes for canonizations and the examination of doctrine.

It would have been possible in such an approach to meet the demand (which in fact has in good measure been met) for a greater responsiveness to modern juridical sensitivities and for a greater attention of other juridical traditions of non-Roman and non-Germanic origin (such as the common law tradition), thus yielding an image of the Church and its authority that resembles less closely that of the state.

6. These observations make it possible to say in recapitulation that the binding methodological and epistemological directive of OT (16, § 4) has been received only in the three central books of the Code, although it must be acknowledged that the epistemological change effected in these parts of the Code makes irreversible the break between the present canonical regulations of the Church and the preceding Roman-law tradition.

The reasons for this serious inadequacy are obviously numerous. I cannot here give an exhaustive list of them, but neither can I fail to mention some of the more important ones.

The first, which was inseparable from the political need of showing the Holy See's determination to proceed expeditiously to the reforms called for by John XXIII and Vatican II, was that the appointment of the Commission for the Revision of the Code of Canon Law came too close on the heels of Vatican II. The Commission lacked the necessary distance from the conciliar event and, instead of undertaking a work of comprehensive comparative interpretation of the conciliar texts, preferred to make a selection. This had the serious consequence that others were neglected.

The second reason, connected with the first, was that the members of the Commission were drawn from a generation of canonists who had been trained before the Council and who for the most part regarded continuity with the preceding juridical tradition as indispensable.

Finally, there is the fact—rarely taken into consideration up to now, but in many ways disconcerting—that the norms for revision that were approved by the Synod of Bishops in 1967 obscured rather than helped to clarify the central problem of the epistemological and theological approach to be taken in the new canon law. They did so because they strengthened the conviction—already present among the council fathers but meanwhile largely transcended in part of the conciliar teaching— that the existence of a canon law originates in the societal nature of the Church. This explains why the Synod so readily proposed the application of the principle of subsidiarity,[23] which had been imported by canonists from the philosophy of law or the Church's social teaching, and overestimated its potential homogeneity with the principle of communion. It also explains why the Synod so emphatically supported as necessary a judicial protection for the rights of the faithful, but also saw this protection as modeled on civil administrative justice.[24]

7. In this situation, the inevitable question is what alternative systematic solutions were available besides the one adopted in the Code.

The first step would obviously have been to reject codification as a tool and to choose instead (on the assumption that the idea of a single body of law—not necessarily a code—was to be retained) an *ordo Ecclesiae*. This would have had the advantage of further emphasizing the constitutional character of canon law over the civil-law character that is still very strongly felt in the Code, and of making superfluous any attempt at a *Lex fundamentalis*. Acceptance of the category of *ordo*, which has been favored especially in Protestant theology,[25] would have meant a valuable ecumenical opening in this vital area of church life, and not implying (contrary to what has been claimed)[26] the acceptance of the opposition

23. See *Communicationes*, 5:80–82.

24. Ibid., 7:83.

25. See, as representative, K. Barth, *Die Ordnung der Kirche. Zur dogmatischen Grundlegung des Kirchenrechtes* (Munich, 1955); E. Wolf, *Ordnung der Kirche. Lehr- und Handbuch des Kirchenrechtes auf ökumenischer Basis* (Frankfurt, 1961).

26. For example, W. Aymans, "Ekklesiologische Leitlinien in den Entwürfen für die neue Gesetzgebung," *AfkKR*, 151/1 (1982) 27–57.

between *ius divinum* and *ius humanum* in which Protestant teaching is still bogged down.[27] The rejection of codification would have meant the rejection of the idea of "general norms," which gives structural dominance to an epistemological principle derived from philosophical and juridical reason over an epistemological principle derived from theology. As a matter of fact, the directive (which in any case was superfluous) of the 1967 Synod that the Code should retain a juridical character[28] in no way requires the acceptance of the method of abstract codification; in any case the Code was forced to some extent to renounce the application of this method.

There are evidently many possible ways of developing an *ordo Ecclesiae*. It is not possible in the present context to propose a fully articulated system, but it will be worthwhile to state at least a few criteria.

An *ordo* tends by its nature to translate the constitutional structure of the Church into institutional forms. Inasmuch as the essence of the Church's constitution is part of the content of the faith, the standard of purely disciplinary norms cannot be applied to it so as to give it a purely functional role in the subjective faith of the believer. An *ordo Ecclesiae* will by its nature highlight those elements that are based on *ius divinum* and therefore reveal both the sacramental, as opposed to societal, origin of canon law and the dependence of human norms on divine law.

The conciliar model of the *tria munera* has not only not been integrally respected by the Code but has not even become the basis for the Code's systematic structure. In light of this, I remain convinced that a systematic approach based on the sacraments would have been a valid alternative.[29] In any case, the hastily made claim is incorrect that such an approach would not have been inspired by the Council.[30] In LG 11 the institutional description of the Church begins precisely by following the succession of the sacraments. The same procedure is also sketched in SC 6 and LG 10, § 2, and 25, § 3.

The more difficult technical problem that then arises is to find a place in the system for the word.[31] The difficulty should be met not by separating word and sacrament but by respecting their inseparability. Word and sacrament are in fact only two formally different ways in which the one presence of Christ becomes a reality in the Church.[32] On the other

27. See A. Rouco Varela, "Was ist 'katholische' Rechtstheologie?," *AfkKR*, 153/2 (1984) 530–43; idem, "Die katholische Rechtstheologie heute," ibid., 145/1 (1976) 3–21.

28. See *Communicationes*, 1:78–79.

29. The idea has been proposed (even in the Commission for the Revision of Canon Law) by S. Kuttner, "Betrachtungen zur Systematik eines neuen Codex Iuris Canonici," in *Ex Aequo et Bono. W. Plöchl zum 70. Geburtstag*, P. Leisching, P. Pototschning, and R. Potz, eds. (Innsbruck, 1977), pp. 15–21.

30. Thus J. Beyer, "Il nuovo codice di diritto canonico," *SCatt*, 112 (1984) 130–33.

31. This is the problem raised by W. Aymans, "Ekklesiologische Leitlinien" (n. 26, above), p. 38.

32. On the problem, see E. Corecco, "La 'Sacra Potestas' e i Laici," *Studi Parmensi*, 27 (1980), 5–26.

hand, the word does not have a structural autonomy of its own, for the institutional existence of the Church begins with the exercise of the first sacrament, baptism. What exists apart from the sacramental structure is not the Church but the "Christian religion." The word always has its own specific place and manifestation (preaching, catechesis, magisterium) in every sacrament.

Beyer's recent proposal is not without its interest,[33] if we prescind from the conceptual overlappings it contains, but it tends to reduce the entire institutional structure of the Church to a purely functional role in the subjective faith of the believer. Its role as he conceives it belongs more in a pastoral directory than in an *ordo iuridicus*.

Reception of the Ecclesiological Contents of Vatican II

An exhaustive appraisal of the phenomenon of reception would require a quantitatively far more extensive analysis of the data in Council and Code than is possible here. But a selective examination of some basic ecclesiological contents of the Code is enough to bring out some salient traits and to lay bare the ambiguity present in them. There were other factors, over and above the twofold epistemological approach sketched in the preceding section of this essay, that contributed to this end result.

On the one hand, some conciliar contents were not received or were received only partially; on the other, not all the contents materially received in the Code have completely retained the formal value and dynamism that is theirs in the conciliar texts. A judgment on reception must therefore take into account the way in which the Code has dealt with both the formal and the material aspects of the conciliar contents. Although it is true that a content requires a satisfactory formal expression in order to have its full value, it is also true that form always has an impact on the material element as well. When form takes precedence over content, the latter takes on a meaning different from its original meaning; when content takes precedence over form, the latter becomes ineffective.

Both of the phenomena just described are to be seen in the reception of the ecclesiological contents of the Council. Because the relationship between the two is reciprocal and convertible, they are both ultimately reducible to the epistemological problem.

If we take Vatican II as our point of reference, it is possible to identify in the Code cases in which the conciliar form has taken precedence over

33. See Beyer, "Il nuovo codice," p. 133. Numbers I–IV in Beyer's plan have different titles but deal substantively with the sacraments.

the contents of the Code, and cases in which the conciliar contents have not found an adequate form in the Code. The paradigmatic example of the first type of case is the conciliar schema of the *tria munera*, which has imposed severe limits on many institutional contents of the three central books of the Code, as, for instance, on the sacraments.[34] A typical example of the second series of cases is the idea of the common priesthood or that of the *sensus fidelium*, both of which have been taken over materially from the Council but have not been used in the Code in a way that allows their ecclesiological meaning to deploy its full formal potentiality.

To avoid this ambiguity the process of reception would have had to deal more freely with the fact that Vatican II not only did not intend to develop a comprehensive ecclesiology, but also did not offer a systematic organization of the doctrine of the Church with the intention of providing at the institutional level a systematic model that would be valid for a reform of canon law, to say nothing of a recodification of that law.

The Faithful in General

1. The ambiguity of which I have spoken comes out quite clearly in the way in which the Code tackles the problem of the faithful.

There is no doubt that in the central three books of the Code the legislators were able to profit by the essential lesson of the Council and to substitute the faithful for the clergy as the principal protagonists in the organization of canon law. This central achievement influences, at least potentially, the entire Code, despite the inconsistencies already brought to light (above) in Books I and VII with regard to *persona physica*.

In so doing, the Code has quite gone beyond the material data verifiable in the Council. This is true, first of all, in that Book II, implementing the insight of LG 10 (which the Council itself was unable to follow up fully), begins its entire treatment of the juridical constitution of the people of God with a broad set of norms covering the status common to all the faithful (can. 204–223). Secondly, in can. 204 the Code defines the faithful without identifying them with the laity, as is done in LG 31, § 1. Thirdly, can. 208, unlike LG 32, § 3, gives a doctrinal clarification of the principle of equality *in dignitate et actione* (one of the most important ecclesiological achievements of Vatican II) by applying it no longer directly to the laity but to all the faithful.

Finally, by listing together at the beginning of Book II almost all the

---

34. Except for baptism, which in can. 96 and 204 begins the treatment of physical persons and the faithful, respectively, the Code does not locate the sacraments in a systematic context that brings out their genetic relationship to norms. Thus the norms for the clerical state (can. 232ff.) are unconnected with the sacrament of orders; those for the universal and local churches (can. 330ff. and 368ff.) have no connection with the Eucharist; and the family, of which the Code says little and this in an unorganized way, is not seen in context as the outcome of the sacrament of matrimony.

main obligations and rights (scattered throughout the conciliar documents) of the faithful, the Code strongly emphasizes the inalienable juridical heritage of the faithful and thus breaks, at least in principle and despite possible inconsistencies, with the constitutional hegemony the hierarchy has always enjoyed in canon law. Moreover, this has been done without introducing the principle of "fundamentality" (still used by the *LEF*), which is applicable to the rights of the person in the constitutions of modern states, but not to the obligations and rights of the faithful in the constitution of the Church.[35]

Thus, instead of creating an artificial formal hierarchy of norms—characteristic of the constitutional principle in modern states—the list of the obligations and rights of the faithful, almost all of which are based in divine or natural law, makes clear the existence of a material hierarchy of norms that the ecclesiastical hierarchy too must respect.[36]

This coherent explanation of the status of the faithful is undoubtedly reinforced by the emphasis put on the constitutional character of the state of those practicing the evangelical counsels. Can. 207, § 2, like LG 44, § 4, does not intend to face directly the long-standing question of whether the evangelical counsels have their origin in *ius divinum*.[37] On the other hand, the Code repeats in can. 575 the basic passage in LG 43, § 1, where the evangelical counsels are defined as "a divine gift the Church has received from the Lord." It also places the norms for "Institutes of Consecrated Life" in part 3 of Book II, away from the juridical context of "Associations of the Christian Faithful." By doing so, it highlights the ecclesiological importance of the consecrated state, making it parallel, from an institutional standpoint, to the lay and clerical states that have been dealt with in parts 1 and 2 of the same book.[38]

The constitutional parity thus assigned to the evangelical counsels makes it possible to move beyond the barren bipolarism of the clergy-laity relationship which has always led either to the dominance of the former over the latter or to the reductive identification of the faithful with the laity. The circular relationship within the new trilogy makes it possible to recognize each state as having a specific ecclesiological function that belongs to it in a primary way: secular responsibility to the laity, responsibility for the unity of the Church to the clergy, and responsibility for the eschatological dimension to the evangelical counsels. At the same time, the circular relationship allows the common equality of the three to emerge more clearly.[39]

35. On the problem, see E. Corecco, "Considerazioni sui diritti fondamentali del cristiano nella Chiesa e nella società," in *I diritti fondamentali* (n. 12, above), pp. 1219–22.

36. See C. Mirabelli, "Protezione giuridica dei diritti fondamentali," ibid., pp. 397–414.

37. See H. Urs von Balthasar, *The Christian State of Life* (San Francisco, 1983).

38. W. Aymans, "Ekklesiologische Leitlinien" (n. 26, above), pp. 43–45, adopts the surprising view that the evangelical counsels belong under the laws governing associations and not under the laws of the Church's constitution.

39. See H. Urs von Balthasar, *The Christian State of Life*.

2. All this is on the positive side. It must also be admitted, however, that the Code has dropped certain elements of the Council that are indispensable in defining the ontological and juridical structure of the faithful, or at least has not been able to turn to full account the entire formal meaning of these elements.

The most important of these neglected elements is that of charisms.[40] The faithful are constituted as such not only by their sacramental structure, thanks to which they share, though in varying ways, in the *tria munera* of Christ and the Church, but also by the possibility of becoming the rightful subjects of charisms. When this potential charismatic dimension is omitted, the ecclesial and juridical identity of the faithful (and therefore the entire people of God, which is the Church) is seriously impaired. The Council, which frequently refers to the presence of charisms in the Church, does not hesitate to regard the right to exercise charisms as one of the principal rights of the faithful;[41] this right is completely neglected by the Code.

The Code certainly does contain propitious references to the presence of the Holy Spirit in the Church: for example, in can. 879 in connection with the sacrament of confirmation; in can. 369 to the Spirit as ingathering the particular Church; in can. 375, § 1, to the Spirit as establishing the apostolic succession of bishops; and in can. 747, § 1, to the Spirit as assisting the Church in its universal teaching office; as well as in the norms for institutes of consecrated life, where, however, the more soothing expression "gifts of the Holy Spirit" is used instead of "charisms," which was removed for good after the schema of 1982.[42] This substitution induces doubt about the ecclesiological significance of charisms. Charisms are not the same as the grace of the Spirit's presence in the faithful, nor can they be looked upon as gifts given preferentially to categories of the faithful (for example, members of the institutes of consecrated life) that are by definition more readily subject to institutional and juridical control.[43]

The Code yielded to the repeated objection that no juridical value can be assigned to charisms and did not have the courage to penetrate to the heart of the Church's constitutional structure by tackling the ontological essence of the faithful in all its aspects. If we consider that charisms never exist autonomously but are always bestowed on the two polar groups in the institutional Church—namely, those possessing the common priesthood (which also finds expression in the ways proper to

40. On this point, see the criticisms already leveled at the projected Code of 1980 by J. A. Komonchak, "The Status of the Faithful in the Revised Code of Canon Law," *Concilium*, 147 (1981) 37–45.

41. The principal passage on this point in AA, §§ 3, 4.

42. See can. 605. In the project of 1982, charisms were still mentioned in can. 580, 590, § 3, 631, § 3, 708, 716, § 1, 717, § 3, 722, §§ 1 and 2.

43. It is of interest to note that Vatican II never speaks of charism in reference to members of the Institutes of Consecrated Life (i.e., religious).

the *sensus fidei*) and those possessing the ministerial priesthood—then it must be recognized that here again the institutional approach has prevailed over the approach determined by the mystery of communion.

In point of fact, contrary to what is true of the structure of modern states, the constitution of the Church is not identifiable with the institution. By its very nature, the presence of charisms freely bestowed by the Spirit relativizes the hegemony of the hierarchy in the Church, because, like the obligations and rights of the faithful, it sets imprescriptible limits for the exercise of *sacra potestas* by authorities. Their *sacra potestas* gives them the responsibility not only of passing judgment on the authenticity of charisms but also, and above all, of not extinguishing them.

3. Emphasis on the ecclesiological centrality of the faithful would have been much more effective if the Code had once again penetrated to the deeper roots of the Church's existence and made the common priesthood and the *sensus fidei* (both bestowed on all the faithful by their baptism) the basis for its systematic and doctrinal organization.

These two factors, which in LG 10 and 12 are of primary importance for understanding the constitutional structure of the Church, are the ontological presuppositions onto which the derivative doctrine of the *tria munera* of Christ and the Church is grafted. The Code, however, limits itself to repeating them in a purely material way in brief references in can. 836 (*De munere sanctificandi*) and 750 (*De munere docendi*), and makes no formal use of the full ecclesiological dynamism proper to them.

Even if we prescind from the fact that in receiving the *sensus fidei* the Code seriously mutilates its meaning,[44] it must be admitted that if the Code had defined the faithful primarily as rightful subjects of the "common priesthood" and the *sensus fidei*, it would have brought out the imprescriptible structural connection of all the faithful with the sacraments and the word (see LG 35, § 1)—that is, with the factors that generate the church itself and are also the root of the distinction between the functions of order and jurisdiction in the *sacra potestas*, functions in which the specific participation of ordained ministers in the mystery of Christ takes concrete form.

The essential difference (LG 10, § 2) between the common priesthood and the ministerial priesthood would likewise have emerged in all its

---

44. LG 12, § 1, reads as follows: "Universitas fidelium, qui unctionem habent a Spiritu Sancto . . . in *credendo falli nequit*, atque hanc suam peculiarem proprietatem mediante *supernaturali sensu fidei totius populi manifestat*, cum 'ab Episcopis usque ad extremos laicos fideles' universalem *suum consensum* de rebus fidei et morum *exhibet*. Illo enim sensu fidei . . . Populus Dei sub ductu sacri magisterii, cui fideliter obsequens . . . *indefectibiliter adhaeret*" (italics added). Can. 750 reads: "Fide divina et catholica ea omnia credenda sunt quae verbo Dei scripto vel tradito . . . continentur, et insimul ut divinitus revelata proponuntur, sive ab Ecclesiae magistero solemni, sive . . . ordinario et universali; quod scilicet communi *adhaesione* fidelium sub ductu sacri magisterii *manifestantur*" (italics added). On the question of the *sensus fidei*, see R. Bertolino, "'Sensus fidei' e consuetudine nel Diritto della Chiesa," in *Studi in onore de Pietro Gismondi* (forthcoming).

relevance, even if the emphasis were placed on the participation of the faithful and ordained ministers in the word.

In addition to providing a stronger systematic arrangement for the norms governing the faithful, the reception of these two elements with their full formal value would have allowed the Code to avoid having recourse to certain compromise formulas that are not free of all ambiguity: *cooperatio in exercitum potestatis regiminis*[45] (can. 129, § 2) and *cooperatio in exercitum ministerii verbi* (can. 759), which are used in order to bring out the difference in the participation of laity and ordained ministers in the *munus regendi* and the *munus docendi*, that is, the ministry of the word.

4. Omission of the charisms and failure to assign full value to the common priesthood are also the source of the ambiguity in the Code's way of dealing with the phenomenon of associations, which is likewise basic for an understanding of the ecclesiological status of the faithful. Associations have a significance transcending the social and juridical as such, because in addition to being, in many cases, concrete manifestations of charisms (as historical experience shows), they are also a sign of communion among the faithful and of the unity of the Church (AA 18, § 1).[46]

In this area the new Code advances beyond the Code of 1917, for the latter did not explicitly acknowledge the right of association, as the new Code does in can. 215.[47] But this progress cannot hide the subtle regression of the new Code in relation to the Council, despite the more modern juridical style of the new apparatus. Whereas Vatican II fully appreciates the variety and multiplicity of the forms of association (see esp. AA 18 and 19), the Code unhesitatingly follows the lead of the 1917 Code in treating them as uniform and forcing them into the traditional corporative mold. It takes no account of the special characteristics of the communal forms of apostolate that swarm in the contemporary Church—the movements, the societies, the base communities (which

45. These formulas do not by themselves permit an unambiguous interpretation of the mind of the legislators, even though it seems clear that to "cooperate" (*cooperare*) does not mean to "participate" (*participare*) in the nature of a power or office that rightfully belongs to another. In fact, even priests (presbyters), who are the *fidi cooperatores* of the bishop (can. 245, § 2), help him in virtue of the degree of sacred orders bestowed on them, but they do not share the fullness of the bishop's sacrament. It follows that interpretation must be based on an ecclesiological presupposition. Those who tend to divide *sacra potestas* into two powers—one of orders, the other of jurisdiction—will inevitably maintain that the power of jurisdiction may be delegated to laypersons; see, e.g., G. Ghirlanda, "De laicis iuxta novum codicem," *Per*, 72 (1983) 53–70; idem, "I laici nella Chiesa secondo il nuovo diritto canonico," *Aggiornamenti Sociali*, 7–8 (1983) 485–96.

46. Feliciani, "I diritti e i doveri," in *In Nuovo Codice di Diritto Canonico* (n. 1, above), pp. 266–69.

47. Can. 268 of the 1917 Code adopted a nonconstitutional juridical approach and limited itself to praising those of the laity who join associations established or recommended by the hierarchy. Obviously, the existence of "recommended associations" implicitly supposes that the faithful have a right to join them.

are recognized not only by the Medellín and Puebla documents but even by *Evangelii nuntiandi*)[48]—and that in defense of their own spiritual identity refuse to be subsumed under the juridical category of association or, if they must accept this subsumption, treat it as a formal juridical superstructure that lacks real content and is therefore foreign to them.

The distinction made by the Code between public and private associations (a distinction borrowed from civil law and applied also to juridic persons) relegates the vast majority of associations to the private sphere and thus promotes the growth of a distorted ecclesial mentality. In the state, private associations exist because it is possible to distinguish between society and the organization of state power.

In the Church, however, it is impossible to demote the common priesthood, which is the first and irreplaceable pole of the Church as an institution, to the sphere of private life, once it is realized that the function of representing the institution cannot be assigned exclusively to the other pole, namely, the ministerial priesthood, as it can be assigned to the public organs of power in the structure of the state. Because the common priesthood continues even in the ministerial priesthood, and because the ministerial priesthood exists only to serve the common priesthood, which is primary in relation to it, it is not possible to split their unity and structural reciprocity by using the criteria of public and private.

The concern to control the phenomenon of associations by applying typically societal and legitimist criteria also surfaces in can. 299, § 3, which was introduced into the Code only in the 1982 schema. Inasmuch as no norms are furnished that would require Church authorities to follow objective criteria in granting or refusing juridical recognition of public status, can. 299, § 3, is in danger of removing all formal value from the principle of association, which was proclaimed by Vatican II (AA 19, § 4) and is materially accepted in can. 215.[49]

The Laity

From the systematic viewpoint, the Code fully recognizes the position of the laity, inasmuch as it reverses the approach of the 1917 Code and even improves on the systematization found in *Lumen Gentium*, where the laity is still discussed after the clergy, and inasmuch as it formulates a list of the principal obligations and rights of the laity, paralleling the list provided for the faithful generally. At the same time, however, it is impossible not to see that, in accordance with a promotional policy that is by its nature contingent, the list tends more to emphasize the impor-

48. See, e.g., the apostolic exhortation *Evangelii nuntiandi* (Dec. 8, 1975), § 58.
49. See Feliciani, "I diritti e i doveri," pp. 270–73.

tance of the laity than carefully to define its ecclesiological and juridical status. In fact, of the seventeen particulars listed in can. 225–232 only eleven can be assigned strictly to the laity, to the exclusion of clerics.[50]

A comparison with the Council reveals moreover the existence of some uncertainties and ambiguities in two areas: the participation of the laity in the *munus regendi*, and the secular identity of the laity.

Contrary to what it does in dealing with the participation of the laity in the *munus docendi et sanctificandi*, which is expressly asserted in can. 759 (first phase) and 835, § 4, on the basis of LG 34 and 35, the Code provides no specific canon that explicitly asserts the participation of the laity in the *munus regendi* as taught in LG 36 and 37. It therefore becomes necessary to fall back on the more general norm in can. 204, which, though valid for all the faithful without distinction, in the final analysis includes the laity only according to the sacramental definition of the laity, as formulated in LG 31, § 1. The immediate reason for the lack of a special canon must be looked for in the decision not to have a book *De munere regendi* in the Code. Above and beyond the possible difficulties of a technical kind that may have inspired it, the decision also points to the difficulty the lawmakers felt in accepting the idea that the participation of the laity in the office of governance is as essential, from the constitutional point of view, as the participation of the clergy—even though the co-essentiality was acknowledged with regard to the other two *munera*. In Book II, therefore, there has been a reabsorption, not only systematic but to some extent substantial as well, of the *munus regendi* of the laity into the *munus regendi* of the hierarchy.[51]

Even can. 129, § 2, which is the only norm in the context of *sacra potestas* that shows any ambition to make a doctrinal statement, does not help us understand the real scope of the problem. In the compromise formulation adopted in this canon, a formulation not identical with the one in LG 33, § 3, which focuses more on the possibilities available,[52] participation of the laity in the *munus regendi* is not seen as the exercise of a native, personal qualification bestowed upon them in baptism, but as an extrinsic cooperation with the exercise of a *potestas* possessed by others, namely, the hierarchy.

From the standpoint of concrete solutions, however, it cannot be said that the Code is ungenerous in acknowledging a broad responsibility of

---

50. The number of obligations and duties will obviously vary depending on the criteria used in identifying them. In any case, those not assignable exclusively to the laity seem to be these: can. 225, § 1 (first part of the sentence), 229, §§ 1–3, 231, §§ 1–2.

51. The reply given by the president of the Commission in the *Relatio* of 1982 to Cardinal Palazzini's objection to the lack of a book *De munere regendi* was, to say the least, evasive. See *Communicationes*, 14/2 (1982) 123. See also the text published in *Communicationes*, 13/4 (1981) 12.

52. The conciliar text (LG 33, § 3) reads: "Praeterea [laici] aptitudine gaudent, ut ad quaedam munera ecclesiastica, ad finem spiritualem exercenda, ab hierarchia *adsumantur*"; can. 129, § 2, on the other hand, reads: "In *exercitio eiusdem potestatis* [regiminis] christifideles laici ad normam iuris *cooperari possunt*" (italics added).

the laity in all areas of ecclesial activity. On the contrary, if we add all the norms presupposed by the exercise of the *munus regendi* to those in which the *munera docendi et sanctificandi* are concretized, we get an image of the layperson henceforth difficult to distinguish from that of the deacon. Nonetheless a symptomatic fact remains. On the one hand, the Code avoids making more obligatory the establishment of pastoral councils, whether diocesan (the divergence from CD 27, § 5, is clear)[53] or parochial; on the other it refuses to promote with greater determination the activity of laypersons even within those institutions in which by their nature it is appropriate for all the faithful (and therefore the laity as well) to assume not only a responsibility as individuals but a co-responsibility for "synodal" government that has much more impact on the daily operation of the Church than that expected from particular councils and diocesan synods.

The second area in which a gap emerges between the Council and the Code is that of secularity. The Council did not intend directly to define the *indolis saecularis* (LG 31, § 2) as a theological constitutive of the *status laicalis*.[54] On the other hand, this "secular quality" cannot rightly be interpreted, as some theological teaching interprets it, as simply a sociological dimension of the laity. For, on the one hand the secular involvement of clerics is supplementary and is not identical, even in concept, with the idea of secularity proper to the laity; and on the other the clear predominance of conciliar texts on this secular quality (LG, AA, and AG) over those in which the Council defines the laity on the basis of its sacramental structure (LG 31, § 1) seems to allow no doubt on the point.[55]

Even if we are willing to leave this matter unsettled, it is surprising to see that in LG 36 and 37 the Council had already taken the secular modality to be the predominant characteristic of specifically lay participation in the *munus regendi*. This explains the very important statement in LG 37, § 4, that pastors, "helped by the experience of the laity, are in a position to judge more clearly and more appropriately in spiritual as well as in temporal matters." To this statement corresponds another that is no less important for understanding the role of laity and clergy in the Church; it occurs in LG 35, § 2, in connection with the prophetic office: "This evangelization [the laity's profession of faith, joined to a life of

53. CD 27, § 5, has the expression "valde optandum"; can. 511 says simply" . . . quatenus pastoralia adiuncta id suadent, constituatur consilium pastorale."

54. On the difficulty of interpreting the conciliar texts, see E. Schillebeeckx, "The Typological Definition of the Christian Layman according to Vatican II," in his *The Mission of the Church* (New York, 1973), pp. 90–116; F. Danneels, *De subjecto officii ecclesiastici attenta doctrina Concilii Vaticani II. Suntne laici officii ecclesiastici capaces?* (Rome, 1973), pp. 19–45.

55. A purely sociological interpretation is given by K. Mörsdorf, "Die Zusammenarbeit von Priestern und Laien in ekklesiologisch-kanonistischer Sicht," in H. Gehrig, ed., *Grundfragen der Zusammenarbeit von Priestern und Laien* (Karlsruhe, 1968), pp. 13–26; idem, "Die andere Hierarchie. Eine kritische Untersuchung zur Einsetzung von Laienräten in den Diözesen der Bundesrepublik Deutschland," *AfkKR*, 138/2 (1969) 461–509.

faith] . . . acquires a specific property and peculiar efficacy because it is accomplished in the ordinary circumstances of the world."

The Code clearly ignores these two statements, which are essential for understanding the specific, constitutional contribution of the secularity proper and peculiar to the laity, in the sphere of lay involvement not only in the world, but also in the Church. The statements enable us to overcome the dualistic temptation of maintaining that secularity, as the ecclesiological dimension in which the primary role of the lay state as compared with the other two states finds expression, manifests itself only in lay involvement in the world and not in any involvement within the ecclesial structure. The laity in fact ensures the unity of the mission of the whole Christian people in both the Church and the world (LG 31, § 1) because the laity is the point at which Church and world, that is, the economy of creation and the economy of redemption, come together. This is why marriage, wherein creativity is sacramentally fused with the supernatural (can. 1055), belongs by its innermost essence to the lay state. For secularity is in fact not operative with the same intensity and the same ecclesiological relevance in laypersons who live in the world and laypersons who live in the clerical state or the state of the evangelical counsels (in religious or secular institutes). In the case of clerics and followers of the counsels, secularity lacks its essential and constitutive elements (property, marriage, and freedom) and is almost completely absorbed by the sacramental dimension common to all the faithful.

The problem is therefore not reducible to a matter of urging the laity in a general way to assume its responsibilities in the Church and in the world, as the Code exhorts the clergy generally (can. 275, § 2), bishops (can. 394, § 2) and parish priests (can. 529, § 2) to do. The problem is rather to accept the fact that the *indolis saecularis* sets certain limits within which the ministerial priesthood must carry out its mission. The "secular quality" thus makes it possible to determine more precisely not only the ontological nature of the laity but indirectly that of the ordained minister as well.

In view of the fact that the Code has not formally received the idea of *indolis saecularis*, it is not surprising that the detailed set of norms aimed at fostering the participation of the laity in the life of the Church in the areas of the *munera docendi et sanctificandi* (a participation that directly presupposes the sacramental definition of the layperson: LG 31, § 2) is not adequately balanced by the few norms dealing with the area of lay co-responsibility that has as its direct doctrinal presupposition the definition of the laity in terms of secularity (LG 31, § 2). In fact, only four norms (or groups of norms) relate to the laity as defined by its *indolis saecularis*. Two are contained in the general list of lay obligations and rights (the duty of imbuing the temporal order with the spirit of the Gospel: can. 225, § 2; and the right to the freedom needed for carrying out this mission: can. 227). The third asserts the right of association to this end (can. 327). The fourth has to do with the obligations and rights of the family in the education of its children (can. 226, 793, 796–799).

In proceeding as it does, that is, not fully in step with the most basic position of the Council, the Code has allowed itself to be influenced by the postconciliar theology of the laity. This theology has neglected the problem of secularity (which alone opens up truly new ecclesiological perspectives) and has gotten bogged down in an effort to attribute to the laity competences ever closer to those of the ministerial priesthood, thus setting itself on the course of a subtle but distortive clericalization of the laity.[56] The Council itself, by backing (in AA 20 and 24, § 4) the outdated doctrine of the collaboration of the laity in the mission of the hierarchy by way of a mandate (itself not a very clear notion), has certainly not helped to do away with the ambiguity.

Communio Hierarchica

Vatican II uses the technical expression *communio hierarchica* only to describe the nature of the sacramental and synodal relationship that unites ordained ministers (except for deacons) with one another. It must be admitted, nevertheless, that the element of hierarchy pervades all levels of *communio*:[57] the fundamental level, which is the *communio fidelium*; the level of the *communio ecclesiarum* (which also includes the relationship between the Catholic Church and the separated churches and ecclesial communities); and the level of the *communio ministeriorum*. Therefore, prescinding from the question of whether *communio hierarchica* insofar as it is *hierarchica* is conceptually suited for expressing in all its complexity the nature of all the levels of *communio*,[58] the term can be accepted as a tool for appraising, in a minimally systematic way, the reception by the Code of the conciliar ecclesiology in which the principle of communion rather than the societarian principle comes to the fore.

To the extent that it is possible to distinguish clearly between the doctrinal and the institutional aspects of these problems, I shall analyze them separately.

The Doctrinal Aspect

1. At the level of *communio fidelium*, only can. 209, § 1, can be regarded as sufficient evidence that the Code has not only materially received the

56. See E. Corecco, "Profili internazionali dei movimenti nella Chiesa," in *I movimenti nella Chiesa negli anni '80* (Milan, 1982), esp. 221–34.

57. See W. Aymans, *Einführung in das neue Gesetzbuch der lateinischen Kirche*, published by the Secretariat of the German Episcopal Conference (Bonn, 1983), no. 31, 7–28.

58. See G. Alberigo, "Istituzioni per la communione tra l'episcopato universale e il vescovo di Roma," in G. Alberigo, ed., *L'ecclesiologia del Vaticano II: dinamismi e prospettive* (Bologna, 1981), p. 248.

substance of the conciliar teaching that makes *communio* an ontological structure constitutive of the faithful, but has also been able to exploit the full formal value of the teaching, to a greater extent even than the Council itself was able to do.

In its catalogue of the obligations and rights of the faithful, the Code lists in first place the obligation to live, interiorly and exteriorly, in communion with the whole Church (can. 209, § 1). It thus shows that communion is the factor determining the anthropological and ecclesial identity of the faithful. The priority of this obligation over all the others in the catalogue is not due simply to the fact that it heads the list of obligations and duties common to all the faithful; its position at the head could, after all, have been due simply to chance, given the lack of order in the list as a whole. Its priority is due rather to the fact that it is the ontological and logical foundation of a series of other obligations and rights, such as the obligation and right to seek holiness (can. 210), to collaborate in the spread of the gospel (can. 211 and 225, § 1) and in apostolic undertakings (can. 216), to receive the sacraments (can. 213), and to help in the promotion of the Church's life (can. 212, § 3; 228). These obligations and rights are in turn the source of almost all the other particulars that make up the juridical patrimony of the faithful.[59]

The hierarchic structure of the *communio fidelium*, which shows itself in the duty of the faithful to obey their pastors as formulated in can. 212, § 1 (this canon is the point of convergence for other similar dispositions of the Code: can. 750–754; 846, § 1; 1311), shows its negative side in the many precautionary and preventive clauses in the catalogue. Taken singly, these clauses might have been justified, but all of them together poison the atmosphere of trust and magnanimity with which the Council generally treated the relationship between faithful and pastors.[60]

2. Thanks to its inclusion of the most important ecclesiological formula of the Council (LG 23, § 1), according to which the universal Church comes into being *in* and *from* the particular churches, it can be maintained that the Code has recieved the substance of the conciliar doctrine on the *communio ecclesiarum*.[61] And in fact from this basic statement all the other constitutive elements of the doctrine can be derived by a process of explicitation. The reason is that the formula *in quibus et ex quibus* defines the source of the *communio* on the basis of a hermeneutical model marked by a paradigmatic clarity. For although *communio* includes a

---

59. For a more analytical discussion of the question, see E. Corecco, "Il catalogo dei doveri-diritti del fedele," in *Atti del V Colloquio Giuridico* (n. 1, above).

60. See J. Bernhard, "Les droits fondamentaux dans la perspective de la *Lex Fundamentalis* et de la révision du code de droit canonique," in *I diritti fondamentali*, (n. 12, above), pp. 367–95.

61. On the interpretation of this formula, see K. Mörsdorf, "Das synodale Element der Kirchenverfassung im Lichte des 2. Vatikanischen Konzils," in R. Bäumer and H. Dolch, eds., *Volk Gottes. Festgabe J. Höfer* (Frieburg/Basel/Vienna, 1967), pp. 568–84; W. Aymans, *Das synodale Element der Kirchenverfassung* (Munich, 1971), pp. 318–24.

whole range of meanings that vary in importance and correctness, it consists essentially in a relationship of immanence that applies to all the structural elements in the Church's constitution: the mutual immanence of the universal and particular dimensions of the one Church of Christ; the immanent reciprocity in the relationship of the faithful and the Mystical Body; the immanence marking obligation and right; and the relationship of reciprocity between common priesthood and ministerial priesthood, and between word and sacrament.

The Code should, however, have made clearer the two ways in which the *communio ecclesiarum* becomes a reality. It does not arise solely from the hierarchic, constitutive relationship between particular churches and the Roman church (can. 331, 349, § 3, 431, § 1), but also from the reciprocal relationship between the individual particular churches. This second relationship, even though derivative compared with the first,[62] is no less essential for understanding the nature of the *communio ecclesiarum* that is the direct ontological and gnoseological foundation of "episcopal collegiality." The Council, unlike the Code, brought out this "horizontal" aspect of the *communio ecclesiarum* at the level of the universal Church in UR 14, § 1 (where the relationship of communion in faith and sacramental life is defined as a relationship between "sister" churches), and especially in LG 23, § 2, where the Church is expressly said to be a *corpus Ecclesiarum*.

Ignoring, however, these passages in which other analogous doctrinal suggestions of the Council combine in an especially effective way,[63] the Code—even more than the Council itself—does give a glimpse of this same dimension at the level of the particular churches. For such institutions as ecclesiastical provinces and regions (can. 431ff.) and particular councils (can. 439) are not thought of as resulting from a convergence of individual bishops, as is true of episcopal conferences (can. 447), but rather as a product of the *communio ecclesiarum* that exists among the particular churches.[64]

Clearly present in the Code, on the other hand, is the conciliar idea of the *communio ecclesiarum* with its reversal of position on the relationship between the Catholic Church and the separated churches and ecclesial communities. The reversal is basic to an understanding of the nature of this Church as embodiment of the one Church of Christ. It appears in the Code both in can. 844, §§ 3–4, 908, and 1124, and in can. 204, § 2, which cites the laboriously elaborated passage in LG 8, § 2, according to which the one Church of Christ "subsists" in the Catholic Church. This

62. See K. Mörsdorf, "Uber die Zuordnung des Kollegialitätsprinzips zu dem Prinzip der Einheit von Haupt und Leib in der hierarchischen Struktur der Kirchenverfassung," in L. Scheffczyk, W. Dettloff, and R. Heinzmann, eds., *Wahrheit und Verkündigung. Michael Schmaus zum 70. Geburtstag* (Munich/Paderborn/Vienna, 1967), pp. 1435–45.
63. See G. Alberigo, "Istituzioni per la communione," (n. 58, above), pp. 236–42.
64. See J. H. Provost, "Particular Councils," in *Acts of the 5th International Congress*, (n. 1, above).

that because it embodies *communio plena*, the Catholic Church represents the "hierarchic" high point of the gradual self-realization of the Church of Christ.

The conciliar teaching on the oneness of the Church of Christ (e.g., LG 8, § 2, and UR 3, § 2), which is received without further development in can. 96 and 369 of the Code, returns to the ecclesiological thinking of the time before the age of controversy (it had survived in can. 87 of the old Code). The idea that *communio* can be realized in stages has led to specific reversals within the Catholic Church itself, as can be seen in the idea of excommunication or the exclusion from eucharistic communion of faithful who are in a state of serious sin (can. 915 and 916), and in the doctrine of the *tria vincula* required for full membership in the Church; the latter teaching is taken over in can. 205 but with the omission of the conciliar phrase *Spiritum Christi habentes* (LG 14, § 2).[65] This last-named very important pruning of the conciliar text is a further example of the tenacious resistance offered by juridical positivism to the reception at the institutional level of the full formal dynamism inherent in the ecclesiological principle of *communio*, which has its roots in the mystery of the Trinity.

Communitas plena, which is the ultimate point of reference for membership in the Church, is found in the Catholic Church precisely because in the latter there is by definition (even if the fact is not always historically evident) a total immanence of the universal and particular dimensions of the Church; in this it differs from the separated churches and ecclesial communities.

Only an ecclesiology that takes the one Church of Christ as its generative point of departure is in a position to avoid the impasse in which an ecclesiology exclusively of the universal Church or one exclusively of the particular Church lands itself. At the same time, an ecclesiology of the one Church of Christ must distance itself from the view (which can be found in the Council) according to which the universal Church and the particular Church are different concrete, material entities; instead it must look upon them as the two constitutive formal dimensions of the one Church of Christ.[66] For the universal Church as such does not materially exist in a place other than that in which the Church of Christ exists as particular.

---

65. On the debate over the interpretation of the conciliar phrase *Spiritum Christi habentes*, see, on the one side, W. Aymans, "Die kanonische Lehre der Kirchengliedschaft im Lichte des II. Vatikanischen Konzils," *AfkKR*, 142/2 (1973) 397–417, and V. De Paolis, "Communio et excommunicatio," *Per*, 70 (1981) 271–302 (who argue that the text is juridically unimportant) and, on the other, F. Coccopalmerio, "Quid significent verba 'Spiritum Christi habentes,' Lumen Gentium 14, 2," *Per*, 68 (1979) 253–76, and H. Müller, "Zugehörigkeit zur Kirche als Problem der Neukodifikation des kanonischen Kirchenrechts," *ÖAKR*, 28 (1977) 81–98 (who rightly assign a constitutional significance to the text).

66. In his teaching Pope John Paul II moved in this direction in his homily at Lugano on June 12, 1984: *I discorsi del viaggio di Giovanni Paolo II in Svizzera, 12–17 guigno 1984*, published by the Secretariat of the Swiss Episcopal Conference (Fribourg, 1984), p. 17, no. 3.

In view of this, it is symptomatic that the Code has not made its own the passage in LG 26, § 1, which says: "In these [altar] communities, though they may often be small or poor, or existing in the diaspora, Christ is present through whose power and influence the One, Holy, Catholic, and Apostolic Church is constituted." The reference to the Eucharist, which is the source and summit of Christian life (can. 897), might have caused the legislators some doubt about the priority given to the universal Church over the particular Church in the systematic organization of Book II of the Code.

3. In regard to collegiality (or *communio ministeriorum*), the Code must once again be said to have struck closely to the teaching of Vatican II and made no effort to note factors (admittedly, already absent from the Council's treatment) that might suggest possible structural limits set for the primacy by collegiality.[67] Like Vatican II, the Code uses (but how could it have done otherwise?) a terminology whose predominantly juridical character and cultural presuppositions prevent a clear grasp of the fact that collegiality is not exercised only when it finds expression in the formal juridical mode of a collegial act (as defined in can. 119 among the general norms) but in other ways as well. In the abstract, the term "synodality" is equivalent to "collegiality." But in fact it makes it possible to give the idea of collegiality a less reductive meaning.[68]

On the other hand, the adverb *conjunctim* (and indeed the very words *collegium* and *collegialis*), which can. 447 takes materially from the Council (CD 38, § 1) with reference to episcopal conferences, excuses the Code from the obligation of making it clear that the principle of collegiality applies not only at the level of the universal Church but also at the level of the particular churches. This is an obligation, however, that can no longer be avoided twenty years after the Council.

But the Code has not remained completely deaf to the ecclesiological developments of the past twenty years. In their systematic organization of the material, the lawgivers have located the intermediate collegial agencies (particular councils, episcopal conferences) no longer after the universal Church, as in the old Code, but after the particular churches. They did so in order to show that the power that these agencies exercise is of episcopal, not primatial, origin.

The Code also deals with the relationship between the college of bishops and the pope without leaving room for very much discussion. The reason is that in its systematization the Code unvaryingly gives priority to the pope over the college. The Council, on the other hand, at least in passages in which the ecclesiological problem is not looked at primarily from a collegial institutional standpoint but remains imbedded

---

67. On the discussion of this problem (defined by the author himself as *ius cogubernii*) at Vatican II, see A. Acerbi, *Due ecclesiologie* (n. 6, above), pp. 485–553; G. Alberigo, "Istituzioni" (n. 58, above), pp. 249–56.

68. On the problem of synodality, see G. P. Milano, *Il sinodo dei vescovi* (forthcoming).

in broader theological reflection, repeatedly does not hesitate to give the college of the apostles priority over Peter and the college of bishops over the pope. The consistent way in which the Code has instead put the pope before the college (can. 330ff., 746, 749, 782)[69] gives the impression that, at least for itself, it preferred to ignore the doctrine of the one subject of supreme power in the Church.[70]

This doctrine, unlike that of the two (inadequately distinct) subjects, gives a clearer glimpse of how the supreme and full power of the college over the universal Church could lead to the concentration of primacy in a single person.[71] The application of the adjective *immediata* to the *potestas* of the pope does not change the nature of this power in relation to the power of the college, once it is granted that the college, in which individual pastors directly represent their particular churches, necessarily has a *potestas immediata* over these churches.[72] This approach is dominated by the typically juridical and not necessarily ecclesiological principle that the universal takes precedence over the particular. It degenerates even more into verticalism by reason of the fact that the Code, adopting the same civil law (rather than constitutionalist) outlook as the 1917 Code, begins its series of norms regarding the pope without locating them in the ecclesiological context of the universal Church as it does for intermediate agencies, whether personal or collegial, that is, for bishops and parish priests. Can. 330, which was introduced at the last moment, is important but it does not substantially alter for the better the direction of the overall trajectory.

The idea of *communio hierarchica* also regulates the relationship between bishop and priests within the presbyterium. It must be acknowledged that Vatican II itself shows a good deal of terminological fluctuation and doctrinal uncertainty in this area.[73] In LG 28, § 2 (at the end) and

69. Priority is given to the college of bishops over the pope by, e.g., LG 17, § 1, 18, § 2, 19, 20, 21, 23, § 3, 24, § 1. At the concrete level it must be acknowledged that precisely when taking the principle of collegiality into account, the Code imposes some timid but nonetheless significant limits on the free exercise of the primacy when it requires the supreme authority to consult the episcopal conferences before erecting personal prelatures (can. 294) and personal dioceses (can. 372, § 2). Are we to suppose that this same law has been forgotten when it comes to the erection of territorial dioceses (can. 373)? The same tendency surfaces, though in a less compelling way, when the Code allows episcopal conferences to propose the establishment of ecclesiastical regions (can. 433, § 1) or a triennial list of candidates for the episcopate (can. 377, § 2) and allows the presidents of episcopal conferences to propose candidates when a diocesan bishop or coadjutor bishop is to be appointed (can. 377, § 3).

70. Can. 755, § 1, is the only place in the Code where the college of bishops is mentioned before the Apostolic See.

71. See K. Rahner, "On the Divine Right of the Episcopate," in K. Rahner and J. Ratzinger, *The Episcopate and the Primacy* (Quaestiones Disputatae, 4; New York, 1962), pp. 64–135.

72. On the meaning of these terms in Vatican I, see J.-P. Torrell, *La théologie de l'épiscopat au premier concile du Vatican* (Paris, 1961), e.g., pp. 105–62.

73. On this question, see O. Saier, "Die hierarchische Struktur des Presbyteriums,"

PO 2, § 2, the presbyterium is seen as a universal college of priests, parallel to the universal college of bishops. In PO 2, § 1, and CD 11, § 1, on the other hand, it is seen as a community of presbyters who form a body distinct from the bishop, somewhat as does the cathedral chapter. The passages in LG 28, § 2 (at the beginning), PO 8, § 1, and AG 13, § 3, in which the issue is resolved and the presbyterium emerges as the community of presbyters with the diocesan bishop at its head (he is therefore a member of the presbyterium) were not received by the Code. It might indeed be admitted that if can. 713, § 3, and 400, § 2, are analyzed simply in terms of syntax, they suppose the image of the presbyterium as a college of priests that includes the diocesan bishop. But the image of a separate body is to the fore in all the other canons dealing with the presbyterium (369, 245, § 2, 529, § 2, 754), including the fundamental canon (495, § 1), which prescribes the obligation of setting up a presbyteral council.

This striking lack of formal exactitude is due in the final analysis to the Code's failure to understand that the synodal structure of the presbyterium is an analogous projection of the synodal structure of the universal Church in the particular Church.[74] The universal Church, with its characteristic synodal structure, could not be embodied in an ontologically true way in a particular church that was structured exclusively around a single person.

The reason for the Code's inattention is that among the many conciliar texts asserting that presbyters are "cooperators" of the bishop (or the episcopal order) and received in can. 245, § 2, and especially in can 384, in which the bishop is ordered to "attend to" (*audiat*) his presbyters, the Code neglects the most important, namely, the passage in PO 7, § 1, in which presbyters are defined not only as *fidi cooperatores* but also as *cooperatores necessarii* of the bishop. Here, in a nutshell, is the ecclesiological justification for the presbyterium. The hearing the bishop is to give to the presbyters does not reflect simply a moral, legal, or vaguely communional obligation, but flows from the ontological structure of *communio* itself, which implies an immanence of the component parts. The adjective *necessarii* defines the nature not only of the presbyteral ministry but of the episcopal ministry as well. It follows that the obligation to have a presbyteral council is not justified merely by corporative principles, but has its raison d'être in the fact that the ministry of the diocesan bishop is not purely personal but essentially synodal, although the analogy probably does not justify us in thinking that the presbyterium is the single subject of *potestas* in the particular Church, as the college of bishops is in the universal Church.

AfkKR, 136/2 (1967) 351–60; see also H. Müller, "De differentia inter episcopatum et presbyteratum iuxta doctrinam Concilii Vaticani Secundi," *Per*, 59 (1970) 614–18.

74. See E. Corecco, "Sacerdozio e presbiterio nel CIC," *Servizio Migranti*, 11 (1983) 354–72.

The Institutional Aspect

1. With regard to the *communio fidelium* I have already pointed out that in response to the line taken by the Council the Code provides many areas for participation, individual and collective, by the laity, which makes up by far the largest sector of the faithful but has traditionally been the most marginalized. But in doing so the Code has not avoided useless exclusions and important omissions.

In the area of individual lay participation, the basic institutions that convey this recognition and were to some extent anticipated by postconciliar law, both common and particular, are: ecclesiastical office, which is defined in such a way as to include nonordained and "collective" ministries (can. 145, § 2); and the possibility of laypersons filling the office of judge (can. 1421, § 2), chancellor (can. 482, § 1), missionary (can. 784), pastoral leader of a parish (can. 517, § 2), official witness at a marriage (can. 1112), and preacher (can. 766). The exclusion of women from the regular ministry of reader and acolyte (can. 230, § 1) has no theological basis. On the other hand, the exclusion of all laypersons from the office of homilist (can. 767, § 1), can at least be based on the fact that there is some theological doubt in this area.[75] As far as omissions are concerned, it cannot be denied that the Code has neglected the necessity of establishing new forms of lay ministry, some of which have won approval in the practice of not a few particular churches.[76]

In the area of "collective" participation, there are some important achievements and omissions. On the one hand, there are the norms establishing the optional participation of laypersons in particular councils (can. 443, § 4) and their obligatory participation in diocesan synods (can. 463, § 1, no. 5), as well as their nonexclusion in principle from ecumenical councils (can. 339, § 2). On the other, there is the merely optional establishment of pastoral councils, diocesan (can. 511) and parochial (can. 536, § 1). If we take into account the fact that at the diocesan level the problem concerns not only the laity but the clergy as well, and that the Code allows not only for the establishment of a diocesan pastoral council (without, however, hoping for it, as Vatican II did) but also of parochial councils (for which Vatican II did not provide), then the failure to establish these representative structures in common law as forms of expression required by the common priesthood can be interpreted only as an unnecessary penalization of the laity, especially in

75. Laypersons never preach with the same formal authority as an ordained minister, because in them the word is not connected with the sacrament of orders. This is probably the only reason that can be given to justify excluding laypersons (in ordinary circumstances) as potential homilists. In fact, it is in the celebration of the Eucharist that the word and the sacrament of orders manifest in the highest degree their unity and reciprocity. See K. Mörsdorf, "Wort und Sakrament als Bauelemente der Kirchenverfassung," *AfkKR*, 134/1 (1965) 80–88.

76. See, e.g., S. Dianich, *Teologia del ministero ordinato. Una interpretazione ecclesiologica* (Rome, 1984), pp. 259–74.

light of its basic qualification, recognized by the Code itself (can. 228, § 2), for filling synodal offices.

When the Code came to translate the various roles of bishops, presbyters, and laypersons in the celebration of the Eucharist into institutional terms, it found no detailed leads in Vatican II. It therefore adopted the traditional solution, anticipated in the motu proprio *Ecclesiae sanctae* (I, 16, 2), of distinguishing between deliberative vote and consultative vote.

General theory recognizes other technical ways of expressing varieties of participation in the exercise of power: a deliberative vote for everyone, combined with the right of veto or the reservation of consent to qualified members, or the granting, *ad nutum* of the superior (in certain areas or in individual cases), of a deliberative vote to those to whom the law grants only a consultative vote. Although the right of veto, which is a more massive expression of the freedom enjoyed by those who possess or usurp power (consider the United Nations), is alien to canon law, the reservation of consent and the granting *ad nutum* of a deliberative vote are institutions that conceptually imply a negation of the truly juridical character of a deliberative vote.

The fact that bishops in their role as witnesses, not only constitutive but necessary, of the apostolic faith express themselves in a deliberative vote, which they have in virtue of divine and not simply human law, keeps the reservation of consent, which the pope enjoys in the college, from downgrading their deliberative vote to a merely consultative vote. But in the canonical order the consultative vote likewise possesses a certain necessity, thanks to the relationship of immanent reciprocity that exists between the common priesthood and the ministerial priesthood. This vote can be described as consultative only because the witness given by presbyters and laypersons to the faith, though being, like that of the bishops, inherently constitutive (thanks to the *sensus fidei*), is not binding in the same way. It follows from this that despite the alternative technical and terminological ways available for expressing the participation of the laity in the decisions of the Church, this participation cannot be misunderstood, as Acerbi, for example, misunderstands it,[77] as a simple "help" given by the laity to ordained ministers. The role of the common priesthood (and of the *sensus fidei*) is not to help the ministerial priesthood but to express its own witness and its own views on the faith and on church discipline.

The common priesthood is in fact primary, even in relationship to the ministerial priesthood. Consequently, the latter cannot ignore the witness of the former without violating the principle of communion. Although the deliberative vote and the consultative vote are institutions that do not succeed in translating into juridical terms the full ecclesiological dynamics of *communio hierarchica*, they are in fact the most trans-

---

77. A. Acerbi, "L'ecclesiologia sottesa alle istituzioni ecclesiali post-conciliari," in *L'ecclesiologia* (n. 58, above), pp. 226–28.

parent and therefore least inadequate technical means of expressing it.[78] Moreover their application can always be nuanced or strengthened by technical expedients of various kinds, as postconciliar particular law has always shown itself able to do.

The Code could have done greater justice to the different relationships that exist between, on the one hand, the laity and bishops and, on the other, the laity and presbyters, if it had, for example, explicitly allowed for an appeal to the bishop by a parochial pastoral council in case of an unjustified refusal by the pastor to comply with a consultative vote that had the backing of a qualified majority.

2. The institutional concretization of the *communio ecclesiarum* can be evaluated by taking as point of reference the legislative, administrative, and judicial autonomy of the particular churches.

The revisers of the Code could obviously have been more courageous in the legislative area, if they had had a more decisive grasp than they actually show of the volume of common law.[79] From a quantitative standpoint two areas of discipline that are especially vital and responsive to every reforming impulse—as shown by the upheaval and suffering of the years after the Council—can be regarded as symptomatic of a certain attitude adopted by the legislators toward the problem of autonomy. I am referring to institutes of consecrated life and to the formation of the diocesan clergy. In the former the degree of legislative autonomy granted to the *ius proprium* is very great, whereas in the latter it has clearly been reduced.

Not the least reason for the latter reduction is that the *institutionis sacerdotalis rationes* of the episcopal conferences find in the *ratio* of the Holy See (can. 242) a barrier that precludes the possibility of adequately diversifying the training of the diocesan clergy to fit the spiritual, ethnic, and cultural context of the individual groups of particular churches. It must be observed, moreover, that from the viewpoint of its material reception of the Council, the Code has preferred to draw its inspiration from *Optatam Totius* rather than from *Presbyterorum Ordinis*.[80] As a result, the educational model it proposes is calculated to ensure that the candidates will live lives befitting the *status clericalis* rather than that they will be prepared to exercise the pastoral ministry. Although it is true that the existence of the presbyteral ministry, based as it is on the sacrament of orders, is not merely a functional organization of the *status fidelium*, it is also true that the pastoral purpose of the sacrament must determine the preparation for its exercise.

On the other hand, the exemption granted to institutes of consecrated life has been much less extensive than the discussion at the Council

---

78. See E. Corecco, "Parlamento ecclesiale o diaconia sinodale?," *Strumento Internazionale per un lavoro teologico. Communio*, 1 (1972) 32–44.

79. See A. Scheuermann, "Das Neue im CIC 1983," *AfkKR*, 152/1 (1983) 132–34.

80. See also the observations of F. Coccopalmerio, "La formazione al ministero ordinato," *SCatt*, 112 (1984) 219–51.

would have suggested. Consequently, the legislative autonomy given to them takes the form not so much of freedom in relation to the particular churches as of an area of freedom within their relationship with the Holy See, which, however, possesses the necessary means of controlling this freedom at the administrative level (as the norms set down in can. 573–606 show). It must therefore be concluded that here again the final result does not differ greatly from that achieved in the area of the training of the diocesan clergy, where autonomy is already precluded at the legislative level.

After these observations, which can to some extent be extended to other areas of discipline, it must be acknowledged that in the new Code reference to particular legislation is no longer contingent and to be decided case by case by the legislator (as in the 1917 form of government), but has become a structural principle of the canonical order.[81] The dominant concern no longer seems to be to ensure the uniformity of legislation required by the medieval principle *unum imperium, unum et ius*, as in the old Code. The concern is rather to establish a new constitutional balance between the universal and particular dimensions of the Church of Christ.

In the administrative area the reception of the Council has perhaps been more thoroughgoing, thanks to the application, in can. 87, of CD 8 a and b.[82] The strictly juridical principle of the old discipline, that only the author of a law (or his superior) can dispense from it, has been replaced by the ecclesiological principle that the diocesan bishop has all the faculties needed for providing for the spiritual good of his faithful. The shift from a system of concession to a system of reservation has thus brought about an almost Copernican revolution within the canonical order. Here again, however, the most stubborn resistance to decentralization shows itself in regard to the obligations inherent in the state of the evangelical councils and in the clerical state (see, for example, can. 291, 686, 691, § 2, 700, 1078, § 2, 1079–1080).

If we prescind from the simplification of procedures (which is, however, something that also concerns the universal Church), we find that no progress has been made beyond the Code of 1917 in the area of the judicial function. The jurisprudential autonomy of the particular churches was acknowledged in can. 19 of the 1980 draft as a means of filling in legislative lacunas, but it was suppressed at the last moment. If the problem was to ensure, in the judicial area as elsewhere, an equality before the law that was rendered doubtful by an often excessively free and easy local jurisprudence, this could have been accomplished by expe-

81. On this problem, see H. Schmitz, "Gesetzgebungsbefugnis und Gesetzgebungskompetenzen des Diözensanbischofs nach dem CIC von 1983," *AfkKR*, 152/1 (1983) 62–75.

82. See H. Schmitz, "Einleitung und Kommentar zu den Vollmachten der Bischöfe und Ordensoberen," *Nachkonziliare Dokumentation*, 16 (Trier, 1970), pp. 1–8.

dients of an administrative kind, without directly attacking the value of the jurisprudence of the particular churches.

3. The institutional reception of the *communio hierarchica ministeriorum* is to a great extent identifiable with the problem of synodal or collegial structures.

In discussing the collegial relationship of the bishops and the pope, the most recent literature has shown in sufficient detail that, instead of receiving the doctrinal formulas of *Lumen gentium* that allow the greatest range of possibilities and are most respectful not only of the historical experience embodied in the ecumenical councils of the first millennium but also of the practice of Vatican II itself,[83] the Code has preferred the institutional interpretations given in the "prefatory note of explanation" (*nota explicativa praevia*), which, as it were, encloses the college of bishops in a rigid hierarchic wrapper.[84] The tendency to place excessive emphasis on the primacy evidently surfaces in other contexts as well, as, for example, in the assignment to the pope of the right to administer and dispose of all ecclesiastical goods, instead of allowing him a simple right of control (can. 1273).

It is true that, apart from any possible political intentions, the Code has in fact shunted ecumenical councils into a systematic position of secondary importance, even in comparison with the position given councils in the 1917 Code. But this does not make any more plausible the claim that it gives the college of bishops a substantial and systematic priority over councils.[85] The subject of *plena et suprema potestas* is admittedly not councils as such but the college of bishops, and this is true even when councils are in progress. On the other hand, there is no doubt that a council should be regarded as an institutional expression of the most binding as well as the most solemn form of episcopal collegiality. But this must not be understood as meaning that in order to be real, collegiality must take the form of "conciliarity," if "conciliarity" implies a permanent or ongoing ecumenical council.[86] From the standpoint of terminology the abstract idea of "conciliarity," which has been taken over from theology, only increases the ambiguity inherent in the term "college." Though used by Vatican II as an alternative for juridically less ambiguous terms (*coetus, ordo*), "college" prevents the elimination from theological and canonical thinking of the conviction that, if collegiality is to be genuine and real, it must necessarily find expression not only in

83. See G. Alberigo, "Una cum patribus. La formula conclusiva delle decisioni del Vaticano II," in *Ecclesia Spiritu Sancto edocta. Mélanges théologiques. Hommage à Mgr. Gerard Philips* (Gembloux, 1970), pp. 291–419.

84. See J. A. Komonchak, "The Ecumenical Council in the New Code of Canon Law," *Concilium*, 167 (1983) 100–105.

85. See the statement of the Concilium Foundation, "Anxiety about the Council," ibid., pp. 111–12.

86. The term is used by, e.g., Y. Congar, "The Conciliar Structure or Regime of the Church," ibid., pp. 3–9, and G. Alberigo, "Istituzioni," (n. 58, above), pp. 235–62.

technically collegial acts but also in the most binding form, the deliberative vote.

As a matter of fact, the ecclesiological reality we call *communio hierarchica episcoporum* is not conceptually reducible to the juridical notions of
college and deliberative collegial act. The reason for this is not so much
the hierarchical structure of the college (as the "prefatory note," no. 1,
would suggest), but that the bishops are bound by the synodal dimension of their office even when they act outside strictly collegial structures. Even prescinding from the fact that, according to the juridical
technicalities of a collegial juridical act, a consultative vote can have a
place in, for example, a synod of bishops, where the acting subject is not
the individual bishops or even the majority of bishops but the synod as
such, it must be admitted that the word "synodality" is in the final
analysis better suited than "collegiality" to convey a correct idea of the
ecclesiological reality.

Because it is not prejudiced by historical and juridical preconceptions,
"synodality" can include all the levels at which the *in solidum* responsibility of the college of bishops is expressed:[87] from concelebration, which
takes the form of parallel actions, to the concern of individual bishops
for the universal Church; the ordinary magisterium, which finds expression in collective actions; the acts of episcopal conferences in matters not pertaining to their competence as collegial agencies; the consultative actions of the synod of bishops, the college of cardinals, or
presbyteral and pastoral councils; and other possible juridical forms not
yet used, all the way to the deliberative collegial actions of the college
and ecumenical councils.

In order to be in a position to evaluate potential institutional forms
that would be alternatives to the solutions adopted in the "prefatory
note," and even new by comparison with the historical relationships between college and pope, one would have to provide theoretical explanations for a series of other theological data and problems. First of all,
there is the fact that synodality, even when exercised consultatively in
service to the primacy, is not without a profound ecclesiological value,[88]
for such activity tends to enhance not only the primacy but also the position of the episcopate.[89] Secondly, there is the ecclesiological significance
to be given to the fact that ecumenical councils have never been permanent. In light of this, is it possible that Vatican II called for conciliarity if
the latter is to be regarded as the basic institutional embodiment of the
limits that collegiality possibly places upon the primacy?

It certainly cannot be denied that in theory the college of bishops can

---

87. See W. Aymans, *Kollegium und kollegialer Akt im kanonischen Recht* (Munich, 1969),
pp. 88–91.

88. See G. P. Milano, *Il sinodo dei vescovi* (forthcoming).

89. This aspect of the question seems to have been neglected by J. M. Tillard in his *The
Bishop of Rome* (Wilmington, Delaware, 1983), when he speaks of the "solitude" of the
pope, p. 43.

commit itself to celebrate a council at fixed intervals. But if it be accepted that a council, to be effective, presupposes the emergence of a need of the Church that can be formulated in a sufficiently organized way, then such a course evidently runs the risk of starting a formal synodal practice that is counterproductive—to say nothing of the fact that the college would remain in authoritative control of its own commitment. Even in the hypothesis suggested by the theory of a single subject of authority in the Church, namely, that the pope exercises the authority of the college itself, it must be admitted that the pope would probably retain his freedom in face of the norm established by the college.

The limits that collegiality places on the primacy cannot in fact be understood as materially reducing the *plena potestas* but only as limits on the modality of its exercise. The hypothesis that the synod of bishops is authorized to represent the entire college is not a plausible one,[90] because no one in the Church, and therefore not even the bishops, can be represented by others in the act of bearing witness to their own faith. The compromise formula of can. 343, thanks to which the pope can allow the synod a deliberative vote, and the thesis that allows for the possibility of appealing from the synod, invested by law with deliberative power, to the college of bishops or a council, are juridical substitutes, useful perhaps for encouraging a more intense synodal practice, but incapable of providing a theoretical solution to the problem of the limits that collegiality places on the primacy. Any limitation or self-limitation of papal authority that prescinded from the intrinsic objective truth of the college-pope relationship could only result from a voluntaristic nominalism that would be unable to establish a practice epistemologically capable of revealing the intrinsic nature of the relationship itself.

If the principle be accepted that ecclesial practice can give rise to a process of doctrinal development only on condition that the practice is based on doctrinal elements already clearly possessed, and if it is permissible therefore to express dissatisfaction with the Code's reception of the "prefatory note," rather than the more open and surer formulas of *Lumen gentium*, it can only be hoped that in the future the synodal practice of the episcopal college at the level of the synod of bishops will develop as fully as possible the potentialities present in the doctrinal truth that is already possessed with certainty.

4. The final institutional element in the *communio ministeriorum* is the presbyterium. The existence of this collegial entity around the diocesan bishop is required not simply by the need to provide the bishop with helpers, as though he were not in a position to carry out by himself the

90. On this point, see the draft constitution for the synod of bishops proposed by G. Alberigo, "Appunti per organi collegiali nella Chiesa cattolica," in *L'ecclesiologia* (n. 58, above), pp. 262–66. But see also the observations made by J. Lécuyer on this proposal in "Istituzioni in vista della communione tra l'episcopato universale e il vescovo di Roma," ibid., pp. 267–70.

many tasks inherent in his ministry, but by ecclesiological considerations, as we have seen. The presbyterium takes institutional form first of all in the presbyteral council, which in turn leads to the college of consultors (can. 496ff.); but in another whole series of juridical institutions it has the factors that more or less directly contribute to making more organic the unity of the presbyters among themselves and with their bishop.[91] I am referring to institutions that were accepted by Vatican II or are given shape directly by the Code and that tend to dismantle structures established in the course of history in order to ensure the clergy an increasingly greater autonomy of the corporative type over against the bishop. In the process, they destroyed the very idea of a presbyterium.

Not all the institutions foreseen by the Council have, however, been received by the Code in an equally decided way. For example, the principle of a communion of goods, which is suggested in PO 8, § 3, and 17, and by CD 28, § 3 and § 4, has been completely neglected, and the principle of common life has been taken over by the Code (can. 245, § 2, 280, 533, § 1, 550, §§ 1–2) with even less conviction than Vatican II itself showed (OT 11, § 2, and PO 8, § 3). On the other hand, the Code has made obligatory a common diocesan fund for the support of the clergy (can. 1274, § 1), which PO 21, § 1, proposed as optional, and it has specifically stated the right of association for all the faithful (can. 215), including the clergy, although it favors, in a discrete way, associations of diocesan clergy within the presbyterium as distinct from those open to everyone in the Church (can. 278).

Other factors of basic importance because of their impact on the bishop-presbyter relationship are, on the one hand, the radical relativization of the principle of territoriality, the application of which is excluded by the theological definition of a particular church and a parish (can. 368–369, 374, § 1, 515, § 1, and 518), and, on the other, the removal from common law of the benefice system (can. 1272), with the consequent suppression of the principle of irremovability (can. 522), called for by PO 20, § 2, and CD 31, § 3, respectively. These institutions had contributed greatly to fragmenting dioceses into small parochial entities by guaranteeing the clergy the material conditions for the economic self-sufficiency that their juridical and pastoral autonomy presupposed. With the abolition of the benefice system is connected, at least in fact, the suppression of the rights of presentation and popular election and the institution of concurrence, as decreed by CD 28, § 1, and ES, I, 18; these two texts are the basis for interpreting can. 523, which establishes a clear juridical presumption in favor of the free conferral of parochial offices by the bishop. Related to the elimination of irremovability and to the norms for the resignation of parish priests who have reached the age limit (accepted by can. 538, § 3; see CD 31, § 4, and ES, I, 20, § 3) are the

91. For a more detailed treatment of the problem, see E. Corecco, "Sacerdozio" (n. 74, above), pp. 365–70.

norms of the Code for the removal and transfer of parish priests (can. 1740–1752), as called for by CD 31, § 3, and ES, I, 20 § 1.

All these institutions are clearly connected both with greater mobility, for which the clergy is to be prepared by seminary education (can. 257), and with the relaxation of the discipline of incardination (can. 265–272), as provided for in PO 10, § 2, and ES, I, 23. There is question in the main of norms that, in addition to urging upon all presbyters a sense of responsibility for the universal Church, at the same time emphasize the fact that the clergy is structurally defined in its apostolic mission by a constant reference to the bishop and the presbyterium.

This transformation in the identity of the diocesan clergy is effected through an organic change in structures, which are now able to bring out better the ontological, sacramental, and jurisdictional bond among all the members of the presbyterium. The transformation makes clear the principle that the pastoral mission in the diocese is entrusted to the presbyterium as such, with responsibility for it being individually differentiated but synodally reciprocal. This means a radical change in the meaning of pastoral coordination. Coordination is called for not on grounds of efficiency but for ecclesiological reasons. It is in this setting that two other institutions, new even in relation to the Council, have their place: the entrusting of one or more parishes to several priests *in solidum* (can. 517, § 1), thus making the *communio ministeriorum* of the presbyterium a reality at the parochial level, and the establishment of a college of diocesan consultors (can. 502), which, to the extent that it replaces the cathedral chapter, does away with the corporative element that contributed so much in dioceses to creating the image of a clergy competing with the bishop.

Sacra Potestas

1. Another content important for evaluating the Code's reception of the teaching of Vatican II is *sacra potestas*.[92] The Council carefully avoided taking a position in the doctrinal debates on the existence of two powers, one of orders, the other of jurisdiction, and of a possible third power, that of teaching. In principle it left the traditional distinctions untouched.[93] On the other hand, it is undeniable that Vatican II chose to express itself, when dealing with the Church's power, by means of the unitary idea of *sacra potestas*, which is outside the tradition of the 1917

92. On this whole section, see E. Corecco, "Natura e struttura della 'Sacra Potestas' nella dottrina e nel nuovo Codice di Diritto Canonico," *Strumento Internazionale per un lavoro teologico. Communio*, 75 (1984), esp. pp. 44–52.

93. LG 28, § 1, and PO 2, § 2, in which the expression *consecrationis missionisque* is used of Christ, cannot be interpreted, as Beyer interprets them in his "Il nuovo codice" (n. 30, above), p. 134, as a proof of the existence of two powers, for it is not possible to speak of Christ as having a power of orders and a power of jurisdiction.

Code and avoids the ideas of "power of orders" and "power of jurisdiction." Except for LG 23, § 2, where the term *actus iurisdictionis* seems to be a synonym for *potestas iurisdictionis*, in all the other passages in which *iurisdictio* has a canonical and not merely a civil law meaning, it can be replaced, without any change of meaning, by the unitary and general term *potestas* or *auctoritas*, without the limiting genitive *iurisdictionis*.[94]

The Code has not adopted this line either materially or formally, but has chosen to follow three sources that differ in their inspiration but have in common a preconception of the Church as a *societas* and therefore an idea of ecclesial power with secular overtones. The three sources are: the doctrine that underlies the "prefatory note" but is not necessarily part of its dogmatic content;[95] the teaching that the power of orders and the power of jurisdiction differ in their nature; and, finally, the division of the power of jurisdiction into legislative, administrative, and judicial, a division closely linked to the philosophical and constitutional theory of the separation of powers. An irrefutable sign that the Code has not made any effort to treat *potestas* as unitary entity is undoubtedly the removal from can. 1213 of the idea of *sacra potestas*, which was part of it in the 1982 draft. Admittedly, the context in which the term appeared there was doctrinally irrelevant. It is highly significant, nonetheless, that the Code should have decided at the last moment to replace the formula according to which the bishops are free to exercise *sacra potestas* in their churches with the formula couched in the plural, and now—more ambiguous than ever—according to which the bishops are free to exercise *suas potestates et munera* (sic!) in their churches.

2. In the sacramental area of the exercise of *potestas*, the Code renounces both the term *potestas* and the institution of *delegatio*, which has traditionally been used to denote the transmission of the material content of a power. The most important context here is undoubtedly the sacrament of penance (can. 872ff.), which is regarded by the school of canon law of which Mörsdorf is the most illustrious contemporary representative[96] as the most telling instance of collaboration between the power of orders and the power of jurisdiction as two causes together producing a single sacramental effect, namely, reconciliation with God and with the Church. Contrary to the 1917 Code (can. 872ff.), the new Code regularly replaces the word *potestas* (*iurisdictionis, absolvendi, audiendi confessiones*) with the word *facultas*, thereby also renouncing the institution of *delegatio* (can. 966ff.). Thus the Code seems explicitly to suggest in can. 966 that absolution from sins is the effect solely of the

---

94. The passages in which the Council speaks of *iurisdictio* can be tracked down with the help of X. Ochoa, *Index verborum cum documentis Vaticani Secundi* (Rome, 1967), s. v. *iurisdictio*.

95. On the interpretation of the *nota explicativa praevia*, see A. Acerbi, *Due ecclesiologie* (n. 6, above), pp. 460–74.

96. See, e.g., his "Weihegewalt und Hirtengewalt in Abgrenzung und Bezug," *Miscelanea Comillas*, 16 (1951) 95–110.

potestas ordinis. As a result, it becomes very difficult to interpret *facultas* as meaning *potestas*.

The same phenomenon occurs over and over: in the sacrament of confirmation, where instead of *delegatio potestatis* the term *concessio facultatis* is used (contrary to the old Code, can. 782, §§ 2 and 5), as a more appropriate expression of authorization or *licentia*; in the sacrament of matrimony, where however the word *facultas* is combined with *delegatio*, the result being the same terminological contradiction found in the old Code (can. 1094); finally, in the sphere of the sacramentals. For sacramentals that can be administered by laypersons the Code uses the word *potestas* (can. 1168), thus presupposing the possession of a delegated power; for consecrations, however, which presuppose possession of the power of orders, it uses the word *concessio* (can. 1169, § 2), which is correlated with *facultas*.

The conclusion must be that the Code no longer maintains (as the old Code could be said to maintain) that the administration of the sacraments is a joint act of the power of orders and the power of jurisdiction (understood as having two material contents), but thinks of it as being rather the effect exclusively of the power of orders. The *potestas iurisdictionis* would thus no longer operate as an intrinsic factor, but only extrinsically, alongside the properly sacramental power, as a social power that is purely formal in character and sees to the correct administration of the sacraments. It seems clear, therefore, that from a doctrinal standpoint the Code has adopted the solution that also underlies the "prefatory note" (no. 2) and is inspired by the theory of which Bertrams is the principal exponent among contemporary canonists.[97]

Neither the "prefatory note" nor the Code gives a theologically plausible explanation of how the *potestas iurisdictionis*, understood as purely formal in nature, can in case of need annul the operation of the power of orders (which alone has a material content), without the latter ceasing to exist conceptually as a true power. The system at work here, then, is one that assigns an ecclesiological priority to the social power of jurisdiction over the sacramental power of orders.

3. In the nonsacramental area, on the other hand, the Code seems to regard the *potestas iurisdictionis* as having a material content of its own that differs from that of the *potestas ordinis*.

Like the Code of Pius X and Benedict XV, the new Code uses the word *potestas (iurisdictionis)* in strict relationship to those acts of ecclesial authority that have traditionally been looked upon as evident operations of the power of governance. Thus it uses the word in connection with the granting of indulgences (can. 995), where there is no doubt that the *potestas* is to be understood as power of jurisdiction, inasmuch as the college of bishops *(suprema Ecclesiae potestas)* cannot express itself collegially

97. See, e.g., his "De potestatis episcopalis exercitio personali et collegiali," *Per*, 53 (1964) 455–81.

according to the communicative logic proper to sacramental signs but only according to that proper to the word, that is, to jurisdiction; or again in connection with the *potestas dispensandi* from vows (can. 1196), oaths (can. 1203), and matrimonial impediments (can. 1079, §§ 2–4). The same language is used for the remission of canonical penalties in the external forum (can. 1354, § 2). The exception in this area confirms what was said above about the use of the word *facultas* in the context of the sacraments: can. 1357, § 3, uses *facultas*, not *potestas*, when, speaking of a confessor empowered to remit penalties, it says that he must be *facultate praeditum*.

The analysis of these two areas—the sacramental and the nonsacramental—shows that the Code distinguishes in a clearly inflexible way between the two *potestates* of orders and jurisdiction, assigning a material content to the former and making the latter a purely formal control. By using the word *facultas* in connection with the sacraments and *potestas* for the nonsacramental sphere, the Code gives two different meanings to the power of jurisdiction itself: one formal and the other material, depending on the area with which its operation is concerned. This double dualism, which betrays beyond any doubt the two ecclesiologies of *communio* and of *societas* that are at work, is already contained in a nutshell in can. 130, which establishes the principle that has behind it the authority of the 1967 Synod of Bishops,[98] namely, that the *potestas regiminis* is normally to operate in the external forum and only exceptionally in the internal. This closely resembles what was thought good by the 1917 legislators (can. 202), who, however, took the *societas perfecta* as their model of the Church.

4. It is possible to move beyond this positivist position only if we interpret the pointers given by Vatican II in regard to the unity of *sacra potestas*, which have led the majority of theologians and some canonists to claim that all power in the Church originates in the sacraments, and in regard to the teaching according to which there are different degrees of communion in the one Church of Christ (a doctrine that the Code too accepts; see, e.g., can. 844).

Mörsdorf has seen that the distinction between orders and jurisdiction has its origin in the distinction between the two factors in the Church that produce institutions: the sacraments and the word.[99] These are the two formally different ways in which God has revealed and communicated salvation, which itself is not only something single but is as one and indivisible as the person of Christ himself, the Word who through the incarnation became a sacrament of salvation. Just as Christ communicates himself in his totality in sacrament and word, which are

98. See *Communicationes*, 2 (1969) p. 79, n. 2.
99. See his "Wort und Sakrament als Bauelemente der Kirchenverfassung," *AfkKR*, 134/1 (1965) 72–79.

structurally reciprocal, so the oneness of sacrament and word is manifested and concretized in two institutional ways that canonical theory
has described terminologically as "power of orders" and "power of
jurisdiction." In orders the logic of communication proper to symbolic
sacramental signs prevails, whereas in jurisdiction the prevailing logic is
the formal logic of spoken language, that is, of the word (iuris dictio).
Orders and jurisdiction are thus the institutional instruments in which
the whole of *potestas sacra*, not merely a part of it, is at work. *Potestas
sacra* therefore does not act according to two material contents but
according to two different formal modes having an identical salvific content. It follows that the distinction between power of orders and power
of jurisdiction is formal, not material.

This makes it possible to move beyond the two traditional theories in
this area. The one maintains that orders and jurisdiction bestow two
complementary parts of *sacra potestas*, and that the Church need only not
give, or need only withdraw, jurisdiction in order to keep sacraments
from being valid (Mörsdorf). The other holds that the power of orders
contains the entire material context of *sacra potestas*, whereas jurisdiction
is purely formal in nature (Bertrams). For even in this second theory
control over the power of orders is exercised in accordance with a voluntaristic theory: jurisdiction puts the Church in a position to loose or bind
the power of orders to the point of determining the validity of its exercise.

If we distinguish between the transmission of *sacra potestas*, which can
take place only through the sacrament of orders, wherein the word is
present (a fact that explains why apostolic succession is connected in its
full expression with the sacrament of orders), and its exercise, which follows the two logics of communication proper to the sacrament and the
word, then we must conclude that when *sacra potestas* is exercised within
the limits of the *substantia sacramenti* and the *substantia verbi* it is always
sufficiently effective to bring the Church of Christ into being. In virtue of
sacra potestas, which thus exercises a control over itself, the Church
establishes what essential elements are required by *ius divinum* for a
sacrament to be a sacrament and for the word to be sufficiently complete
so as still to be the word of God. In the hypothesis that these two elements are substantially present, the Church cannot prevent their effective operation even outside *communio plena*, in a degree that varies with
the completeness of their content.

Vatican II teaches that the Church of Christ subsists in the full communion of the Catholic Church in virtue, among other things, of the total immanence in that Church of the universal dimension (all the sacraments and all the doctrine) and the particular dimensions, but that it is
also found in various degrees outside the boundaries of the Catholic
Church. This teaching makes it intelligible that *sacra potestas*, through
which salvation finds binding expression, should also operate with
varying degrees of effectiveness. This approach enables us to avoid all

voluntaristic views in appraising the validity or invalidity of the sacraments and the word. *Communio* becomes the setting for judging the validity or invalidity of the actions both of the Catholic Church and of the separated churches and ecclesial communities, because on the one hand it is the ecclesiological reality within which *sacra potestas* must be exercised if it is to be efficacious and, on the other, it is the reality that *sacra potestas* helps bring into being. *Communio* either is or is not, and the Church is called to pass judgment on it in virtue of *sacra potestas* itself, but it is different both conceptually and ontologically from *sacra potestas*, which it both precedes and follows upon.

If a Catholic minister exercising the functions of orders and jurisdiction that belong to *sacra potestas* were to go beyond the limits set for him by *communio plena* (limits established in principle by the canonical order), his sacramental and jurisdictional acts would no longer be capable of bringing about *communio plena* and therefore of being binding on the Catholic Church. This does not necessarily mean that these acts are null or invalid as nullity or invalidity is understood in the general theory of law. When the *substantia sacramenti* and the *substantia verbi* are respected, any positive intervention declaring the sacramental or jurisdictional act of a minister (acting according to the degree of orders that he has received) to be invalid instead of simply illicit is a dubious one. Such, for example, are the norms declaring that the sacraments of penance (can. 966, § 1) and confirmation (can. 882) are invalid when administered by a priest who lacks the necessary *facultas*.

5. A final proof of the positivist approach taken to the problem of *sacra potestas*, and one that makes clear the absence from the Code of any concern to give even a minimum of theological and conciliar direction to a matter so centrally important to ecclesiology and the canonical order, is the introduction on a massive scale of juridical terminology unabashedly smacking of civil law. For in the Code *sacra potestas* comprises not only *potestas ordinis et iurisdictionis* but *potestas legislativa, potestas executiva, potestas iudiciaria*, and even *potestas interpretandi* (can. 129ff.). The intention may have been to make clearer than in the 1917 Code the various areas of the exercise of power in the Church and the various criteria governing this exercise. The result has certainly been to give the impression that the "powers" exercised are not different functions of a single *sacra potestas* but powers really and truly separate, as in the juridical organization of states.

Conclusion

It is not possible to appraise adequately the process of the reception of Vatican II by the Code of Canon Law simply by applying the positive scientific method. If one were simply to compare the material contents of the respective texts without reference to a comprehensive interpretation of the deeper tendencies at work in the Council, one would have to allow that the Code has received, in approximately equal measure, both the ecclesiology of *societas* and the ecclesiology of *communio*. At most, one would have to note the fact that the different systematic requirements of the Code as compared with those of the Council have made even clearer the unbridgeable gap between the two ecclesiologies.

Those therefore who maintain that the two ecclesiological models used by Vatican II are necessary structures and cannot be eliminated from theology may well be satisfied with the conclusion that the Code only acted prematurely in accepting the two as equal. The fact that at this level the Code already shows many limitations and omissions of details (these, admittedly, of varying importance) in its material and formal takeover of individual texts is something that cannot be gainsaid, but it is secondary in relation to the overall judgment. This is true especially if we take into account the fact that Council and Code, with their different roles in the Church, are not really reducible to documents or sources, because they are events[100] in the Church's oral tradition and are therefore not susceptible of a purely positivist interpretation.

Those on the other hand who reject the established theological practice of recent centuries and maintain that the Church is not a human society "elevated" to the supernatural sphere but a social entity generated by *communio* (the formal constitutive element in the entire institutional reality of the Church)[101] will inevitably have a different set of criteria for evaluating reception. It is in fact no longer possible to think that the institutions and laws of the Church are produced by the "spontaneous [biological] dynamics" of human life in community, as is the case in the state; they are produced rather by the social dynamics specific to communion and are knowable in their essence only through faith.

If the essence of ecclesial sociality and canon law differs profoundly from that of human sociality and state law, because the former has its origin preeminently in the sacraments, then neither can *sacra potestas* be regarded as a social power having the same nature as the social power of the state. *Sacra potestas* is in fact identical with the binding salvific power inherent in word and sacrament, which together and in the same degree, though according to different formal logics of communication, produce the Church itself together with its sociality, for the purpose of bringing about an eschatological salvation that is already present in history.

If we may legitimately think that the ecclesiology of communion is

100. See Cardinal Karol Wojtyla (Pope John Paul II), *Sources of Renewal: The Implementation of the Second Vatican Council* (San Francisco, 1980), esp. pp. 15–41.

101. See A. Rouco Varela and E. Corecco, *Sacramento e Diritto: antinomia nella Chiesa? Riflessioni per una teologia del diritto canonico* (Milan, 1971), pp. 59–62.

destined gradually to absorb the scraps of natural law that serve as cues
for the ecclesiology of the Church as society and to integrate them into a
theological synthesis capable of shutting the door against every dualistic
approach, then the Code was clearly not in a position to receive this conciliar datum with all its power of expansion and to identify it as the only
factor binding in the future. The fact that twenty years after the council
the Code did not avoid this ambiguity is clearly not a reason for any
sense of satisfaction.

Our judgment on the Code will inevitably be even more severe when
we consider the discontinuity manifested by the Code in applying the
epistemology proper to faith (and called for by the ecclesiological principle of *communio*: OT 16, § 4) in its overall systematic organization of the
legislative material and in its approach to each content. Severity is also
warranted by the discrepancies between the conciliar texts and the
normative texts of the Code (discrepancies surfacing in the material and
formal reception of many institutions). The severity is justified even
when it is based, as it is here, on only a partial analysis, though one that
deals with some basic areas of legislation.

The limited question of the reception of Vatican II cannot, of course,
be made the sole and exclusive criterion for evaluating the Code. Many
other points of view would have to be taken into consideration, not least
the suitability of promulgating it at the present moment in the history of
the Church. In any case, one point is certain: the Code represents a transitional stage of major importance for the life of the Church. Its novelty,
even if only partial, in relation to the 1917 Code, is such that it will irreversibly affect the institutional image of the Church and the methodol-
ogy of the science of canon law. Well before the last two decades this
science had indeed already entered upon the fourth stage of its development (despite the resistences of many kinds persisting in a doctrinal
approach that can still claim justification in various—outdated—elements of the Code). This fourth phase is the theological phase and is
based on the acceptance of theology as co-essential for the development
of a general theory of canon law. It was preceded by the sapiential phase
of the first millennium, the techno-juridical phase of the golden age that
had its origins in Roman law, and the apologetic phase of the *ius publicum ecclesiasticum* that was based on natural law.

Only the distance given by the years will make it possible to evaluate
in an adequately balanced and magnanimous way the impact of the new
Code on the consciousness and practice of the Latin Church and the universal Church. For the moment, my impression is that the attempt of the
Code to put order into Church discipline by accepting many of the innovative impulses of Vatican II, while also trying to contain the disloca-
tions and profound tensions that emerged in the postconciliar period, is
like trying to put the lid on an already operating pressure cooker whose
safety valve is the principle implied by Pope John Paul II, namely, that

the Code is to be interpreted in the light of Vatican II.[102] This is the principle that must control the work of the Pontifical Commission for the Interpretation of the Code of Canon Law.

When the turmoil has died down and it becomes possible to get a clearer grasp of the doctrinal and institutional problems presently distressing the Church, it will also be possible to begin a new page in the history of the Church.

102. See the apostolic constitution *Sacrae Disciplinae Leges* on the promulgation of the new Code (Jan. 25, 1983), in *The Code of Canon Law: A Text and Commentary* (n. 1, above), pp. xxiv–xxvi.

Christian Duquoc

14. Clerical Reform

The closing exhortation of the Vatican II "Decree on the Ministry and Life of Priests" (Dec. 7, 1965) shows how seriously the bishops had taken the subject:

This sacred Council, while keeping in mind the joys of the priestly life, cannot pass over the difficulties too which priests encounter in the circumstances of their life today. It knows also how much economic and social conditions, and even men's morals, are being transformed, and how much men's sense of values is undergoing change. Hence it is that the Church's ministers, and even sometimes the faithful, in the midst of this world feel themselves estranged from it and are anxiously seeking suitable methods and words by which they may be able to communicate with it. The new obstacles opposing the faith, the apparent fruitlessness of the work done, the bitter loneliness they experience—these can bring for priests the danger of a feeling of frustration.[1]

Twenty years after it was written the passage still gives a true picture and remains relevant, and a rereading of the decree is therefore not a useless exercise. In it the bishops give an idea at once lofty and modest of the priestly ministry. They do not mask the reality behind utopian visions or pious phrases, but at the same time they show their determination to convey the meaning of this ministry in all its nobility, that is, to present it as what it really is. To this end they connect its exercise with the three titles given to Christ: teacher, priest, and king (§ 1). This ministry is thus assigned three main functions: preaching of the word, administration of the sacraments, and exercise of leadership.

This lofty idea of the threefold function of the ministry is tempered, however, by a reminder of the frailty of the one who carries it out: a priest does not preach or sanctify or govern on his own account or by reason of his intrinsic abilities; rather he fulfills his functions through and for another, namely, Christ. The Latin text expresses this unique situation in a lapidary phrase: *in persona Christi*. This qualification means

---

1. "Decree on the Ministry and Life of Priests," in A. Flannery, ed., *Vatican II: The Conciliar and Postconciliar Documents* (Collegeville, Minn., 1975), p. 901. This translation will be used henceforth for citations from *Presbyterorum ordinis*.

concretely that the sole purpose of the priest's ministry is to lead the believers entrusted to his pastoral care to Christian freedom (§ 6). The more fruit his activity bears, the less necessary it becomes. The ministry phases itself out.

I repeat therefore that the text is still relevant. The fissures that have developed in the clergy since the end of the Council may cause their abiding positive contribution to be forgotten and the radical challenge they are now facing to be underestimated. A return to the passage quoted and an appraisal of its effectiveness or failure are not motivated by an archaizing smugness, but are simply a matter of honesty, because the questions it expresses are still our own.

The text is also relevant because the antagonisms and challenges that were to bring turmoil to the subsequent history of the Roman Church cast their shadow before them in this passage. What I mean is this: at work in the discussion of the three focal points that define the role of the priest is a theory pregnant with danger: the theory of a preestablished harmony between the goals and interests of the faithful and those of priests, provided that the latter carry on their pastoral activities in an honorable and disinterested way. The theory is never stated as such but it is operative at every point, despite the mention of present-day difficulties in the exercise of the priestly ministry. It veils potential conflicts or denies in advance their possible legitimacy (such conflicts cannot but be sinful in their origin).

This inability to accept in a clear-eyed way the social contradictions existing in the Church was to have serious consequences for the juridical application of the text itself and of other texts later based on it. The inability was thus not unconnected with the drifts that occurred later on. For this reason I must make clear how this dramatic aftermath cast its shadow before it in the structure of the text.

The decree emphasizes three basic aspects of a priest's ministry: his openness to nonbelievers, his profound involvement in everyday life, and his service of the poor, the downtrodden, and the outcast (§ 6). Despite the high praise of liturgical preaching, sacramental activities, and the exercise of an authority rooted in Christ, the text is serenely but firmly critical of the kind of pastoral practice predominant at the time: the sacral management of religious needs. The decree thus pays heed to pastoral experiments that until then had been marginal, for example, those of the priest workers (§ 8).

Admittedly, the decree issues no detailed challenges, but in my opinion its general direction, accentuated by many allusions, is unmistakable: the necessity of a conversion in classic pastoral practice. This practice is judged to be excessively taken up with meeting the everyday demands of the faithful and not sufficiently stirred by the growing unbelief or the injustice found everywhere. Thus a rather classic theology of the priesthood is assumed and meshed with a quite untraditional presentation of ministerial activity. The frequent appeals to scripture or the data of tradition in order to show the legitimacy of these ministerial requirements does not successfully hide the difficulty of making classic theology a basis for meeting new needs.

My meaning, more concretely, is this: the post-tridentine theology of priesthood is here the foundation for subsequent reflection. In the nineteenth century this theology led to a prevailing practice that was more focused on the administration of the sacraments and on sacral government than it was inspired by missionary ideals and intentions. In the decree, however, these missionary ideals and intentions become the criterion for the authentic exercise of priestly ministry! Some passages of the decree develop this approach to such an extent that the reader is forced to ask whether the classical picture of the priesthood—though accepted by the decree—is still valid. The text says absolutely nothing to suggest this latent opposition, but subsequent events and contradictory interpretations of the decree have revealed the fault line running through it. Thus it has proved impossible to revive the old style of pastoral practice by appealing to the decree, for the document calls not for restoration but for conversion. And because this conversion, though called for in practice, has not been given its necessary intellectual basis, the structure of the decree prefigures the breakup that has been taking place ever since the Council in the socio-juridical organization of the Catholic Church.

The hypothesis I shall develop in this essay is the following: the Council called for changes—for example, clerical reform—that could not in fact be implemented, in the course of the decree's reception, but the failure has been due less to external or administrative factors (though I do not underestimate their importance) than to the indecisiveness of the decree itself. In the particular instance I am discussing here, the Council wished to keep unaltered the post-tridentine theology of the sacrament of orders, while radically reorganizing the exercise of the priest's pastoral functions. The result was the failure of reform. For, by reason of the indecisiveness of the documents and the artificial linkage of two alien requirements, attempts at an effective change in the ministry or the manner of life of priests have gotten bogged down in ideological and theological debates for which there can be no resolution. As a result, no reform has been possible; and when there has in fact been a change in practice, it stands in a schizophrenic relationship to the still dominant theology. To avoid the failure of the desired reform, the Vatican II decree would have had to offer a more flexible doctrine of the hierarchy and the ministry. The unfortunate effects of some pre–Vatican II changes have indeed been corrected to some extent by a greater ethical and evangelical sensitivity, but this could not substitute for structural deficiencies.

In arguing my hypothesis I shall proceed in stages: after describing the impasses in which we find ourselves today, I shall recall the desires expressed by the Council. I shall then show the inability of the classic theology of orders to satisfy these desires. In my conclusion I shall suggest a way in which the present schizophrenic relationship between theological theory and pastoral practice may be overcome.

Present Impasses

For almost two decades since the close of Vatican II, the Catholic clergy has been experiencing a profound unrest. Many causes have been invoked as explanations of the phenomenon. Some observers have spoken of a crisis of identity, but this is too general a notion to shed any real light. Others have appealed to the difficulties inseparable from the preaching of the faith in an indifferent or derisive world. Others have pointed out the contradiction inherent in the social status of priests.

These explanations are not negligible, but, rightly or wrongly, I do not think they account for the indecisiveness and, at times, the irritability that have taken hold of the clergy. A further element must, I think, be added: the incoherence between the evangelical intentions of authorities and the institutional reality.

Let me give an example. Invoking the gospel, hierarchical authorities urge priests to exercise their de facto power, not as though it were a possession to which they had a right, but as a service to the poor; they are to do away with all repressive threats in the exercise of the power given to them. The hierarchy is here applying to clerics the attitude that Jesus symbolizes in his washing of his disciples' feet. Clerics are to live among the faithful as those who occupy the lowest place and act as servants.

No one denies the evangelical validity of this appeal. But the appeal runs up against an obstacle that effectively banalizes the good intention: I mean the de facto juridical organization of power and authority in the Catholic Church. Priests who struggle to keep the idea of ministry as service from being just a pious wish, in their parishes and in the diocese beyond, find that present institutional structures do not promote the practice of what is preached.

The events of 1968 affected to a greater or lesser extent the social balances and mores of the developed countries. They had extensive repercussions in the churches, especially among clerics and religious. The French movement *Echange et Dialogue*, which sought to establish a trade union of clerics in order to achieve "declericalization," had its birth in the utopian vision of 1968. But the movement would never have seen the light of day if the ground had not been prepared for it by trends in Vatican II that were then given a concrete focus: a clerical reform aimed at introducing into clerical life the democratic ideals shared by the majority of Catholic believers. As a matter of fact, however, relationships between priests and their bishops, on the one hand, and the faithful and their priests, on the other, were schematized according to a hierarchical, pyramidal structure that justified a division of roles in the Church at odds with the positive demands then being heard in civil society.

Thus all the talk, based on the Gospel, that made the legitimate exercise of power depend on effective service was contradicted by the logic inherent in hierarchical relationships. In addition, these relationships were rooted in the centralizing Roman tradition, the functioning of which was supposedly guaranteed by the dogma of infallibility (contrary to the original meaning of the dogma). In these circumstances, priests felt themselves excluded from meeting the requirements and fulfilling the hopes expressed at Vatican II in their relationships with the faithful and with their bishops: over the former they possessed an authority from which there was no appeal; in the eyes of the latter, priests were themselves subjects who had not reached their majority. Priests were well aware, moreover, that the bishops were in the same situation in relation to their clergy, on the one hand, and to Rome, on the other. The institutional impasse thus turned all the fine talk into empty words and was leading to an explosion. The explosion did occur. Unfortunately, the sensational and journalistic character of certain challenges obscured the broader issue.

Challenges to the general law of priestly celibacy, questions about the validity of the exclusion of women from the priestly ministry, demands by the clergy to be recognized as professionals with the right to form a trade union are only secondary symptoms of a more general uneasiness springing from the separation of the clergy from the people. Priests look upon the separation as a shameful disease; it is an insult and an injustice. They believe they can dispel this feeling of being exceptional and marginal by an ever greater identification with the people. The idea of a declericalization of the priesthood—which provided the slogan for the *Echange et Dialogue* movement—has its roots in this desire for immersion in the people. Some have laughed at this kind of phraseology, but, be it clumsy or not, it bears witness to real suffering caused by a real problem.

Unfortunately, hierarchical authorities have not understood, or have not been willing to understand, the question; their response has simply been to remind priests of their institutional obligations. These, however, have come to seem regressive in relation to the wishes of Vatican II. The shutdown thus produced by opposing the immutability of the clerical institution to the hopes of clerics has led to a sense of helplessness and an explosion with a resultant decline in the number of new recruits.

It is now possible to gauge the harm done by institutional resistance to challenges: many priests have left the ministry; the reduction in numbers has meant a heavier pastoral burden for the remaining older men; the higher average age of priests and their isolation have been obstacles to recruitment. Priestly life has come to seem, humanly speaking, quite insecure, so that families and priests no longer encourage young men who are inclined to choose the ministry.

The harmful effects on the number and distribution of the clergy provoked by institutional resistance have been intensified by a determination to keep doctrine unchanged. Rome has felt it must justify its refusal to change the clerical discipline of celibacy by having recourse to traditional arguments. It has also rejected the priesthood of women by arguing from a male-female symbolism rooted in the Bible. The documents defending these positions give the appearance of being ideological justifications for the status quo. The determination to maintain the status quo by appealing to an ideal priesthood eliminates the institutional question, but it hardly cures the restlessness; rather it increases it.

In effect, the appeal to an ideal order closes the debate, because the transcendent data supporting empirical decisions are regarded as beyond discussion. Apart from this recourse to an ideal, the empirical decisions might be argued; after this recourse they are in principle no longer debatable. Thus the various openings of Vatican II seem to have been betrayed by a dogmatic justification of institutional immobility. More recent Roman decisions have focused the entire debate on celibacy and priesthood for women, thus turning attention away from the approach to the problem that was taken at Vatican II, or so at least the majority of the clergy see the situation.

At the present time there is still a serious sense that a democratic debate on the pastoral issues has been unjustly frustrated. That debate has been broken off, and the hierarchic and antidemocratic image of central authorities has been strengthened. The challenge arose from the rejection of a centralizing monopoly in 1968; more recent Roman decisions and the helplessness of the episcopal synods held in Rome have intensified the feeling of powerlessness and accentuated the drift toward uncontrolled ways of exercising the ministry. Were the hopes placed on Vatican II real or imaginary? Have they in fact been betrayed, or has there been a turning away from them? These are questions on which I shall try to shed some light by studying the wishes of Vatican II regarding the priestly ministry.

The Wishes of the Council

The structure of *Presbyterorum ordinis* presupposes the classical theory of the sacrament of orders, though with one rather important shift, inasmuch as Vatican II, unlike the Council of Trent, decided to take the episcopate as its starting point. The classic schema remains operative, however, according to which the sacrament of orders gives the priest a participation in the activity of Christ. The priest thereby becomes the instrument of Christ in Christ's exercise of the three offices of teacher, priest, and king that have been attributed to him.

Having recalled this doctrine of the rootedness of ministerial activity in the action of Christ himself through the mediation of the sacramental "character" of orders, the document moves on to a practical description of priestly activity: an explanation of the nature of priesthood is not one of its purposes. The henceforth predominant place of the episcopate in the consideration of the sacrament of orders explains the importance assigned to the ministry of the word. This represents a new departure in relation to traditional explanations and entails a profound revision of them.

Thus the priest is seen primarily not as the president of the liturgical eucharistic assembly but as one who, after the manner of the bishop, is in charge of evangelization. Worship and the exercise of governance are fitted into this priority, even though it is in the Eucharist that the community's acceptance of the Gospel is celebrated. This move away from the central place that liturgical presidency has in the tridentine theory and toward evangelical mission influences the way in which the priest's manner of life is conceived. His manner of life no longer follows from the sacrality of the liturgical action, but instead from the mission assigned him of preaching the gospel of Jesus Christ in a way that will make it intelligible to both believers and nonbelievers.

Once evangelization is made the primary goal of priestly activity, the situation of the hearer, whether Christian or non-Christian, becomes a decisive determinant of the form the mission is to take. This element was missing from the sacral structure of Trent's liturgical theory of priesthood. In the Vatican II doctrine the specific note of priestly ministry is no longer the almost abstract power to consecrate bread and wine, but the interconnection between the way in which this ministry is exercised and the situation of human beings. Thus the ancient sacral idea of apartness that had so influenced the determination of the priest's concrete manner of life here moves to the purely spiritual level: apartness or separation is now an ascetical and ethical requirement that does not by its nature entail particular juridical or sociological forms.

In the traditional description of priestly life, a socio-juridical framework served to ensure the priest's holiness. In the decree of Vatican II there is no longer any question of ensuring this holiness by means of a socio-juridical apartness: the priest's holiness of life flows rather from his fidelity to the requirements of his evangelical mission. If the Gospel leads to a separation, it is a separation that applies not to the priest alone but to all who want to bear witness to the relevance of the Gospel in their lives. A priest may take on a form of employment that makes him part of the worker world; he is nonetheless still required to integrate into his life the evangelical demands laid on him by his mission. Consequently the socio-juridical separation from the laity that has done much to make the clergy a social caste must now be assessed in light of the evangelical mission proper to the priesthood, rather than that this mission should be judged by whether or not it is compatible with a life of separation from the laity and the world. In principle, there are no longer any specific laws cutting the priest off from the Christian community.

This elimination of the traditional idea of separation that was so firmly entrenched in the sacral theory of the sacrament of orders led to challenges that the authors of the document had certainly not anticipated. They do indeed expressly admit that it is legitimate for a priest to be engaged in a profession (they refer to the experiment of the worker priest) because evangelization now takes priority over all other goals. But recall the obstacles that were in fact put in the way of the worker priests. They were blamed, for example, for not being able to hold in esteem the priestly way of life in which the praying of the breviary was very important. In those days the liturgical office was seen as sustaining the priest in his juridical and spiritual position; in the Sulpician tradition the priest was regarded as "God's religious." This aspect of priestly life even took precedence over the demands made by pastoral care. The stir caused by missionary pastoral experiments in the years before the Council had its basis in this liturgical vision of the priesthood.

Vatican II settles that debate by modeling priestly activity on the mission of the bishops: concern for evangelization is the criterion that must determine one's manner of life. In the older tradition the position of the priest had been defined a priori in terms of his relationship to God. The Vatican II decree on the priesthood allows a way of life to emerge from the priest's relationship to actual or potential believers (§ 4). Not long before, the priest's position had been defined in a way that allowed for no alteration; he thus had a fixed place in society. Today there is no question of a fixed position, because the changing character of priestly involvement in evangelization is the primary norm. As a result, the position of the priest continually evolves, because it is no longer determined in advance by his liturgical functions but by his always contingent relationships with the human beings to whom the word of the Gospel is addressed.

Can this reversal of perspective be sustained by the classic theology of the sacrament of orders? Has the decree of Vatican II managed to establish a harmonious connection between the old theology, which serves as an ideological justification for a sacral view of the priesthood, and the missionary perspective to which the new situation of the Church has given rise? I shall discuss these questions in the next section.

Classical Theology and the Wishes of the Council

The sections of *Presbyterorum ordinis* devoted to the other two ministerial functions of the priest—the administration of the sacraments and government (§§ 5–6)—fit in with the traditional theology.

The description of the priest's sacramental and liturgical ministry (§ 5) shows a very obvious continuity with the preconciliar tradition. The text repeats, for example, the doctrine of the Eucharist as sacrifice and as praise. Also repeated is the Thomist thesis that all the other sacraments are ordered to the Eucharist. This borrowing from the medieval or Tridentine tradition has an unfortunate consequence: one symbolism of the Eucharist that is fundamental for ecclesiology, namely, the fraternal meal, is passed over in silence. The omission gives the figure of the celebrating priest a sacral aura that is out of harmony with his position as presiding over a communion fellowship, but fits in very well with the ideology of sacrifice and victim that the text emphasizes several times.

In view of this drift toward a theology of sacrifice, the reader of the conciliar decree is doubtful of the meaning to be given to the statement that the Eucharist is the high point of evangelization because it is both its source and its goal. The statement can be understood in two ways. The mention of evangelization may be a reference to what has been said earlier in the section on the ministry of the word, in which case the allusion indicates a transformation in the dominantly sacral viewpoint of the section on the administration of the sacraments. But it is possible that the phrase "preaching of the gospel" is here interpreted in light of the acknowledged purposes of the liturgical office and of the sacrament, in which case the omission of the fraternal symbolism of the Eucharist to the advantage of self-offering and praise would indicate a shift of ground in relation to the section on the word and a return to a preconciliar perspective. A decision on the real meaning is all the more difficult because the texts of these two sections have not been brought into harmony. For this reason I turn to a third section, the one on the role of the priest in governing the faithful (§ 6).

Even a first reading shows the presentation here to be at once very classic and somewhat polemical. It is classic because it is based on the idea of power: the priest runs his community in a way that hardly seems democratic, inasmuch as he does not have to render any account to the people. It is also polemical: the power exercised is kept from being authoritarian by the ethic that controls its exercise, namely, an ethic of service to the faithful and especially to the poor and the outcast.

As a matter of fact, the authors of the text, who had inherited a hierarchic doctrine of the priesthood that did not allow for any democratic exercise of the office, are hard put to it to include the wishes that are at least suggested in the section on the ministry of the word. The purport of these wishes is that believers or nonbelievers be viewed as partners in a dialogue, not as subjects. The bishops were aware of how obnoxious the unrestrained exercise of authority is, and so they very strongly emphasize the ethical finality of the ministerial power of government: its aim cannot be domination or exploitation, but only the service of the faithful. They write in an inspired vein:

It is the priests' part as instructors of the people in the faith to see to it either personally or through others that each member of the faithful shall be led by the Holy Spirit to the full development of his own vocation in accordance with the Gospel teaching, and to sincere and active charity and the liberty with which Christ has set us free. Very little good will be achieved by ceremonies however beautiful, or societies however flourishing, if they are not directed towards educating people to reach Christian maturity [§ 6].

This ethical corrective to a possible drift of the theology of power is all the more necessary inasmuch as § 5, on the sacramental ministry of sanctification, describes the people as subjects of priestly activity. But the corrective is inadequate: it forestalls potential abuses but does so at the private level; it says nothing of a socio-juridical regulation of the power given to priests over the faithful. Nor is it accidental that nothing of this kind is said, because the hierarchical theory that is an intrinsic part of the post-tridentine theology of the sacrament of orders forbids that kind of regulation. The hierarchical theory presupposes a preestablished harmony between ministerial activity and the authentic wishes of the people. Because it can imagine no discrepancy between the exercise of the ministry and the desires of the people that is not due to a sinful failure at some point, the theory has no need of including any regulation of ministerial power except an ethical directive.

It is precisely this absence of rights for the people that explains to some extent the uneasiness of the clergy. But the Tridentine theology of orders is unable to include such rights except in the form of correctives for abuses. It does not directly structure the ministerial relationship to the unordained faithful, for to do so would be to pave the way for turning them into active and responsible subjects in the concrete exercise of the ministry. The response of the people that is mentioned in § 4 finds expression in the "Amen" of the liturgy.

In short, the failure to establish a juridical correlation between the rights and duties of ministers and those of the people in ecclesial society is due to the post-tridentine hierarchic theory. That theory is still dominant despite the radical challenge issued to it in the section on the ministry of the word where the idea of evangelization is normative. The disquiet of the clergy springs from the ongoing inability of the Catholic Church to give an effective role to the laity in its system of government, an inability that is due in turn to the traditional theory of the sacrament of orders.

Vatican II calls for the proclamation of Christian liberty, but the juridical organization of the community restricts this proclamation to the private or the extraecclesial sphere. This lack of connection between proclamation and practice is corrected only by an ethical directive. It remains a source of uneasiness; it signals the failure of a conciliar reform of the clergy.

Conclusion

Is it possible to do away with this alienation of proclamation from socio-ecclesial practice? In other words, can the disquiet of the clergy be relieved by an abandonment of the hierarchic theory? I shall not venture to forecast the future, nor shall I offer solutions. I should like simply to end by setting forth a hypothesis: the development in the theology of ministry expressed by the inversion of priorities among its objectives in § 4, where the main options of the document are set forth, led to the removal of the effects of the post-tridentine theology and to a different version of the priest-laity relationship in ecclesial society. If there is to be a reform, it is here that it must take hold.

The document does in fact state a principle that opens the way to a different conception of the relationship:

[Priests] could not be the servants of Christ unless they were witnesses and dispensers of a life other than that of this earth. On the other hand they would be powerless to serve men if they remained aloof from their life and circumstances [§ 3].

The challenges of all kinds that have arisen among the clergy for about twenty years now have never been concerned with their obligation to bear witness to another life; they have been concerned solely with the means of making this witness heard. The challenges have therefore had to do with the second half of the principle just stated, for, contrary to what the Council called for, the clergy, by reason of its position in the Roman Church, has always been alienated from the life and circumstances of the laity. And if the challenge has been directed especially at Rome's decision to maintain celibacy and to refuse the ministry to women, this is because these two points best bring out the limitations imposed on a clerical sharing of the common human condition.

Because of these limitations the "other life" that clerics preach has inevitably seemed tainted with dualism: it is not so much a different way of living our common condition as it is an attempt to substitute for it a way of life that is under the egis of ecclesiastical jurisdiction. This dualism infects the clergy-laity relationship: clerics alone have the power of governing, without any controls except those imposed by ethical norms or obedience to a higher authority in the hierarchy. Thus the limits placed on accession to the ministry define in advance the framework of a possible reform: there can be no application to Roman ecclesial society of socio-juridical considerations that would detract from the hierarchical structure that was given its ideological justification by post-tridentine theology.

As long as this obstacle has not been removed, attempts at democratizing relationships between priests and bishops, and between bishops and the central authorities, will appear to be simply ways of coping with hierarchic abuses too obvious to hide, and not a challenge to the dominant ideology. Any effective challenge could come only from a different relationship between ministers and laity in canon law.

Priests continue to occupy an ambiguous position: they resent the exclusion felt by the laity as a result of decisions by higher authorities over which they have no control. At the same time, however, they themselves exercise an unrestricted hierarchical power over the laity, analogous to that which higher authorities exercise over them. The conciliar document in no way corrects this situation; instead it aggravates it by proclaiming principles that do not produce any corresponding theology and code of rights. This is all the more regrettable because of the moderation and wisdom shown in the passages on relationships between priests and others, and on their manner of life. Chapter 3 (§§ 12–22), which is devoted to the life of priests, is remarkable for its humane spirit and levelheadedness, its acknowledgment of human qualities, and its concern for a well-balanced life. But because of its literary genre the chapter is restricted to the ethical realm; the question of the juridical organization of ecclesial society is not raised.

The failure of reform is not due to any lack of inspiration at the level of intention. It is due to a failure to bear in mind the real functioning of a society that out of excessive fidelity to tradition, cannot rid itself of a hierarchic theory of government, even though this is radically at odds with, on the one hand, the demands of advanced societies and, on the other, the evangelical principles that it repeatedly proclaims. The great error of the fathers of Vatican II was to underestimate the role of law. The challenges that have arisen have not been leveled directly at the faith or the demands of the Gospel, but at the way in which principles remarkable in themselves function ideologically, that is, socially, by reason of the archaic character or the deficiencies of church law.

As long as the hierarchic principle supported by post-tridentine theology has not been revised in terms of the goal of ministry, namely, evangelization, there is little chance that desires for reform will be fulfilled. The desire to do away with the separation between clergy and laity, which is one of the causes of the present malaise, will lead only to declarations of ethical principles. The extension of the structure found in the liturgy to the entire organization of the Church must therefore be rejected. The elements of a different theology of ministry that allows this restriction of the liturgical model are present in *Presbyterorum ordinis*. They must be exploited all the more urgently because the determination, already expressed in practice, to change the situation of the clergy in the Church is manifesting itself everywhere. If this is not done, we shall end with restoration, not reform—the very thing that Vatican II wanted to avoid.

Luis Maldonado

15. Liturgy as Communal Enterprise

The Council and History

When the Vatican Council voted almost unanimously on December 7, 1962, to accept chapter 1 of the liturgy constitution, Yves Congar wrote: "Something irreversible has happened and has been affirmed in the Church."[1]

As a matter of fact, *Sacrosanctum Concilium*, the constitution on the liturgy, was not only the first of the many that were to be approved by the Council (it was promulgated on Dec. 4, 1963); it was also one of the most important from a theological standpoint *(lex orandi lex credendi)*. As such, it contributed in a decisive way to the spectacular change that has taken place in the contemporary Church since the Council of 1962–1965.

Since that time there has been a radical change in the way that Catholics pray and celebrate the liturgy. There has been a shift from the devotionalism, subjectivism, individualism, and privatism that characterized preconciliar liturgical life to a sacramental life that in fundamental ways is more objective, biblical, and community-oriented.

More community-oriented? This is the point I should like to analyze here because it is in this area that we now encounter sharply critical judgments, as well as a sense of disappointment, frustration, and disillusionment.

One of the principal contributions of the postconciliar period has been the realization that no important question regarding the liturgy is either simple or "innocent," but always involves serious theological and anthropological issues. Liturgical action is conditioned by them and in turn influences them. There is no such thing as liturgical "autonomy" in either pastoral practice or theoretical reflection. For example, what goes on in liturgical prayer is inseparable from the image of God that it presupposes and that is, as it were, acted out in it.

The role of community in the liturgy is an even more complicated mat-

1. *ICI*, 183 (Jan. 1, 1963).

ter. We realize today that three major questions and pastoral activities play a part in it: the ecclesial question (the conception and practice of the Church), the question of evangelization (Christian initiation, catechumenate, the relationship between faith and sacrament), and the question of celebration (what it means to celebrate; the laws of Christian anthropology that govern celebration). Just as there is a felicitous harmony between *Sacrosanctum Concilium*, on the liturgy, and *Lumen gentium*, on the Church, so too there is in practice a close relation between pastoral care that is authentically geared to community and pastoral care that is truly liturgical.

The reason why liturgy that is not community-oriented is still a relatively widespread phenomenon is the persistent survival of a model of the Church that is not focused on communion. It takes no great effort or sociological analysis to show the existence of numerous eucharists that are celebrated for large, passive congregations and in which priests play an unduly predominant role. We also see Christians being given access to the other sacraments without satisfying the required preconditions, namely, an authentic understanding that they are thereby being linked to the Church, and an authentic initiation into a commitment to the mediation of the ecclesial community that is inseparable from the commitment of faith.

In the contemporary liturgy of the Church, at least two divergent models for celebration coexist. They correspond to the two models of the Church that likewise coexist in the practice of the community as a result of a lengthy development in ecclesiology and the magisterium in recent decades.

In celebrations for large, passive congregations in which the faithful "attend" mainly as spectators, the underlying model of the Church is the "societal" model; that is, the Church is regarded as a "perfect [complete] society" in which the hierarchy is dominant to the point of absorbing all activity. In this model, the hierarchy is the Church; ecclesiology is therefore reduced to hierarchology. (Yves Congar has shown very clearly that since the high Middle Ages the laity has been relegated to a secondary place in the Church and even reduced to silent passivity.)[2]

The faithful do at times play a part in the liturgy by answering, singing, and reading, but all this remains at the level of external formalism. There is no corresponding authentic commitment to the community outside the celebration and in the whole of ecclesial and civil life. In other words, there is no commitment to justice and love.

These liturgies do not reflect the other model of the Church that has been revived in our day: the Church as communion and community. My point is not that there must be an opposition between hierarchical society and community-communion, but that the two must be integrated.

2. See Y. Congar, *Ministères et communion ecclésiale* (Paris, 1971); idem, *L'ecclésiologie du haut Moyen-Age* (Paris, 1968).

And in any case priority must be given to the model to which Vatican II gives it. As I have already indicated, Vatican II achieved a noteworthy convergence and harmony in its constitutions on liturgy and Church, *Sacrosanctum Concilium* and *Lumen gentium*, respectively. The dominant theme of the former, namely, the participation of the entire assembly in the celebration, is matched by the dominant theme of the latter, namely, the idea of the people of God, of a church in which the center of gravity is not the apex but the base.

The course chosen by Vatican II was to understand the Church in terms of the people of God, not of the hierarchy. *Lumen gentium* has a whole chapter on the people of God and, more importantly, puts this chapter before the one on the hierarchy. This great contribution of the Council was based on biblical studies. Thanks to them we now have a new awareness of that which is the core of all ecclesial and liturgical life: not only the people of God but communion or *koinōnia* (Acts 2:42–45), brotherhood or *phratria* (Matt. 23:8–11), and service or *diakonia* (Luke 22:24–27).[3]

More concretely, recent publications make clear the importance of the house church, and therefore of house liturgies, in the early Church.[4]

Eucharistic Celebrations

As a result of these studies and on the basis of these presuppositions, the end of the Council was followed by a proliferation of house eucharists, just as it was by a great surge in new communities.

The two phenomena are in fact closely connected. The house eucharists often were and are the principal liturgical and sacramental celebration of the communities, and the communities celebrate house liturgies because they have a smaller membership.

The peculiarity of house eucharists is not simply that they are celebrated in homes rather than in church buildings (note the importance of

---

3. P. C. Bori, *Koinonia. L'idea della communione nell'ecclesiologia recente e nel Nuovo Testamento* (Brescia, 1972); S. Dianich, *La Chiesa mistero di communione* (Turin, 1975); M. J. Sieben, M. Manzanara, et al., *Koinonia, communauté, communion* (Paris, 1975); J. M. R. Tillard, "L'Eglise de Dieu est une communion," *Irén,* 53 (1980) 451–68; M. Legido, *Fraternidad en el mundo. Un estudio de eclesiología paulina* (Salamanca, 1982); L. Lescrauwaet, "Koinonia. L'asemblée comme signe caractéristique de l'identité de groupe des chrétiens," *QL,* 2 (1984) 85–97; C. Floristán, *La Parroquia communidad eucarística* (Madrid, 1961); J. Hamer, *The Church Is a Communion* (New York, 1965); D. Bonhoeffer, *The Communion of Saints. A Dogmatic Inquiry into the Sociology of the Church* (New York, 1963); J. A. Möhler, *Die Einheit in der Kirche* (1825).

4. H. J. Klauck, *Hausgemeinde und Hauskirche im frühen Christentum* (Stuttgart, 1981); R. Banks, *Paul's Idea of Community. The Early House Churches in Their Historical Setting* (Exeter, 1980); J. H. Elliot, *A Home for the Homeless. A Sociological Exegesis of I Peter, Its Situation and Strategy* (Philadelphia, 1981).

the *oikia* as another central New Testament category and word) but also that the participants form a microgroup. They are neither a mass of people nor a fortuitous and heterogeneous assemblage, but a group that must be described as primary, inasmuch as they all know one another, and speak and intervene and communicate in depth.

An important part of these eucharists is the dialogue homily and shared prayer, although the priest continues to be president of the celebration. In these assemblies, greater attention is paid to horizontal communication (among those present) than to vertical (between priest and congregation).

The house liturgy was the characteristic mark of the Christian communities that came into being after the Council. On the other hand, this whole movement often fused with the traditional parish, thereby turning the parish into a community of communities.[5] As a result, the parish liturgy took over some of the typical elements and values of the house celebration; these made possible the formation of macrogroups.

In other instances, however, the traditional parish was left out and thus did not experience the dynamic influence of the house liturgy and the community movement. It remained a clerical enterprise; that is, both its overall management and its type of liturgy were characterized by the focus on the priest.

In my opinion, this is the main reason for the rigidity, formalism, and passivity that are clear marks of many parish Masses both on Sunday and during the week. Rather than forming a community, the faithful resemble a public that remains somewhat detached from what the priest is doing in the santuary. They form not an active, involved group but an assemblage of individuals who passively receive something—and wait for the rite to end so that they can return to their lives outside the church: lives that they view as utterly different from and unconnected with what goes on in the celebration.

Meanwhile, however, the community movement has itself undergone a noteworthy development that must be described and taken into account.

As time passed, these communities began to describe themselves as base communities or communities of the people. The vocabulary reflected an important development in the theology of the Church. "Base" and "people" referred not only, and not so much, to the membership as distinct from the hierarchy, but to the poor and marginalized of society.

This "partisan" sense of the word "people" prevailed over the inclusive, national sense; that is to say, "the people" came to mean the economically feeble and unfairly treated sector of the nation.[6]

5. F. Connan and J. C. Barreau, *Demain, la paroisse* (Paris, 1966).
6. L. Maldonado, "Religiosidad popular," in C. Floristán and J. J. Tamayo, eds., *Conceptos fundamentales de Pastoral* (Madrid, 1981), pp. 874–86.

This shift in meaning represents an effort to revive one of the main thrusts in the message and plan of Jesus for the reign of God. Poverty and marginalization here cease to be an ascetical and moral issue, and become central in the theology of Church and sacraments. This has evidently been one of the main contributions of the theology of liberation.[7]

This development in the community movement has not meant and need not mean that only the poor can celebrate the liturgy, any more than that the communities are made up solely of the poor and the marginalized. What does follow from this new way of looking at things is that the cause of the poor, which is inseparable from the cause of Jesus, ought to be and is present in all aspects of the Christian celebration (as anamnesis of the forgotten and the victimized, their sufferings, and sacrifice, their unsuccessful struggles; as actualizing proclamation of Christian salvation at work against wretched conditions and death, as well as of commitment to the fight against injustice; and, finally, as prevision of hope).[8] To the extent that this change has not occurred, our liturgy is defective; it lacks one of its principal components.

One evident concrete corollary of what I have been saying is that the liturgy should reflect as clearly as possible the culture of the people and, to some extent, the culture of poverty. Recent studies of popular religion can help in bringing about this liturgical inculturation.[9] This major task is inseparable from the issue of liturgical creativity as well as from the sensitive subject of a greater decentralization in the legislative entities of the hierarchy.

I can sum up the thoughts of this section in the term *koinōnia*. In the liturgy, and especially in the Eucharist, there ought to be a sacramental communion with Christ and the Church, and a concomitant sharing of temporal goods or, in other words, a commitment to *agapē*. Where these are missing, we succumb to a dangerous sacramentalism. This "reified" view of the sacraments, for which Protestant theologians so strongly criticized the Catholicism of the preconciliar period, is still to be found in various groups. The reason is the continuing disregard of evangelization, the second of the three factors I mentioned in the beginning as playing an important role in a community-oriented approach to the liturgy.

7. J. Sobrino, *The True Church and the Poor* (Maryknoll, N.Y., 1984); L. Boff, *Ecclesiogenesis: The Base Communities Reinvent the Church* (Maryknoll, N.Y., 1986); idem, *La fe en la periferia del mundo. El camino de la Iglesia con los oprimidos* (Santander, 1981); G. Gutiérrez, "Theology from the Underside of History," in his *The Power of the Poor in History. Selected Writings* (Maryknoll, N.Y., 1983), 169–221.

8. J. B. Metz, "The Church and the People," in his *Faith in History and Society. Towards a Practical Fundamental Theology* (New York, 1980), pp. 136–53; see also 88–99.

9. S. Galilea, *Religiosidad popular y pastoral* (Madrid, 1980); L. Maldonado, *Religiosidad popular. Nostalgia de lo mágico* (Madrid, 1975); idem, *Génesis del catolicismo popular* (Madrid, 1979).

Celebration, Faith, Involvement of All

Evangelization is a major theme that has been extensively developed in the postconciliar period and has produced some practical fruits—for example, the rise of an extensive catechumenal or neocatechumenal movement in connection with the celebration of the sacraments.[10]

The point that interests me here in this movement is the new awareness it has created that the sacraments are signs of faith and presuppose a development of faith. Theologians in recent years have been emphasizing the indissoluble link between faith and sacrament.[11] There must be a corresponding revival in pastoral practice of a concern not to admit to the sacraments those who have not yet opened themselves to the Christian faith. Otherwise, those who take part in our sacramental celebrations will do so for sociological reasons (the pressure of their environment, or sociological Catholicism) or with attitudes inspired by magical ideas. The result will be a breakdown in the community dimension of the liturgy. In parishes where no real effort is made to evangelize and where each major step in the sacramental life is not preceded by neocatechumenal meetings of the community for the purpose of stimulating an authentic commitment to Christ and the Church, we will continue to have the kind of liturgy that is individualistic, privatized, and more or less focused on personal devotion.[12]

Let me pause for a moment to analyze the reasons, located in the very structure of the celebration, why large sectors of the Church have not yet achieved a truly community-oriented liturgy. Here again it can be said that the Council set down some principles and established some new criteria, but that these were not subsequently applied and therefore failed to bear fruit in practice.

The first question to be asked today with regard to the structure of liturgical celebration is: Who is the subject (agent) of Christian celebration? The answer of some contemporary liturgists is that the subject of the celebration is the assembly, the entire assembly.[13] The active subject is therefore not the priest (bishop or presbyter) considered in isolation from the rest of the faithful, as was thought before the Council when in discussion of the "celebrant" mention was made only of the priest or bishop.

There has now been a change of vocabulary, terminology, of the ru-

---

10. C. Floristán, *El catecumenado* (Madrid, 1972); J. Vermett and H. Bourgeois, *Seront-ils chrétiens? Perspectives catéchumenales* (Paris, 1973).

11. L. Villette, *Foi et sacrement* (Paris, 1959–64, 2 vols.).

12. R. Coffy, *Eglise signe du salut au milieu des hommes* (Paris, 1972).

13. A. Verheul, "L'assemblée célébrante et ses services," *QL*, 2 (1984) 135–52; Y. Congar, "L''ecclesia' ou communauté chrétienne sujet intégral de l'action liturgique," in *La liturgie après Vatican II* (Paris, 1967), pp. 241–82; A. G. Martimort, *Mens corcordet voci* (Paris, 1983), pp. 193–246; H. Legrand, "Grace et institution dans l'Eglise," in *L'Eglise: institution et foi* (Brussels, 1979), pp. 139–72.

brics. In referring to the priest the new sacramentary speaks not of "the celebrant" but of "the celebrating priest," thus suggesting that there are other celebrants as well. In addition, it may be recalled that until the high Middle Ages "celebrant" referred to the entire community.[14]

A liturgical action is a celebration of the *ecclesia* of gathered assembly. All its members are or should be involved and participate in the celebration. The subject or chief agent of the celebration is the entire ecclesial body, that is, those who are gathered and form a group of persons united among themselves by the bonds of faith and sacrament. For this reason the conciliar constitution on the liturgy says:

Liturgical services are not private (*particulares*) functions, but are celebrations belonging to the Church, which is the "sacrament of unity," namely, the holy people united and ordered under their bishops.

Therefore liturgical services involve the whole Body of the Church; they manifest it and have effects upon it; but they also concern the individual members of the Church in different ways, according to their different orders, offices, and actual participation.[15]

There is a principal celebrant, of course, but he is Christ, who is present in the liturgical action under various signs. The Council lists among these signs not only the persons of the priests and more important ministers but the assembly as such, gathered as a believing and praying community:

Christ is always present to his Church, especially in its liturgical celebrations. He is present . . . in the person of the minister . . . He is present in his word. He is present, lastly, when the Church prays and sings. . . .

From this it follows that every liturgical celebration . . . is an action of Christ the Priest and of his Body which is the Church.[16]

This declericalized view of the subject of liturgical action has led to another important change of vocabulary since the Council. No longer do we speak, as before the Council, of the active participation of the faithful or say that the faithful should participate actively in the liturgy. That was clerical language, for it seemed to presuppose that the priest does what is important and that the faithful take a subsidiary part in that principal action. It suggested that the priest did not participate, with the faithful, in the saving action of Christ. It is clear now, however, that he acts not only *in persona Christi* but also *in persona Ecclesiae*.[17]

This is why all the presidential prayers (the formularies of the priest, in preconciliar parlance) are written in the plural. They must also be endorsed and "received" by the assembly through its "Amen." Formular-

14. B. Droste, *"Celebrare" in der römischen Liturgiesprache. Eine liturgietheologische Untersuchung* (Munich, 1963), pp. 11.

15. *Sacrosanctum Concilium*, § 26 (*DOL*, 1, no. 26).

16. Ibid. (*DOL*, 1, no. 7).

17. B. D. Marliangeas, "In persona Christi. In persona Ecclesiae," in *La liturgie après Vatican II* (Paris, 1967), pp. 283–88; idem, *Clés pour une théologie du ministère* (Paris, 1978).

ies written in the singular were creations of the Middle Ages when, as I pointed out above, the sense of the assembly was lost.

Since the Council, then, we have ceased to speak of participating and have begun to speak of celebrating. In a celebration all are active subjects. Insofar as they form an assembly, all are the principal subject at the sensible, perceptible level in the structure of the celebration. The liturgical assembly is a structured community made up of individuals and subgroups carrying out various ministries or services; among these, of course, the priestly role of presidency stands out.

A glance at the "General Instruction" or general introduction to the new Missal makes it immediately clear that preeminence is given to the part played jointly by president and faithful as a single unit, and not to the various specialized functions. These joint activities are mentioned twice as often as are the specialized.[18] Thus it is the entire community, including the celebrant, that recites the Confiteor, sings Glory to God in the highest, the Creed, Sanctus, and Lamb of God, listens to the readings, gives the responses to them, and receives the body and blood of Christ.

The eucharistic prayer is admittedly a presidential prayer the priest alone is to say. But in its commentary on the main elements of this prayer the "General Instruction" adds:

In the epiclesis the Church calls down the Holy Spirit on the eucharistic gifts; in the anamnesis the Church remembers the paschal mystery of Christ; the Church offers the spotless victim to the Father.[19]

But, despite all these theological and pastoral instructions, the twenty years since the Council have not witnessed the calm, balanced acceptance of responsibility for the liturgy by the assembly as such, that is, by the entire group of faithful who are present and take part in a series of ministries, of diversified but interrelated roles. Many assemblies continue to resemble amorphous masses. They do not become structured groups actively involved in various specialized ministries or functions assigned to various members. There has been a persisting, or revived, liturgical clericalism in which the priest monopolizes all these functions and thus serves as a "one-man band."

According to the mind and norms of the Council, the role of the priest in the celebration is fundamental and indispensable, but it is also to be unobtrusive and restrained. It consists in performing certain essential actions and reciting the presidential prayers, which are few in number.

18. A. Goossens, "Het aandeel van de celebrant en de gemeenschap in de eucharistieviering," *Tijdschrift voor Liturgie*, 67 (1983) 16–38.

19. See the "General Instruction of the Roman Missal," 29, 31, 44, 55b, 56e, 33–34, 56i, 55c, 55e, 55f. Also to be mentioned is the constitution on the liturgy, § 14, which speaks of the priesthood of the faithful and contains another important biblical approach to the doctrine of the assembly that I am presenting here.

The priest is also to show the relevance of the word that has been proclaimed (his homiletic function) and issue various cautions or exhortations to the assembly.

All the other actions are to be shared by other liturgical ministers who vary according to circumstance and occasion. Always fundamental are the ministries or services of reading, prayer (intentions, exhortations), singing, the altar, communion, welcome, and preparation. Some of these ministers have traditional names: deacon, lector, psalmist, cantor, acolyte, porter, candlebearer. Others are new and represent shifts in emphasis: commentator, leader of song—instituted and noninstituted ministries.

There can obviously be no question here of expounding a detailed theory of what the liturgy as a communal act ought to be. I am concerned only with what has been and is going on after twenty years of conciliar reform.

Present Concerns

It is important, of course, to take note of the possibilities opened up by the new conciliar constitution on the liturgy; I refer to the principles and norms cast like seeds into the life of the Church. It is no less important, however, to try to get a closer look at some of the undertakings that have succeeded or proved abortive after twenty years.

I cannot provide the reader with the results of sociological surveys; none have as yet been undertaken. I can, however, profit from a few studies and general testimonies that reflect with some accuracy the general state of affairs. In a recent volume published in Italy, for example, a layperson raises precisely the question that concerns me here: What could the laity have done, or done better, in these twenty years to apply and give practical embodiment to the principles and norms of the Council?[20]

Here is a summary of his opinions, which are realistic, modestly proposed but also critical and unsparing. They yield a list of things not done, of things that could be improved and are desirable, and, above all, of things that are concrete:

1. Working with the priest to choose passages of scripture well adapted to the celebrating assembly.

2. Organizing the "ministry of welcome." In society, even the simplest symposium, the most modest congress, has a "hospitality committee" to welcome participants. But the Church neglects this task and allows its place of worship to look like a kind of open marketplace.

20. See *Concilio e riforma liturgica* (Milan, 1984), pp. 59–72.

3. Organizing the ministry of song, not only by restoring or improving a choir, but also by providing leadership for the singing of the congregation.

4. Preparing much more seriously for the ministry of reading.

5. Restoring the procession with the gifts, after the manner, for example, of black Africa.

6. Helping the priest or deacon to prepare the homily for a better application of the Gospel to daily life and contemporary circumstances.

7. Taking the initiative in the prayer of the faithful, which is not meant to be a prayer supplied by a functionary in the episcopal curia who must periodically send out generic, abstract formularies.

8. Those in charge of the ministry of welcome should also take charge of the procession with the gifts.

9. Bestowing special care on the "commentaries" so that they do not degenerate into a kind of pseudo sermon.

10. Receiving suggestions and proposals for activities, so that the liturgical celebration may not be simply an experience of thanksgiving or contemplation, but can also be translated and prolonged into deeds.

11. During this period of application of the liturgical reform, the laity, like the entire Christian community, should have been giving living witness to what they celebrate under sacramental signs.

12. But, before all and above all, the laity should have grasped more fully and put more fully into practice the truth that all are and form a true celebrating community; that all are active, including those who have no special ministry. What is at issue here is a state of soul, a disposition, an attitude the laity should have acquired before asserting any claim to roles, however necessary and important these may be.

This is a summary of the testimony of a layperson who, in my view, can be taken as quite representative of the prevailing state of opinion in many parish communities.

As the final part of my analysis, I should like to raise a question that is in one sense quite limited but in another quite comprehensive and that today plays a determining role in the life of the Church as a community. It brings together several of the themes touched on in the preceding pages, but also brings to light new aspects of what has been happening since the Council. In what follows, therefore, I shall be expanding and developing in a particular direction the observations I have been making up to this point.

I shall take as my starting point some lucid observations of the bishop of Breda on the observance of Sunday.[21] He points out two phenomena in this area: first, the loss of the Christian religious sense of Sunday in

21. W. Ernst, "Mon souci d'évêque pour la célébration liturgique du dimanche," QL, 2 (1984) 129–33.

developed societies; secondly, the diversity among Catholics in regard to attendance at the Sunday assembly.

As a matter of fact, in broad areas of "developed" societies, Sunday is no longer the Lord's Day. Christians do not gather in vast numbers in the name of the Lord. Only a dwindling minority continues to do so. In any case, the gathering or assembly of Christians does not put its mark on the life of contemporary civil society. This is true of all secularized milieus.

The masses no longer attend the Sunday gathering, because they have a misconception of the fact of secularization. Due to its negative influence on consciences, secularization amounts in fact to a dissipation of the sense of faith.

There are, however, those who have ceased to attend the Sunday Eucharist but continue to think of themselves as openly Christian and faithful to the gospel message, the latter being accepted in what they regard as its authentic secular version. They help the needy, fight for justice, work for peace. These, too, are a minority, like the minority faithful to the eucharistic assembly on the Lord's Day.

There is thus a new form of division in the Church today: the existence of two minorities or groups thinking and behaving in very different ways with regard to the celebration of the liturgy. For one group the real liturgy is life itself, and temporal and political involvement. For the other it is the explicit confession of faith, the sacramental thanksgiving, the weekly meeting with brothers and sisters at the Eucharist. There is thus a dissociation between Christian liturgical life and the socio-political commitment of Christians in some secularized nations of the West. Does not this dissociation mean a break in communion?

Instead of offering a discursive or speculative appraisal of these two positions,[22] I prefer to report more directly and literally the thinking of the Dutch bishop I have been citing; his thought shows pastoral wisdom and respect for individuals.[23]

He begins by expressing a wish, not a condemnation. He does this in truly paternal language that allows a deep sense of Christian hope, confidence, and even ingenuousness to shine through.

It would be, he says, a tremendous boon to the Church and to society if the convinced Christians who celebrate the Lord's Day and the convinced Christians who seek justice and peace were to meet and unite. Only if they join together can the continued existence of the Church in the world of today and tomorrow be ensured.

22. As everyone knows, there is an extensive literature on the secularization of the cultic sphere in the New Testament; see L. Maldonado, *La secularización de la liturgia* (Madrid, 1969), for a synthesis and appraisal.

23. The French episopate has provided a very complete treatment of this problem of division among Christians with regard to the Sunday assembly. See R. Coffy *Une Eglise qui célébre et qui prie* (Paris, 1974).

When the Church celebrates the Sunday eucharist, it remembers that Jesus the Christ was raised from the dead by God. It confesses that the divine promise of salvation and life was embodied in the trustworthy action of Jesus and that through his resurrection a life-giving power that saves from death has manifested its presence in the world of human beings. Sunday, the Lord's Day, is the day that gives hope where there is no hope.

Moreover, it is of vital importance for society that there be kept alive the hope that sustains action for justice and peace, and keeps human beings working in the service of others. The Church, which lives by hope, has for its duty to make faith in God the root of faith in justice and peace; to strengthen these commitments for perseverance in adversity; and to fortify against discouragement those who may grow weak from their efforts in the struggle.

It is in this perspective (Bishop Ernst continues) that we should view the Sunday celebration. When Christians who accept responsibility amid the events of society draw energy for their commitment from the life of faith, and when Christians who celebrate Sunday extend the celebration into actions and responsible deeds, we shall see the Church built up *and* society served. Sunday will then become a source of salvation for the human world.

The Church not only keeps the memory of the death and resurrection of Jesus alive through history. It also has the task of establishing peace in the world of human beings and of doing this in such a way that all will have justice done to them. The Sunday celebration signifies that the two missions are connected.

The bishop of Breda voices two concerns. The first and more important is that the Sunday assembly of Christians go on being held and that it develop. The Sunday gathering in the name of the Lord is necessary for the community of Christians, which in this way bears witness to Jesus Christ. It is also necessary for the faithful if they are to keep their faith alive. Those who remain faithful to the Sunday assembly carry on the Church's task of remembering Jesus the Christ until he comes again; they also offer those who do not do this the opportunity of doing it. Moreover, they will have to exercise their societal responsibilities in union with this remembrance of Jesus Christ.

The second concern is that two kinds of Christian community may develop: one exclusively liturgical and catechetical, the other exclusively social and political.

The pastoral goal is clear: those who give priority to the remembrance of the death and resurrection of Jesus and those who follow Jesus Christ by promoting understanding among human beings, alleviating wretchedness, fighting against injustice, forming communities, and preaching peace, must celebrate Sunday together and thus build up the Church among their fellow men and women.

If these two groups could discover that the liturgy and social responsibility are closely linked in the celebration, then both those whose goal is social action and those whose first concern is the liturgy could alike play a role in preparation for the celebration and in the celebration itself. The liturgy must of course retain its proper character and not be turned into a political meeting. At the same time, however, those whose lives are filled with commitments to society must be able to find in the liturgy the deepest of their reasons for temporal activities.

The liturgy must be able to lead persons back from their immediate concerns to the roots of their existence, that is, to those depths at which all can see that they are united in a single faith. At the same time, they can find there the fulcrum for their lives and an indication of the direction they are to take.

What is lacking is a liturgical style that can bring out the relationship between faith and human responsibility, offer human beings solid grounds for trust in God, and reveal to them the meaning of their lives— a meaning in which the path taken by God in coming to human beings becomes the path by which human beings are to go out to their fellows.

This kind of celebration and celebratory language must form a way to union between Christians now divided in their views of the liturgy. In it the traditional elements of liturgical action will be retained, although renewed and made more relevant. Those taking part will listen to "all that the scriptures say about him" (Luke 24:27) and will answer by means of the psalms of Israel and other songs expressing the whole life of human beings in their relationship to God. The language of symbols, witness to life, preaching based on the faith of the Church according to the scriptures, traditional prayer and spontaneous prayer, the sacramental signs—all these can provide a fertile ground for union and encounter among all Christians.

It is evident that the ultimate goal of this episcopal document from the world of Central Europe is basically the same as what the theology of liberation looks for in a community-oriented liturgy.

The First and Third Worlds are in agreement despite their different perspectives. This is a sign of unity amid the plurality and even division of Catholics.[24]

24. Attempts at an appraisal of these twenty years of postconciliar liturgy can be found in special issues of journals: *Phase*, 137 (1983); *La Maison-Dieu*, 157 (1984). See also Bishop F. Favreau, *La liturgie* (Paris, 1983).

V. REJECTIONS OF THE COUNCIL

Daniele Menozzi

16. Opposition to the Council (1966–84)

The Several Faces of Opposition to the Council: Limits of this Study

It is not an easy task to reconstruct in even a summary way the history of opposition to the Council during the twenty years since its close. To begin with, the positions taken in open and declared rejection of the Council compose a varied and composite montage of groups, currents of thought, political and religious movements, and periodicals, which as a whole has attracted very little scholarly attention.

In this montage we find, on the one side, a radical outlook shared, despite divergent approaches, by a number of circles ranging from the followers of Abbé Georges de Nantes and their journal, *Contreréforme catholique au XXe siècle*, to the Dominicans of the *Cahiers de Cassiciacum*; from E. Gerstner's *Liga katholischer Traditionalisten* to the readers of the various national editions of the periodical *Fortes in fide*, edited by N. Barbara; from the groups that follow the messianic priest J. Saenz y Ariaga to the groups that draw their inspiration from the biweekly *The Remnant* or the ideas of philosopher P. Scortesco.[1] All these (the list gives only a few examples) have a basic thesis that is pretty much the same in all cases: inasmuch as the pope promulgated the acts of a Council that is opposed to tradition under various headings, his schism and heresy have in fact created a *sede vacante* situation, which can be ended only if Rome emends the conciliar texts.[2]

---

1. There is a list, though quite incomplete, of traditionalist periodicals and movements in W. Siebel, *Katholisch oder Konziliar. Die Krise der Kirche heute* (Munich/Vienna, 1978), pp. 449–56. An analysis of the directions they take (with special reference to the German-speaking world) is given in A. Schifferle, *Marcel Lefebvre. Ärgernis und Besinnung* (Kevelaer, 1983), pp. 271–313.

2. G. des Lauriers, "Le siège apostolique est-il vacant?," *Cahiers de Cassiciacum*, 1 (1979) 5–111. For indications of the ground that these various positions share, see *Cahiers de Cassiciacum*, 2 (1980) 47–90; *Itinéraires*, 27/162 (1971) 243–60; *La contreréforme catholique au XXe siècle*, 190 (1983) 10–12; 193 (1983) 15–16; 196 (1984) 4; 197 (1984) 13; *Relazioni religiose* for March 29, 1977.

On the other hand, opposition to the Council is present in associations (*Una voce, Opus sacerdotale, Credo, Silenziosi della Chiesa*, and others) that profess obedience to the hierarchy but are fighting for a return to the Church of Pius XII. In their view, the decisions of Vatican II, which was a valid but exclusively pastoral synod, have no dogmatic value and are therefore not binding.[3]

Between these two extremes there is a broad gamut of tendencies that are in dialogue or, more often, disagreement with one another.[4] How, then, can a writer assume that he can provide reliable information on the dynamics at work in opposition to the Council unless he has first placed at the reader's disposal a sufficiently detailed map of a world divided and interrelated as I have indicated and a systematic list of what it has produced?[5] And there are still other factors that make analysis even more difficult. For it is clear that the reception of Vatican II does not necessarily imply acceptance of the new direction that the majority of the council fathers wanted to give to the life of the Church.

After returning to their dioceses, the members of the *Coetus internationalis*, for instance, emphasized those passages that the minority had succeeded in introducing into the conciliar documents in order to nullify their deeper thrust, while paying lip service to their wording. Thus R. Graber, bishop of Regensburg, based his pastoral activity on an extrapolation from the text of those passages that allowed him to present Vatican II as desiring a rigidly counter-reformational church.[6] Others, like Cardinal Siri, backed a broader thesis: the postconciliar crisis has its roots in the discrepancy between the letter of the Council and the interpretations of it that were being purveyed by those sectors of the episcopate which during the Council had tried in vain to negate the tradition.[7]

3. *DC*, 66 (1969) 1094; 67 (1970) 249; 68 (1971) 139–41 and 1071; 72 (1975) 241 and 690; 73 (1976) 788; 75 (1978) 692. Data on associations of priests can be found in *La pensée catholique*, 24/122 (1969) 55–62; 25/124 (1970) 5–7; 26/133 (1971) 14–27.

4. See the efforts of the periodical *Itinéraires* to bring various traditionalist groups together in agreement on a minimal common line: 27/155 (1971) 1–11; 28/159 (1972) 143–52; 29/169 (1973) 224–26; 29/173 (1973) 259–61. Documents from these circles have been collected in A. Figueras, *Les catholiques de tradition* (Fontenoy-sous-Bois, 1983).

5. Studies concentrating on individual nations do exist. I shall mention only G. Tassani, *La cultura politica della destra cattolica* (Rome, 1976); C. Antoine, *L'intégrisme brasilien* (Paris, 1973); I. Baumer, "Die Frömmigkeitsbild der Traditionalisten," in J. Baumgartner, ed., *Wiederentdeckung der Volksreligiosität* (Regensburg, 1979), pp. 53–81.

6. See his statements in *Hirtenbriefe aus Deutschland, Österreich und der Schweiz*, published by the Institut für kirchliche Zeitgeschichte, Salzburg: 1966, pp. 253–56; 1971, pp. 180–81; 1972, pp. 206–8; 1973, pp. 254–57; 1977, pp. 206–14; 1981, pp. 350–74. The idea of a return to the preconciliar Church finds fuller expression in Graber's book, *Am Vorabend des Konzils* (Abensburg, 1973); see the review of the French translation in *La pensée catholique*, 29/148 (1974) 93–95. Finally, it is worth mentioning that it was the Regensburg diocese that gave the imprimatur for the German translation of Dietrich von Hildebrand's *The Trojan Horse in the City of God* (Chicago, 1967), which develops themes of anitconciliar traditionalism.

7. The theme shows up in statements published in the review *Renovatio*—e.g., 7 (1972) 491–94—and in writings now collected in G. Siri, *Opere. 1. La giovinezza della Chiesa* (Pisa,

One example may stand for all: G. de Proença Sigaud, archbishop of Diamantina, Brazil, who on the morrow of the Council's closing proposed to follow in his future acitivity the line of purely formal adherence to its decisions: attempts at innovation in the Church were to be met by pointing to the passages that the minority had managed to get included in the decrees and constitutions.[8]

On the other hand, the refusal to see in Vatican II a decisive change of direction for the Church won approval in an area extending far beyond the members of the *Coetus* and their sympathizers. I need only recall in this context the attitude of such movements as *Communion and Liberation*, concerned exclusively with finding in the conciliar texts confirmation of positions developed independently of it.[9]

References to renewal of the Church, however, although making it possible to identify modes of apparent, limited, or alleged acceptance of the Council, do not seem helpful in discerning more subtle forms of anti-conciliarism. It is well known that the very large sector of the Church that is in favor of the conciliar aggiornamento has not given a homogeneous interpretation of it. For example, some circles, influenced by writers who before and during the Council fought for reform (for example, J. Maritain, J. Daniélou, H. de Lubac, and H. Urs von Balthasar), subsequently grew fearful that the Council itself would lead to a secularization of Catholicism[10] and a collapse of church authority.[11] The result was an

1983); see esp. pp. 175–97. There is thus a broad agreement in traditionalist circles on the theses expressed here; see the review of Siri's *Opere* in *Sí sí no no*, 11/2 (1985) 4–5.

8. G. de Proença Sigaud, "Le concile et le prêtre traditionnel," *La pensée catholique*, 21/100 (1966) 13–24.

9. *Realizzare il concilio. Il contributo di Communione e liberazione*, a supplement to *Litterae communionis*, 11 (1982).

10. J. Maritain, *The Peasant of the Garonne. An Old Layman Questions Himself about the Present Time* (New York, 1968). Maritain's views are repeated by Charles Journet in *Nova et vetera*, 41 (1967) 255–74, and 43 (1968) 245–73. It is no accident that *La pensée catholique*, which had always opposed Maritain's philosophical views, showed appreciation for this book: 22/108 (1967) 64–76. The same worry about tendencies emerging from the Council was shown in J. Daniélou, *Prayer as a Political Problem* (New York, 1967), and in an article answering criticisms leveled at the book by circles open to the wishes of Vatican II: "Religion et civilisation. Réponse à quelques objections," *Etudes*, 326 (1967) 418–20. To be noted again is the favorable reaction of *La pensée catholique* to these works—22/107 (1967) 5–18—and the fact that this journal gave sympathetic emphasis to the fixism of Daniélou's vision of the church-world relationship (see esp. 30/154 [1975] 20–28). This journal of French traditionalism showed similar synpathy for the writings of H. Urs von Balthasar, esp. *Cordula oder der Ernstfall* (Einsiedeln, 1966; Engl. trans., *The Moment of Christian Witness* [New York, 1969]), which expressed fear that the Council might occasion a movement away from the direct opposition between Church and world; see *La pensée catholique*, 23/117 (1968) 104–8. In addition, from 1972 on, the periodical *Communio* would enable the Swiss theologian to make clear his tendency (shared by broad sectors of the Church) to throw obstacles in the way of possible innovations resulting from Vatican II.

11. H. de Lubac, "The Church in Crisis," *Theology Digest*, 17 (1969) 312–15 (complete text); idem. *The Motherhood of the Church (and) Particular Churches in the Universal Church* (San Francisco, 1982); J. Daniélou, "La profession de foi de Paul VI," *Etudes*, 329 (1968) 599–607,

educational effort by these circles to spread an interpretation of *Gaudium et spes* as legitimizing recourse to a secular Christendom as model for defining the relationship between Christianity and the world, and an interpretation of *Lumen gentium* in the light of traditional Roman monarchist ecclesiology. Shall these positions too be the subject of my investigation?

At this point we run into a difficulty that is inherent in the conciliar texts themselves: they do not form a monolithic whole, but—I prescind from the reception of the theses of the minority, usually not a matter of great importance—are the product of impulses coming from various tendencies present within the majority itself. Sometimes these impulses led to homogeneous compromise formulas, but in other cases the conciliar fathers settled for a juxtaposition of heterogeneous ideas. It is therefore understandable that the postconciliar period should show rather divergent judgments on renewal. This does not mean, however, that it is impossible to discern some basic directions by which to measure the conciliar call to aggiornamento. In fact, on the morrow of the Council's closing, M. D. Chenu pointed out the hermeneutical criteria to be used in a correct interpretation of its work: a synoptic reading of successive redactions of the documents in order to identify the underlying intention; location of the texts within that historical thrust, so unequivocally approved by the Council, toward self-understanding by the Church and definition of its relationship with history.[12]

Against this background, the tendencies I mentioned can indeed find in the final documents elements that support their vision of the direction enjoined by Vatican II, but they seem nonetheless to disregard its spirit. It was at bottom this very outlook that Cardinals Suenens and Alfrink were denouncing, in 1969 and 1971, respectively, when they said that Rome itself was providing the model for an application of the Council that nullified its inner logic.[13] How, then, am I to avoid including in an analysis of opposition to the Council these subtle, yet real and influential forms of resistance to Vatican II that have been developing within the framework of acceptance of it?

But a further problem makes the picture to be studied even more complex and elusive. As is well known, the congress held in Brussels in 1970 by *Concilium*—the periodical founded expressly to take up, study more fully, and broadcast the themes discussed during the Council—closed with a seemingly surprising watchword for the future: "Beyond the

---

in which the writer judges the pope's creed to be "an essential complement to the work done by the Second Vatican Council" and thus lends credit to the thesis that the Council needs to be completed by papal statements. On this point, too, see C. Journet in *Nova et vetera*, 40 (1965) 120–31 and 44 (1969) 161–66; although Journet distances himself from traditionalism, he argues for an interpretation of the Council in the light of Roman ecclesiology.

12. M. D. Chenu, "La chiesa nella storia: fondamento e norme della interpretazione del concilio," *Idoc Dossiers*, 1 (1966) 19.

13. J. de Broucker, *The Suenens Dossier* (Notre Dame, Ind., 1970); and Alfrink's statement in *Idoc Internazionale*, 2/20 (1971) 13–14.

Council!"[14] And, more generally, the theologies of earthly realities that arose as a result of rethinking the Church-world relationship proposed by *Gaudium et spes* gave currency henceforth to the thesis that the Council, although positive as far as it went, was linked to a moment of history now irretrievably past and had little contribution to make to the resolution of the problems it had even helped to raise.[15] But does not the call to go beyond Vatican II imply a questioning of its entire value? To what extent can the abandonment of a fixed vision of Christianity be said to have a place within the perspective of the Council itself?

The questions that a first approach to opposition to the Council has successively brought out not only shed light on the multiform and composite character of this opposition; they also allow me to define the limits of my essay. The lack of specialized studies of the positions taken in the various tendencies I have been pointing out in the Church and, at the same time, the limited space at my disposal will not allow me to embark on the comprehensive presentation that is both desirable and needed. I do think it possible, however, to deal with the subject through some illustrative cross sections, that is, to trace some important aspects of opposition to the Council in each of the main settings in which this opposition seems to manifest itself.

In the area of explicit rejection, for example, the attitude of Archbishop Lefebvre to the Council seems important by reason of the objective influence it has had.[16] In the area of formal acceptance, the denunciations of Cardinals Suenens and Alfrink call for special attention, rather than the basically discounted positions of the members of the *Coetus* or the intellectual work of those theologians who have been rather appropriately described as "repentant prophets": I shall therefore examine the judgment that the papacy has passed on the Council.[17] Finally, among those who propose going beyond Vatican II, it seems to me that a clear separation from conciliar positions can be seen especially in those sectors in the Church that have set out to interpret the Council in light of the Marxist view of history: The "Christians for Socialism" movement therefore provides a privileged vantage point (I am well aware that it is not the only one) for entering into this perspective.[18]

14. *L'avvenire della chiesa. Bruxelles 1970. Il libro del congresso* (Brescia, 1970). See also the articles in *Le Monde* for Sept. 15 and 19, 1970, which summarized the moods of the meeting. The theme had already been proposed by K. Rahner and J. B. Metz in *La risposta dei teologi* (Brescia, 1969), pp. 61–62.

15. There is a survey in R. Winling, *La théologie contemporaine (1945–1980)* (Paris, 1983), pp. 363–90.

16. The Lefebvre case is discussed in E. Poulat, *Une église ébranlée. Changement, conflit et continuité de Pie XII à Jean-Paul II* (Tournai, 1980), 266–81, and in Schifferle, *Marcel Lefebvre* (n. 1, above), pp. 33–195, where, however, the approach is more systematic than historical. On the other hand, Schifferle has an updated bibliography.

17. An attempt to synthesize this judgment is made in R. Laurentin, "Paul VI et l'après-concile," in *Paul VI et la modernité dans l'Eglise* (Rome, 1984), pp. 569–601.

18. A history of this movement, told from within, is given in J. Ramos Regidor and A. Gecchelin, *Cristiani per il socialismo* (Milan, 1977).

Having thus limited the field of inquiry, and having explained that I am examining only one aspect, even if an obviously important one, of a much more complex phenomenon whose parts are interconnected, I shall attempt a historical reconstruction of the anticonciliar movement that can serve as groundwork for more complete and comprehensive studies.

The First Manifestations of Anticonciliarism

The initial phase of anticonciliarism can be located in the period between the close of the Council and the beginning of the 1970s. The first point to be made about this period is that the positions taken by Lefebvre differed markedly depending on whether they were public or private.

His public judgments implied a substantial acceptance of the Council, although he had his own interpretation of it. Thus, in the homily he delivered in March 1966, on occasion of the annual pilgrimage of the Croisés de Notre Dame, the archbishop asked what was the basic direction of the renewal intended by Vatican II.[19] In his answer he made two points: on the one hand, the Council showed the faithful the path of interior personal change as contrasted with renewal understood as transformation of the world and structural reform of the Church. On the other hand, the council fathers proposed not a change but an intensification of traditional post-tridentine modes of behavior. Without issuing any direct challenges to the Council, the prelate concluded that that body had wanted only to promote a deeper understanding and more general application of the model of holiness proper to the Counter-Reformation period.

In private, however, he expressed a quite different attitude. In his reply of December 1966 to Cardinal Ottaviani's circular letter asking for information about truths now being called into doubt in the Church, he said that by rejecting the preparatory schemata Vatican II had opened the door "to the worst tragedy that the Church has ever experienced."[20] From Pius IX to Pius XII the popes had condemned in turn Catholic liberalism, modernism, the tenets of Le Sillon, communism, and neo-modernism. It would be going against all the evidence to deny that "the Council has allowed those professing errors and tendencies condemned by the popes . . . to believe in good faith that their teachings are now approved." An impassable gulf had thus been opened between the innovations encouraged by the assembly and "the truths which the authentic magisterium of the Church has taught as definitively belonging to the treasury of tradition."

19. The homily was published in La pensée catholique 21/102 (1966) 38–43.
20. M. Lefebvre, J'accuse le concile (Martigny, 1976), pp. 107–12.

The reasons for this discrepancy are not difficult to identify. In all his public statements of this period, Lefebvre was in fact telling the reigning pope to work toward keeping the Church on the track that he, Lefebvre, was pointing out.[21] Even in his 1969 address to the Autonomous Faculty of Economics and Law in Paris, on the crisis in the contemporary Church (an address in which the attack on the Council emerges more clearly), the rigidity of his views was tempered by the thought that the activities of Paul VI were providing an adequate answer to the attempted subversion of tradition.[22]

On the other hand, during these same years circles close to the archbishop were speaking out along the same lines. To see an outlook comparable to his we need only page through the volumes of La pensée catholique, a periodical that provided ample space for his statements and with which he had long-standing close ties.[23] The editor of La pensée catholique was the pugnacious L. J. Lefèvre. In his opposition to Concilium, which he charged with forcing the texts of Vatican II in order to make them show an openness to errors of the modern world that had been repeatedly condemned by the popes,[24] Lefèvre did not restrict himself in his editorials to insisting that a correct interpretation of the conciliar documents could be achieved only by reading them in continuity with the decrees of Trent and Vatican I. He claimed in addition that the pope himself was presently endorsing this interpretation.[25]

The periodical did at times undoubtedly seem to show some impatience with Rome for its failure to issue legislation that would irrevocably determine the ways in which the Council was to be implemented and thus put an end to the effort of the "neo-modernists" to adapt the documents to their views.[26] The prevailing tendency, however, was to regard the statements of Paul VI—especially his Creed, Humanae vitae, and some addresses on the crisis in the contemporary Church—as giving secure backing to the basic thesis advanced by the periodical, namely, that Vatican II did not break with the past but was in complete continuity with the preconciliar Church.[27]

It can be said in summary that, although Lefebvre and his followers had during this period already reached the point of substantial rejection

21. M. Lefebvre, A Bishop Speaks. Writings and Addresses, 1963–1975 (Edinburgh, n.d.), pp. 49–55.

22. Ibid., pp. 69–70.

23. A founder and co-director of the journal was V.-A. Berto, who was Lefebvre's personal theologian at the Council and then secretary of the Coetus. His interventions on the schemata have now been published in Pour la sainte èglise romaine (Paris, 1976).

24. La pensée catholique, 22/110 (1967) 20–25; 24/118 (1969) 8–19.

25. L. J. Lefèvre, "Petrus locutus est," La pensée catholique 23/115–16 (1968) 15–19; idem, "Et le pape . . . a t'il encore le droit de parler?" ibid., 24/119 (1959) 5–17.

26. La pensée catholique, 21/103 (1966) 20–26; 24/119 (1969) 61.

27. This view found expression especially in connection with Cardinal Felici's reply to Cardinal Suenens's interview in Osservatore romano, July 3, 1969: see L. J. Lefèvre, "Y a-t-il eu un concile Vatican II? Oui ou non . . . ," La pensée catholique, 24/121 (1969) 5–21.

of the Council precisely because it meant a decisive shift of direction in the life of the Church, they still thought they could turn it into a confirmation of their vision by an effort at interpretation that had a definite basis in the direction being given to the Church by the pope. Was this simply an attempt to turn the papal magisterium into a support for opposition to the Council? Or was there rather an objective convergence in lines of thought? We are thus brought to the problem of the judgment of Paul VI on the ecumenical council.

It may seem even paradoxical to ask what was the attitude to Vatican II of a pope who at the beginning of his ministry had actively worked to promote the punctual conclusion of its labors and who shortly before his death had said, in a kind of testamentary review of his activity, that he had had but a single program: the Council.[28] And yet the question becomes relevant even if we remember only that in his programmatic encyclical *Ecclesiam Suam* Paul VI, although assuring the fathers of the Council that they were completely free, had also reminded them that the pope was not bound by the decisions of the assembly.[29] This position was then exemplified concretely by the *nota praevia* he ordered introduced into *Lumen gentium*. In short, the substantial agreement of the pope with the directions being taken by the majority turns out to be a real question.

Furthermore, some aspects of this problem had already been brought into the open. As early as 1965, E. Schillebeeckx, for example, observed with concern that the program of ecclesial aggiornamento emerging from the pope's addresses was based on a letter-oriented vision of the conciliar documents and was in substantial contrast to the dynamism the majority of the council fathers had intended the documents to embody.[30] And in fact it cannot be denied that Paul VI regarded the closing of the Council as also bringing an end to the effort to understand the limits and modalities of Church renewal. In his opinion, all that was needed was the juridical and administrative application of the decisions reached.[31] But this was simply to evade the plea that the Council, basing itself on what John XXIII had said in his opening discourse as he looked to the future, expressed in some passages of its documents, namely, that there should be a continuous rereading of Christianity in the light of the signs of the times the Gospel was making visible in the contemporary world.[32]

28. *Insegnamenti di Paolo VI*, 15 (1978) 489.

29. *AAS*, 56 (1964) 622.

30. E. Schillebeeckx, "Bilancio del concilio," *Idoc Dossiers*, 4 (1966) 1. A historical synthesis of the pope's attitude to the Council is given in B. Ulianich, "Concilio e magistero di Paolo VI," *Il Regno–Documenti*, 21 (1976) 136–40, and G. Miccoli, "Note su cristianesimo e chiesa cattolica in Italia," in *Chiesa in Italia. 1975–78* (Brescia, 1978), pp. 16–19.

31. *Insegnamenti di Paolo VI*, 5 (1967) 302–10. One of the most faithful interpreters of the Council along this line seems to have been Cardinal G. H. Garrone; see his *Tempête sur l'Eglise* (Paris, 1969) pp. 163–72, and esp. his *L'Eglise* (Paris, 1972).

32. G. Alberigo, "Cristianesimo e storia nel Vaticano II," *Cristianesimo nella storia*, 5 (1984) 577–92. On the approach outlined by Pope John and its limited reception at the

At this level, however, the pope's perspective always remained one of substantial fidelity to the decisions of the Council, even if fidelity was given a narrow and minimalist interpretation as a result of his prevailing concern. This attitude of the pope, however, might have been adequately explained by the exigencies of government and the necessities imposed by governance of the Church. But the problem becomes a more thorny one as soon as we examine more closely Paul VI's judgment on the meaning and value of the Council precisely in relation to an aggiornamento of the Church. The pope repeatedly stated that the assembly had not intended either to transform or to reform, but only to renew. He dwelt even more frequently on the character of the renewal proposed: the faithful are called to an interior and spiritual renewal. Moreover, the pope contrasted this kind of change with a structural reform of the Church.[33] It is easy to see here a broad similarity to the Lefebvrian interpretation of Vatican II, even though Paul VI carefully avoided linking the spiritual renewal intended by the Council with a greater emphasis on the Counter-Reformation model.

On the other hand, anticonciliar circles could find support in another aspect of the pope's outlook. While the Council was in progress the pope had often mentioned the twofold danger to be avoided in interpreting its work: the attempt to understand it as doing away with the traditional patrimony of truth, and the attempt to hold on to old and outmoded ways.[34] But from 1966 to 1967 the pattern changed, as Paul VI showed himself concerned exclusively with changes being made in tradition in the name of the Council. His reading of the contemporary Church, which until then had been based on an identification of three fundamental orientations, was now simplified into a vision of a key dualism: the opposition in the Church between those who remain faithful to the decisions of the Council, and those who make the conciliar aggiornamento an excuse for questioning everything.[35]

It is true that on a few occasions the pope also issued warning to

---

Council, see G. Alberigo and A. Melloni, "L'allocuzione *Gaudet Mater Ecclesia* di Giovanni XXIII (11 ottobre 1962)," in *Fede Tradizione Profezia. Studi su Giovanni XXIII e sul Vaticano II* (Brescia, 1984), pp. 187–283.

33. See Paul VI, "Address to a General Audience (January 15, 1969)," *TPS*, 14 (1969–70) 53: "In particular, there has been, and still is, a good deal of talk about Church 'structures,' with intentions that are not always aware of the reasons justifying these structures and of the dangers that would arise if they were changed or destroyed. It should be noted that interest in renewal has in many cases taken the form of insistence on the exterior and impersonal transformation of the ecclesiastical edifice, and of acceptance of the forms and spirit of the Protestant Reformation, rather than the essential and principal renewal desired by the Council: moral, personal and inner renewal. . . . Beloved sons, We would like to invite all of you to meditate on this fundamental intention of the Council: to bring about our inner and moral reformation." For comparable statements see *Insegnamenti di Paolo VI*, 3 (1965) 797–98; 4 (1966) 510; 5 (1967) 237; 6 (1968) 762; 7 (1969) 122, 947–50, 994–97.

34. *Insegnamenti di Paolo VI*, 3 (1965) 728; 998–99; 1116–18.

35. Ibid., 4 (1966) 823–24, 844; 5 (1967) 325, 463, 834–35; 7 (1969) 683, 1051–52, 1106–8.

another quarter: to those conservative sectors that were criticizing Rome and the hierarchy for not taking drastic repressive measures against the innovators who in the guise of fidelity to the Council were guilty of introducing into the Church a disorder that would lead to its self-destruction.[36] But the pope's statements on these occasions came down to a call for greater trust in the church authorities to whose prudential judgment such steps must be left. Such a call seemed to imply a fundamental agreement in positions, the practical consequences of which had to differ depending on the level of responsibility involved.

As a matter of fact Paul VI adopted a rather clearly anticonciliar attitude in an address of March 1969. Here the pope asked sorrowfully whether the present evils in the Church were not due to the fact that Vatican II, with its emphasis on the Church, had not failed to develop ideas essential to the personal practice of religion and to interior spirituality.[37] His answer was essentially affirmative: the council fathers had only alluded to points central to Christian life, and therefore their decisions had to be completed by an appeal to the inheritance of tradition. What we see emerging here were ideas fairly widespread in anticonciliar circles. To begin with, the pope was lending authority to the thesis that the crisis in the contemporary Church was a direct result of the Council's work. In addition, and most importantly, he was maintaining that the decisions of the Council needed not only to be applied but to be completed as well. Finally, he was saying that this completion required a return to the preconciliar past.

It is a fact, of course, that the judgments that appear in this address are rarely to be found elsewhere in papal statements, and when they do occur they are rather subdued. In addition, beginning in 1970, Paul VI abandoned the practice of interpreting the situation in the Church according to a pattern in which only two positions were identified: supporters of the Council and opponents of it. Instead, he returned to the idea of a correct intermediate position, which was represented by church authorities and was opposed both by innovators desirous of emancipating themselves from tradition and by conservatives incapable of distinguishing correctly between customs to be abandoned and traditions to be preserved.[38] But one gets the impression that even when

36. Ibid., 7 (1969) 860–61, 1142.
37. Ibid., 7 (1969) 897–99: "If, on the contrary, we try to synthesize the characteristic aspects of the Council's treatment of the spirituality it seeks to foster, we would find that its attention was focused less on the personal and interior religious formation of believers than on that of the social body, the Church. . . . This is why some complain that personal piety emerged weakened from the Council and that there is observable in some circles and at some moments a certain decline in the interior religious spirit within the sanctuary of the individual soul. . . . We ought therefore do two things: first, we ought to make a closer study of the Council's teachings, and second, we ought to bring them into harmony with that essentially religious, mystical, ascetical, and moral patrimony of doctrine which the Council in no way repudiated."
38. Ibid., 8 (1970) 26–29, 46–48, 723–26, 780–83, 1418–26.

adopting this stance the pope regarded the position of the conservatives as more legitimate. As a matter of fact, not only is the amount of space given to condemnation of the innovators much more extensive, but the conservatives are accused of nothing more than an "excessive love" for the Church.

In conclusion, it seems possible to say that the confidence that conservative circles placed in Rome had some foundation during this early period. The judgment passed on Vatican II by the papacy and the conservatives was certainly not completely the same, but there were affinities and correspondences. It was symbolic, moreover, that the conference of European intellectuals at Strasbourg in 1971—to which the pope sent his apostolic blessing—had been suggested by the *Silenziosi della Chiesa* and reflected the basic wishes of this group.[39] But was there a real basis for Roman fears that aggiornamento might develop into subversion? Did forms of opposition to the Council really spring from the soil of fidelity to the Council?

The openness to the world that the Council decreed had in fact encouraged various Christians to involve themselves in the rebellious youth movements of the second half of the 1960s. These Christians had then made their own the radical demand for political and economic liberation that was the mark of these movements. A first reflection on the situation in the Church in the light of this experience led to one conclusion: there was a basic opposition between the existence of ecclesiastical structures and the possibility that the faithful could participate fully in key choices made in the Church as they did in those of society.[40] In light of this analysis, the aggiornamento proposed by the Council came to seem utterly inadequate: it simply reformed ecclesiastical structures and left them in place.

When Marxism eventually made its way into these Christian circles, its methods of ideological criticism were applied precisely to the conciliar aggiornamento. As a result, Vatican II and its retrieval of such values as liberty and conscience, which historically had developed outside the Church, were seen as simply "an attempt to integrate the Church into the value system of our society, almost without challenging this society in any way."[41] The conclusion was drawn that to spend time on carrying out the conciliar renewal (which had served only to expose a Church henceforth incapable of disclosing the Gospel message in terms intelligible to contemporary humankind) was to betray the task of universal liberation to which Christians were called.[42] This kind of analysis would be further systematized by the organized groups that emerged from the

39. *Fidélité et ouverture*, G. Soulages, ed. (1972). The positions of Soulages, who led the conference, were clearly expressed later on in his article, "Lettre à un évêque de France," *La pensée catholique*, 31/165 (1976) 15–19.
40. J. Mansir, "I cristiani francesi in una situazione rivoluzionaria," *Idoc*, 1 (1968) 48.
41 T. Veerkamp, "La distruzione del tempio," *Idoc Internazionale*, 1 (1970) 9–16.
42. H. Assmann, *Diskussion zur Theologie der Revolution* (Munich, 1969), pp. 218–48, and

ashes of the youth movement. By then, however, a new phase had begun in the history of anticonciliarism as a whole.

Maturation of Anticonciliar Thematics

Beginning in June of 1970 Archbishop Lefebvre began to make public the position he had been maintaining in private since immediately after the Council. He started by publishing a 1964 manuscript in which he had bitterly attacked the work done by Vatican II up to that time. In publishing it he added a complementary note in which he said that some contemporary catechisms containing doctrines that were Protestant, not Catholic, were based on schemata approved by the Council.[43] The article still showed a degree of conceptual uncertainty: the protestantization of Catholicism was attributed now to the Council, now to the preparatory documents, now to equivocal sentences that survived into the final texts. In any case, the attack on Vatican II was open and unambiguous.

It is difficult to give an exhaustive explanation of the reasons for this change on the basis of the available documentation. The timorous reforms, especially the liturgical and catechetical, that ecclesiastical authorities promoted despite their confirmed agreement with conservative circles; the failure of the *Lex fundamentalis*, to which these circles had looked as a means of applying the Council in a way that would preserve continuity with tradition; the encouragement given by the right wing of the Curia to ruptures that would block the process of reform—all these may provide at least a partial explanation of the shift. Whatever the explanation, Lefebvre steadily hardened his position during 1972.

In April of that year, in a lecture to the traditionalist Claretian Association of Priests and Religious, he once again indicted the conciliar renewal in a global way, that is, without distinguishing between Vatican II and conclusions drawn from it. The renewal, he said, was the work of the devil and even Satan's master stroke: he used obedience to it to produce disobedience to tradition.[44] By August, in a retreat to French priests, the archbishop was making the Council solely responsible for the crisis in contemporary Catholicism. He therefore urged his audience to work for a return to the preconciliar Church, undeterred by fear of seeming disobedience. Once the criterion of fidelity is defined as faithfulness to tradition, the acts of Vatican II, like those of the pope, are to be examined and accepted to the extent that they are conformed to tradition.[45]

"Notas a margem do projeto romano para un Diretorio catequético general," *Catequesis latinoamericana*, 4 (1969) 48–64.

43. Lefebvre, *A Bishop Speaks* (n. 21, above), pp. 73–84.
44. Ibid., p. 101.
45. Ibid., p. 116.

Finally, in an address at Rennes in November, the prelate's judgment on the Council was given its most fully organized and systematic presentation.

Following the lead of R. Wiltgen in *The Rhine Flows into the Tiber*,[46] Archbishop Lefebvre here described the texts produced by the Council as the fruit of maneuvering by the French and German episcopates.[47] This group in the assembly, which controlled economic aid to the bishops of the Third World and took advantage of widespread anticurial feeling, had (in the archbishop's view) gathered around itself the majority of the council fathers and persuaded them to join in an unparalleled act of rebellion, namely, to reject the preparatory schemata redacted in Rome, offering solutions to the problems of the Church in light of the teaching of Pius XII. The purpose of the group was to reverse the attitude taken by the papacy toward the modern world since the French Revolution. And in fact, by accepting the group's wishes, Vatican II introduced the very principles of the Revolution into the Church itself, for collegiality corresponds to *égalité*, religious freedom to *liberté*, and ecumenism to *fraternité*.

In the following years the position set forth here was to receive only slight modifications taken over from the cultural world of intransigent Catholicism. As everyone knows, during the nineteenth and twentieth centuries the intransigents had developed the thesis that modern history is a lengthy chain of errors let loose in the world by Satan in order to gain control of the Church: the Reformation had led to the French Revolution, and the latter in turn first to liberalism, then socialism, and finally communism.[48] Lefebvre simply added the Council as a final link in the genealogical chain. This most recent attack on the Church seemed to him all the more serious because it came, not from declared enemies as the previous ones had, but from within its own ranks. Moreover, the hierarchy, instead of firmly rejecting it (as Pius X, by condemning Modernism, had rejected a similar attempt of the enemy to infiltrate the city of God), encouraged and even promoted it.[49]

This view of the matter found widespread agreement in circles connected with the archbishop. *La pensée catholique*, for example, not only gave a good deal of space to a review of Wiltgen's book, but repeatedly

46. R. Wiltgen, *The Rhine Flows into the Tiber. The Unknown Council* (New York, 1967). Wiltgen limited himself, in fact, to pointing out the interventions of Paul VI in correcting certain trends among the majority. From this fact the traditionalists inferred the existence of maneuvering that had its roots in those historical movements—Protestantism, Freemasonry, communism—that Satan had raised up against the Church; see *La pensée catholique*, 29/149 (1974) 85–93, and *Cristianità*, 4 (1976) 19–22.

47. Lefebvre, *A Bishop Speaks*, pp. 131–36.

48. G. Miccoli, "Chiesa e società in Italia tra Ottocento e Novecento: il mito della cristianità," in *Chiese nelle società* (Turin, 1980), pp. 153–245.

49. Lefebvre, *J'accuse le concile* (n. 20, above), unpaginated preface, and *Le coup de maître de Satan* (Martigny, 1977). See also the homily delivered at Lille on Aug. 29, 1976, and reported in J. A. Chalet, *Monseigneur Lefebvre* (Paris, 1976), pp. 205–26.

338   THE RECEPTION OF VATICAN II

asserted that Vatican II had been the outcome of a conspiracy to have the age-old objective of Protestantism and Freemasonry triumph at last in the Church, namely, to substitute the deification of the human for the principle of authority.[50] Seen in this light, the Council could only be regarded as satanic. There was doubtless a noteworthy ambiguity in the line taken by the periodical: some articles referred simply to the Council as such, whereas others focused rather on the interpretation of Vatican II forced on the Church by progressive theologians with the aid of the mass media and sectors of the hierarchy. During these years, nonetheless, the claim was no longer, as it had been in the earlier period, that Rome gave legitimacy to the theses being maintained; on the contrary, the pope was asked, in respectful but unyielding terms, to intervene and correct the conciliar documents in the light of tradition.[51]

In November 1974, moreover, Archbishop Lefebvre sent a profession of faith to the members of the Fraternité Sacerdotale S. Pie X, which had been established under his authority in 1970. In this document he declared that he gave his fealty to eternal Rome, the guardian of faith and tradition, but rejected "the Rome of neo-Modernist and neo-Protestant leanings that clearly manifested itself in the Second Vatican Council and after the Council in the reforms issuing from it."[52] This statement was the basis for the objections raised against the archbishop by a commission of cardinals that finished its assigned work by canonically suppressing the Fraternité.[53] It is worth noting here that in defending himself the prelate acknowledged that in his manifesto he had used excessive language about the Council and that he would limit himself to asking for correction of the conciliar documents on specific points.[54] But in the bulletins of the Fraternité his position was unambiguous: fidelity to the Church required disobedience to a council that had been defiled by Protestantism, liberalism, and Modernism.[55]

The archbishop's exchange of letters with the pope and his clear distancing of himself from the theses of Abbé Georges de Nantes show that his proclaimed submission to Rome did not imply changes in his view of Vatican II.[56] Shortly after his suspension a divinis in July 1976, he would say: "On the basis simply of internal and external criticism of Vatican II, I believe we can say that this council turned its back on tradition and

50. L. J. Lefèvre, "La foi . . . aujourd'hui?," La pensée catholique, 28/146 (1976) 5–6; "La conjugaison des forces qu'entretiennent les nourritures terrestres contre la primauté de Pierre," ibid., 29/150 (1974) 5–13; "Un complot à ciel ouvert," ibid., 30/157 (1975) 5–17.
51. La pensée catholique, 27/138 (1972) 5–8; 28/147 (1973) 9–16; 29/151 (1974) 53–54.
52. DC, 71 (1975) 544–45.
53. There is a careful reconstruction of the incident in J. Anzevui, Le drame d'Ecône (Sion, 1976).
54. DC, 72 (1975) 740.
55. Anzevui, Le drame d'Ecône, pp. 58–59. And see p. 63 for the supposed supernatural revelations that confirm Lefebvre's views. But the whole subject of miraculism in traditionalist circles deserves a study, the content of which I cannot even begin to suggest here.
56. DC, 73 (1976) 811–12.

broke with the Church of the past and that it was therefore a schismatic council."[57] This was the high point of Lefebvre's opposition to the Council. As we shall see shortly, this judgment was quickly withdrawn. Meanwhile we must inquire whether, in the light of the proceedings begun against the archbishop, the pope's judgment on the Council underwent modification.

In a letter to the archbishop, Paul VI had in fact written a sentence that was to scandalize traditionalist circles: "The Second Vatican Council . . . is no less authoritative . . . and is even in some ways more important than the Council of Nicaea."[58] But alongside this clear assertion of the normative character of the Council—an assertion the pope repeated on public occasions[59]—there were other statements in the 1970s that were certainly not displeasing to the Lefebvrians.

I am not referring solely to statements that are fairly significant in themselves: for example, that Pius XII must be regarded as precursor of Vatican II;[60] or that it is the role of those governing the Church to bring into unity tradition and the impulse to renewal coming from the Council;[61] or that aggiornamento must be understood not as a break with the preconciliar Church but as a continuation of it.[62] Also to be considered are statements whose logic openly undermines the importance and role of Vatican II.

The first statement to be mentioned in this category is the address of June 1972, in which the pope maintained that Satan's intervention was the reason why the Council failed to produce the ecclesial springtime expected of it. He added that, instead, the fumes of Satan had entered the Church through crevices.[63] In light of what was said above, and without any need of describing in detail the propagandistic use made of these sentences by the traditionalist periodicals and by conservative circles generally,[64] it is readily understandable that one of Lefebvre's characteristic theses gained considerable credit. Even though the pope did not apply the traditional scheme of the intransigents to Vatican II, he seemed to make a connection between the energies set in motion by the

57. Interview in *Le Figaro*, Aug. 3, 1976; the language used is essentially repeated in the statement released in *L'Europeo*, Sept. 3, 1986, p. 20.

58. Anzevui, *Le drame d'Ecône*, p. 110 (the ensuing rebukes for departing from the Council are in *Insegnamenti di Paolo VI*, 14 [1976] 380–82, 647–48, 811–23). See the reply to the pope's position on the normative value of Vatican II, in *Supplément-Voltigeur*, 42 (1976) of *Itinéraires*, a journal that had already been maintaining that the most recent ecumenical council could not be put on the same level as its predecessors: 27/157 (1971) 339–41, and 29/169 (1973) 224–26.

59. *Insegnamenti di Paolo VI*, 11 (1973) 631; 13 (1975) 676, 1438–41.

60. Ibid., 13 (1975) 216.

61. Ibid., 8 (1970) 1418–26; 9 (1971) 725; 10 (1972) 651.

62. Ibid., 10 (1972) 672–73, 1135–38; 12 (1974) 493.

63. Ibid., 9 (1971) 707–8.

64. Ibid., 10 (1972) 707–8. *Osservatore Romano* paraphrased the address but it put the words "the fumes of Satan have entered the temple of God through some crevices" in inverted commas.

Council and a movement not aimed at the good of the Church. In addition, he often emphasized the theme—already seen in his earlier addresses and openly maintained in anticonciliar thinking—that the ecumenical council marked the beginning of a period of crisis in the life of the Church.[65]

Moreover, in the reflection on the Council that Paul VI undertook in connection with the tenth anniversary of its close, one point seems to be made with greater forcefulness and decisiveness: the need for a timely review of what the Council had produced, the need of ending the period of criticism and experiment, and developing, on the solid foundation of tradition, whatever had emerged from that period as truly valid.[66] At work here, though not explicitly stated, was the view that Vatican II contains heterogeneous elements, some of which are to be accepted, others to be rejected. It was not by chance that Lefebvre himself, appearing before the commission of cardinals that interrogated him, appealed to this aspect of papal teaching on the Council in order to show that his call for the correction of some texts was well founded.[67]

In conclusion it may be observed that the proclaimed adherence of Paul VI to the directives of the Council was located in a troubled and complex setting in which some of the tendencies voiced by traditionalist opponents of the Council also made their appearance. This observation acquires its full significance if we bear in mind that in giving an account

65. Ibid., 14 (1976) 176–77: "The Council . . . seems to have paved the way for an outburst of the doubts and uneasiness that the disputatious heritage of the Reformation had introduced into the subconscious of some scholars and not a few of the faithful. The innovating spirit is open to two characteristic temptations. One has to do with the human and hierarchical structure of the Church, which is formally defined according to the model of a perfect or complete society; the temptation is to think of the Church as therefore completely like civil society. The other has to do with the religious and transcendent content of the Church; the temptation here is to look upon this content as entailing an unnecessary or even harmful flight from the social reality in which the life of the Church is immersed" (see ibid., 8 [1970] 723–26, and 10 [1972] 158–59). To be noted in this passage, as also in the one cited in n. 33, above, is the establishing of a connection (different but no less real than that claimed by Lefebvrian circles) between the Reformation and the Council. Also to be noted is the fact that the thesis according to which Vatican II produced an unprecedented crisis in the Church has received an authoritative denial from a historian: J. Delumeau, *Le christianisme va-t-il mourir?* (Paris, 1977). It was no accident that *La pensée catholique* launched a series of attacks on this book: 32/169 (1977) 11–21; 32/170 (1977) 64–67; 32/171 (1977) 20–22.

66. "Bull *Apostolorum limina* Proclaiming the 1975 Holy Year (May 23, 1974)," TPS, 19 (1974–75) 151 and 156: "The same [need of conversion] applies to the Church as a whole. At a distance of ten years from the ending of Vatican II, We view the Holy Year as the close of a period devoted to reflection and reform, and as the beginning of a new phase devoted to solid development in the theological, spiritual and pastoral fields. . . . We consider it a fitting time for this work [of renewal] to be examined and carried further. If we keep in mind what Church authority has approved, we should be able to see and single out the valid, legitimate elements to be found in the many varied experiments that have been carried out all over the world. We should be able to put these elements into practice with even greater alacrity."

67. The text of the conversation is given in R. Gaucher, *Monseigneur Lefebvre. Combat pour l'Eglise* (Paris, 1976, pp. 215–61. The point mentioned here is on pp. 243–44.

of the Lefebvre case the pope made renewed use of the reading grid we have already seen: the life of the Church is endangered both by those who reject the Council in the name of tradition and by those who invoke it to justify criticism of existing church structures.[68] Proponents of these contrary extremes at work in contemporary Catholicism forget that the supreme magisterium alone has authority to determine the ways in which the conciliar decisions are to be implemented.

The pope, in short, was claiming to have made his own the outlook of Vatican II and at the same time was reserving interpretation of the Council to Rome as sole depositary of its true meaning.[69] But, even if we prescind from the serious question of the compatibility of this view with the collegiality described in *Lumen gentium*, it does not seem possible to attribute the pope's approach solely to the need of gradually carrying out the Council's wishes in the face of anticonciliar resistance, while restraining the impatience of more advanced currents of thought. The pope may also have thought that in the situation of conflict in which the Church found itself, only a mediating authority could ensure the introduction of certain novelties. In any case, the fact remains that his judgment on Vatican II undercut the reformist thrust of the Council and its potential influence on the Church by allowing value to the theses and positions characteristic of opposition to the Council.

On the other hand, we must not overlook the fact that progressives, too, not only held and acted on anticonciliar positions but had been consolidating them at the levels both of ideological development and of organization. In the final statement of the meeting in honor of Camilo Torres at L'Avana, there appeared the thesis that the documents of Vatican II were a tool for deceiving peoples in quest of liberation, because these documents were spreading a false idea of social justice, trying to reconcile the irreconcilable, that is, to eliminate antagonism between classes.[70] In the writings that paved the way for the formation of Christians for Socialism groups in Latin America, it was asserted that Vatican II had represented the high point in the Church's effort to adapt itself to the bourgeois form of society.[71] Concentration on intraecclesial reform and the proclamation of the Church's detachment from politics amounted (it was said) to a concealment of the opposition between the classes and thus to a sanctioning of the now tottering bourgeois control of society. The need, therefore, was to move beyond the Council and to test the historical potential of Christianity within revolutionary struggle.

---

68. *Insegnamenti di Paolo VI*, 14 (1976) 388–90, 500, 1087–88.

69. The emphasis on authority as providing the only sure point of reference in applying the directives of the Council pervades almost all the papal statements; for one example, see *Insegnamenti di Paolo VI*, 11 (1973) 715–16.

70. *Idoc Internazionale*, 2/15–16 (1971) 31–33.

71. J. P. Richard Gúzman, "Razionalità socialistica e verifica storica del cristianesimo," *Idoc Internazionale*, 3/8 (1972) 26–31. See also passages of other articles in the same periodical: 3/1 (1972) 401; 3/4 (1972) 38.

It is doubtless true that more nuanced positions were voiced at the 1971 convention in Santiago, Chile, which launched the Christians for Socialism movement in Latin America. Some participants defended Vatican II as having played a historically positive role and having had the merit of opening the door to criticism within the Church and thus to the development of new perspectives. Others even defended the continuity between the new movement and the directions taken by the Council, which the institutional Church was at bottom now betraying. Nonetheless, both the inaugural address and the final document of the convention clearly asserted the thesis that the ecumenical council had decreed only formal changes and that the result had been to bolster the established system against which Christians were called to struggle.[72]

These views of the Council were very quickly echoed on a wide front in Europe, where, however, the call for a demythization of the Council developed chiefly in the area of ecclesiology. Here the Council was pictured as the work of the ecclesial aristocracy (the episcopate), which was concerned chiefly to increase its own power in relation to the pope and the Curia, and paid no heed to the fact that the real collegiality is that which binds not the bishops but all Christians together.[73] In any case, the establishment in Europe of Christians for Socialism groups was accompanied by the reassertion of a well-defined anticonciliar argument: although Vatican II did open the door to some new needs, it reached conclusions that were in the service of neocapitalism and thus set the faithful on an erroneous path; there was need, therefore, of radical revision.[74]

It is true that from the mid-1970s on the repeated defeats that the movement suffered and the ever clearer emergence of a church whose characteristic traits were quite unconciliar led the Christians for Socialism to some rethinking of positions. Vatican II was henceforth seen not as an incident to be left behind, but as an event that had brought into the open two types of ecclesiastical policy—one focused on innovation, the other on restoration. Without denying the limitations of the first type, it

72. The texts of this meeting are in *Idoc Internazionale*, 3/12–13 (1972). Examples of nuanced positions: p. 9, 19, 45; positions of the official documents: pp. 5 and 29–35. See also *Christians for Socialism. Documentation of the Christians for Socialism Movement in Latin America*, J. Eagleson, ed. (Maryknoll, N.Y., 1975). In the theology of liberation, on the other hand, the debate about this appraisal of the Council still goes on: J. Comblin, "El tema de la 'liberación' en el pensamiento cristiano latinoamericano," in *Panorama de la teología latinoamericana* (Salamanca, 1975), 1:229–45), and P. Richard, *Mort des chrétientés et naissance de l'Eglise* (Paris, 1978), pp. 155–57; Engl. trans., *Death of Christendoms and Birth of the Church* (Maryknoll, N.Y., forthcoming).

73. Examples of this thinking: B. Besret, *Tomorrow: A New Church* (New York, 1973), and J. C. Barreau, *Questions à mon église* (Paris, 1972).

74. M. Cuminetti, "Dal concilio a 'Cristiani per il socialismo'" *Idoc Internazionale*, 4/20 (1973) 31 and 38. Comprehensive survey in B. van Onna, "La désintégration du catholicisme politique," in M. Xhaufflaire, ed., *La pratique de la théologie politique* (Paris, 1974), pp. 155–77.

was in the channel cut out by it that the Christians for Socialism now tried to situate the activity of their organization.[75]

Spread of Traditionalist Anticonciliarism

After the furious charges leveled at Vatican II in August of 1976, Lefebvre adopted a calmer tone, although he made no substantial changes in his position. It was in this new atmosphere that the attempt was begun to obtain a review of his canonical status. Public shows of solidarity from other bishops were rare,[76] but the traditionalist press mounted an intense campaign of support. Here, in addition to widespread talk of the irregularity of the proceedings to which the archbishop had been subjected,[77] the question of the Council kept surfacing as the crucial issue in the whole situation. One reason for this was that in a letter of October 1976, the pope showed himself open to canceling the measures taken against Lefebvre, provided he declare his acceptance of Vatican II.

These publications, however, did not introduce any new factors beyond those found in the disquisitions aired in previous years. Instead, there was an evident effort to go more deeply into certain aspects. The conspiracy theory was supported by a reconstruction of what had happened at the Council,[78] and supplemented by the accusation that representatives of the majority had been Freemasons.[79] Further arguments were adduced in support of the thesis that Vatican II represented the final stage in a plan, begun at the Protestant Reformation, to break down authority in the Church.[80] Further details were introduced into the picture of the Council as a synod that had been exclusively pastoral and therefore had had nothing to say pertaining to faith.[81] On this last point

75. M. Cuminetti, "Uno scacco salutare," *Idoc Internazionale*, 5/10–11 (1974) 5–6; J. A. Viera-Gallo, "Chiesa e fascismo ieri e oggi," ibid., 6/7 (1975) 52–60.

76. There was uncertainty even among the members of the *Coetus:* Siri openly distanced himself (see *Renovatio*, 11 [1976] 126–30), while de Proença Sigaud supported Lefebvre, although cautiously (see *Ansa. Bolletino informazioni religiose*, July 9, 1977). Bishops who had an anticonciliarist attitude tended in this context to raise rather the issue of the crisis that Vatican II was causing in the Church; see the statements of Bishop R. J. Dwyer in *Cristianità*, 5/28–30 (1977) 4–7, and Bishop Pintonello in *Sí sí no no*, 3/6 (1977) 1 and 3/9 (1977) 3.

77. *Cristianità*, 4/19–20 (1976) 3–6; *Sí sí no no*, 2/3 (1976) 6; *La pensée catholique*, 32/166 (1977) 57–58.

78. Especially emphasized was communist infiltration of the Council: *Cristianità*, 5/32 (1977) 3–4; *Sí sí no no*, 8/21 (1982) 1–2.

79. *Sí sí no no*, 2/2 (1976) 1 and 2/6 (1976) 1.

80. *La pensée catholique*, 31/162 (1976) 64–70, and 32/166 (1977) 46–52. See also J. Ploncard d'Assac, *L'église occupée* (Chiré-en-Montreuil, 1976).

81. *Cristianità*, 3/9 (1975) 7; *Sí sí no no*, 2/1 (1976) 2. The latter periodical, in addition to using the weapons of personal defamation on leaders of the majority, did not hesitate to

the articles of L. Salleron in *La pensée catholique* are worth noting; they are perhaps the most complete and original contribution to the subject. In Salleron's opinion, the Council was an attempt to replace ecclesiastical power with evangelical freedom in every area of church life. In carrying out this plan, however, its supporters had done away with all authority, including that of the Council itself, so that the only recourse left is to give its decisions a unified meaning by applying to them the only valid hermeneutical norm, namely, tradition.[82]

Beyond the repetition of the usual anticonciliar arguments there was one striking new note: a change in attitude that corresponded to a change in the pope's attitude. *La pensée catholique*, in particular, abandoned its direct attacks on Vatican II and returned to the theme that the Council had been valid in itself but had been betrayed by malevolent interpreters.[83] This shift was undoubtedly to be explained by Roman reconsideration of the Lefebvre case.

At the instigation of Paul VI, the Congregation for the Doctrine of the Faith had in fact sent the archbishop a questionnaire in which he was asked to explain not only his infractions of discipline but his entire opposition to the Council.[84] His answers on this second point (even though they did not alter his long-held positions) must have been regarded as satisfactory: under the new pope, John Paul II, he was invited to an interview during which the objections against him were reduced to a request for an explanation of the choice he made among the conciliar texts, rejecting some and accepting others. Lefebvre's answer was simple: "I am ready to sign an acceptance of Vatican II as interpreted in accordance with tradition." This formula was accepted by the pope during a personal meeting, at the end of which the archbishop stated that Rome no longer found his judgment of the Council unacceptable, although there were still differences in positions on problems of a canonical kind.[85] And in fact the Vatican press office indirectly confirmed Lefebvre's statement by issuing a communiqué saying that because of Lefebvre's violations of canonical discipline his position remained unchanged.[86]

The attitude adopted by *La pensée catholique* cannot, however, be at-

---

describe the Council as an "ill-starred orgy": 2/7–8 (1976) 3. Articles in *La pensée catholique* adopted a more measured tone but continued to ask for Roman intervention to correct or interpret the conciliar documents: 31/163 (1976) 7–11; 31/165 (1976) 5–12; 32/167 (1977) 36.

82. L. Salleron, "Dialogue autour d'Ecône," *La pensée catholique*, 31/164 (1976) 27–35; "Reparlons du concile," ibid., 32/170 (1977) 43–54; "Dialogue sur la politique et l'Eglise," ibid., 33/175 (1978) 53–60.

83. *La pensée catholique*, 34/178 (1979) 5–6, with a significant reference to editorials that had appeared before Lefebvre's canonical suspension. See also the editorial in 34/183 (1979) 5–14; in the same issue (pp. 63–64) L. Salleron insisted on the correction of the conciliar texts but seemed to be expressing a personal opinion.

84. "Mgr. Lefebvre et le Saint-Office," *La pensée catholique* 35/233 (1979) 10–174.

85. *DC*, 76 (1979) 243.

86. Ibid., p. 896.

tributed solely to the dismissal of the charges against the archbishop.[87] The editors began by disagreeing, for the first time since the close of the Council, with those traditionalist groups that maintained the *sede vacante* thesis.[88] The periodical went on from there to face the question of John Paul II's position on the Council. In its view, the pope's statement that he intended to be fully faithful to Vatican II was not a problem, because he had added that he intended to interpret the Council in the light of tradition.[89] Moreover, it was impossible not to share his attitude—often expressed during his years as bishop of Cracow—on the conciliar opening to the world: the documents of the Council are a vade mecum for Christians insofar as they are soldiers fighting to win society.[90] Admittedly, the pope undoubtedly did accept certain values contrary to tradition—religious freedom and human rights—which the Council had promoted. But there was no need to reject his position, because this acceptance did not imply any yielding to the secular city. Not only was the pope's defense of these values a tactical move against the anti-Christian nations that denied them; in addition, he situated them within the traditional context of the principle that every expression of social life is in need of legitimation by religion.[91]

La pensée catholique did think that the pope was too slow in effecting a restoration, but it urged its readership to allow the successor of Peter to decide on the times and ways for carrying out the program; they could be confident that the thinking it had so long championed was now shared at the summit of the Church.[92] In fact, there even seemed to be a growing disagreement between the periodical and Lefebvre on this point.[93] In various interviews given between 1980 and 1982 the archbishop acknowledged that there was widespread Roman agreement with his positions, but he added that the solution of every problem depended on the correction of some of the conciliar documents, *Dignitatis*

---

87. The change was also visible in other traditionalist periodicals: for example, *Cristianità* (see nos. 81, 85, and 92 of 1982) tended to emphasize the continuity between the teaching of Pius X, Pius XI, and Pius XII, on the one hand, and John Paul II, on the other, and showed a favorable attitude to the pope, which was quite new. It was, however, toward the thinking represented by Cardinal Ratzinger that it showed the greatest favor: 10/96 (1982) 5–11.

88. *La pensée catholique*, 35/184 (1980) 54–56, and 35/185–87 (1980) 107–10.

89. Ibid., 37/206 (1982) 5–14. In his address to the college of cardinals on Nov. 6, 1979 the pope had linked his program with the integral teaching of the Council, but he added: "the integral teaching of the Council as understood in the light of sacred tradition and the constant teaching of the Church itself" (*Insegnamenti di Giovanni Paolo II*, 2/2 [1979] 1051).

90. L. Salleron, "Jean-Paul II expliqué par Karol Wojtyla," *La pensée catholique*, 36/192 (1981) 62–69.

91. Idem, "Dialogue sur le pape," ibid., 36/190 (1981) 52–61; and see the statements of Fr. André-Vincent, ibid., 36/195 (1981) 32–39, and 39/211 (1984) 21–28.

92. Ibid., 36/193 (1981) 5–10, and 37/199 (1982) 38–43.

93. There are, of course, other traditionalist circles that have not ceased to criticize the pope, for they maintain that the hopes raised by the new pontificate quickly died: *Sí sí no no*, 9/11 (1983) 2, and 10/8 (1984) 3–4.

humanae in particular.[94] One had the impression, however, that this assertion of principle hid a much more prosaic set of negotiations in which the issue was not the judgment to be passed on Vatican II but the future fate of the works and institutions now controlled by the archbishop, as well as the canonical status of the so-called Mass of Pius V, which he did not want to see simply put on the same level as the *novus ordo Missae* promulgated by Paul VI.[95]

In addition, despite the new pope's declared intention of following in the steps of Paul VI, his statements on Vatican II showed a greater accord with the conservatives. On the morrow of his election he had said that he intended to implement the conciliar decrees in a dynamic way that would take the movement of history into account. "The fruitful seeds which the fathers of the ecumenical council . . . sowed in good ground must grow to maturity after the fashion of dynamic, living things."[96] But in his address to the college of cardinals in November of the following year his outlook has already changed radically. His recall of the Montini heritage now signified a takeover of the latter's schema for interpreting the Church's life in the postconciliar period. To the two deviations represented by the progressives and the traditionalists there is opposed the correct path marked out by church authorities.[97] On the other hand, John Paul II lays much greater emphasis than his predecessor on continuity with tradition as a criterion for interpreting the decisions of the Council. Furthermore, he does not limit himself to insisting that the Council was essentially asking the faithful for a personal, interior, and spiritual transformation; he also stresses the penitential aspects of this conversion, showing thereby a clearer acceptance of the counter-reformational model of holiness. And it is to these same norms that he refers in the following years when he expresses his judgment on the ecumenical Council.[98]

What we see here is admittedly a difference in tone and emphasis rather than in content from the line taken by Paul VI; but this difference seems to imply a broader agreement with the characteristic arguments of conservative anticonciliarism. Moreover, the very emphasis on the role of the pope (something that Wojtyla does not so much thematize in his statements as make clear in the concrete way he carries out the Petrine

94. See the interview given to K. G. Peschke in 1983 (text transcribed from the tape in the archives of the periodical *Il Regno*, Lefebvre epistolary, 2).

95. Lefebvre explained the terms of the negotiations in *Lettre aux amis et bienfaiteurs*, 13/24 (1983) 1, and in the interview in *Présent*, Dec. 6–7, 1982. Moreover, Cardinal Ratzinger had already stated that Lefebvre's position on the Council was acceptable: Kipa dispatch of Oct. 30, 1980, in the archives of *Il Regno*, Lefebvre epistolary, 2.

96. "Radiomessage Urbi et Orbi (October 17, 1978)," *TPS*, 24 (1979) 8.

97. *Insegnamenti di Giovanni Paolo II*, 2/2 (1979) 1060–69; see also 1182–83.

98. Ibid., 3/2 (1980) 1292, and 4/1 (1981) 235; *DC*, 79 (1982) 1032–33. The recent reintroduction of the "Mass of Pius V" was accompanied by a rejection of the Lefebvrian thesis that the Tridentine rite is preferable to the *novus ordo Missae*, but the action nonetheless seems to suggest this.

ministry) lends credence to one of the theological claims made by circles opposed to Vatican II. Nor is it an accident that the overall climate of the Church has changed with the coming of the new pope; we need only think how sectors that were committed to the renewal of the Church have developed a new slogan, "The meta-council," in order to question the orthodoxy of the interpretation of the results of the Council given by those who reject a legalistic or fixist reading of its documents.[99]

This situation underscores the reappraisal of the Council by groups that see themselves as following in the steps of the Christians for Socialism. They still maintain the thesis that it was the historical and political developments of the 1960s, rather than Vatican II, that caused the maturation of the Christian conscience in relation to problems of the Church and of society. But they now acknowledge more fully the positive role of the Council in the emergence of evangelical ways within some ecclesial communities.[100] Perhaps even further revision might be stimulated by consideration of the paradoxical results achieved by a certain sociology inspired by Marxism: although repeating the view that the Council represented an adaptation of Catholicism to contemporary neocapitalism, some writers tend to combine it with a very positive reappraisal of popular religion of the traditional kind and an evident nostalgia for the preconciliar Church.[101]

Is Traditionalist Thinking Becoming More Widespread?

Does all this mean that anticonciliar thinking has been spreading in recent years? Can it be said that the neoconservative tendencies at work today have fostered the spread of typical traditionalist themes beyond the small associations of priests and those minority groups on the political right that were the solid base of traditionalism during the 1970s? The limits of my inquiry—which, let me remind the reader, has been selective and focused on examples—will not permit answers to these crucial questions. Certainly the manifesto that Archbishop Lefebvre and A. de Castro Mayer, former bishop of Campos and longtime spiritual leader of the archconservative group "Tradition, Family, Property."[102] jointly

99. I shall mention only P. Delhaye, *La scienza del bene e del male. La morale del Vaticano II e il "metaconcilio"* (Milan, 1981).

100. M. Cuminetti, *Il dissenso cattolico in Italia* (Milan, 1983, pp. 103–12.

101. A. Lorenzer, *Das Konzil der Buchhalter. Die Zerstörung der Sinnlichkeit* (Frankfurt, 1981).

102. The bishop had long been a supporter of this movement—see his pastoral letters published in *Cristianità*, 5/26–27 (1977) 3–5, and 6/38–39 (1978) 3–16. Its theorist, P. Correa de Oliveira, described Vatican II as "one of the greatest, if not the greatest, disaster in the history of the Church," in his *Rivoluzione e controrivoluzione* (Piacenza, 1977, 3rd ed.), pp. 181–83. The movement now publishes a bulletin making it possible to follow its activities

addressed to the pope in December 1983, implies a hardening of positions (in the repetition of violent accusations against Vatican II) that seems to suggest a consciousness of new strength.[103] But only the coming years will be able to tell us whether the strength flows from despair at being substantially isolated in the Church or from the assurance of extensive support among the faithful and powerful backing in the hierarchy.

---

in the various countries in which it is present; the bulletin claims that the movement is following the social teaching of the Church.

103. "Lettera al papa. Manifesto episcopale," *Sí sí no no*, 9/17 (1983) 1–4. See also the report of the press conference in which Lefebvre introduced the manifesto: ibid., 19/11 (1984) 1–3; and an interview given by de Castro Mayer in which he applies the name of heretic to the Church that follows Vatican II: ibid., 10/12 (1984) 3.

Appendix
Avery Dulles, S.J.

The Reception of Vatican II at the Extraordinary Synod of 1985

The Extraordinary Synod of Bishops, when it met at Rome from November 24 to December 8, 1985, made a number of important contributions to the reception of Vatican II. First of all, one must mention the reports of the various episcopal conferences; they were submitted in advance and further elucidated by the oral and written interventions of bishops at the Synod. These reports and interventions represent, on the whole, a very honest and informative self-appraisal of the state of the Catholic Church all over the world in our day. It was high time for an assessment of the Council, which had given rise to various and conflicting interpretations and reactions. The bishops acknowledged some difficulties and confusions, but almost all reflected enthusiasm and gratitude for the work of the Council. This strong endorsement should put to rest any lingering suspicion that many bishops are unhappy about Vatican II.

The reports of the episcopal conferences were in principle intended to be confidential, and the majority remain unpublished. Nearly a score, however, have been printed in various languages, including a rather small sampling in English.[1] Others have circulated in manuscript form. Most of the Synod speeches are likewise inaccessible, but summaries of all of them were published in *L'Osservatore Romano*, and a full collection of these summaries has been printed in Italian.[2] Together with the conference reports, these speeches should be extremely useful to ecclesiastical authorities in setting priorities for the years to come.

The most tangible contribution of the Synod consists in its two official documents, the "Message to the People of God" and the "Final Report,"

---

1. The United States bishops' report, presented by Bishop James W. Malone, is in *Origins*, 15/15 (Sept. 26, 1985) 225–33. The report of the episcopal conference of England and Wales is in the *Tablet* (London), 239/7569 (Aug. 3, 1985) 814–19 and in *Origins*, 15/12 (Sept. 5, 1985) 177–86. The most valuable larger collection of synod documents thus far published is *Synode Extraordinaire. Célébration de Vatican II* (Paris: Cerf, 1986).

2. Gino Concetti, ed., *Il Sinodo della Speranza. Documenti ufficiali della seconda assemblea straordinaria del sinodo dei vescovi* (Rome: Logos, 1986).

both of which are easily accessible in English translation.[3] Without ignoring the real difficulties, these documents both attest that Vatican II, in the judgment of the bishops, has been a great grace for the Catholic Church in the present century and remains the magna charta for the future.

For the reception of the Council future writers will have to take particular note of the principles for the interpretation of Vatican II laid down in the "Final Report" (part I, § 5.). These principles may be paraphrased as follows:

1. Each passage and document of the Council must be interpreted in the context of all the others, so that the integral meaning of the Council may be rightly grasped.

2. The four major constitutions of the Council are the hermeneutical key for the other decrees and declarations.

3. The pastoral import of the documents may not be separated from, or set in opposition to, their doctrinal content.

4. No opposition may be made between the spirit and the letter of Vatican II.

5. The Council must be interpreted in continuity with the great tradition of the Church, including earlier councils.

6. Vatican II must be accepted as illuminating the problems of our own day.

These guidelines may be criticized as being skewed toward harmonistic readings and thus as minimizing the tensions between different passages or between different documents, or between Vatican II and earlier church teaching. But the contrasts had been unduly emphasized in many earlier commentaries, which stood in need of a corrective. If the Synod's principles are followed, the Council need no longer be brought into discredit by one-sided interpretations, as has sometimes happened in the past. The Synod's hermeneutical principles will make it clear that, notwithstanding some real shifts and developments, Vatican II is fundamentally self-consistent, stands in substantial continuity with earlier church teaching, and remains valid in its essentials for our own day.

The "Message to the People of God" and especially the "Final Report" give concise and updated syntheses of the basic teaching of Vatican II, particularly in the realm of ecclesiology. These syntheses are useful both because the teaching of the Council is scattered throughout sixteen constitutions, decrees, and declarations, and because the Council was addressing the situation of the 1960s, which is no longer precisely our own.

To a great extent the Synod documents repeat the principal themes of Vatican II's ecclesiology, making use of images such as body of Christ,

3. The "Message to the People of God" and the "Final Report," together with several important synodal addresses, are published in *Origins*, 15/27 (Dec. 19, 1985). Another translation of the "Message to the People of God" and the "Final Report" is given in Xavier Rynne, *John Paul's Extraordinary Synod* (Wilmington, Del.: Michael Glazier, 1986).

bride of Christ, temple of the Holy Spirit, and family of God. As in the constitution on the church (*Lumen gentium*), so in the "Final Report," these images are all read against the background of the Church as mystery. Yet the Synod in some ways moved beyond the Council, at least in what it chose to emphasize.

Rather surprisingly, the Synod scarcely uses the term "people of God" except in the title of its "Message." It presents the Church as a mystery of grace, a supernatural communion of sacramental life. Recovering an almost forgotten theme of Vatican II, found chiefly in chapter 5 of the Constitution on the Church, the Synod makes much of the universal call to personal holiness. In speaking of the Church's relationship to nonmembers, the Synod gives relatively more importance to missionary witness and evangelization than did the Council. The intent is evidently to counteract the tendency in some quarters to emphasize interfaith dialogue and secular service at the expense of explicit proclamation of the Gospel, with a view to conversion to Catholic Christianity.

Another shift can be seen in the way that the signs of the times are mentioned. The Synod provides a new list of such signs, less optimistic than the ones alluded to at Vatican II, with the result that the line of distinction between Church and world is more sharply drawn. In this connection the Synod makes much of the theology of the Cross, a theme not explicitly mentioned at Vatican II. The point seems to be that Christians are to expect suffering, even martyrdom, in their dealings with the world.

The idea of inculturation, discussed at some length in the "Final Report," is a development beyond Vatican II, which never used the term, and also beyond the secular theology of the late 1960s, which was accommodationist in spirit. The Synod picks up the term as used by John Paul II, and interprets it with the help of Paul VI in his apostolic exhortation, *Evangelii nuntiandi* (1975).

The final documents of the Synod do not attempt to report everything that was said at the meeting itself or contained in the preparatory papers. Aiming at universalism, they make no distinction between different parts of the world and thus might give the impression, to unwary readers, that all their statements are equally applicable everywhere. Aiming at unanimity, the authors have deliberately omitted not only minority opinions but even majority opinions that fell short of general consensus. For example, no reference is made to problematic issues such as birth regulation, the status of divorced and remarried Catholics, clerical celibacy, the powers of the Synod of Bishops, and the question of Roman centralization, all of which came up for discussion. The question of theological dissent is treated only by a passing recommendation for improved communication and dialogue between bishops and theologians. Although they state that the talents of women should be more effectively utilized in the apostolate, the Synod documents do not tackle the questions whether women should be installed in official, nonor-dained ministries (such as lector and acolyte) or whether they might even be ordained, at least to the diaconate.

Some critics are disappointed that these problem areas are not openly discussed in the "Final Report," but it may be argued that the Synod showed good judgment in not trying to solve everything at once. Some questions are too complex and divisive to be treated with any degree of adequacy at a brief gathering of two weeks, such as the late Synod. Besides, these disputed questions are only tangentially connected with the main theme of the Synod, the review of Vatican II.

The Synod has been particularly reproved for having practically suppressed the theme of the People of God in its final documents. It is indeed surprising that the Synod, which purported to be reaffirming the Vatican II ecclesiology, should have so distanced itself from what many regard as the dominant ecclesial image of the Council. Some have even suggested that the devaluation of this image was due to "some outside agents who have put pressure on the synod to rework the council in this crucially important point."[4] But if one keeps in mind the intention to produce a consensus document, the reticence seems to be explicable without recourse to conspiratorial theories. Although some of the Synod material was favorable to the image of the People of God, a number of criticisms were voiced.

Among the conference reports, the Dutch and Belgian papers both complained that "People of God" was being played off against other images, such as body of Christ, with the result that civil democratic thinking was being encouraged in the Church. The French episcopal conference likewise reported that chapter 2 of the Constitution on the Church had sometimes been subjected to political readings in the light of secular trends. "The presentation of the People of God should be reinserted between the first chapter, which shows the trinitarian grounding of the Church, and chapter 3, which brings out its ministerial structure."[5] Cautions such as these may sufficiently explain why Cardinal Danneels, in his initial report, noted: "Above all, the concept of the Church as People of God has been defined in an ideological manner and detached from complementary concepts in the Council: body of Christ and temple of the Holy Spirit."[6] This report also took note of the tendency to make false oppositions between the hierarchical Church and a "people's Church."

At the Synod itself, the direction taken by the initial report received considerable confirmation. Archbishop Christian Tumi of Garoua, Cameroon, stated that in his country the concept of "People of God" had led

4. Peter Hebblethwaite, "Exit 'The People of God'," *Tablet*, 240/7596 (Feb. 8, 1986) 140–41. He points the finger at Cardinal Ratzinger, who would hardly have been an "outside agent."

5. *Synode Extraordinaire*, p. 201.

6. "Initial Report" (part 2, section C, § 3), p. 345.

to confusion regarding the distinction between the common priesthood of all Christians and the ministerial priesthood.[7] In the language group discussions, French-speaking group A and the German-speaking group both remarked that the image of "People of God" stood in need of being protected against socio-political deformations. Thus it is not surprising that the term is practically absent from the final documents. Other terms used—such as body of Christ, family of God, and communion—function, as would "People of God," to offset a one-sided concentration on the hierarchical aspect of the Church, which the Synod surely did not espouse.

It is legitimate to ask whether the Synod documents represent a victory for any particular party or tendency among the bishops. The differences of opinion at the Synod cannot be simplified in such a way as to classify all the members under quasi-political headings such as progressive and reactionary, liberal and conservative. There were many different perspectives, reflecting concerns from a variety of nations and continents. One may, however, call attention to two major schools of thought, each of which had prominent leaders.[8] The first of these, led by figures such as the German Cardinals Ratzinger and Hoeffner, had a markedly supernaturalistic point of view, tending to depict the Church as an island of grace in a world given over to sin. This outlook I would call neo-Augustinian.

These bishops, without opposing Vatican II, were inclined to think that the Council had spoken somewhat naively in a situation that no longer exists, when secular society all over the world seemed to be converging toward greater freedom, prosperity, and universal harmony. The signs of the times today, according to these bishops, are almost the contrary. The world is falling into misery, division, and violence. It is manifestly under the power of the Evil One. Catholics who seek friendship with the world easily fall into materialism, consumerism, and religious indifference. Striving for openness to the world, the Church in the postconciliar period allowed itself to be contaminated, with the result that much of the faith was called into question. Many priests and religious abandoned their vocations, and fewer young people felt called to the service of the Church.

Under these circumstances, according to the neo-Augustinians, it would be a mistake to persist in the reform and modernization of church structures, which was attempted after Vatican II. In consequence of the efforts already made, they maintain, the Church has become excessively bureaucratized. Paralyzed by staff, committees, and agencies, pastors can no longer perform a personal ministry. The Church fails to appear as a sign of Christ's love and to beckon its members to the life of evangeli-

7. Ibid., p. 445.
8. For the following analysis I am in part indebted to Hermann-Josef Pottmeyer, "The Church as Mysterium and as Institution," published in *Concilium*, 188, *Synod 1985—An Evaluation* (Edinburgh: T. & T. Clark, 1986), pp. 99–109.

cal perfection. The Church today must take a sharper stance against the world and seek to arouse the sense of God's holy mystery.

The second major school of thought was represented by Cardinal Hume of England and many others, including Bishop James Malone and Bishop Bernard Hubert, the respective presidents of the United States and Canadian bishops' conferences. This group of churchmen, taking their inspiration from Pope John XXIII and Vatican II, had a more humanistic and communitarian outlook. Convinced that great progress had been made as a result of the Council, they attributed the main difficulties to the failure of conservative prelates to carry through the reforms of Vatican II. If there is disenchantment among youth, these bishops maintain, it is not because excessive attention has been given to structural reform but rather because the necessary reforms have been resisted and partly blocked. The Catholic Church has not yet succeeded in giving its laity an adequate sense of participation in, and co-responsibility for, the mission of the Church. The urgent need today is for a further development of collegial and synodal structures so that the Church may become a free and progressive society, a sign of unity in diversity, at home in every nation and every sociological group.

The two points of view I have described implied vastly different programs for the future. The neo-Augustinians, putting the accent on worship and holiness, wanted a church more separate from the world, more manifestly united in itself, more taken up with the cultivation of a direct relationship with God. The communitarian school—if one may so describe the second orientation—wanted the Church to become more involved in the promotion of peace, justice, and reconciliation. The first group used the term "mystery" as a kind of code word; the second group, "communion." The first group was eschatological and other-worldly; the second, incarnational and this-worldly.

Not all the bishops and conferences taking part in the Synod could be neatly fitted into one or the other of these two orientations. For example, the leading advocates of liberation theology, coming from Third World countries, shared neither the sacralism of the Augustinians nor the secular optimism of the communitarians. They wanted a politically involved church that was confrontational and militant.

The "Final Report" of the Synod refrained from taking a definite position in favor of any one of the dominant schools. It preferred to strive for consensus. In certain sections the "Final Report" seemed to be inclining more toward one school than toward another, but on balance it is difficult to say that any one party was victorious. In its opening sections (part 1, and part 2, sections A and B) the "Final Report" underscores mystery, love for the sacred, and the quest for personal holiness—all themes characteristic of neo-Augustinianism. The section on the sources of faith emphasizes the authority of tradition and of the hierarchical magisterium, the need for mystagogical catechesis, for interiority, and for heroic fidelity even to the point of martyrdom.

Then follows a long section (part 2, section C) in which the emphasis shifts from mystery to communion. This section begins with the words, "The ecclesiology of communion is a central and fundamental idea in the documents of the council." The following paragraphs celebrate the variety of particular churches and insist on pluriformity as a feature of true catholicity. Then the document goes on to discuss collegiality, affirming that the Synod of Bishops and the episcopal conferences are partial realizations of the collegiality of the episcopate as a whole; that they are signs and instruments of the collegial spirit. The same section then takes up the themes of participation and co-responsibility at all levels in the Church, advocating greater collaboration of laypersons in the apostolate and a more adequate use of the distinctive gifts of women. Basic ecclesial communities are here characterized as a positive development offering great hope for the revitalization of the Church. In its concluding paragraph this section on the ecclesiology of communion contains a strong endorsement of ecumenism, which is presented as a process that presupposes a measure of communion in Christ and aims to achieve full sacramental and ecclesial communion.

In part 2, section D, the focus of the "Final Report" shifts again, this time to speak to the concerns of the Third World, especially inculturation, interfaith dialogue, and the Church's service toward the poor and the oppressed. All these concerns are encouraged, but only with certain reservations that seem to reflect the outlook that I have called neo-Augustinian. In this portion of the "Final Report" the point is made that the favorable signs of the times, so prominent in the documents of Vatican II, have yielded to the ominous signs mentioned above. It is therefore more necessary than ever to adhere to the "theology of the cross" (a term reminiscent of Luther but here applied to the struggle for human rights). Strengthened by its Lord, the Church must not retreat into itself. In the face of opposition it must fearlessly defend and promote authentic human values, such as personal dignity and freedom from oppression, including the right to life.

Inculturation, according to this section, is to be pursued but it must not be understood as an easy acceptance of whatever cultural forms happen to exist. Interreligious dialogue is accepted and approved with the proviso that it not be set in opposition to mission and evangelization. Service to the world is encouraged, but only with the caution that it should not infringe on the Church's spiritual mission. In part 2, section A, evangelization had already been identified as the primary mission of the Church.

The "Final Report" thus incorporates numerous concerns of the neo-Augustinians, who emphasize mystery and sacred authority; of the communitarians, who value communion and participation; and of the liberationists, who prize the option for the poor and the oppressed. So artfully is the "Final Report" constructed that the reader hardly perceives the transition from one portion to another. All are woven together with great skill so that the document reads as a coherent whole. The Vatican II concept of the Church as sacrament is used to weave together the diverse elements. Sacrament may be seen as a manifestation of mystery, as a source of communion, and as an instrument of transformation. Thus the "Final Report" can declare, in a pregnant sentence: "The Church as communion is the sacrament for the salvation of the world" (part 2, section D, § 1).

In the nature of the case, the "Final Report" could not have given full satisfaction to the concerns of any one party or school. Like the documents of Vatican II itself, it is a compromise. But compromises can often be useful in effecting reconciliation between groups that would otherwise be hostile. The "Final Report," if it is taken as seriously as it deserves to be, can become a unifying and stabilizing factor in a divided and turbulent church. At least some legitimate aspirations of all the major tendencies are affirmed, with suitable cautions to prevent them from becoming mutually antithetical. If the Catholic Church has a will to survive—and all the evidence suggests that it does—it would do well to heed the prescriptions of the Synod.

Looking toward the future, the Synod made a number of suggestions. At the end of each section of the "Final Report" there is a paragraph detailing recommendations growing out of the preceding analysis. The following recommendations may be mentioned by way of sampling: a pastoral plan should be drawn up by particular churches for the better dissemination and implementation of Vatican II; better use should be made of the mass media of communication; more thorough philosophical training should be given to future priests; catechesis is to be oriented toward liturgical life in the church; and the changing signs of the times are to be subjected to continual reexamination.

Among the suggestions of the "Final Report," four deserve special consideration because of their immediate practical implications for the Church as a whole. They are: the early completion of the Code of Canon Law for the Eastern-rite churches, the preparation of a universal catechism or compendium of Catholic doctrine, a study of the nature and authority of episcopal conferences, and a study of the applicability of the principle of subsidiarity to the internal life of the Church.

The preparation of a revised Code of Canon Law for all Eastern Catholic Churches has been under way since 1972, when Paul VI established a commission to undertake this task.[9] But progress has been slow and difficult. The recommendation in the "Final Report" may be seen as a response to the oral intervention of the Melchite patriarch of Antioch, Maximos V Hakim. He concluded his address with an appeal to the pope:

9. For a concise survey explaining some of the points at issue, see John D. Faris, "The Codification and Revision of Eastern Canon Law," *Studia Canonica*, 17 (1983) 449–85.

I ask the Lord to give you the strength, health, and length of life to convoke on the occasion of the jubilee of Vatican II, five years from now, a new Extraordinary Synod. I hope that then all our Eastern Churches and I myself—or my successor, if I am no longer alive—may thank you for having given us at length an Eastern canon law. Not any Code at all, but one impregnated with our venerable traditions. May this new Code realize the wish of the first President of the Commission for the Reform of Eastern Law, Cardinal Massimo, who said, "You will see that our new Code will be so Oriental that our Orthodox brothers and sisters will be happy to adopt it at the same time as yourselves."[10]

The "Final Report" expressed great esteem for the institutions, liturgical rites, ecclesiastical traditions, and disciplines of the Eastern-rite churches. Its suggestion that the codification of law for these churches be completed as soon as possible should be understood in this context.

Pope John Paul II in his closing address at the Synod took up this suggestion. He said that the Code should be according to the traditions of the Eastern churches and the norms of Vatican II. In his annual address to the Roman Curia, on June 29, 1986, the pope described this proposal as one of the three priorities for the universal Church growing out of the Synod. He stated that the commission charged with drawing up the Code of Eastern Canon Law will be ready, in a relatively short time, to issue "a code in which they can recognize not only their traditions and disciplines, but also and above all their role and mission in the future of the universal Church and in the broadening of the dimension of the Kingdom of Christ *Pantocrator*."[11] I take this to be, in part, a warning that any false particularism or anachronistic adherence to the past will be avoided in the forthcoming Code.

The second suggestion that requires our attention has to do with the preparation of a universal catechism or compendium of all Catholic doctrine regarding both faith and morals. The "Final Report" specified that this work should be a point of reference for all regional catechisms or compendiums, that the presentation of doctrine should be predominantly biblical and liturgical, and that the work should be adapted to the present-day life of Christians.

The idea of a universal catechism had been discussed at Vatican II and rejected in favor of a general catechetical directory (*Christus Dominus*, § 44). This was in fact composed after the Council and finally promulgated in June 1971. A number of national and regional catechisms, including one for the United States, have been drawn up according to the general directory and approved by Rome.

At the Synod the suggestion for a universal catechism was made rather tentatively in the United States episcopal conference report and, more definitely, in the Korean conference document and in several Afri-

10. Text in *Synode Extraordinaire*, pp. 393–94.
11. In *L'Osservatore Romano*, Weekly Edition, July 7, 1986, p. 3.

can reports, notably that of Senegal and Mauritania. In his eight-minute intervention at the Synod Cardinal Bernard Law, archbishop of Boston, stated:

I propose a Commission of Cardinals to prepare a draft of a Conciliar Catechism to be promulgated by the Holy Father after consulting the bishops of the world. In a shrinking world—a global village—national catechisms will not fill the current need for clear articulation of the Church's faith.[12]

Archbishop Joachim Ruhuna of Burundi requested "a model catechism issuing from Vatican II," and the Latin patriarch of Jerusalem, Giacomo Beltritti, in his intervention called for a single catechism for children to be used by the entire church, adaptable to the needs of various countries.

Cardinal Silvio Oddi, then prefect of the Congregation for the Clergy, apparently gave his support to this movement, which he may have to some extent inspired. At any event the idea of a universal catechism or compendium of doctrine came up in one form or another in six of the nine language-group reports: the Italian, English group A, both French groups, Spanish group B, and the Latin group. The "Final Report" followed most closely the wording of the Spanish group.

The pope in his closing address picked up this suggestion, which he said corresponded to a real need both of the universal and of the particular churches. On June 10, 1986, he was able to announce the creation of a special commission composed of twelve cardinals under the presidency of Cardinal Ratzinger, prefect of the Congregation for the Doctrine of the Faith. The two Americans on this commission are Cardinal Baum, prefect of the Congregation for Education, and Cardinal Law, archbishop of Boston.

In his report to the Curia on June 29, the pope further explained that the commission was to prepare, with due consultation, the draft of a true and proper catechism, which should be presented at a forthcoming regular session of the Synod of Bishops and promulgated, if possible, on the twenty-fifth anniversary of the close of Vatican II.

It is too early to predict the precise character of the proposed manual. Notwithstanding the intervention of Beltritti, it would appear that most of the advocates were not thinking of a catechism for children but rather of a manual of doctrine composed for adults—possibly something similar to the Catholic adult catechism issued by the German Bishops' Conference in 1985. The new document is evidently not intended to be a substitute for national and regional catechisms but to be a sort of model for them—possibly doing for the contemporary church what the Tridentine catechism did for the Church several centuries ago. According to the "Final Report," the presentation of doctrine is to be "biblical and liturgical" and thus, it would seem, not primarily philosophical or scholastic. Spanish-speaking group B had called not for a detailed catechism

12. Ibid., Dec. 9, 1985. This is a summary of Cardinal Law's intervention.

but for a common point of reference for Catholics, "an integral synthesis of the doctrine of the Church concerning faith and morals in the new pastoral perspectives of Vatican II."[13] French-speaking group B, in similar fashion, had recommended a catechism or compendium containing the essential doctrines of Vatican II, presenting the "good news" of Jesus Christ as the way of life and not as an ideology.[14] The Latin language group, on the other hand, was especially concerned with orthodoxy. It requested that the new catechism take into account the "Credo of the People of God" issued by Paul VI in 1968.[15]

It remains an open question to what degree the new commission will satisfy the intentions of the different groups that had requested the new manual. Will it be a catechism in the traditional sense of the word? Will it be biblical, pastoral, and liturgical in tone, or will it be predominantly doctrinal? Will it leave room for significant pluralism in national and regional catechisms, or will it set a uniform pattern for all?

The third major project recommended by the "Final Report" had to do with the episcopal conferences. This institution was welcomed with enthusiasm in many of the conference reports, notably those of Brazil, Canada, England and Wales, France, Indonesia, North Africa, Switzerland, and the United States. Several of these reports asked for greater autonomy for the conferences. At the plenary meeting of the college of cardinals held immediately before the Synod, Cardinal Jérôme Hamer, prefect of the Congregation for Religious, gave a talk in which he quoted Henri de Lubac and Willy Onclin to the effect that the national and regional conferences were not true instances of collegiality.[16] In their eight-minute presentations the presidents of the conferences of Brazil and the United States strongly favored the growth of the conferences. In the group reports, however, a division of opinion appeared in some of the language groups, such as English-speaking group A. The Latin-speaking group warned against excessive autonomy of the conferences. Further study of the conferences and their teaching authority was requested by English-speaking group B and by French-speaking group A.

The "Final Report" commended the conferences as useful and indeed necessary. It called them partial realizations of collegiality and authentic signs and instruments of the collegial spirit. But at the same time the report called for further study of the theological status of the conferences and, in particular, of their doctrinal authority. In his closing address at the Synod Pope John Paul II welcomed this as a valuable suggestion. Then, in a letter of May 19, 1986, he entrusted this study to the cardinal prefect of the Congregation for Bishops, Bernardin Gantin, who was instructed to consult with local churches and to collaborate with the competent organs of the Roman Curia.

13. *Synode Extraordinaire*, p. 516.
14. Ibid., p. 529.
15. Ibid., p. 541.
16. Ibid., p. 601.

The results of this study will be of great importance for the future of the universal Church. The subject is a highly controversial one because many regional churches feel that they have not been accorded the freedom and autonomy that seemed to be promised by Vatican II. On the other hand, a number of excellent theologians, together with influential Roman cardinals, fear that the growth of the national conferences could introduce an unhealthy nationalism and separatism within the Church. Others have objected that the conferences tend to stifle the pastoral responsibility of the individual bishop for the flock committed to his care. These criticisms should not be dismissed as groundless.[17]

The fourth major suggestion that requires attention in the present context has to do with the principle of subsidiarity. The principle was first set forth by Pius XI in his encyclical *Quadragesimo anno* (1931) in the following terms:

It is a fundamental principle of social philosophy, fixed and immutable, that one should not withdraw from individuals and commit to the community what the individuals can accomplish by their own enterprise and industry. So, too, it is an injustice and at the same time a grave social evil and a disturbance of right order to transfer to the larger and higher collectivity functions that can be performed and provided for by lesser and subordinate bodies.[18]

The point was therefore that the higher authority is to be seen as a *subsidium* (support) for the lower when the latter is incapable of handling a given problem by its own resources.

Does the principle of subsidiarity apply to the Church? Pius XII, in a consistorial allocution of February 20, 1946, after expounding what Pius XI had had to say on subsidiarity, added: "These very enlightening words are valid for social life at all levels and also for the life of the Church, without prejudice for the latter's hierarchical structure."[19] Some interpret this as a positive endorsement of subsidiarity in the Church; others regard it as a warning that subsidiarity does not apply to the Church without notable qualifications.

At the first meeting of the Synod of Bishops, in 1967, Cardinal Pericle Felici presented ten basic principles for the revision of the Code of Canon Law.[20] The fifth of these was the application of the principle of subsidiarity. When this fifth principle, as formulated by the code commission, was submitted to the Synod fathers in 1967 for their reaction, 128 voted *placet*; only one voted *non placet*; and 58 voted *placet iuxta*

17. For some of the past developments and present problems, see Avery Dulles, "Bishops' Conference Documents: What Doctrinal Authority?," *Origins*, 14/32 (Jan. 24, 1985) 528–34; see also Ladislaus Orsy, "Episcopal Conferences: Their Theological Standing and Their Doctrinal Authority," *America*, 155/13 (Nov. 8, 1986) 282–85.

18. *AAS*, 23 (1931) 2–3; cf. DS, 3738.

19. *AAS*, 38 (1946) 145.

20. For the ten principles in English translation, see James A. Coriden et al., *The Code of Canon Law: A Text and Commentary* (New York: Paulist, 1985), p. 6.

modum.[21] At his press conference on October 5, 1967, Cardinal Giovanni Urbani, president of the Italian episcopal conference, reported that the principle of subsidiarity had been received by the Synod with universal favor.[22]

At the Extraordinary Synod of 1969 the principle of subsidiarity again came up for consideration. It was extensively discussed in presentations by Archbishop Carlo Colombo, by the theologian Gérard Philips, and by Cardinal François Marty, all of whom regarded it as applicable to the life of the Church. Colombo, however, explained that, although the local church has a certain priority in pastoral matters, in which the particular bishops are the first and immediate judges, the reverse obtains for doctrinal matters: "The ultimate judgment in matters of doctrine or in the teaching of the faith and of the moral law, without being withdrawn from the authority of individual bishops, by its nature falls primarily and per se under the competence of the supreme authority of the magisterium"—that is, the college of bishops under the direction of the pope, or the pope himself acting as visible head of the universal Church.[23]

Cardinal John Francis Dearden, in reporting for the first English-language group on October 21, 1969, declared: "Taking their direction from what is said in *Christus Dominus,* no 8, all admit that, although there are some limits to the power of the bishop imposed by reason of unity of faith and communion, and the need for a common ordering of certain matters concerning the whole Church," the principle of subsidiarity nevertheless does apply. "Its actualization, urgently required today, will lead to a radical transformation in the concept and practice of granting faculties."[24]

In an interview published in *La Documentation Catholique* on the eve of the 1969 Synod, Cardinal Julius Döpfner of Munich gave a carefully worded formulation of the principle of subsidiarity as applied to the Church:

Subsidiarity—an important principle of Christian social doctrine, which holds equally for the Church—signifies that the higher instances and organisms must respect the capacities, competences, and tasks of individuals and communities, in theory and in practice. In this way a healthy and vigorous life, adapted to different situations, can develop. This holds also for the Church as a whole, for the pope and his curia, for the bishop and his ministers, for the pastor and the government of his parish. On this point much remains to be done on all levels.[25]

At the Synod of 1985 the principle of subsidiarity was mentioned favorably in the conference submissions from Brazil, Canada, England

21. See René Laurentin, *Le premier Synode* (Paris: Seuil, 1968), p. 305.
22. See Gino Concetti, *Bilancio e Documenti del Synodo dei Vescovi* (Milan: Massimo, 1968), p. 103.
23. Giovanni Caprile, *Il Sinodo dei Vescovi 1969* (Rome: Civiltà Cattolica, 1970), p. 127.
24. Ibid., pp. 166–67.
25. Quoted from *DC*, 66/1546 (Sept. 7, 1969) 789.

and Wales, Indonesia, North Africa, Scandinavia, and (by implication without actual use of the term) Switzerland. In oral reports at the Synod, bishops from Brazil, Kenya, and Norway all spoke in favor of the principle and even recommended its extension. The group discussions, however, were less favorable. The German-speaking group asked for further study to determine to what extent the principle was appropriate to describe the life of the Church. English-speaking group A was about evenly divided as to whether or not to recommend that ways of furthering subsidiarity in the Church be explored. The Latin-speaking group cautioned against understanding subsidiarity in such a way as to imply that local churches should be independent of the primacy of Rome. French-speaking group A observed that any general appeal to subsidiarity was a false trail, because the principle was not applicable to the sacramental and liturgical life of the Church. One member of this last group was Cardinal Hamer, who had said at the plenary meeting of cardinals immediately preceding the Synod that subsidiarity does not apply to the Church, because the universal Church is not a mere support (*subsidium*) for the particular Church.[26]

Reflecting the general trend of the discussion, the "Final Report" recommended that a study should be made "to determine whether the principle of subsidiarity in use in human society can be applied to the Church and to what degree and in what sense such an application can and should be made" (part 2, section C, § 8). The report here referred to the statement of Pius XII quoted above.

In his closing address John Paul II made no reference to the recommendation of a study of subsidiarity. In his speech to the Curia on June 29, 1986, he observed that the question of subsidiarity is a very complex and subtle one, already treated to some degree at the Extraordinary Synod of 1969 and in connection with the revision of the Code. The revised Code, in the preface to the Latin text, left "to particular legislation or to the executive power that which is not necessary to the unity of the discipline of the universal Church." The Secretariat of the Synod, added the pope, had asked for more time to establish the precise state of the question and the point at issue before embarking on a full study of subsidiarity. In his personal reflections the pope seemed to suggest that, because of the unique nature of the ecclesial society, the principle of subsidiarity as generally understood could not be applied to the Church without being modified.

All four of the main agenda items left by the Synod are of major importance for the reception of Vatican II. The Council, by its recognition of the relative autonomy of regional and cultural entities, encouraged the idea of an internally diversified Catholicism. The Synod of 1985

26. "L'Eglise universelle n'a pas simplement un rôle de suppléance." The text of Cardinal Hamer's speech to the plenary meeting of cardinals is given in *Synode Extraordinaire*, pp. 598–604; quotation from p. 604.

made it evident that there is as yet no full agreement as to the necessary measure of visible unity and the limits of permissible variety. The Oriental Code, the catechetical manual, and the two studies recommended by the Synod may cast further light on the disputed questions. Much depends, however, on how the Synod proposals are executed. Will there be free and open processes based on a recognition of the desirability of input from below? More specifically, will subsidiarity be utilized or excluded in the conduct of the study of subsidiarity? As this example indicates, it will be difficult to find ways of carrying out the Synod agenda that do not prejudice the solution of the very questions that are to be settled.